TJ Lee and Lee Hudspeth's

Absolute Beginner's Guide to

PC Upgrades

201 West 103rd Street
Indianapolis, Indiana 46290

T.J. Lee and Lee Hudspeth's Absolute Beginner's Guide to PC Upgrades

International Standard Book Number: 0-7897-2417-0

Library of Congress Catalog Card Number: 00-101712

Printed in the United States of America

First Printing: December 2000

02   01   00   4   3   2   1

Trademarks

Warning and Disclaimer

Associate Publisher
Greg Wiegand

Senior Acquisitions Editor
Jill Byus Schorr

Senior Development Editor
Rick Kughen

Managing Editor
Thomas F. Hayes

Project Editor
Tricia Sterling Liebig

Copy Editor
Megan Wade

Indexer
Mary SeRine

Proofreader
Maribeth Echard

Technical Editors
Vince Averello
Erik Mandel

Interior Designer
Kevin Spear

Cover Designer
Trina Wurst

Layout Technicians
Ayanna Lacey
Heather Hiatt Miller
Stacey Richwine-DeRome

Contents at a Glance

Table of Contents

Dedication

To my wife Loretta, who grows more beautiful every day; to my kids Andreana, Jason, Vicky, and Lillian; and to my friends, all of whom have had to put up with me while I write books.—T.J.

To my wife Liz, my children Tate and Aaron, and my parents Eloise, George, and Gloria for their unwavering support. Special thanks to Danny Dunham for all those soul-renewing shuttle trips to the Cove.—Lee

About the Authors

T.J. Lee and **Lee Hudspeth** are coauthors of *The Unofficial Guide to PCs* and six books about Microsoft Office, the most recent being *Outlook Annoyances*, *Office 97 Annoyances*, *Excel 97 Annoyances*, and *Word 97 Annoyances*. They routinely contribute to *eBay* and *PC Computing* magazines; at *PC Computing*, T.J. and Lee were contributors to the feature story that won the prestigious National Magazine Award, also known as the "Ellie." They are cofounders of PRIME Consulting Group, Inc., a firm that provides consulting, software development, training, and add-ins for Microsoft Office and Windows. They have written countless courseware packages and manuals, coauthored a Microsoft Education Services software development course, and taught thousands of developers and end users in classes and seminars the world over. In their spare time, T.J. and Lee publish *The Naked PC*, an e-zine with a circulation of more than 55,000, which is dedicated to the concept of being the good neighbor who's also a computer consultant. They have been developing add-ins for Microsoft Office since before it was Office. Their numerous award-wining add-ins— PRIME DocLauncher 2000, PRIME for Excel 2000, PRIME for Word 2000, and versions for prior releases of Office—are featured on Microsoft's celebrated Office Update site (http://officeupdate.microsoft.com).

You can find out more about the authors, this book, and other amazing stuff at http://www.primeconsulting.com/teachpc/.

T.J. Lee is a certified Microsoft trainer, and has been focusing on computer and management consulting for more than a decade.

Lee Hudspeth is also a certified Microsoft trainer. He got involved in the computing industry two decades ago as a student at the USC School of Business while also working part-time as a consultant at the computer center.

Acknowledgments

We sincerely appreciate the efforts of Jill Byus Schorr and Rick Kughen at Macmillan for steering us safely and sagely through the editorial shoals, Vince Averello (Microsoft Outlook MVP extraordinaire) and Erik Mandel for their quintessential technical-edit flair, and Claudette Moore and Debbie McKenna for their artful agency representation. Thanks and a tip of the hat to Jim Baker, Bill Bradley, Vic Brzezinski, Dan Butler, Mike Craven, Al Gordon, Jack Jonaitis, Kevin Keele, Christian Schock, Peter Simmons, and M. David Stone for their superb technical expertise. Thanks to Steven H. Short (Intel) and Dr. David Corey (Massachusetts General Hospital) for giving permission to reprint photos and other figures throughout the book. We appreciate Brittney Stone's Electric Library support. Special thanks to Al Gordon for his gracious eleventh-hour work on the scanner chapter, and to Donna Ortiz de Anaya and Liz Harsch for their splendid contributions to the glossary.

Tell Us What You Think!

As the reader of this book, *you* are our most important critic and commentator. We value your opinion and want to know what we're doing right, what we could do better, what areas you'd like to see us publish in, and any other words of wisdom you're willing to pass our way.

As the publisher for Que, I welcome your comments. You can fax, email, or write me directly to let me know what you did or didn't like about this book—as well as what we can do to make our books stronger.

While I cannot help you with technical problems related to the topics covered in this book, you may email our user support group at support@mcp.com or visit or support Web site at http://www.mcp.com/support.

When you write, please be sure to include this book's title and authors as well as your name and phone or fax number. I will carefully review your comments and share them with the authors and editors who worked on the book.

Fax: 317-581-4666

Email: hardware@mcp.com

Mail: Greg Wiegand
Que Corporation
201 West 103rd Street
Indianapolis, IN 46290 USA

INTRODUCTION

Do You Need This Book?

When it comes to pulling the cover off a PC and tinkering with its innards, plenty of folks get the shakes and try to convince themselves maybe what they need is a whole new computer. But we're here to tell you, "You can do it!" You can successfully upgrade a variety of your computer's components and live to tell the tale. This not only gives you great bragging rights at the water cooler, but saves you some money in the process.

T.J. Lee and Lee Hudspeth's Absolute Beginner's Guide to PC Upgrades shows you which upgrades are worth undertaking at all, which upgrades you can perform yourself, and how to perform them in step-by-step fashion. That's what's unique about this book—we use plain English to carefully explain the steps of preparing for an upgrade, performing an upgrade, testing your work, and cleaning up afterward. We also tell you which upgrades to pass up and when it's time to call in a professional to avoid getting in over your head. Although we're here to preach the upgrade gospel, very credible computers are available in the $600–$1,000 range, which makes it all the more tempting to toss the baby out with the bathwater. With PC prices dropping like the proverbial lead balloon, you need to know when it makes more sense to buy a new system than to upgrade an existing one.

T.J. Lee and Lee Hudspeth's Absolute Beginner's Guide to PC Upgrades explains what other books omit or overlook—for example, we provide a simple checklist of exactly which tools and resources to have on hand before you perform any PC upgrade. This book will help you achieve the confidence you need to perform your own upgrades, gain valuable insights into how your PC works, and save bucks along the way. We also call 'em as we see 'em, so we explain the formula for when *not* to attempt a particular upgrade and instead call in an expert. You should know that *T.J. Lee and Lee Hudspeth's Absolute Beginner's Guide to PC Upgrades* isn't just about hardware; we also offer hard-won insider tips and tricks on upgrading to a different operating system (such as from Windows 98 to Windows 2000) or upgrading applications, say, from Microsoft Office 97 to Office 2000. We're strong believers in preventive medicine, so we'll show you what to do now to ensure that upgrades later go smoothly.

You might be a computer user who doesn't want to buy an entirely new PC just to get the latest CD-RW drive, DVD drive, or screaming video card. Perhaps you're someone who is quite capable of upgrading your computer but have been put off by what you perceive as too difficult for a mere mortal to achieve. You might be annoyed by the fact that your two-year-old PC has slowed to a crawl under the weight of increased Internet activity and bloated applications. We're here to guide you along the road to upgrade nirvana.

You have our decades of practical, in-the-trenches experience at your disposal. We have hardware and software consulting notches in our belts, have written eight computer books, and regularly write for *PC Computing* and *eBay* magazines. We also publish our own electronic bulletin: *The Naked PC* (55,000+ circulation), a labor of love in which we tell the unadulterated truth about all things PC. Our biweekly *Naked PC* journeys run the gamut from the Internet to Microsoft Office and Windows, software, hardware, system warts, and low-tech solutions for high-tech problems; plus we offer regular recommendations of useful books, Web sites, and products. We use that same unadulterated approach in this book by giving you friendly, accurate, no-nonsense advice about PC upgrades just as though we were sitting right there at your office or home, advising you in person.

How This Book Is Organized

The average PC user perceives a personal computer as a complex, delicate, often belligerent creature hiding inside a little gray box, a box that works much like the wizard in *Wizard of Oz*—a wizened being scurrying around madly behind a red curtain to make the smoke puff and the mirrors twirl. This perception is wrong, *but it's not your fault!* The blame lies squarely on the shoulders (and pointy heads) of the PC industry's bigwigs, pundits, and chest-pounders. These folks have gone out of their way to litter the PC arena with jargon, obtuse explanations, and a perverse fascination with features that have nothing to do with the PC being your tool and serving your will. Naturally, we fall into the opposite camp; we fervently believe you are the boss and the PC is your tool. The goal of this book is to demystify the little gray box, give you the information you need to make it serve you better, and have fun along the way.

Part I, "The Lay of the Land," explains precisely which steps to take before you touch anything. It doesn't make sense to upgrade a component without knowing what your system was like before the upgrade, so we provide a soup-to-nuts inventory form (downloadable in Excel format or hard copy from Appendix C, "PC Inventory Form"). As we walk you through the form, you learn about the various components of your PC. We use plain English to describe the various types of peripheral buses so you'll know which bus to use for which component, and we offer tips on buying hardware online. Part I concludes with a step-by-step checklist for performing an upgrade on any component. Subsequent chapters drill further down on this checklist as it applies to each specific component in a modern PC.

Part II, "The Core Upgrades," is the meat-and-potatoes part of the meal. Here we cover upgrading the BIOS, system memory, motherboard, microprocessor, hard disk, and Internet connections, and how to connect PCs into a network.

Part III, "Upgrades to Consider," covers the two most common upgrades: UPS and USB. These two areas are often considered optional or even unnecessary, but we disagree vehemently. For a few dollars more, adding an uninterruptible power supply (UPS) increases your peace of mind regarding power fluctuations and outages that can easily—and permanently—wreck your system. We feel that a UPS, properly matched to its constituent hardware, is a mandatory component for any modern system. The second member of the family is USB, an acronym for Universal Serial Bus. This medium-speed peripheral bus primarily offers ease of use with a simple cable/port design, automatic reconfiguration upon connection or disconnection of any device, and no use of sparse IRQs. USB has been built into most systems for the last several years, and you should be taking advantage of it.

Part IV, "Upgrading Peripherals," sets out to soothe your eyeballs and appease your ears—with a new video setup, printer, and sound setup. How many hours per day do you sit staring at your monitor; eight hours, ten hours, or more? You're definitely a candidate for a sharper, flickerless monitor with more screen real estate, conformity to the latest energy safety specifications, and support for power management in all its incarnations. Oh, and a light-speed graphics card to drive it. If your printer is more than a few years old, you can buy a new one with features that make the current one seem like a deadbeat, and for about half the price of the original! And then there's your sound setup. If you want to listen to streaming audio on a speakers-sound card combo that barely competes with the radio in a 1975 Pinto, fine by us. But you can get near-audiophile quality today for prices that get the attention of even the most cost-conscious PC lover.

Part V, "Adding the Extras," covers the remaining devices you might choose to add or upgrade: CD-R/RW drives, DVD drives, other removable media drives, tape drives, and scanners.

Part VI, "Solving Problems," tackles operating system and application upgrades. We also address how to partition a hard disk so you can run multiple operating systems on the same PC—a process called *multi-booting*. This gives you the ability to turn one PC into two or three PCs, each with its own operating environment. This is an ideal way to safely beta test software without placing your production partition at risk, and it's a cost-effective way to meet client project requirements without investing in multiple PCs. Third-party partitioning tools are also useful for cloning a partition, meaning, take a snapshot of a partition and set it aside in case you need to roll back in the event of a problem with your production partition. This section also discusses strategies and tools you need to efficiently solve software and hardware problems. Topics range from a discussion of common problems and how to fix them, step by step, to Registry restoration tricks. Plus, we cover an area that other hardware books ignore: getting good technical support. Over our collective three decades of computer consulting experience, we've placed literally thousands of calls to technical support engineers. We refined the checklist on how to handle these calls, right down to the gnat's eyebrow, and present it for your use in this section of the book. By using our calling techniques, you'll get better answers and solve your problem much more quickly.

Part VII, "Appendixes," covers a gamut of special topics including how to build a PC from scratch, upgrading your laptop, and how to inventory the hardware and software that makes your computer tick. We've also included a glossary of common technobabble terms. Use this glossary to help steer your way through a sea of difficult terms and acronyms.

We hope you find this book a good resource for saving your valuable time, increasing your PC's work capabilities and its fun factor, and reducing the upgrade stress factor. We wrote this book for you, and look forward to hearing from you. ·

Conventions Used in This Book

We've designed some special elements that appear throughout this book. We've written them to give you a short burst of information flavor along several different themes. In some cases, you really won't want to miss them (Do It Yourself); in other cases, you can skip over them (you might already know the jargon being demystified in a Plain Speaking blurb).

NOTE

NOTES

A Note is a snippet of information that elaborates on the current section's theme. In some cases, a Note will provide a Web address or product suggestion. The idea here is to whisper in your ear an example or product that adds value to the subject at hand, should you want to pursue it.

READ MY TIPS

A Tip presented this way deserves your special attention. We suggest you read these.

Do It Yourself

This element gives you step-by-step instructions on how to accomplish a small, well-defined task. We're do-it-yourselfers from way back, so come on in and join us.

PLAINSPEAKING

One of our pet peeves with this industry is the inordinate use of acronyms. Sure, some amount of shorthand is reasonable, but how is a consumer expected to keep her or his eyes from glazing over when the salesperson says, "And the really neat thing about this system is the built-in IEEE-1394 port for DV, plus the very latest AGP port in 4x mode, and loads of SDRAM DIMMs." Say what? These Plain Speaking blocks attack jargon with a vengeance. BTW (okay, we couldn't resist), here are some excellent Web sites for looking up acronyms and emoticons. ;-)

- Smileys and Acronyms Dictionary page at `http://wellweb.com/behappy/smiley.htm`

- Webopedia Online Computer Dictionary for Internet Terms and Technical Support page at `http://webopedia.internet.com`

- Freeware Hall of Fame's Acronyms Used in the Computer Community page at `http://www.freewarehof.org/acronyms.html` (beware—while very complete, many acronyms listed here include profanity). ■

ANOTHER FINE MESS

Occasionally, we present a personal or professional anecdote that reeks of poor judgment (on someone's part, occasionally ours), manufacturer misinformation, or a full-on bug. Of course, we always end with a moral to the … mess. ■

OFF THE WALL

Sometimes, boys just want to have fun. (With a tip o' the hat to Cyndi Lauper and songwriter Robert Hazard.) ∎

T.J. Lee and Lee Hudspeth

California, USA

PART

I

THE LAY OF THE LAND

1

DECIDING TO UPGRADE

Have you ever upgraded your toaster? Woke up one morning and decided that adding some extra slots to the chrome wonder on your countertop would be a great idea? Or maybe you've thought of popping the back off the old television out in the garage and upgrading that mature black and white set to color picture-in-picture? It's doubtful you've given these types of appliance upgrades any thought. But the chances are good that you *have* thought of upgrading your personal computer.

An Upgradable Appliance

Personal computers are unlike most other consumer electronic devices. When you buy a television or a toaster, it comes out of its box, gets plugged into an electrical outlet, and works. You expect years of reliable service until the unit either wears out through normal use or you replace it altogether with something newer that has more features than the original item you purchased.

The current state of computer hardware is more akin to the audio components from back when "hi-fidelity" was the buzzword and audiophiles were all agog over woofers and tweeters. The ultimate stereo back then was something you tinkered together from a wide array of different hardware choices, and you could "upgrade" your system by replacing one part with another. Sound familiar? Stereo systems and computer systems still have a lot in common today in that you can upgrade different parts of the system and mix and match components from different manufacturers.

While it's becoming more and more possible to buy a system that comes complete with everything you need and is up and running by just plugging it in, chances are good that at least one component exists that you'll want to upgrade at some point. For instance, the monitor that came with your computer might be a little smaller than you'd like. Or you might discover right after you bought your system that you can get a bigger hard drive, more memory, or whatever for less than you just paid. You also might decide to discard the system's computer speakers, keyboard, sound card, network card, and so forth and upgrade to another brand or model with a better or different feature set. Perhaps the nifty gizmo you didn't get with your system because it was too expensive comes down in price and you decide to add it to your computer. Yes, it's safe to say that an upgrade is probably in your future if you own a personal computer.

Unlike the toaster, which is probably at the apex of its development, computer technology is still developing so quickly that anything you buy today has already been made obsolete by

PLAINSPEAKING
PCS ARE NOT APPLIANCES

Computers are not yet in the ubiquitous "appliance" category as toasters and televisions are. In our opinion, computers are still in the do-it-yourself domain of the techno-hobbyist. Starting with the original IBM PC, personal computers have always been cobbled together from a plethora of off-the-shelf parts. When you purchase a complete system, you are just getting a box someone else cobbled together for you. Computer companies such as Dell and Micron are not really manufacturers so much as box assemblers. Because the PC is a collection of assembled parts, you can disassemble it and replace some parts with upgraded parts. ■

the new generation of machines and components coming out soon afterward. And *soon* does not mean the new stuff is years away from the showroom floor. No, your screaming fast, bleeding-edge power machine becomes a quaint PC that barely totters along when compared to what rolls off the conveyor belt only months after you uncrate yours.

OFF THE WALL
OLDER PCS RETIRE

Something else we'll talk about is what you can do with a PC you decide to "retire" as your primary machine. A number of things can be done to still get functionality from an older PC even though you've decided to get a new one. Even when you make the decision to buy a new system, you don't necessarily have to walk away from your original investment in your existing computer. ■

Because most of us can't afford to discard our systems every six months, more and more computer users are giving serious thought to rolling up their sleeves and pulling the covers off their systems to see whether an upgrade can breathe some new life into their personal computers. We're here to tell you that this is an excellent idea, and you don't have to be a computer expert to do so. You can keep your current system humming along with the right upgrades.

The Cost of Upgrading

The decision to upgrade is not as simple as it once was. Prices are such that you can purchase an entire new system today for what a hard disk cost just a few years ago. Does that mean you should forget upgrades, toss the whole computer, and buy a new one? Not at all, but you must be careful when planning upgrades so you don't wind up in a situation in which either the upgrade won't get your system to the performance/function level you want, or you spend so much money on the upgrade that it makes more sense to buy a new system.

The trick to a successful computer upgrade is not limited to knowing how to correctly plug card A into slot B. What makes a good upgrade is deciding on new components that make sense given your budget and the age and features of the system to be upgraded, all the while staying focused on the tasks for which you intend to use your improved computer.

Throughout this book, we'll stay mindful of the "upgrade or buy new" question and point out when you might be crossing the line and when a new computer would be a more economical option.

Total Upgrade Costs

Another important point to consider is that an upgrade will cost you not only the price of the components—hard disk, motherboard, memory, peripheral card, and so on—but you'll also be adding and installing into your system. One significant additional cost must factor into your upgrade decision. That cost is *the value of the time you'll spend getting the new component to work with your system.* This cost is often overlooked, and what's worse is that it's often doubled by the havoc of a poorly planned upgrade.

A simple "plug this in and go" type of upgrade can turn into a very different type of project if, in the middle of the install, you find that your current system's BIOS doesn't support the new component. Or if you find, after installing the new component, that you don't have a free interrupt request (IRQ) to which to

ANOTHER FINE MESS
POWER PROBLEMS

You can run into a number of problems when performing an upgrade if you don't think it all the way through before you begin. Power problems are an often-overlooked area. Does your system have sufficient power to run one more internal or USB component? Can your current UPS handle that new printer in addition to everything else you've got plugged into it? Have you overloaded the wall plugs or the amperage available on the circuit to the point where you're creating an overload or a fire hazard?

Physical size concerns exist, too. Does the chassis have room inside for your new gizmo? Should you have gotten an external version instead? Do you have a bus slot available, and is it the right type for your new card?

At one time or another, we've run into each of these situations while upgrading computers. While each can be dealt with in various ways, you want to avoid discovering a problem such as these when you have a production system disassembled all over the floor on a Sunday night after all the stores are closed and you need the machine working bright and early Monday morning. ■

assign it or that it requires a specific IRQ that's already in use. Now, you're juggling IRQs and uninstalling and reinstalling components that were working fine—all in a frantic effort to find a combination of peripherals and IRQs that works.

Therefore, the rule is not to jump into an upgrade haphazardly. Doing your homework can prevent a simple upgrade from becoming a huge, costly time investment. We'll cover these and other upgrade homework items, such as taking an inventory of your PC, planning the upgrade steps and procedures, selecting the right component, tools and spare parts checklists, backing up, performing the upgrade, and testing the upgrade, in detail in subsequent chapters. We'll point out the potential time-swamps for which to watch out and show you how to avoid them whenever possible. We'll also talk about all the little things a specific upgrade will require, which often are not included with the component, so you don't wind up with your computer's guts strewn all about your workspace only to realize you're missing a Y power cable.

Determining the Correct Upgrade

When deciding to upgrade a system or component, you must ensure that what you wind up with when you are finished is a solution for the problem you had when you started. If you don't accomplish your goal, you've wasted the money and effort expended performing the upgrade.

The most important step is defining the specific performance goal you want to reach or the exact feature you want to add to your current system. Sometimes this might require adding a component you do not currently have, in which case you must ensure you have the necessary resources (slots, BIOS support, IRQs, and so on) so the new item will work with your system. Some upgrades require replacing an existing component with a newer or enhanced version of the same thing—for example, replacing a 2D graphics card with a newer 3D or combo card.

It doesn't make sense to add more disk space or a new motherboard if what you are trying to improve is your Internet surfing speed. That's like trying to improve your car's performance by changing the air in the tires. If you're going to be using the same dial-up connection, modem, and ISP to connect to the Internet, a new system isn't going to address the sluggish Internet connectivity problem you want to solve.

Before deciding to perform a PC upgrade, you must do the following:

Determine Source of Problem First

1. Define the problem or shortcoming in the existing system you want to improve.

2. Find the component upgrade that addresses that problem or shortcoming.

3. Determine whether the necessary component will work with your existing system or whether ancillary upgrades will also be required; if so, define those requirements.

4. Locate the component and determine the cost of it, *including the value of your time spent performing the upgrade.*

5. Compare the total cost of upgrading to the cost of a new system that addresses the problem defined in step 1.

If you follow these guidelines, you'll find plenty of ways to extend the life of your existing system and give it the features you require, without having to buy a new system.

Buying Upgrade Components

When it comes to buying upgrade components for your computer, you have four choices:

- Mail order
- Brick-and-mortar superstores
- Local system integrator
- Auction, swap meet, or person-to-person

In this section, we'll discuss the advantages and disadvantages of each channel and show you the best options.

Mail Order on the Internet

There's been a lot of talk about e-commerce like it was some new form of acquisition science, but trust us, it's just mail order. Instead of poring over a catalog and then talking to a human being over the phone, you're looking at Web pages and placing the order using a script tied to a Web form. It's still the same basic process, though, with the same primary benefit of lower prices and sometimes the avoidance of sales tax. Plus, it has a few added benefits, but with all the same old pitfalls of mail order.

With mail order, you don't get to kick the tires. You can't see the item you're purchasing and it gets shipped to you, putting it at the mercy of whatever delivery method is used to get the component to your doorstep. If a problem exists with the item, you must go through an administrative procedure (read: hassle for you). This procedure usually involves calling customer service, waiting on hold for a while, getting a return merchandise authorization (RMA) number, and arranging for shipment back to the supplier (sometimes covered by the manufacturer, sometimes not). If you return the item because you ordered the wrong gizmo (say, a SCSI drive when you really wanted an IDE drive), you'll probably have to pay a restocking fee. With mail order, you can get customer support only over the telephone or via email or a Web site—never eyeball to eyeball. However, these issues shouldn't deter you from mail order; just be aware of the potential for problems.

What Internet mail order gives you over traditional mail order is the ability to search for a given component across many retailers and wholesalers quickly. Let's say you want to buy a new hard disk. If you go to the Ask Jeeves site (www.askjeeves.com) and inquire, "Where can I find information on hard disks?" you could jump to the following retail suppliers:

> Value America: http://www.valueamerica.com
>
> NECX: http://necxdirect.necx.com
>
> Dell: http://gigabuys.us.dell.com

The number of vendors you can query with very little effort using the Internet makes finding a bargain much easier and faster than traditional catalog shopping. If you do your homework and know exactly the component you are after, mail order is a great option.

ANOTHER FINE MESS
MAIL ORDER SYSTEMS

We've had entire systems purchased via mail order show up dead on arrival (DOA). This can really take the fun out of ordering a computer over the Internet. You uncrate your new PC, set it up (hopefully following the guidelines in our book *The Unofficial Guide to PCs*, published by Que, ISBN: 0-7897-1797-2), flip the switch, and nothing happens. At least, nothing you want to have happen. Calls go back and forth with the manufacturer, they have you do fun things such as pulling out every card in the machine and disconnecting and reconnecting cables, and they even have you try flashing the BIOS with an upgrade (on a brand-new system, mind you)—none of which does any good. Ultimately, you must recrate the system and send it back, after a somewhat heated discussion as to who is going to pay the shipping.

However, this is a worst-case scenario; the system usually comes up fine and you feel very good knowing you saved some substantial dollars using this channel to buy your computer. ■

Review Sites

Research is something you must do no matter where you wind up buying your computer upgrade components. The Internet makes researching reviews of given products and product categories easy. For example, if you were researching which drive in particular you should buy, you could find reviews for individual drives at sites such as the following:

- PC Magazine (http://www.zdnet.com/pcmag/filters/pclabs/)
- PC World (http://www.pcworld.com/top400/0,1375,,00.html)

NOTE

WEB SITE REVIEWS
Both PC Magazine and PC World post hardware and software reviews on their Web sites.

- Tom's Hardware Guide (`http://www.tomshardware.com`)—Here you'll find reviews of hardware, systems, and peripherals, plus columns and a message board where you can post questions.

- MaximumPC (`http://www.maximumpc.com/index.html`)—Provides great information on buying, upgrading, and fixing computers. Click the Reviews button to access their review search engine.

- Computing Review.com (`http://www.computingreview.com/reviews/`)—This site features reviews by actual users who post their experiences with a given product.

- CNet Computers.com (`http://computers.cnet.com/hardware/1,10121,0-1092-402-0.html`)—Publishes its own reviews and combines the editorial content with the ability to compare prices across several suppliers of the component in question.

- ReviewBooth.com (`http://www.reviewbooth.com/hardware/pr_review_hardware.asp?SearchString=storage&SearchString2=365`)—An *aggregator site*, which is a site that pulls together information from a number of other Web sites. Here you'll find product reviews from *InfoWorld*, *PC Week*, *Storage Review*, *Windows Magazine*, and *Computer Shopper*, just to name a few.

- Sharky Extreme (`http://sharkyextreme.com/hardware/`)—In-depth technical reviews of a wide variety of computer hardware can be found at this site, along with ratings across a number of categories. We were impressed with the volume of technical specifications provided in the Sharky Extreme reviews.

Shopping Bots

If you know the exact model and manufacturer of the drive you want (or at least the general type of drive, size, and type), you can use a shopping bot site to find the best price on the Web. A *shopping bot* is a bit of programming that goes out on the Web and finds places you can buy what you're looking for and lets you compare prices.

The CNet Computers.com site mentioned earlier does some price comparisons, but sites such as MySimon enable you to enter your search criteria and then search across a larger number of Web merchants, showing you the prices and letting you compare to find the best deal available.

Some of the more popular shopping bots that search across multiple sources on the Web are as follows:

- MySimon (http://www.mysimon.com)

- BottomDollar.com (http://www.bottomdollar.com)

- CNet Computers.com (http://shopper.cnet.com)

- Price Watch (http://www.pricewatch.com)

- Tech Shopper (http://www.techshopper.com)

- MyGeek.com (http://www.mygeek.com)

- Street Prices (http://www.streetprices.com/)

- Price SCAN (http://www.pricescan.com/)

MyGeek.com is unusual in that it enables you to fill out a "You Need What?" form with information such as the price you'd want to pay, the quantity to purchase, the brand, and other information specific to the type of item for which you are looking. Then, it sends your request to all the sellers who have registered with MyGeek. You then get an email response from one or more retailers interested in filling your order.

Volume Discounts for a Quantity of One

Even more extraordinary is the Volumebuy site (www.Volumebuy.com) where you can pool your purchase with others to develop some volume buying power. Volumebuy has three types of groups you can join to purchase an item listed on their site: Time, Flex, and Group.

- **Time Pools**—In a Time pool, you get a locked-in price for the item you're buying. The longer the length of time until the pool closes and you actually close the transaction and purchase the item, the cheaper the item is. This is because the longer a pool runs, the more people might sign up for it. More units mean a lower purchase price by Volumebuy, so it can in turn pass along that savings to pool members. However, no matter how many or few enter the pool, your price will remain the same.

- **Flex Pools**—Flex pools have a tiered pricing structure. The current price is where you can "jump in" and the pool will run for a fixed length of time, although, as more people enter the pool, the price can drop to the next-lower tier price. If more people join the flex pool, the price can fall to the next-lower level and so on until the pool closure date is reached.

■ **Group Pools**—In a Group pool, an item is available for a fixed price that does not change. Instead, a stated number of people must join the pool before the pool expiration date for everyone who has joined to receive the item at the stated price. Should the number of participants in the pool fall short of the required number when the pool expires, the item is not shipped.

You'll find shopping on the Internet gives you a variety of vendors and lets you find the best price around quickly.

Brick-and-Mortar Superstores

The new breed of consumer electronics superstores such as CompUSA, Fry's, Circuit City, and Best Buy makes it possible to not only pick up a quart of milk at the grocery store on the way home but also get a new sound card, hard drive, or entire system as well.

These retail super-outlets offer you the chance to speak face-to-face with a person. The downside is, of course, that the salesperson you speak to might not know beans about computers in general or the specific upgrade you want to purchase in particular. You'll still have to do your homework so that a fast-talking salesperson who babbles impressive TLAs (three-letter acronyms) won't bamboozle you into buying something you don't want or need.

Keep in mind that brick-and-mortar stores stock inventory, and in the time-accelerated world of computers where a hot new technology is only "hot" and "new" for weeks or months, pressure exists to push the old "new" stuff to make way for the new "new" stuff. This can create some really good bargains if you know what you want to buy and watch the local classified ads.

For components such as monitors and speakers, a retail store can provide the opportunity to "test drive" the upgrade item you are considering. Just be aware that the lighting and acoustics in these stores will not be anything similar to your home or office. However, being able to see what you're buying before laying out the cash can be comforting and helpful.

Taking a page from the Web e-tailers, many superstores such as Best Buy (www.bestbuy.com) and CompUSA (www.compusa.com) now have their own online Web sites. You can find advertised specials, get store locations, search for specific products, or even (in the case of CompUSA Auctions) bid on computer systems and peripherals.

Local System Integrator

A *local system integrator* is a small shop where systems are custom-made to your specifications. An integrator usually performs repairs and upgrade work, too. Having a good relationship with the staff at a local shop can come in very handy when you are trying to decide about a particular upgrade. They usually are quite knowledgeable about the latest hardware available, and more importantly, they know about the glitches and gotchas that might not be discussed in the hardware reviews you've read.

These folks can answer your questions and recommend the brands and parts for a particular system with which they have experience and that you can reasonably expect to be compatible.

ANOTHER FINE MESS
FRUSTRATING REPAIRS

You might decide that the comforts afforded by dealing face-to-face outweigh the risks of mail order where you don't get the benefit of eye contact. Be aware that we've had just as many problems with brick-and-mortar vendors as with our worst mail-order fiasco.

We've had store managers tell us to take the problem we encountered directly to the manufacturer, only to have the manufacturer tell us all returns must go through the retail outlet. We've made countless calls, had our calls not returned, experienced delays, and heard numerous excuses. Although we've usually gotten everything resolved to our satisfaction, the angst and frustration levels are much the same when we've had a problem with purchased hardware be it via a retail store or from a Web site. ■

Some integrators will order parts for you even though you're going to perform the upgrade yourself. Oftentimes, they can get you a particular part for a bit less than the superstores. In addition, if an upgrade you are performing yourself runs into unexpected problems, a local shop can sometimes save the day.

The biggest problem with local shops is that they tend to go out of business, sometimes unexpectedly. You should find a shop that has been around a while, does not turn over the entire staff every few weeks, and has no open Better Business Bureau complaints against it.

Auction, Swap Meet, or Person-to-Person

This is one of the riskiest ways to acquire an upgrade component, but it also can be the cheapest. Auction sites such as eBay (www.ebay.com) offer used, new, and refurbished equipment in a bewildering array of prices. You can buy an entire system, a computer case, motherboards, power supplies, and so on—you name it and there's an auction somewhere for it. The following are some of the auction sites available:

■ eBay (http://www.ebay.com)

■ Amazon (http://www.amazon.com/auctions/)

- Auctions.com (`http://www.auctions.com/categories/AZBONAOGWA/computers/computers.asp`)

- Egghead (`http://www.egghead.com/atauction/computers/computers.htm`)

- uBid (`http://www.ubid.com`)

- Yahoo! (`http://auctions.yahoo.com/`)

- CNet (`http://auctions.cnet.com/`)

OFF THE WALL
PROTECT YOURSELF WHILE BUYING ONLINE

Be mindful that when participating in an online auction as a buyer, you could be doing business with anyone, ranging from an individual who wants to sell some unused equipment to a retailer looking to dump unwanted inventory to someone who might never ship the product you purchased. Although auction sites are doing all they can to ensure that sellers behave ethically and are requiring sellers to sign binding agreements that they'll ship the product to the highest bidder in the condition the product was advertised, this is difficult to enforce.

The 911.com site has a fairly good beginner's tutorial to online auctions at `http://www.service911.doc` (search on `auctions`).

To protect yourself when buying via an auction, you can use a service called iEscrow (`www.iescrow.com`). This service can be used to avoid the problem in which you pay for something but the seller never sends you the product. With iEscrow, you send the money to iEscrow and they hold the funds until the seller sends you the merchandise and you accept it. If the seller never ships you the product, iEscrow returns your money. In addition, you can reject the product because it is in a different condition from what was promised, in which case you return it to the seller and iEscrow sends you back your money. ■

The uBid site is not your traditional auction site because you don't deal with different sellers; instead, you deal with a single reseller who lets you bid on items they carry. The opening bid is the floor price below which uBid will not sell the product in question. We've found some very good deals on the uBid site from time to time.

Computer swap meets are still a big business in various parts of the country, and bargains can indeed be found here. At your local computer swap meet, the deals usually are cash-and-carry, so you can wind up with a great deal or a real nightmare with little recourse—very similar to buying something at a flea market or garage sale. At a swap meet, you must be very knowledgeable about what you want and be willing to assume the risk of transacting business with a vendor you might never see again.

Buying a component from a friend or co-worker is something we see more often now that so many households have a computer (or two) and more and more people are upgrading.

The main problem with these alternative methods of finding upgrade components is that you have to know exactly what you want and be able to determine whether a deal being offered is legitimate or "too good to be true." Deals that are too good to be true usually aren't true at all. Warranty can also be an issue. Say your friend buys a computer system, pulls out the 2GB drive, and pops in a monster 20GB drive in its place. You'd love to have a 2GB drive for your old system, so you buy the drive. But, if something goes wrong, will the drive manufacturer honor the warranty? Someone else made the original purchase, and he might or might not have the original invoice. In addition, the warranty work might have to go through the original vendor who sold the complete system. As you can see, no pat answers exist, so just be aware of the issues involved.

Overall, we don't recommend buying your components this way because of the potential dangers involved. Instead, you should stick with one of the other three methods discussed in this section. That won't guarantee you success, but it should increase the odds a bit.

2

PREPARING FOR AN UPGRADE

This chapter describes how to inventory your PC from BIOS to Zip drive. You must know everything possible about what you already have on hand to avoid compatibility and other upgrade snags. In the process, you'll fill out an inventory list and learn about the various components of your PC, including tips on how to find manufacturers and track upgrades. We describe the various types of peripheral buses, offer tips on purchasing hardware online, and conclude with a checklist of what to do before performing any upgrade.

Finding Out What's Inside

Little bits and pieces of descriptive information about your PC's components are scattered throughout your operating system—assumed to be Microsoft Windows (95, 98, or Millennium Edition) for this book—and your PC itself. You must travel a bewildering trail to discover everything important about a particular component. The trip starts with the System Properties dialog box, specifically the Device Manager tab. From there, you can select a component and double-click it, or click the Properties button, or right-click it and then choose Properties; any of these actions displays the Properties dialog for that device. That dialog box typically offers three tabs you can study: General, Resources, and Driver (see Figure 2.1).

NOTE

WINDOWS 95, 98, AND MILLENNIUM SPOKEN HERE

Most operating system–related discussions in this book will apply to Windows 95, 98, and Millennium Edition (Me). Your mileage might vary if you're running Windows NT or Windows 2000.

FIGURE 2.1

The Device Manager's *<device name>* Properties dialog box enables you to view and change a device's internal settings.

But the Properties dialog box doesn't provide a thorough inventory. It does not include the following important items: serial number, Web site (for a component's technical info, FAQs, and drivers), warranty terms and conditions, what type of slot it occupies (if any), what bus it uses, and manufacturer's model number (which might differ from the text Windows uses to describe it, but more on this later). For these specifics, you need to get your fingernails dirty—figuratively speaking.

To help you inventory your system, we have developed a Microsoft Excel workbook called PC Inventory.xlt. The *t* in xlt isn't a typographical error. Standard Excel workbooks do have an extension of xls (not xlt), but PC Inventory.xlt is a special type of workbook. The xlt extension indicates that it's an Excel *template*. We set things up this way on purpose. You can use this Excel template to create a standard Excel workbook—one for each of your PCs—that contains all the template's boiler-plate headings and formatting. Then, all you have to do is enter the relevant data for your first PC, create another workbook based on PC Inventory.xlt for your second PC, and so on.

Here are the steps for using PC Inventory.xlt.

NOTE

WHERE TO FIND OUR PC INVENTORY FORM
A blank, paper-based version of the inventory form is included in Appendix D, "PC Inventory Form," so that you can photocopy it. It is also available for download as the Excel files described earlier; browse to our firm's Web site at
http://www.PRIMEConsulting.com.

1. Copy PC Inventory.xlt to your Microsoft Templates folder. In Office 97, it's typi-cally C:\Program Files\Microsoft Office\Templates. In Office 2000 it's typically C:\Program Files\Microsoft Office\Templates\1033. (The last folder's name is a four-digit code determined by Microsoft to indicate which language Office is using; 1033 represents English.)

2. Start Excel.

3. Select File and then choose New.

4. You should now see the New dialog box. In the General tab's list, select PC Inventory.xlt and click the OK button. This creates a new workbook based on PC Inventory.xlt.

5. Save the new workbook with whatever name you want. For example, if you have a PC named Pterodactyl then name the file Pterodactyl.xls.

6. Fill out the worksheet's cells for this PC. See the next section for information about the worksheet's rows and columns.

Using Our Excel Workbook to Inventory Your PC

The following sections describe the workbook's general information area, columns, and rows.

PC Inventory Form: General Information

Before doing an inventory of the PC's components, you need to fill out information about the PC as a unit.

PC Name

Right-click your desktop's Network Neighborhood icon, choose Properties, select the Identification tab, and look in the Computer name field, as shown in Figure 2.2. (You also can find this value in the Registry. For a Windows 98 PC, look at the value for
`HKEY_LOCAL_MACHINE\System\CurrentControlSet\Control\ComputerName\`
`ComputerName`.)

Viewing the contents of your Registry is a relatively safe procedure. Simply click Start, Run, and type `regedit.exe`. Then, click OK.

CAUTION

BE CAREFUL!

Of course, you should always be careful not to edit or delete any entries while browsing. If you know you're going to modify your Registry, do so carefully and while you're not distracted. Be sure that you know exactly what you're doing and have backed up your Registry before making even a single change. We also suggest you never leave your Registry open for editing for an extended period of time; make your changes and then close the Registry Editor immediately.

For more information about viewing and editing the Registry, study the "Changing Keys and Values" help topic in the Registry Editor's (Regedit.exe) help file. For information about how to recover your Registry, see Microsoft's article "How to Manually Restore the Windows 98 Registry" at `http://support.microsoft.com/support/kb/`
`articles/Q221/5/12.asp`.

FIGURE 2.2

This obscure dialog box tab is where you view and change your PC's name, workgroup, and description.

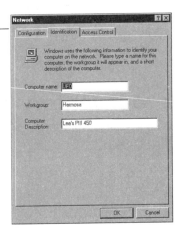

PC Username

Enter the name of the person who uses or is responsible for this PC.

Manufacturer Technical Support

Enter the PC manufacturer's technical support phone number. We can't tell you how many times we've desperately needed this phone number but couldn't find it. And if you're thinking, "I can just get it off their Web site," that doesn't work if this is the only PC on the floor, house, whatever, and it's belly up, leaving you with no way to connect to the Internet.

Manufacturer Customer Service

Enter the PC manufacturer's customer service phone number. You'll need this for return merchandise authorization (RMA) numbers for bad components and copies of your paperwork, or to complain about inadequate technical support.

Manufacturer Service/ID Number

Some manufacturers use a unique code to help you identify your PC. You must have this code to get information about your PC whether on their Web site or by phone.

NOTE

HOW DELL ELECTRONICALLY TAGS ITS PCS

Dell maintains a System Service Tag for each PC it sells. The tag is burned into the BIOS during manufacturing so you can get to it via your system setup program or from a sticker on the system's back panel. In Dell's case, a second value called the Express Service Code is a conversion of the alphanumeric System Service Tag into a strictly numeric value to make it easy to key in to Dell's automated call-routing system.

Order Number

The PC's original order number is available from your invoice or packing list.

Order Date

The PC's order date is available from your invoice or packing list.

Customer Number

Your customer number is available from your invoice or packing list.

Internal Asset Number

If your employer has assigned an internal asset number to your PC, enter it here.

PC Inventory Form: Column Headings

Figuring out the correct values for a component's properties ranges from easy (Manufacturer) to occasionally obscure (Serial No.). For tough columns, we provide tips on where and how to look for the answers.

Component

This column identifies the type of system component—for example, CPU, Motherboard, RAM, Hard Drive #1, and so on.

Bus/Interface

This column indicates the component's bus or interface—for example, SCSI, ISA, PCI, Parallel, and so on. This field applies to only a few of the components.

All the modern—and some retired—peripheral buses you might encounter are covered in the section "Available Peripheral Slots."

TIP

WHAT BUS IS THAT CARD ON?

Start with the motherboard diagram, something any self-respecting PC manufacturer provides in the PC's user manual.

Open up the chassis.

Compare the chassis's actual layout to the diagram in the manual and note which peripheral card is in which slot.

Some motherboards display the slot type's acronym adjacent to the slot itself, for example, "AGP1", "PCI1", and so on. See the section "Available Peripheral Slots," later in this chapter for more information on slot and bus types.

Manufacturer

This column contains the name of the component's manufacturer.

Model

This column identifies the component's model name or number. This might seem simple enough, but occasionally a component will have slightly different model numbers depending on where you look. The documentation that came with the component might not be of much help either because manufacturers typically publish one user's guide that covers several models. In such a case, if you ever need to contact the manufacturer—say, for warranty or registration information—you'll need the exact model number. The place to look is on the component's serial/model number label, not the description displayed by Windows in the Device Manager list.

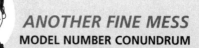

ANOTHER FINE MESS
MODEL NUMBER CONUNDRUM

One of our testing PCs is a Micron Pentium 166 workhorse. It shipped from Micron's factory outfitted with a Plextor CD-ROM drive. According to the Device Manager, the model is PX-8XCS, but a search for "8XCS" on Plextor's Web site gets no hits. The drive's model/serial number label includes the correct model: PX-83CS. A search for "83CS" on the Web site yields a hit. ∎

Quantity

This column indicates the component's size, quantity, or capacity—for example, how many megabytes of system memory. This field applies to only some of the components.

Serial Number

This column stores the component's serial number. You'll need the serial number for any in-warranty technical support. With some manufacturers—Adaptec, for example—you can't get technical support of any kind, not even a simple answer about the component's specifications, without the serial number. A utility called Sandra (more on this shortly), other analysis packages, and some specialized device identification utilities can ferret out this value. We discuss these identification tools later in this chapter in the section "Available Peripheral Slots."

SERIAL NUMBER LABELS

The simplest and most reliable way to determine a component's serial number is to get it directly from the device's serial/model number label, which is affixed to the component.

Driver Info

This column identifies the driver's filename and version number. Start by using Device Manager to examine the device's Properties dialog box, click the Driver tab, click the Driver File Details button, and then look at the name of the first file in the Driver files list. The version is listed below the Provider and Copyright fields. We discuss where to get updated drivers later in this chapter.

Web Site

This column includes links to one or more Web pages that specifically deal with the device, particularly information about technical support or specifications. For example, in the case of Covemeister's motherboard, we store the link `http://support.micronpc.com/faq/mbdfaq/images/ts00835.html`, which goes directly to a diagram of the motherboard. Then, in the Comments field we've entered `See also http://www.micronics.com`.

QUICK FIX FOR DEAD-END WEB ADDRESSES

Web addresses can change unexpectedly and aren't always redirected (although in a perfect world of infinite time for all Webmasters, they should be). So, if you have a problem with a device months or years after completing the inventory and the link is invalid, try this. Lop off the last segment of the address and resubmit it to your browser. For example, truncate from `http://support.micronpc.com/faq/mbdfaq/images/ts00835.html` to `http://support.micronpc.com/faq/mbdfaq/images/`. You might still get an error code such as `HTTP 403 - Forbidden` or `HTTP 404 - File not found`, but keep lopping off the last segment and resubmitting to your browser until you get to a navigable page, which in this case is `http://support.micronpc.com`.

Warranty

This column contains a brief description of the warranty terms, or possibly the date of a warranty's expiration.

COMMENTING CELLS IN EXCEL

If you want to add a special comment to a cell, say, the Warranty cell, it's easy. You add a comment to an Excel cell in the form of a Comment object, which is then hidden "inside" the cell. A Commented cell is marked with a bright red triangle in the cell's upper-right corner. This Comment object's text is separate from the content of the cell. To add a Comment, select the cell, select Insert, choose Comment, and then type in your comment (see Figure 2.3). When finished, click anywhere outside the Comment frame. To see a Comment after you've quit the Comment frame, hover your mouse over the cell. A ToolTip will appear with your text in it. (Note, you don't have to actually click the cell to see its

Comment; you can simply hover over it.) To edit a Comment later, select the cell, select Insert, and then choose Edit Comment. Right-click equivalents exist for all these actions: Right-click the cell and choose the appropriate command. One last comment about Comments: Excel's factory default is for Comments to be displayed, but you, or someone else using your PC, might have turned off this feature inadvertently. If you don't see a Comment and can't figure out why, select Tools, Options, View, and make sure the Comments section's None option button is *not* selected.

FIGURE 2.3

When you anno-
tate an Excel cell
with a
Comment, you
type inside a
resizable frame,
similar to a Post-
it, that points to
the host cell.

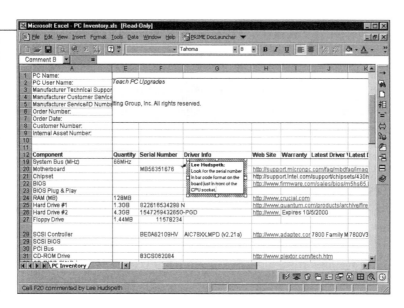

Latest Driver Version

When you're sleuthing for a component's latest driver, type your notes here and, if appropriate, in the Latest Driver Download Info field. If you find an updated driver but decide not to install it right away due to time or other constraints, you can store the driver's version number in this field. Leave this field empty if you already have the latest driver installed. We discuss where to get updated drivers later in this chapter.

NOTE

FINDING DOWNLOADS

A device manufacturer's Web site should include a Downloads link on its home page. If no such link exists, look for a Search link and key in your device name or model number. For example, the Sound Blaster site's home page (`http://www.soundblaster.com`) has a Downloads section with a Drivers link below it, and it also has a Search field.

Latest Driver Download Info

When you're tracking down a component's latest driver and find one but decide not to install it right away, enter the filename and download link information here. Leave this field empty if the latest driver is already installed.

Comments

Use this column for free-form notes.

SiSoft Sandra: A System Analysis Tool

For some components, you can get values either by studying Windows' built-in Device Manager or by visually inspecting the device. In many cases, a system analysis tool such as SiSoft Sandra can be revealing.

This product isn't actually named after a person. The name comes from the phrase *System ANalyser, Diagnostic, and Reporting Assistant*. Sandra is a must-have tool that we recommend for the efficient and thorough cross-checking of a system's inventory.

NOTE

TESTING A SYSTEM

You also can use a tool such as Sandra to burn in or test a new system, or one you've recently upgraded or repaired.

Sandra comes in two flavors. The Standard version is freeware and includes 50 reports called *modules*. The Professional version costs $29 and includes more than 70 reports. The user interface for these reports is similar to the appearance of the applets inside your Control Panel, as shown in Figure 2.4. Double-clicking a module displays a dialog box for the chosen component(s). Sandra's modules are full of documented and undocumented information about your PC and its components. You'll be amazed at how much low-level information Sandra can pry from your system without removing the cover.

For example, say you're curious to see detailed CPU information but aren't in the mood to pop it from its socket/slot. Go into Sandra's CPU & BIOS Information module and, among other things, Sandra reports that this PC's CPU is a P6K Katmai Pentium III 450-700 2V (revision/stepping 7/2; stepping mask kB0; Slot 1), and that the CPU fan is currently rotating at 4018rpm.

Tips at the end of each module offer suggestions and warnings regarding your system. In many cases, this information is too generic to be beneficial, but you can use these items as a checklist for researching your system's behavior. Sandra's Create a

Report Wizard can generate printed, file, or fax reports on any or all of its modules. Sandra provides graphic bar chart benchmarking statistics inside its information dialog boxes. For example, it will compare your CPU performance against four standard CPU configurations. As mentioned previously, you can use the benchmark modules (CPU, drives, CD-ROM/DVD, and memory) to burn in your system. We use the Create a Report Wizard to run all enabled information and testing/diagnostic modules and then gather all that data into a single HTML-formatted list. The Wizard's output comes in one of five formats: standard (text), hierarchical (report), Web HTML, Web XML, and CIM (SMS/DMI).

The Standard version's 2.2MB free download is available at `http://www.sisoftware.demon.co.uk/sandra/`. You can buy the Professional version (downloadable) for $29 at `http://www.beyond.com/PKSN100846/prod.htm`.

FIGURE 2.4

Sandra looks similar to the Windows Control Panel; to run any available module, simply double-click it.

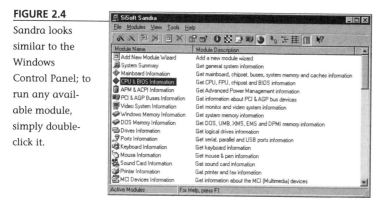

Current Components

The following sections cover individual PC components; each component is represented by a row, and each property is represented by a column.

PC Model

The best source of information about this component is the invoice or packing slip. We put the invoice description in the Model field and any different, alternative model information in the Comments field. For example, one of our Micron Pentium boxes reads "Millennia Plus Series A (430HX)" on the invoice, but the serial/model number label reads "M55HIPLUS-P166-MT" (it turns out that the motherboard model is M55HI+). Regarding your warranty, be sure the invoice lists any add-on warranties you purchased—for example, an additional year of onsite service.

TIP

READ THE FINE PRINT

If your PC has an onsite warranty, print a copy of that warranty's terms and conditions, document it, and study it carefully. A manufacturer's "next-day onsite service" claims, which are so appealing in the form of sexy bullet items and blinking text on its Web site, might actually be constrained by the fine print. Furthermore, some of the components might not be covered by the onsite warranty, even if they were installed in the manufacturer's factory! Buyer beware.

Case

Cases that house the inner workings of a PC come in several different standard sizes. The case determines how much room you have for adding components such as hard disks and DVD or CD-ROM drives. The case also will determine the size of the motherboard that can be mounted in it. Most of the new cases are designed for the ATX motherboard form factor (or micro-ATX, which is a smaller version of the ATX), although you can still get cases for the older Baby AT–size motherboards.

Your invoice or packing slip should list your system's case type. Different cases provide different numbers of front-accessible drive bays. Most unused bays have plastic faceplates covering them that you can easily, and sometimes not so easily, remove when installing another internal drive. You will find some cases, however, that have spare hard drive bays with no removable faceplate. Because you don't need to physically access a hard drive, the faceplate is unnecessary.

A desktop case sits horizontally and typically has four front-accessible bays: two smaller ones suitable for floppy or Zip drives and two full-size bays.

Tower cases come in several flavors. A mini-tower has two to three full-size bays; a mini-mid tower has three to four; a mid-tower has four to five; and a full-size tower has between six and seven.

The power supply is part of the case. Newer models have 250- to 300-watt power supplies, whereas older cases run 200–230 watts. It's a good idea to note your case type and the power supply wattage.

CPU

Figure 2.5 shows a Pentium III processor in a Single Edge Contact Cartridge (SECC2) package. If you're interested in seeing what your processor looks like, you're in the right place. In this section, we describe the processor and explain how to get more information about it.

The following are several ways you can get information about your Central
Processing Unit (CPU):

1. For Windows users, you can run the Intel Processor Frequency ID Utility. It
   reports CPUID information, including the processor classification, system configuration, processor features, and cache (see Figure 2.6). It also compares your
   Pentium III processor and system bus's reported frequency to expected frequency and issues a Pass/Fail warning. (The Frequency Test supports only
   processors in the Pentium III family.) See Figure 2.7. You can download this
   tool at `http://support.intel.com/support/processors/tools/`
   `frequencyid/download.htm`.

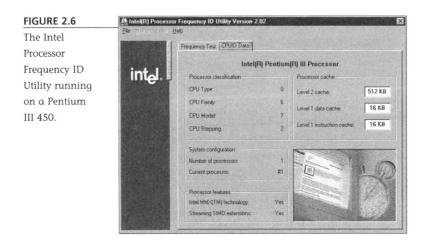

FIGURE 2.7

The Intel Processor Frequency ID Utility has a pass/fail indicator that reports whether your system is operating within Intel's frequency specifications.

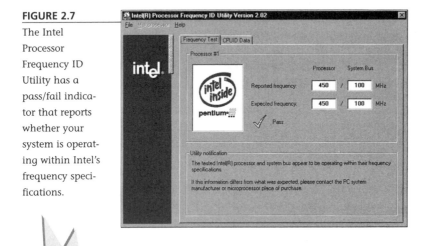

NOTE

FINDING THE AMD CPUID TOOL

The AMD CPUID tool is available at `http://www.amd.com/products/cpg/bin/amdcpuid.zip`.

2. For DOS users, the comparable utility is the Intel CPUID Utility for DOS. You can download this tool at `http://support.intel.com/support/processors/procid/cpuid/cpuiddos.htm`.

3. You also can run Sandra's CPU & BIOS Information module (see Figure 2.8).

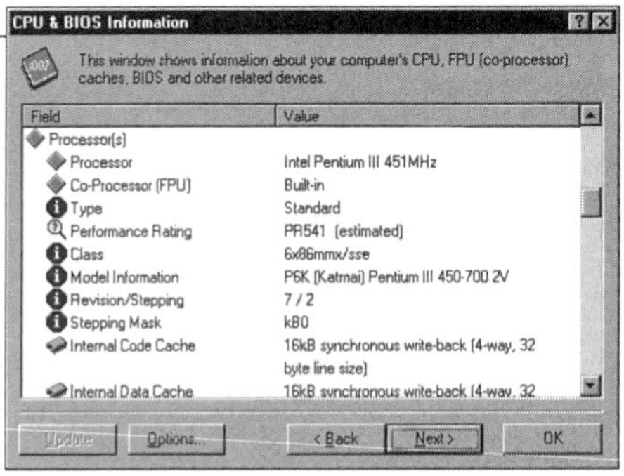

FIGURE 2.8

Sandra provides several screens of data on your CPU.

4. You can examine the markings on the top of the processor. The diagram in Figure 2.9 shows how a Pentium III processor is marked. If you can't see the markings because they're covered by a heat sink/fan attached to the top, don't bother removing the heat sink/fan (except as a last resort, and we mean your

very last resort because it could get ugly). Instead, remove the processor entirely from its slot/socket, turn it upside down—without fussing with the heat sink/fan assemblies affixed to the top of the processor—and look at the duplicate markings on the bottom.

FIGURE 2.9

This is a diagram of a Pentium III's markings.

An Intel processor will typically be marked to include some or all of the following: a product logo, a product code (speed and cache size), country of origin, an FPO # (sometimes referred to as a Test Lot Traceability #), a serial number, and an *S-Spec number*. The last takes the form of a four- to six-digit alphanumeric code—for example, SY037 (more on this important number in a moment). You can glean other information from these markings, depending on the processor.

For more detailed information, perhaps more than any of us mere mortals can really use (because we're not actually implementing the processor in a manufacturing setting), see Intel's Manufacturing Advantage Tips home page (`http://developer.intel.com/design/quality/index.htm`) and Table 2.1.

Table 2.1 Intel's Manufacturing Advantage Tips Web Pages for Pentium and Higher Generations

Processor	Manufacturing Advantage Tips Web Page
Celeron	`http://developer.intel.com/design/quality/celeron/hints_labeling.htm`
Pentium II	`http://developer.intel.com/design/quality/pentiumii/index.htm`
Pentium II Xeon	`http://developer.intel.com/design/quality/pentiumii/xeon/index.htm`
Pentium III	`http://developer.intel.com/design/quality/pentiumiii/`[1]
Itanium IA-64	`http://developer.intel.com/design/ia-64/prog_overview/index.htm`[2]

1. You'll have to follow some links to find the final page at `http://developer.intel.com/design/quality/pentiumii/secc2/shipping.htm`.

2. At the time of this writing, no specific page exists for the Itanium's manufacturing advantage tips.

CAUTION

WHEN ZERO INSERTION FORCE ISN'T

The *zero force* part of a Zero Insertion Force socket is not exactly zero. The lever, by design, is tightly wedged into a clip that holds the processor securely in place. Picture the processor (and motherboard) lying flat on a table. To remove the lever from its clip, you must apply a moderate amount of sideways force to swing it horizontally out and away from the processor. This can be an especially delicate operation if the power supply or anything else is in the way; therefore, either remove what's in the way or be very careful. After the lever is free, the zero insertion force moniker lives up to its reputation.

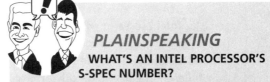

PLAINSPEAKING
WHAT'S AN INTEL PROCESSOR'S S-SPEC NUMBER?

To get additional information from Intel about your Intel processor—information that's not revealed by the Intel Processor Frequency ID Utility—you need the *S-Spec number*. This special number is printed on the top (and sometimes the bottom) of the processor. The S-Spec number is nothing more than an identification code. For example, the S-Spec number SY037 refers to a specific Pentium classic P54C 166MHz microprocessor. See Table 2.2 for more information. ■

Table 2.2   Intel's Processor Family Quick Reference Guide Web Pages

Processor	Quick Reference Guide Web Page
Pentium	http://developer.intel.com/design/pentium/qit/
Pentium Pro	http://developer.intel.com/design/pro/qit/
Pentium II	http://developer.intel.com/design/pentiumii/qit/
Pentium III	http://developer.intel.com/design/pentiumiii/qit/
Pentium III Xeon	http://developer.intel.com/design/pentiumiii/xeon/qit/

After you know the S-Spec number, go to the appropriate processor family's Quick Reference Guide page and click the matching link for that S-Spec number. Note that we refer to an older processor in this scenario; we do this to demonstrate that this infrastructure is in place for Intel's old and new processors. See Figure 2.10.

FIGURE 2.10

This is Intel's Quick Reference Guide page for a Pentium P54C 166MHz processor with an S-Spec number of SY037.

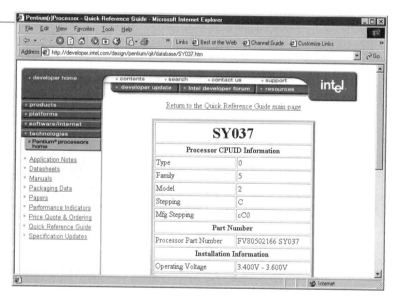

To glean even more detailed information, you need what Intel and AMD call the *datasheet* for your processor's family (see Table 2.3). For example, to retrieve Covemeister's datasheet, a Pentium P54C running at 166MHz, you would go to the Pentium datasheets home page, select the Pentium® Processor link, and then download the file 24199710.pdf. See Figure 2.11.

NOTE

DOWNLOADING ADOBE ACROBAT READER

To read this Adobe Acrobat document, you'll need a copy of the free Adobe Acrobat Reader. You'll find the latest version at
`http://www.adobe.com/products/acrobat/readstep.html`.

FIGURE 2.11

This is what a Pentium P54C 166MHz processor's datasheet looks like when viewed with the Adobe Acrobat reader.

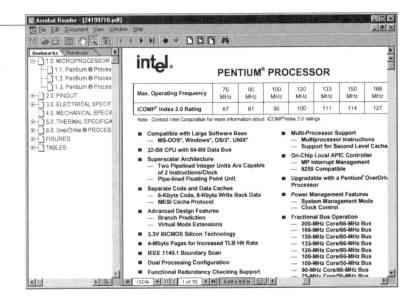

Table 2.3 Intel's and AMD's Processor Family Datasheets Web Pages

Processor Family	Datasheets Web Page
Pentium	`http://developer.intel.com/design/pentium/datashts/`
Pentium Pro	`http://developer.intel.com/design/pro/datashts/`
Pentium II	`http://developer.intel.com/design/pentiumii/datashts/`
Pentium III	`http://developer.intel.com/design/pentiumiii/datashts/`
Pentium III Xeon	`http://developer.intel.com/design/pentiumiii/xeon/datashts/`
AMD-K5	`http://www.amd.com/products/cpg/techdocs/datasheets/18522.pdf`
AMD-K6	`http://www.amd.com/K6/k6docs/pdf/20695.pdf`
AMD-K6-2	`http://www.amd.com/K6/k6docs/pdf/21850.pdf`
AMD-K6-III	`http://www.amd.com/K6/k6docs/pdf/21918.pdf`
AMD Athlon	`http://www.amd.com/products/cpg/athlon/techdocs/pdf/21016.pdf`

SEE ALSO

➤ *For more details on choosing and upgrading a CPU, see Chapter 6, "CPU and Motherboard Upgrades," page 135*

FINDING AMD PROCESSOR TECHNICAL DOCUMENTS

Technical documents for AMD processors—datasheets, technical manuals, and other related documents—are easy to access. Browse to AMD's Technical Documentation page (`http://www.amd.com/support/techdocdir.html`) and drill down on the product of your choice. You also can get a free CD-ROM that contains the technical documentation for all current production and most recent AMD processors (`http://www.amd.com/products/cpg/cdrom/index.html`), and you can even register to have a new CD shipped to you as it is updated.

TOM'S HARDWARE GUIDE PROCESSOR AND CHIPSET TABLES

The diligent folks at the Tom's Hardware Guide site have gone the extra mile in assembling detailed tables on a wide variety of processors and chipsets. The processor tables include the following information: CPU clock speed, system bus speed, multiplier, core voltage, L2 cache, cache frequency, architecture, and micron process. Go to `http://www.tomshardware.com/howto/00q2/000412/index.html` and look toward the bottom of the page for the Table of Contents. Thanks, Tom, Patrick, and Uwe!

Processor Socket/Slot

The processor is connected to the motherboard using either a *socket* (see Figure 2.12) or a *slot*. A socket is a socket and a slot is a slot, meaning a socket connector is square-ish in appearance, whereas a slot is—you guessed it—thin and rectangular (similar in appearance to a peripheral card slot). Socket and slot designs vary somewhat confusingly across several parameters: the actual connector type (socket versus slot), the number of pins, the layout of the pins, and voltage. Adding to the confusion is the cross-section of all these features by processor family. Finally, although very exacting specifications exist for the dimensions of each socket type (Sockets 1, 2, 3, 4, 5, 7, 8, and PGA-370) and each slot type (Slots 1 and 2), those dimensions aren't as important as simply knowing which type of connector your processor uses. Because Intel considers the design specifics of its Slot 1 connection a trade secret, AMD has developed its own connection schemes. One is called Slot A and looks very much like Intel's Slot 1, although by design you can't accidentally plug in the wrong CPU. The upcoming Socket A will house AMD's new line of 1GHz processors.

FIGURE 2.12

A Socket 370 connector.

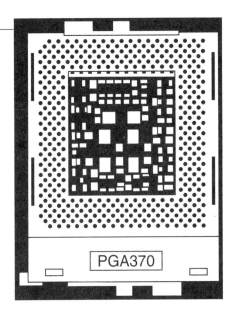

Socket 370

PROCESSOR SOCKET/SLOT SPECIFICATIONS AT YOUR FINGERTIPS

The gurus at Motherboard HomeWorld have put together a marvelous resource to help you sort out socket and slot arcana. Browse to `http://www.motherboards.org/sockets.html` to view a well-organized table full of data on current and future connections, plus write-ups on each one. The HomeWorld site includes plenty of other helpful information and resources, too.

If your processor was manufactured by Intel, you can look at the connector itself, which is usually labeled with the socket/slot type. You also can look at its S-Spec Web page to see what the socket/slot type is.

INTEL PROCESSOR IDENTIFICATION TOOLS

The Intel Pentium III, Pentium II, and Celeron processors' five form factors (types of packaging) are nicely cataloged, along with photos, at `http://support.intel.com/support/processors/procid/ptype.htm`.

L1 Cache

L1 stands for *Level 1*. The *L1 cache* is a memory cache built into the 486 and later-generation processors, so it runs at the processor's full core speed (meaning, faster than any other cache in the system). Synonyms for L1 cache are *internal cache*, *integral cache*, and *primary cache*. A good source for details about your processor's L1 cache is the Intel Processor Frequency ID Utility.

L2 Cache

L2 stands for Level 2. The *L2 cache* is the second memory cache to which a processor turns. Traditionally it is larger in size than its upstream L1 counterpart, and—for P5 generation systems—is located on the motherboard; thus, it runs at the motherboard bus speed (meaning, more slowly than the processor's full core speed). In the P6 family, the L2 cache migrated into the processor (in the Pentium II MMX and Pentium III, the internal L2 cache runs at half the core speed). Synonyms for L2 cache are *external cache* and *secondary cache*. A good source for details about your processor's L2 cache is the Intel Processor Frequency ID Utility.

PLAINSPEAKING
GOT ANY SPARE CACHE?

Cache *n.* 1. A place in which stores of food, supplies, etc. are hidden, as by explorers or trappers.

The term *cache* is used in the computing industry to describe a location for storing frequently used data or instructions, thereby improving system performance. Caches are used for both memory and hard disks. In this section, we'll confine ourselves to a discussion of memory caches, particularly two that are built right into a microprocessor's architecture: the Level 1 cache and Level 2 cache.

These caches use *static RAM (SRAM)*, a type of memory that is much faster than traditional DRAM—so fast that it can keep up with the galloping processor. However, SRAM's fast speed makes it very costly. Also, consider that SRAM is physically much larger than a comparable quantity of DRAM (up to 30 times larger), and you can see why SRAM isn't used for all system memory.

Instead, system designers judiciously use SRAM for these two small caches, which are the processor's first and second stops for data. Compare these numbers to a Pentium III and you can see why even a small amount of Level 1 and Level 2 cache memory provides improved system performance (were the processor to always have to fetch data from the slower system memory). For a Pentium III/550 system, CPU speed is 550MHz; L1 cache speed is 550MHz; L2 cache speed is 275MHz; motherboard speed is 100MHz; and system memory (SIMM/DIMM) runs at 100MHz. So, the L1 cache memory is running 5.5 times faster than system memory. ∎

System Bus (MHz)

It's helpful to be aware of the speed of your *system bus*. The system bus connects the microprocessor and a crucial chipset called the North Bridge (more on this later), and it is the highest-speed bus in a system. Synonyms for system bus are *motherboard bus* and *processor bus*. This can be confusing because you'll often encounter the term *processor core speed* (or *processor full core speed*), the operative word here being *core*. What's going on is that the processor has an external speed matching that of the motherboard, but the processor's internal speed is a multiple of the motherboard speed. For example, a Pentium III Xeon 500MHz system has a motherboard bus (processor bus speed) of 100MHz. Its clock multiplier is 5, so its processor full core speed is 5×100, or 500MHz. It accesses its L1 cache at 500MHz. That's fast! As an example of an older processor, a Pentium 166MHz system has a motherboard bus speed of 66MHz, a clock multiplier of 2.5, and a processor full core speed of 166MHz. Note that Pentium can access its L1 cache 2.5 times faster than when it has to go out to the motherboard bus.

Motherboard

Check the literature that comes with your system for information about the motherboard: manufacturer, model, form factor, jumpers, and so on. Sandra is another good source for information. In some instances, you might need to remove one or more cables and peripheral cards, or remove the motherboard entirely from the case, to get an unobstructed view of the motherboard. You also can access motherboard specifications, diagrams, and FAQs on the Internet at the PC or motherboard manufacturer's Web site.

TIP

DO YOU YAHOO!?

Yahoo! maintains an extensive listing of motherboard manufacturers. See
`http://dir.yahoo.com/Business_and_Economy/Companies/Computers/Hardware/`
`Components/Motherboards/Manufacturers/`.

SEE ALSO

➤ *For more details on choosing and upgrading a motherboard, see Chapter 6.*

➤ *For more details on tools that can help track down manufacturer information about an old, outdated, or esoteric motherboard, see Chapter 4, "Upgrading the BIOS."*

Chipset

In common usage the term *chipset* refers to a motherboard's core functionality, meaning what the motherboard can do in addition to sheltering a microprocessor. Think of it in terms of how the processor communicates with memory, peripherals, ports, and so forth. In the analogy of microprocessor as the brain and PC as the human body, a brain is of little use to a human being without a central nervous system to communicate with the body's organs and limbs. The motherboard's chipsets are its central nervous system.

Technically speaking, a chipset is a group of chips that together perform an interconnected set of operations. You probably won't be surprised to read that, over time, more operations are being conducted by a smaller number of tinier chipsets. For the purposes of our inventory, we're interested in a motherboard's *North Bridge* and *South Bridge* chipsets, terms invented by Intel. See Figure 2.13.

The North Bridge chipset contains these components:

- Cache controller

- Main memory controller

- Interface between the motherboard bus (processor bus) and the PCI and AGP buses

The South Bridge chipset contains these components:

- Interface to the PCI bus

- Interface to the ISA bus

- Dual IDE hard disk controller interfaces

- Interface to the USB

- CMOS RAM and clock

PLAINSPEAKING
KNOW THY CHIPSETS

Chipsets are integrated into the motherboard itself and therefore aren't upgradable. (To upgrade a chipset, you must upgrade the entire motherboard.) But it's important to know which chipsets you have and what their features are. A PC manufacturer's system manual will occasionally be wrong about the system's capabilities, such capabilities being related directly to chipset features. That's why we recommend you determine which chipsets you have and study their documentation enough to at least determine their main features.

For example, we have a Pentium III 450MHz system based on an Epox EP-ZXA motherboard. This board includes a 440ZX North Bridge (82443ZX) and a PIIX4E South Bridge (82371EB). The motherboard manual was poorly written or poorly translated, or both. So, we were a bit suspicious about the motherboard Features section. When we opened up the case and dug around, we verified that in fact it had 440ZX and PIIX4E chipsets. However, some important feature differences exist between the 440BX and the 440ZX. (Note that Sandra was incapable of distinguishing between the big brother 440BX and its little brother 440ZX; it simply reported 440BX/ZX.)

Continued

Good sources for chipset information are your system's documentation, your motherboard's documentation, an analysis by Sandra (use the Mainboard Information module), or a visual inspection of your motherboard. You can look at the markings on the motherboard's chips and compare them to product listings at Intel's chipset page (`http://developer.intel.com/design/chipsets/`). For information on older chipsets—what Intel calls *mature products*—see `http://developer.intel.com/design/chipsets/mature/index.htm`.

On the positive side, both the BX and ZX chipsets support a 100MHz processor host bus. (They also can run at 66MHz, so one North Bridge chipset can be used in a wide range of Pentium II and III processors.) On the downside, the ZX supports only a maximum of 256MB of memory; the BX supports 1GB. Also, the ZX doesn't provide parity or ECC memory; the BX does. Had we not done this research, we wouldn't have been certain about this system's maximum performance capabilities.

Another example involves a system (Pentium P54C 166MHz) with a South Bridge model PIIX3 (82371SB). This was Intel's first South Bridge that supported USB. Although this PC's motherboard has no USB ports, upgrading this system to accept USB devices is as simple as plugging in a PCI card with some USB port connectors on it. ∎

FIGURE 2.13

Block diagram of the Intel 440BX AGPset, a North Bridge chipset commonly used in modern motherboards; also includes the accompanying South Bridge chipset, the ubiquitous PIIX4E. (Diagram courtesy of Intel Corporation)

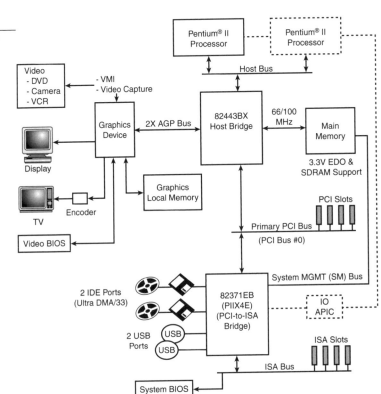

BIOS

You can determine your BIOS manufacturer and version by going into your BIOS Setup utility. You can also watch the power on self test (POST) messages onscreen when you boot your system or use Sandra's CPU & BIOS Information module. Your PC manufacturer's Web site, especially the pages devoted to your particular system and motherboard, should provide links to your BIOS manufacturer's upgrades page(s), if BIOS upgrades are available.

SEE ALSO

➤ *For more details on your system's BIOS, see "Your Current BIOS," page 109*

BIOS Plug and Play

We include this line item in the PC inventory worksheet as a reminder to folks with older systems. If your BIOS does not support Plug and Play (PnP), upgrade it to a version that does, assuming a version is available for your motherboard. This assumes your operating system supports PnP, as do Windows 95, 98, Millennium Edition (Me), and 2000, but not Windows NT. A PnP BIOS makes it much easier to install peripheral cards.

To determine whether your BIOS supports PnP, watch the POST messages onscreen when you boot your system, check your BIOS Setup utility, check your system's documentation, check your motherboard's documentation, or use Sandra's CPU & BIOS Information module.

RAM

See how much physical RAM you have with Device Manager. Look at the last line of the Computer section at the bottom of the dialog box, as shown in Figure 2.14. Other useful values are the memory type, speed, bank configuration, and module configuration. Check your system's packing list or invoice. Sandra reports these values, too.

SEE ALSO

➤ *For more details on choosing and upgrading RAM, see "Memory Upgrade Payoff," page 122*

Hard Drive #1 and Hard Drive #2

The following are good sources of information about this device:

- The Windows Device Manager device list

- Your invoice or packing list

- Any documentation that came with the device

■ The device manufacturer's Web site or technical support department

■ A system analysis program such as Sandra

■ A physical inspection (meaning remove the device from the chassis if necessary to read its model/serial number label)

Note that the Hard Drive #2 column is left blank unless your PC has two hard drives.

FIGURE 2.14

The Windows Device Manager tab is a quick way to see how much physical RAM a PC has.

TIP

FREE IDE DRIVE IDENTIFICATION TOOLS

You might be able to coax additional low-level information out of some IDE drives with a freeware utility such as IDEINFO or IDE-ID (see `http://www.dc.ee/files/utils/`).

NOTE

ONLINE WARRANTY INFORMATION

Some drive manufacturers, such as Quantum, provide a warranty information form on their Web site. Key in your drive's serial number and the form tells you when your warranty expires.

NOTE

DETAILS, DETAILS

For more details on choosing and upgrading a hard drive, see Chapter 7, "Upgrading the Hard Disk."

Floppy Drive

The following are good sources of information about this device:

- The Windows Device Manager device list

- Your BIOS setup information

- Your invoice or packing list

- Any documentation that came with the device

- The device manufacturer's Web site or technical support department

- A system analysis program such as Sandra

- A physical inspection (meaning remove the device from the chassis if necessary to read its model/serial number label)

SCSI Controller

Good sources of information about this device are as follows:

- The Windows Device Manager device list

- Your invoice or packing list

- Any documentation that came with the device

- The device manufacturer's Web site or technical support department

- A system analysis program such as Sandra

- A physical inspection (meaning remove the device from the chassis if necessary to read its model/serial number label)

Your SCSI controller most likely came with some analysis/reporting tools. For example, one of our older Pentium PCs is running an Adaptec AHA-2940/2940U controller. This card came with EZ-SCSI version 4.00, which includes the Adaptec SCSI Interrogator (see Figure 2.15).

SCSI BIOS

During your PC's POST cycle, watch for an onscreen prompt to run the SCSI BIOS utility, at which point you can get the SCSI BIOS version number. That number is usually displayed during POST, but very briefly, so you might have to run the utility just to write down the version.

FIGURE 2.15

Adaptec SCSI
Interrogator dis-
plays informa-
tion about one
of the system's
SCSI devices, a
Quantum hard
drive.

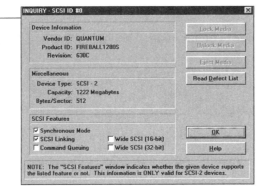

SCSI IN THE WILD

Most folks reading this book have IDE devices in their systems, and only in relatively rare
cases will you be using SCSI devices. In fact, generally you won't have SCSI unless you or a
previous owner intentionally installed a SCSI adapter.

PCI Bus

This value indicates which version of PCI is implemented on your system. A good
source of information about this device is a system analysis program such as
Sandra. You also can read the chipset-level documentation. At the time of this writing, the latest PCI local bus specification is revision 2.2, published by the PCI SIG.

CD-ROM Drive

Good sources of information about this device are as follows:

- The Windows Device Manager device list

- Your invoice or packing list

- Any documentation that came with the device

- The device manufacturer's Web site or technical support department

- A system analysis program such as Sandra

- A physical inspection (meaning remove the device from the chassis if necessary to read its model/serial number label)

NOTE

CD-R OR CD-RW?

For more details on choosing and upgrading a CD-ROM drive, see Chapter 15, "Adding a CD-Recordable or CD-Rewritable Drive."

CD-R/CD-RW Drive

The following are good sources of information about this device:

- The Windows Device Manager device list
- Your invoice or packing list
- Any documentation that came with the device
- The device manufacturer's Web site or technical support department
- A system analysis program such as Sandra
- A physical inspection (meaning remove the device from the chassis if necessary to read its model/serial number label)

DVD Drive

Good sources of information about this device are as follows:

- The Windows Device Manager device list
- Your invoice or packing list
- Any documentation that came with the device
- The device manufacturer's Web site or technical support department
- A system analysis program such as Sandra
- A physical inspection (meaning remove the device from the chassis if necessary to read its model/serial number label)

Zip Drive

The following are good sources of information about this device:

- The Windows Device Manager device list
- Your invoice or packing list

- Any documentation that came with the device

- The device manufacturer's Web site or technical support department

- A system analysis program such as Sandra

- A physical inspection (meaning remove the device from the chassis if necessary to read its model/serial number label)

NOTE

ZIP WHAT?

For more details on choosing and upgrading a Zip drive, see Chapter 17, "Adding Removable Storage."

Tape Drive

Good sources of information about this device are as follows:

- The Windows Device Manager device list

- Your invoice or packing list

- Any documentation that came with the device

- The device manufacturer's Web site or technical support department

- A system analysis program such as Sandra

- A physical inspection (meaning remove the device from the chassis if necessary to read its model/serial number label)

NOTE

MORE ON TAPE DRIVES

For more details on choosing and upgrading a tape drive, see Chapter 18, "Adding a Tape Drive."

Other Removable Media Drive

Good sources of information about this device are as follows:

- The Windows Device Manager device list

- Your invoice or packing list

- Any documentation that came with the device

- The device manufacturer's Web site or technical support department

- A system analysis program such as Sandra

- A physical inspection (meaning remove the device from the chassis if necessary to read its model/serial number label)

NOTE

OTHER REMOVABLE DRIVES

For more details on choosing and upgrading a removable media drive, see Chapter 17.

Modem

The following are good sources of information about this device:

- The Windows Device Manager device list

- Your invoice or packing list

- Any documentation that came with the device

- The device manufacturer's Web site or technical support department

- A system analysis program such as Sandra

- A physical inspection (meaning remove the device from the chassis if necessary to read its model/serial number label)

SEE ALSO

➤ *For more details on choosing or upgrading an Internet connection, see "High-Speed Connections," page 196*

Monitor

The following are good sources of information about this device:

- The Windows Device Manager device list

- Your invoice or packing list

- Any documentation that came with the device

- The device manufacturer's Web site or technical support department

- A system analysis program such as Sandra

- A physical inspection

NOTE

MORE MONITORS COVERAGE

For more details on choosing and upgrading a monitor, see Chapter 12, "Monitor and Graphic Card Upgrades."

Video Card

Good sources of information about this device are as follows:

- The Windows Device Manager device list

- Your invoice or packing list

- Any documentation that came with the device

- The device manufacturer's Web site or technical support department

- A system analysis program such as Sandra

- Your video software's about information (see Figure 2.16)

- A physical inspection (meaning remove the device from the chassis if necessary to read its model/serial number label)

FIGURE 2.16

Diamond
Multimedia
InControl Tools
98's Display
Information
dialog box.

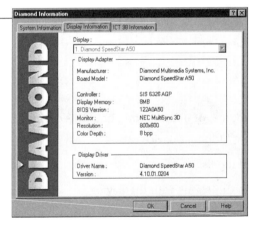

TIP

DEVICE DETECTION UTILITIES

Some graphic chipset manufacturers provide free detection utilities for their products. For example, S3id.exe is available to sniff out S3 video chipsets. You can get S3id.exe at FTP sites everywhere. Go to FAST FTP Search v4.0 at `http://ftpsearch.lycos.com` and search by the exact filename.

SEE ALSO

➤ *For more details on choosing and upgrading a graphics card, see Chapter 12, "Monitor and Graphic Card Upgrades," page 267*

Sound Card

Good sources of information about this device are as follows:

- The Windows Device Manager device list

- Your invoice or packing list

- Any documentation that came with the device

- The device manufacturer's Web site or technical support department

- A system analysis program such as Sandra

- A physical inspection (meaning remove the device from the chassis if necessary to read its model/serial number label)

Speakers

Good sources of information about this device are as follows:

- The Windows Device Manager device list

- Your invoice or packing list

- Any documentation that came with the device

OFF THE WALL
WHERE TO GET TEST CDS

The `rec.audio.*` newsgroup's FAQ includes an informative answer to the question, "What can I get in the way of a CD test-disc?" The FAQ authors suggest several different test disc sources: *Hi-Fi News & Record Review*, Chesky, *Stereophile*, and Denon. Many of these discs are stocked by DB Systems in Rindge Center, New Hampshire. Denon's product is the Denon Audio Technical [CD], part number C397147 in their Pro Audio catalog (see `http://www.del.denon.com`). To read the FAQ, see `http://www.faqs.org/faqs/AudioFAQ/part3/.` ■

■ The device manufacturer's Web site or technical support department

■ A system analysis program such as Sandra

■ A physical inspection

SEE ALSO

➤ *For more details on choosing and upgrading speakers, see Chapter 14, "Speaker Upgrades," page 311*

Keyboard

The following are good sources of information about this device:

■ The Windows Device Manager device list

■ Your invoice or packing list

■ Any documentation that came with the device

■ The device manufacturer's Web site or technical support department

■ A system analysis program such as Sandra

■ A physical inspection

Mouse

The following are good sources of information about this device:

■ The Windows Device Manager device list

■ Your invoice or packing list

■ Any documentation that came with the device

■ The device manufacturer's Web site or technical support department

■ A system analysis program such as Sandra

■ A physical inspection

Solving the Microsoft IntelliPoint Driver Update Mystery

If you use a Microsoft IntelliMouse, the associated IntelliPoint drivers are in a constant state of improvement, so it pays to have the latest version. But determining which version of IntelliPoint you have isn't easy. You can do this in two ways. First, locate the file Mousex32.exe (typically in C:\Msinput\Mouse), right-click it, choose Properties, click the Version tab, select Product Version in the Other version information frame, and note the corresponding value (see Figure 2.17). Another approach—and one that provides more information—is to run the MousInfo utility that comes with your IntelliPoint software (see Figure 2.18).

FIGURE 2.17

How to determine a product's version number by inspecting its Properties sheet in Windows Explorer.

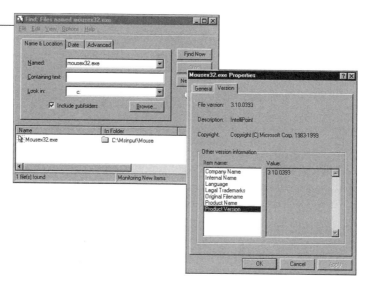

FIGURE 2.18

The MousInfo utility ships with Microsoft IntelliPoint software; it reveals detailed version information, among other things.

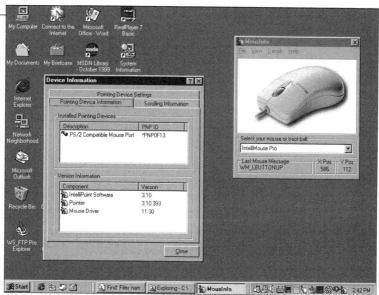

TIP

FINDING MICROSOFT INTELLIPOINT PRODUCT INFORMATION

Microsoft maintains a Knowledge Base article, "Microsoft IntelliPoint Software Available for Download" (Q186389), that describes where to go for a wide variety of Microsoft Intelli-something mouse products. See `http://support.microsoft.com/support/kb/articles/q186/3/89.asp`. The link of interest if you want to update to version 3.1 is `http://www.microsoft.com/products/hardware/mouse/driver/default.htm`.

Network Interface Card

Good sources of information about this device are as follows:

- The Windows Device Manager device list

- Your invoice or packing list

- Any documentation that came with the device

- The device manufacturer's Web site or technical support department

- Any diagnostic, configuration, or reporting tools that came with the device (with some older network cards, you might have to exit Windows and go into MS-DOS mode to run these tools)

- A system analysis program such as Sandra

- A physical inspection (meaning remove the device from the chassis if necessary to read its model/serial number label)

FINDING A DEVICE'S DIAGNOSTIC OR REPORTING UTILITIES

The fastest way to find which file on your card's driver disk provides diagnostic, configuration, or reporting tools is this: Look for a `Readme.txt` or any files with a .doc extension. If you examine them, you'll usually find a file inventory. If not, search on the terms diagnostic and configuration. If you can't find it, contact the manufacturer's technical support staff.

Network Card Detection Utilities

Some network card manufacturers provide a detection utility that examines a system to see whether one of their cards is installed and, if so, provides descriptive information about it. For example, 3Com's NIC detection utility 3LINK-ID is available at `http://support.3com.com/infodeli/tools/nic/index.htm`; the download filename is `crdfind.exe`; and the utility's filename is `3Link-id.exe`.

LEARN MORE ABOUT GETTING CONNECTED

For more details on choosing and upgrading a network, see Chapter 9, "Adding a Network."

Printer

Good sources of information about this device are as follows:

- The Windows Device Manager device list
- Run the printer's self test
- Your invoice or packing list
- Any documentation that came with the device
- The device manufacturer's Web site or technical support department
- A system analysis program such as Sandra
- A physical inspection

SEE ALSO

➤ *For more details on choosing and upgrading a printer, see "General Considerations," page 296*

Scanner

Good sources of information about this device are as follows:

- The Windows Device Manager device list
- Your invoice or packing list
- Any documentation that came with the device
- The device manufacturer's Web site or technical support department
- A system analysis program such as Sandra
- A physical inspection

NOTE

SCANNER DETAILS

For more details on choosing and upgrading a scanner, see Chapter 19, "Adding a Scanner."

Operating System

Use Device Manager's General tab to determine your operating system's precise version number (refer to Figure 2.14).

Slots 1–8

The only columns you need to fill out here are Bus/Interface and Manufacturer. See Figure 2.19 for an example of how we filled it out for a Pentium P54C 166MHz. You've already gathered the details about each card in other records; this small section is just a quick list of which card is in which slot.

FIGURE 2.19

This is how we fill out the Slots 1–8 section of the PC Inventory form.

	A	B	C	D	E
1	PC Name:		Covermeister		
2	PC User Name:		Lee Hudspeth	See *T.J. Lee and Lee Hudspeth Teach PC Upgrad*	
3	Manufacturer Technical Support:		888-349-6972	by T.J. Lee and Lee Hudspeth	
4	Manufacturer Customer Service:		888-642-7662	ISBN 0-7897-2417-0	
5	Manufacturer Service/ID Number:		n/a	Copyright © 2000 PRIME Consulting Group, Inc. Al	
6	Order Number:		#####		
7	Order Date:		5/29/96		
8	Customer Number:		#####		
9	Internal Asset Number:		n/a		
10					
11					
12	Component	Bus/Interface	Manufacturer	Model	Quantity	Serial
47	Operating System		Microsoft	Windows 98 Second Edition (4.10.2222A)	
48	Slots				
49	1	PCI	Video Card		
50	2	PCI	Available		
51	3	PCI	SCSI Controller		
52	4	ISA/PCI Shared	Available		
53	5	ISA/PCI Shared	Available		
54	6	ISA	Available		
55	7	ISA	Sound Card		
56	8	ISA	Network Interface Card		
57	PC Card Slot 1	PC Card	None		
58	PC Card Slot 2	PC Card	None		
59	IDE Bus				

PC Card Slots 1–2

As with the Slots 1–8 rows, the only columns you need to fill out are Bus/Interface and Manufacturer.

IDE Bus

The only columns you need to fill out here are Manufacturer and Model. You've already gathered the details about each IDE device in other records; this small section is just a quick list of which device is on which channel, and their master/slave relationships.

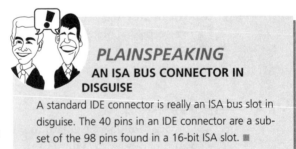

PLAINSPEAKING
AN ISA BUS CONNECTOR IN DISGUISE

A standard IDE connector is really an ISA bus slot in disguise. The 40 pins in an IDE connector are a subset of the 98 pins found in a 16-bit ISA slot. ∎

Manufacturer Information

As you've seen in the previous sections on individual components, the best sources of information about a particular device are as follows. We list the sources in an order that reflects the least amount of work first, to save you time. However, where accuracy counts above all else—say, in figuring out exactly which model of motherboard is in your PC—you'll have to open up the case and get your hands dirty:

- The Windows Device Manager device list

- Your invoice or packing list

- Any documentation that came with the device

- The device manufacturer's Web site or technical support department

- A system analysis program such as Sandra

- A physical inspection

The best place to go for the most detailed, current information is the system or component manufacturer. Keeping track of a dozen or so manufacturers' Web addresses can be daunting, but if you invest the time once and enter it into your PC Inventory worksheet, the payoff will be high. To help you automatically keep track of changes to device drivers, Web-based clearinghouses for these updates are available, as well as third-party software packages that monitor your system and notify you when a relevant upgrade occurs.

ANOTHER FINE MESS
REPLACING A LOST MANUAL
    If you have lost your manual, or never got one, many manufacturers provide images of their devices on their Web sites, along with user manuals, datasheets, and other technical documentation in PDF format for easy downloading. ■

ANOTHER FINE MESS
TRY, TRY AGAIN
    When searching for device information on a Web site, it all boils down to this:

- Perseverance

- Frequent use of a sitewide Search field (if available)

- And more perseverance

Try every sensible link until you've exhausted all possibilities. If all else fails, contact the manufacturer's technical support department. ■

Finding Manufacturers

To find a manufacturer, first check the documentation tucked away in your NEAT box. (NEAT is a term we coined that stands for New computer Emergency catchAll Trunk. It's a storage box for your system's documentation and other odds and ends that we discuss in Chapter 3, "Things You Need.") If the component is software (for example, a video management package), you can probably get contact information in its Help, About dialog box.

A great resource for tracking down drivers is the WinDrivers.Com site at `http://www.windrivers.com`. WinDrivers.Com knows where to find drivers by monitoring peripheral manufacturers; it's up to you to search their database for a given company. Each listing includes links to the relevant Web pages for downloadable drivers, along with the company's mailing addresses, phone numbers, email contacts, and hardware categories.

ANOTHER FINE MESS
SLEUTHING FOR A MOTHERBOARD DIAGRAM

Here's how we unearthed information about a motherboard in a Micron system named Covemeister. We started at Micron's main Web site, drilled down to the MicronPC site (`http://www.micronpc.com`), chose the Home/Home Office link (we made an educated guess that that link would most likely include this particular system), and then chose the Support link. Then, we had to do some reading. Micron has segregated all information about components made before the summer of 1999 into an Archives area. From there we chose the Troubleshooting and Specifications link in the Desktop Technical Support section, the Motherboards link, the Pentium link, and then searched the page for M55. That page offered nine different motherboard topics; we chose Diagram, and there it was. The graphic even includes some hot zones you can click for more detail, such as a port diagram and a connector U50 pin diagram. (For this particular motherboard, connector U50 includes all the front-panel connectors: Reset, Infrared, Soft Power, Turbo LED, Hard Drive LED, Keyboard Lock, Pwer LED, and Speaker.) ∎

You can search for manufacturers alphabetically, by product category, or by entering the FCC ID number affixed to most peripheral cards (more on this in a moment). WinDrivers.Com maintains a page on Windows 95, 98, and NT service packs and driver updates, with links to the appropriate Microsoft Web site pages. You can sign up to receive an email notification whenever your virus software publishes a new update or new set of virus definition files (assuming your virus package is one of the packages WinDrivers.Com tracks).

Tracing a Peripheral with Its FCC ID Number

All peripheral cards are supposed to be marked with an FCC ID number, so even if you can't determine the manufacturer, model number, or other information, you can perform a search on the FCC ID for contact information. Go to http://www.fcc.gov/oet/fccid/, fill in the FCC OET Search Form's grantee and product codes, and you'll see the applicant company's name and address, along with other information—for example, the grant itself for this particular piece of equipment. For an example of our search for an Adaptec SCSI adapter with an FCC ID number of FGTAHA2940-42, see Figure 2.20.

FIGURE 2.20

The FCC ID inquiry about a SCSI adapter card with an ID of FGTAHA2940-42 reveals it was manufactured by Adaptec and provides the manufacturer's address and date of the FCC grant.

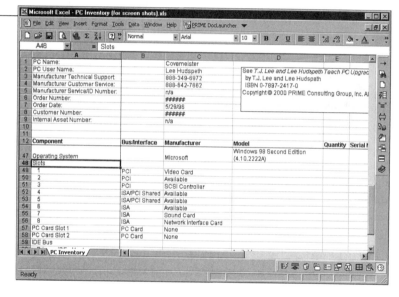

GET DEVICE AND DRIVER UPDATE NOTICES BY EMAIL

While filling in your PC Inventory worksheet, if you see that a component manufacturer's Web site offers an electronic newsletter or email notification when new or updated components are available, sign up. This way, you'll be kept abreast of the latest news.

Two other popular sites for locating drivers are PC Drivers HeadQuarters (http://www.drivershq.com) and the WinFiles drivers database (http://www.winfiles.com/drivers). To locate a company, check out Microsoft's Computer

Company Information Center at `http://library.microsoft.com/compcos.htm`. This database includes more than 1,800 companies. You can search for a specific company or you can browse the entire list.

Another Web resource exists that lists computer companies and contact information, typically the Web site address, FTP site (if any), and telephone number. It's part of a general computer FAQ covering a variety of Internet newsgroups; see `http://www.faqs.org/faqs/pc-hardware-faq/part5/`.

Tracking Upgrades Automatically

Right now, upgrading software via the Internet is a very disorganized process that puts the burden of finding available upgrades squarely on your shoulders. No doubt this process will become more automated and user friendly. Meanwhile, to ease this burden, you can choose a third-party product that tracks updates applicable to your system. These update tracker products are convenient because they enable you to turn to one place for updates. One of the main disadvantages of update trackers is that they aren't likely—at least not today—to be omniscient. If you're a stickler for details and accuracy, you might want to track upgrades yourself. Also, update tracker tools aren't free; you must pay an annual subscription renewal fee. (Catch-UP is the notable exception.)

Here's a quick explanation of how these packages work: The update tracker inventories your system's drivers and applications and checks these against its own online database of drivers and software upgrades. When an item in your system matches an entry in the database, the software determines whether its database contains a more current version, at which point you can decide whether or not to get the update. The following are some of the available tracker tools:

- **Oil Change by CyberMedia**—Sells for $39.95, which includes the first year's subscription. Go to `http://www.cybermedia.com/products/oilchange/` for a registered or trial version (the latter supports only a limited number of applications).

- **TuneUp by Quarterdeck**—Costs $39.95 per year. They offer a 30-day free trial, sort of. Sign up, provide your credit card number, and within 30 days you can cancel your subscription—and they won't charge your card. TuneUp is available at `http://www.tuneup.com`.

- **Catch-UP by Manageable Software Services**—Is freeware and functions as an add-on to your Web browser. After you download and run the Catch-UP executable, it finds your browser and then installs itself. One of Catch-UP's best features is that, before you decide to install it, you can review the software, drivers, and DLLs that Catch-UP monitors. Although not as automated as the two subscription-based services we just mentioned, we recommend Catch-UP as a part of your update arsenal. The lack of automation reminds you that you are ultimately responsible for your system's upgrades. It is available at `http://www.manageable.com`.

TIP

TRACKING UPGRADES OVER THE INTERNET

Ziff-Davis and PDQ Information Systems both offer Web-based services for tracking the current update state of your PC. These services are Updates.com (`http://updates.zdnet.com`) and FileWatch (`http://www.filewatch.com`), respectively.

More vendors providing similar services are likely to proliferate over time. The good news is that you don't have to install any client-side software (well, that's not entirely true in the case of Updates.com; there you have to install an ActiveX control for Internet Explorer users or a plug-in for Netscape users). Nonetheless, we favor Updates.com for its simple and straightforward design.

The bad news is that, depending on your degree of paranoia, you might feel violated by the fact that these services are maintaining information—allegedly anonymously—about your system back on their servers.

These services are equally susceptible to the *can't ever know it all* problem that plagues the PC-based utilities discussed earlier. However, studying the recommended update list can be helpful, as long as you don't go crazy and start updating every single item in one sitting. Be judicious.

Free IRQs

Table 2.4 shows the standard uses for each IRQ in a contemporary PC.

Table 2.4   IRQ Typical Uses

IRQ	Typical Use	Other Common Uses and Comments
0	System timer	Reserved for system use only
1	Keyboard controller	Reserved for system use only
2	Cascade for IRQs 8–15	Reserved for system use only
3	Serial port 2 (COM2:)	Modem
4	Serial port 1 (COM1:)	Modem

Table 2.4 continued

IRQ	Typical Use	Other Common Uses and Comments
5	Sound card	Parallel port 2 (LPT2:)
6	Floppy disk controller	Floppy disk controller
7	Parallel port 1 (LPT1:)	Printer
8	Real-time clock	Reserved for system use only
9	Open	Network interface card (most common)
10	Open	USB, PCI devices, SCSI host adapter, and so on
11	Open	SCSI host adapter, video adapter, PCI devices, and so on
12	PS/2 (motherboard) mouse	PS/2 mouse
13	Math coprocessor	Reserved for system use only
14	Primary IDE channel	Hard disks
15	Secondary IDE channel	CD-ROM, CD-RW, tape, and other removable drives

Here are some suggestions for freeing up one or more IRQs:

1. Go into your BIOS setup program and disable any unused COM ports.

2. If you're not using a PS/2 mouse, this automatically frees up IRQ 12.

3. If your system isn't using the secondary IDE channel, go into your BIOS setup program and disable the secondary IDE controller. On most systems, this frees up IRQ 15.

NOTE

GETTING YOUR SECONDARY IDE CHANNEL BACK
Disabling the secondary IDE controller is a good idea, but remember that if you later decide to add a device to the secondary IDE channel, you will have to do some more IRQ shuffling.

4. If your system supports USB, switch one or more devices to the USB bus. For example, a USB mouse will free up IRQ 12 (if you swap a PS/2 mouse for a USB mouse), and a USB printer will free up IRQ 7.

5. If you anticipate adding more devices to the current system, consider installing a SCSI adapter and let it run your hard disk, CD-ROM, CD-RW, scanner, and so on. While setting up SCSI is not as easy as, say, setting up an IDE device, and you'd have to transfer your system from a current non-SCSI hard disk to a SCSI hard disk, it will definitely save you resources.

Available Peripheral Slots

You need to know the type of peripheral slots you have in your system, if they are being used, and if so by what card. This way, you know how much room you have to expand your system. Dealing with the confusing lingo of buses, slots, and some related terms is the first order of business.

The following terms can be confusing because their meanings overlap but don't mean precisely the same thing. We'll start with some definitions and practical examples and then describe the various types of peripheral buses:

- **Bus**—A set of physical wires that transfer data and other information to and from the various components of a PC. In the computer realm, a bus is primarily characterized by its width—that is, how many bits it can carry at a time. The other key factor is speed, measured in megahertz (MHz). This measurement reveals how many trips data can make along the bus in one second (one megahertz equals one million trips or cycles). Here's an example of this term in a sentence: PCs based on the Intel 8088 processor used an 8-bit–wide bus operating at 4.77MHz to connect to peripheral devices. That bus was named ISA, which stands for Industry Standard Architecture.

- **Interface**—According to *Webster's New World Dictionary, Third College Edition*, an interface is "a point or means of interaction between two systems, disciplines, or groups." In the context of PC hardware, an interface is a card, plug, or other mechanism that connects devices. In fact, the terms *interface card, adapter card, expansion card*, and *peripheral card* are synonymous. An interface card uses one of a PC's peripheral buses; an interface card is not itself a bus. For example, a network interface card is built to use either an ISA bus, a PCI bus, or a USB bus, and is marked accordingly on the box it comes in.

- **Peripheral slot**—A PC ships from the factory (or you build it yourself) with certain components built right in. Expandability has always been a trademark of Windows/Intel (Wintel) PCs, and that expandability is made possible by the existence of peripheral slots. A peripheral slot is a receptacle that accepts a peripheral card and connects it to one of the PC's peripheral buses. These peripheral cards are themselves small, printed circuit boards that provide features such as networking, sound, video acceleration, telecommunications, and support for a plethora of additional devices.

- **Port**—The outlet that acts as a connection between a PC and a device. A bus typically involves (and can expand to include) more than two devices, whereas the term port typically signifies communication between only two devices. For example, a PS/2 mouse port connects the mouse directly to a chipset on the motherboard.

Table 2.5 shows the various types of peripheral buses that have been around since the time of the first PC. Note the following:

■ All Speed and Bandwidth values are rounded to the nearest integer MHz value.

■ The table is sorted by descending bandwidth, except Processor bus, which is in the first row for comparison purposes.

■ Max Bandwidth is defined as a theoretical maximum and can't be reached in some cases, for a variety of reasons.

■ The formula for Max Bandwidth in Megabits/sec is
Max Bandwidth (Megabits/sec) = (Width×Speed)/number of cycles to transfer all data

■ The formula to convert from Megabits/sec to MegaBytes/sec is
Max Bandwidth (MegaBytes/sec) = Max Bandwidth (Megabits/sec)/8

■ The information on EISA and MCA is for historical purposes only; we doubt many folks reading this book have a PC with either of these buses.

Table 2.5   Peripheral Bus Width, Speed, and Bandwidth Characteristics

Bus	Width (Bits)	Speed (MHz)	Max Bandwidth (Megabits/sec)	Max Bandwidth (MegaBytes/sec)
Processor bus (Pentium III)[1]	64	100	6,400	800.00
AGP Mode 4x	32	266 (266.66)[2]	8,512	1,066 (1,066.64)
AGP Mode 2x	32	133 (133.33)[3]	4,256	533 (533.32)
AGP Mode 1x	32	66 (66.66)	2,112	266 (266.64)
PC Card CardBus	32	33	1,056	132.00
PCI	32	33	1,056	132.00
VL-Bus	32	33	1,056	132.00
EISA	32	8 (8.33)	256	32.00
1394 (i.Link/ FireWire)[4]	1 (serial)	200	200	25.00

Bus	Width (Bits)	Speed (MHz)	Max Bandwidth (Megabits/sec)	Max Bandwidth (MegaBytes/sec)
ISA 16-bit	16	8 (8.33)	64	8 (8.33)[5]
ISA 8-bit	8	5 (4.77)	16	2 (2.39)[6]
USB	1 (serial)	12	12	1.50
MCA	16, 32	10–20	-	10–80

1. The processor bus is not an I/O peripheral bus; it is shown here for comparison purposes only.

2. The 66MHz rate also applies for Mode 4x, but four full data transfers are performed each cycle. This yields an effective speed of 266MHz.

3. The 66MHz rate also applies for Mode 2x, but two full data transfers are performed each cycle. This yields an effective speed of 133MHz.

4. There are plans for rates up to 1.0 Gigabits/sec (125 MegaBytes/sec) with a specification called 1394b.

5. Assuming two cycles to transfer all the data.

6. Assuming two cycles to transfer all the data.

Accelerated Graphics Port (AGP)

This bus architecture was initially released by Intel in 1996. Its primary purpose is to give high-performance, memory-hungry video cards faster access to system resources (AGP's base frequency is 66MHz, twice that of PCI). If present, there is only one such slot on the motherboard. The slot is offset slightly from the PCI slots and sports a different connector. When a video card uses the AGP slot, this frees the PCI bus to attend to other devices. (Actually, AGP is really a port and not a bus.) If you're contemplating a graphics card upgrade, this is the only way to go. For more information, see the Accelerated Graphics Port Technology home page at http://developer.intel.com/technology/agp/. AGP has the following features:

- High-speed local bus

- Supports one device

- Well suited to high-performance video cards

- Enables a video card to communicate at a higher bus speed than PCI (at least 2×)

- Gives a video card fast access to system memory to avoid the extra cost of memory on the video card itself

Extended ISA (EISA)

Compaq was the main proponent of EISA, announced in 1988. Compaq and its peers were displeased with IBM's licensing requirements for MCA so Compaq stepped up to the plate, designed a new bus, and then gave it away through a nonprofit EISA committee. The slot is the same size as a 16-bit ISA slot but has two rows of connectors. This enabled the EISA slot to accommodate either an ISA card or an EISA card. The EISA bus floundered and has passed quietly into the footnotes of personal computer history.

i.Link/FireWire (IEEE-1394)

This high-speed serial bus specification was published by the IEEE Standards Board in 1995, and was originally conceived by Apple Computer in 1986. Apple has trademarked the term FireWire in reference to the bus, whereas Sony advocates the term i.Link. IEEE-1394 is not typically available on modern motherboards as of the time of this writing. For more information, see the Energy Conservation Working Group of the 1394 Trade Association page at `http://www.1394-pcwg.org/index.html`. This bus might catch on and become "the next big thing." If so, it will be an upgrade consideration for you in the very near future. It has the following features:

- High-speed serial bus

- Supports up to 63 devices

- Supports Plug and Play

- Supports *hot-swapping* (also *hot plugging*) whereby the device can be plugged in (or unplugged!) at any time, even when the device and PC are powered on, and the system automatically reconfigures itself to support the device

- Provides power to devices on the bus (eliminates bulky power bricks and cables for some devices). IEEE-1394 provides up to 1.5 amps of power to a device on the bus.

- Does not require an IRQ for each device on the bus

- No peripheral cards required

- Supports a type of data-delivery scheme called *isochronous* (data must be delivered at some guaranteed time), which makes it ideal for real-time audio/video applications

- Supports devices operating at differing speeds on the same network

- Connects to the motherboard through a PCI adapter card or an IEEE-1394 interface

- No complex termination requirements (as with SCSI)

- A serious competitor to SCSI

- Does *not* require a PC host connection

FIREWIRE IN A CARD

Evergreen Technologies' fireLINE plug-and-play PCI card enables FireWire on your existing Windows PC. The card includes one internal FireWire connector and three external FireWire connectors, and lists for $99. This is a bargain if you want to use FireWire peripherals today. For more information, see `http://www.evertech.com/products/fireline/`.

ISA (Industry Standard Architecture)

The 8-bit version of this bus was used in the original IBM PC in 1981, and chugged along at a rate of 4.77MHz. For standardization and backward-compatibility reasons, ISA continues to survive (albeit in a 16-bit version operating at 8.33MHz), although it's now in the twilight of its long and loyal life. For new PCs, the ISA bus will eventually be entirely replaced by high-speed, user-friendly buses such as PCI, USB, and IEEE-1394. Its features are as follows:

- It has been the de facto peripheral bus for Wintel personal computers since 1981, but is being eclipsed by modern buses such as PCI, USB, and IEEE-1394.

- It supports Plug and Play (Plug and Play wasn't introduced until 1993, so ISA implementations prior to 1993 don't support Plug and Play).

INTEL OFFERS NON-ISA MOTHERBOARDS

If you've been reading along, wondering when motherboard manufacturers will let go of the vestigial ISA bus and convert to a PCI-only design, wonder no more. Intel has three sizzling motherboard designs out that are PCI-only. For more information, take a look at the Intel Desktop Board VC820, Desktop Board CC820, and Desktop Board CA810E. Go to Intel's Pentium III Processor Desktop Boards page at `http://www.intel.com/design/motherbd/iii_mbd.htm`.

Micro Channel Architecture (MCA)

This bus, invented by IBM in 1987 to replace the performance-constrained ISA bus, has been retired. The architecture never caught on outside IBM for two reasons. First, it was not backward compatible with ISA. Second, other manufacturers weren't fond of IBM's predatory licensing practices. Nonetheless, it was a very cool idea technically; in fact, MCA introduced the idea of self-configuring peripherals eight years before Plug and Play saw the light of day. MCA cards themselves had no switches or jumpers with which to fiddle. Instead, an MCA card was configured solely by communication between the PC's Reference disk and the card's Options disk.

PC Card

The acronym PCMCIA stands for Personal Computer Memory Card International Association, which is a nonprofit trade association and standards body for certain small form factor cards. The PCMCIA was founded in 1989 and is comprised of more than 300 member companies. Initially, credit card–size peripheral cards were all referred to as *PCMCIA cards*. Today, the trend is to use PCMCIA to refer only to the association itself. The PCMCIA issues standards for the following technologies: PC Card, Small PC Card, Miniature Card, and SmartMedia Card. PC Cards come in three flavors—Type I, Type II, and Type III. All PC Card types have the same length and width (3.4×2.1 inches) and use the same 68-pin connector, but with varying thickness (thicker cards accommodate portable disk drives). PC Card slots are found mainly in portable PCs. For more information, see the PCMCIA home page at http://www.pc-card.com. The PC Card has the following features:

■ Small form factor (3.4×2.1 inches) and is therefore highly portable.

■ Supports Plug and Play.

■ Supports hot-swapping.

■ Supports Advanced Power Management.

■ The various card type specifications are backward compatible.

NOTE

USING CARDBUS FOR HIGH-SPEED MOBILE INTERCONNECTIONS

The CardBus provides a 32-bit data path and operates at a speed of 33MHz, thus providing a maximum potential throughput of 132MB/sec. This is equivalent in performance to the PCI bus. The main advantage of the CardBus architecture is its optimization for mobile computing: low-voltage operation (3.5v) to conserve power, high-speed interconnection (a PCI-like 132 MB/sec), small form factor (same as the widely implemented PC Card standard), and PnP and hot-swapping support.

PCI (Peripheral Component Interconnect)

Intel developed this bus architecture in concert with other industry leaders and then created the PCI Special Interest Group to manage and promote it. The PCI SIG published the specifications for PCI version 1.0 in 1992. The latest PCI version is 2.1, published in 1995. For more information, see the PCI SIG home page at http://www.pcisig.com. This is the most common peripheral bus found in modern PCs today. It has the following features:

- High-speed local bus

- Supports Plug and Play

- Can support 64-bit data width

- Widely thought to be the successor to the sluggish, outdated ISA bus

Universal Serial Bus (USB)

The main advocate of the USB bus is Intel, aided by six other companies (Compaq, Digital, IBM, Microsoft, NEC, and Northern Telecom). This group has formed the USB Implementers Forum (for more information, see http://www.usb.org). USB was developed in 1996, but users didn't become interested until 1998 when Apple released the iMac with USB ports in place of serial and Apple Desktop Bus (ADB) connectors. Most motherboards manufactured in the past few years provide built-in USB support, typically in the form of two USB connectors. Many modern monitors and keyboards also serve as USB hubs, which means they use the bus like any other USB device and also provide ports to which more USB devices can be connected. Note that for older PCs, companies such as Entrega Technologies (http://www.entrega.com) make two-port and four-port USB cards in the PCI form factor. We cover this type of upgrade in Chapter 11, "Adding USB Compatibility." It has the following features:

- Has a medium-speed serial bus

- Supports up to 127 devices

- Supports Plug and Play

- Supports hot-swapping

- Provides power to devices over the bus (eliminates bulky power bricks and cables)

- Does not require an IRQ for each device on the bus

- Does not require peripheral cards

- Is supported by Windows 95 B (OEM Service Release 2) and Windows 95 C, but *not* supported by earlier versions of Window 95

- Is supported by Windows 98 and Windows 2000

- Is *not* supported by Windows NT 3.x and 4.x

FREE UTILITY EVALUATES YOUR PC'S USB STATUS

Intel has written a free USB evaluation utility called USBReady. You can get it at `http://www.usb.org/data/usbready.exe`. (See Figures 2.21 and 2.22.)

FIGURE 2.21

Intel's USBReady tool performs an initial system check and report.

FIGURE 2.22

By clicking USBReady's Details button, you get detailed test results.

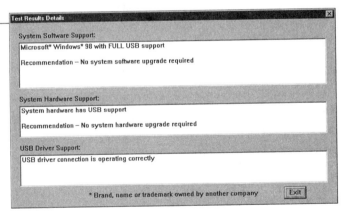

USB ONLINE RESOURCES GALORE

Two excellent Web sites full of USB resources are AllUSB at `http://www.allusb.com` and USB Workshop at `http://www.usbworkshop.com`.

VESA Local Bus

This bus was created by NEC in 1992 in conjunction with the Video Electronics Standards Association (VESA). Its architecture is rather inflexibly tied to the 486 processor family, although theoretically it could be adapted to other processors. This bus has been supplanted by the PCI bus, and for all intents and purposes, is no longer in use.

An Upgrade Checklist

Even with your inventory in hand, you're not quite ready to start ripping and tearing on your system. It's important to be prepared before physically upgrading a component, whether it's a software or hardware component. Believe us when we say that every time we've tried to rush an upgrade or skip a step because we were feeling particularly lucky that day, we've always regretted it. The following checklist also will appear in condensed form at the beginning of every subsequent chapter that involves an upgrade activity. That way, even if you someday open this book up to Chapter 6 and jump right in, the checklist will be there as a friendly reminder:

1. Do your homework.

   The specifics will vary from one component to another; however, research on a component could range from checking the manufacturer's Web site for FAQs, to rereading the relevant chapter in this book, to searching public newsgroups for the device's model name or number. Use your inventory form to ensure that the upgrade you have in mind will work with the system's buses, that the right type of peripheral slot is free, and that no device incompatibility risks exist.

TIP

SEARCHING PUBLIC NEWSGROUPS FOR IN-THE-TRENCHES HARDWARE EVALUATIONS

We were interested in public opinion about a specific Acer CD-RW drive. At the time of this writing, a search of Acer CRW4432A on Deja.com (`http://www.deja.com/ usenet_home.epl`) yielded 700 hits. This research told us that most folks were satisfied with its performance and some complaints about Acer's technical support existed, and yielded suggestions on places to shop for a good price.

2. Determine whether your PC supports the planned upgrade.

   This step is relatively self-explanatory. For example, you can't install a USB device if your system doesn't support USB. Or, your motherboard and its chipsets might limit whether your system is eligible for a particular BIOS upgrade. Again, your inventory worksheet is your roadmap so you don't get lost and try to put a square peg in a round hole.

3. Determine whether you can perform the upgrade.

   Do you have the necessary knowledge, experience, and time to perform this upgrade? Just because you don't have experience with a particular upgrade is no reason to forego it; instead, you'll need to do a bit more homework than someone who has done it a dozen times before (we'll give you plenty of confidence-building tips in Chapter 3). So, if you've got the time and the interest, be sure you do your homework first. On the other hand, if in your judgment the upgrade is beyond you, even given plenty of time and information, don't sweat it. Instead, assign the upgrade to an expert.

4. Purchase or acquire the component.

   Gather together literally everything you need to install the device in one operation. Many an upgrade has ground to an abrupt halt because of a missing doodad: power splitter, power cord, dual ribbon cable, pair of drive rails, set of mounting screws, you name it. If the upgrade involves a hardware component and you decide to shop online, we have some good tips for safe cyber-shopping later in the chapter.

TIP

CARRYING SPARE PARTS AND A KIT BAG

If you're going to be performing PC maintenance and upgrades for a living, a good inventory of spare parts and a hefty kit bag are essential.

TIP

EXCELLENT E-COMMERCE SITE RECOMMENDATIONS

You can get recommendations for a wide range of e-commerce sites at Forrester's Power Rankings (`http://powerrankings.forrester.com`).

5. Organize your tools and workspace.

   See Chapter 3.

6. Back up everything: data, operating system, mission-critical applications, and BIOS.

   The temptation is strong to skip this step, because it can be the longest. Please don't skip this step! Never perform an upgrade without a complete system backup. (We've said it before, but it's worth saying again—every time we've skipped this step, we have regretted it in spades.) At the very least, back up your data. You might choose to make a physical backup of your entire system or have current CDs on hand for your operating system and applications (plus a detailed printed list of which applications are mission-critical) should you have to start from scratch. Keep a current list of your BIOS settings. Although third-party utilities are available that will dump your BIOS settings to disk, we prefer the reliable graphite technology (a pencil) for this critical data.

7. Test your startup disk.

Here's another step we humbly regret ever having skipped. Make sure your startup (emergency boot) disk works. That means insert it into the floppy disk drive, reboot your machine, make sure it boots properly, and ensure that it has access to your CD-ROM drive.

EXPLICITLY TEST A STARTUP DISK'S CAPABILITY TO SEE THE CD-ROM DRIVE
Warning: Don't assume that all is well if the system boots up off a startup floppy disk. You must physically verify that the PC can see—and therefore read from—the CD-ROM drive. To do this, insert your operating system CD in the drive and switch to it by drive letter from the DOS prompt. Note that some operating systems support booting from a CD, notably Windows 98 Second Edition and Millennium.

8. Perform the upgrade.

9. Take good notes and permanently file them in your system log when you're finished.

If some aspect of the upgrade goes wrong, referring to your notes will enable you to quickly reverse course and put your system back in working order. The system log and recording of upgrade steps are discussed in more detail in Chapter 3.

10. Update your inventory documentation to reflect the upgraded or newly added component.

Online Shopping Tips

Some of you might be veteran online shoppers, others might have dabbled, and still others might be curious and ready to give it a try. Whatever your online shopping experience, it can't hurt to review the following list of tips:

- **Conduct online business only over a secure server**—A secure server's address begins with `https://` instead of the more common `http://`. The s suffix indicates you're connected to a secure server. With Internet Explorer or Netscape Navigator, a small padlock icon appears on the status bar.

- **Buy with a credit card**—This gives you the option to dispute a charge if the vendor fails to perform, and it also limits your liability to $50. Plus, few banks actually make you pay the $50.

- **Read the Web site's fine print about all their purchase transaction policies**—This includes studying quoted prices, shipping charges, how back-orders are handled, return policies, and restocking fees.

- **Get the company's physical address and phone number**—If you're in doubt about a site, check it out with a consumer agency, such as the Better Business Bureau (`http://www.bbb.org`).

- **Visit the Computer Economics Internet Shopping Complaint Hotline page**—If you do run into a problem with an online vendor, consider visiting this page (`http://www.compecon.com/new4/helpdesk/hotline.html`).

3

THINGS YOU NEED

*T*he very thought of pulling the cover off your computer and tinkering with its innards has given more than one tough hombre a case of the willies. The insides of a PC look like a prop left over from a *Star Trek* Borg episode. But we're here to tell you that performing hardware upgrades is something even the most timid earthling can do with a little thought and preparation.

A Proper Work Area

Before you start taking your computer apart, be prepared. Much of what we'll talk about in this section might seem obvious, but you'd be surprised how easy it is to overlook the obvious when fussing with computer hardware.

Before you even think of beginning an upgrade, give some serious thought to your work area.

Moving the Computer

Don't pull the cover off a computer that's installed under a desk and start working on it in the dark, lying on your side with a flashlight clenched in your teeth. Please, we've tried this and are here to tell you that it does not save time in the long run even if all you want to do is swap out a sound card.

Take the time to move the PC to a real work area out of the way of pedestrian traffic, preferably up on a solid table (see Figure 3.2). This will go a long way toward saving both your back and your sanity. Getting the PC up off the carpet is a good idea because static electricity and computers do not go together. A good static buildup from rolling around on the carpet can arc from you to a delicate bit of silicon, rendering it useless.

PLAINSPEAKING
IT'S ALL IN THE CARDS

If you've never taken the cover off a computer and gazed at its internal workings, it can be downright intimidating the first time. All kinds of stuff is in there, wires are running this way and that way, and there are strange metal boxes. *Don't panic.* With a little guidance and experience, you'll be popping boards in and out with ease.

Here's the short course to get you started. A number of circuit boards are inside the computer case. These are the green, plastic-looking things with all the weird and shiny stuff sticking out of them. A *circuit board* is just a bunch of electronic flotsam and jetsam stuck together in a base of epoxy on one side and all connected together by spidery lines on the other. These lines are what makes the *circuit* in circuit board. Therefore, it's important not to scratch one of these lines or crack the epoxy of the board.

Each circuit board, also known as a *peripheral card* (or just *card*), performs a function, such as handling the graphics output to your monitor (graphics adapter card) or dealing with sending sound to your speakers (sound card). The board contains the electronics necessary to perform the function, relieving the motherboard of the need to have that function built into it.

Cards connect to the motherboard by plugging into a bus slot and communicate with the motherboard and the central processing unit through that connection. This design makes upgrading possible; you easily can change out one graphics card for another without having to replace the entire motherboard.

Continued

Clearing the Clutter

If you're installing several new components (or setting up a new system from scratch), you'll be amazed how quickly you find yourself up to your elbows in empty boxes and packaging materials. Allow for this and figure out where you'll stack the boxes before you start unpacking. Uncrate one component at a time so you don't wind up with manuals, instructions, spec sheets, CDs, and the like scattered all around, causing you to get lost in the empty boxes and discarded packaging materials.

Remember to handle circuit boards carefully when removing and installing them, and always handle them by the edges. You don't want to twist or stress the boards themselves. Pretend they're old and valued photographs and you don't want to bend them or touch the actual photo part. Figure 3.1 shows an example of a typical circuit board.

The motherboard and various cards can be attached to other devices inside the case by *cables*. Some cables are flat and range from narrow to several inches wide. Other cables are just a number of wires twisted together. Some cards don't connect to anything inside the case but have cables plugged into them where their connectors protrude from the back of the computer.

Don't let the complexity of all the junk inside your computer throw you. You don't need to know how to build a circuit board to remove one from a computer or pop in a new one. ■

FIGURE 3.1

Handle peripheral cards with care.

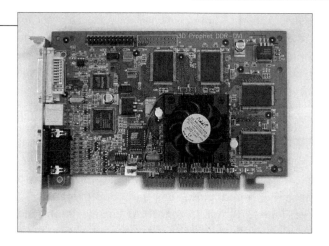

FIGURE 3.2

An uncluttered
work area is
essential to a
smooth upgrade.

FIGURE 3.2

An uncluttered
work area is
essential to a
smooth upgrade.

TIP

SAVE THE BOXES

Open the component's box carefully with a minimum of collateral damage to the box and
any Styrofoam packing blocks that might be inside. Save the original box, packing materials, internal plastic bags, twist ties, and related materials in case you have to repackage the
component and return it to the seller. This is especially important when dealing with
equipment purchased via mail order. Most vendors will always want the item returned in
its original packaging.

Okay, that's easy enough for small boxes, but what about the giant monitor and system
boxes? Granted, they're a pain to store, but you should save them, too—at least for a
month or so. If you have room in the garage, keeping the box for as long as the warranty
runs is not a bad idea. Trust us, you won't be happy trying to box up a monitor for shipment without the original packaging.

While we're on the topic of clutter, be sure you set up a NEAT box (if you don't
already have one) for the system on which you're working. *NEAT* stands for New
computer Emergency catchAll Trunk and can be anything from an old shoebox
to a large plastic trash bag. We, however, highly recommend you purchase a
Rubbermaid (or similar brand) plastic box that's approximately 12" wide, 16" long,
and 8" deep (see Figure 3.3). Add to your NEAT box everything that accompanies
each component—manuals, install disks, specification sheets, instructions, CD-
ROMs, licenses, invoices, packing slips, spare parts, screws, twist ties, cables, connectors, and so on. A NEAT box ensures that you have to search for things in only one
place. Everything that relates to a given system should be stored in its NEAT box. If
you have more than one computer, set up a separate NEAT box for each of them.

FIGURE 3.3

A NEAT box contains everything related to a particular PC.

Importance of Good Lighting and Ventilation

When picking out and setting up your work area, don't overlook adequate lighting. Some cables are color-coded, meaning you need to see the colors to know which side is which. Some of the parts you'll be working with are small and have smaller jumper blocks on them. In addition, they have tiny letters written next to the jumpers so you can identify them, so get as much light as you can. However, you'll still need a good flashlight and possibly a magnifying glass in your toolkit.

Ventilation is a good idea, too, because no matter how well you clean out your system prior to working on it (as we'll discuss shortly), some dust will still be inside the case.

Disconnecting the PC

Most people have a natural reluctance to moving the computer from where it is to the work area. Unplugging all the cables from the system and hauling it out from under the desk can be a hassle. Older computer chassis force you to unplug everything from the back before you can open the case, but more recent designs let you pop the side off the system with everything still connected. Resist the temptation. Instead, disconnect everything and move the system to your work area.

If you're nervous about getting everything hooked back up correctly when you put the system back, don't be. Use a marker to label each connection on the back of your PC and then tape a tag to each cable and label them accordingly. When you are ready to reconnect the system, you just match the cable tags to the connections on the system and plug them in. If you don't want to mark up your computer chassis with a marker, you can tape a piece of paper to the back of the chassis near the connectors and label them that way (see Figure 3.4).

FIGURE 3.4

Labeling each cable and connection port makes it easy to reconnect everything after you've finished your upgrade.

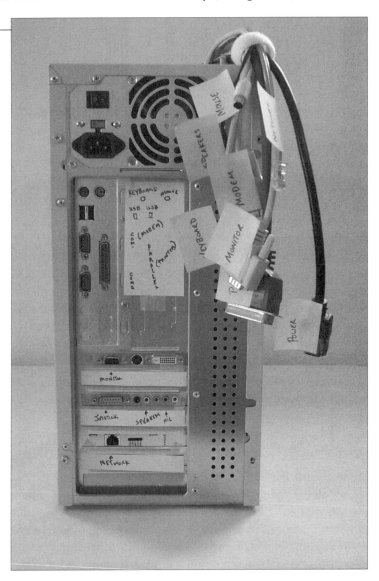

When you're disconnecting a system, be sure to first power down the computer and then unplug the power cord. This is important because some systems are designed so that power is still going to the motherboard even though the switch is off. You can damage your computer, to say nothing of yourself fussing around with a PC that still has the power cord attached. Unplug the cord!

Cleaning the PC

If you've never pulled the cover off your system, you might be amazed at all the dust and dirt that has accumulated inside.

Computer power supplies have fans that suck the air out of the system chassis. This causes air to flow into the system wherever it can. This air is then expelled, creating a current of air flowing over and around the components inside the case. This serves to cool down the electrical components that generate a lot of heat.

CAUTION

COOL OFF FIRST!

Keep in mind that *cool* is used here as a relative term; the insides of your computer get *hot*, so don't ever work on a system until it has been powered down and had time to cool to room temperature.

Dust, dirt, hair, and anything else that can be found on the floor around the system gets drawn in as well, and stays there.

After disconnecting your system and before performing the upgrade, take the computer outside and blow it out with compressed air. Most computer supply stores sell cans of compressed air in various sizes. You definitely want to do this outside if at all possible because billowing clouds of dust will result.

Make sure the entire system has cooled to room temperature before you blow it out because the com-

OFF THE WALL
CLEAN IS COOL

Your computer needs to be cleaned from time to time, not just when you open the case up for an upgrade. Once a quarter, open up the system case and blow out all the dust bunnies. If you're working in an exceptionally clean environment, you probably could get away with twice a year. It's not that we're neat freaks; dust is a real problem because it's a great insulator. Dust builds up on the chips and boards inside your computer and similar to a cozy wool blanket holds in heat, which is the primary enemy of your computer. Heat shortens the life of electronic components and can exacerbate the problem of thermal distortion. When you heat things, they expand. Conversely, when you cool them, they shrink. This happens to everything inside your computer. The more expanding that occurs when things are hot, the more shrinking that occurs when you shut down your system. Things work loose, crack, warp, and so on—all of which are bad for your computer. Keeping your system free of dust helps the cooling efforts of the system fan and increases the life of the system. ■

pressed air chills whatever you spray it at (the air spray can itself actually gets so cold it might become uncomfortable to hold). Hitting something that is hot with an icy blast of cold air causes it to contract suddenly, and that can damage the circuit boards and electrical parts in your system.

You might be tempted to break out the trusty household vacuum cleaner to get dust out of your computer and avoid having to move it outside for cleaning. However, two problems exist with this method.

First, the business end of a vacuum cleaner is hard metal (or a hard plastic attachment) and too large for the purpose, thereby increasing the chance you'll whack something delicate inside the case that should remain whack-free. Second, even if you have a mini-vac designed for this type of work, it simply can't do as effective a job as a can of compressed air. Air cans come with small pipettes (little plastic tubes) that fit the nozzle and enable you to direct the air stream between circuit boards and in very tight places where dust and debris accumulate.

Note, Map, and Label

The first time you remove something from your computer chassis can be unsettling or even frightening. How can you, an unqualified technician, be expected to get everything put back when you're finished? Did this cable-thingy plug in here or over there? Did the whatsit plug in like this or like that? And what about this plug that doesn't plug into anything? Was it like that when I started or did I forget to hook something back up?

Don't get scared; get cautious. Caution is your friend.

Mapping the Layout

Take a moment (and a pad of paper) and sketch out the area of your system on which you'll be working. This might be just a relatively small area of the system (for example, if you're performing a RAM upgrade) or it might be the entire system (if you're pulling out and replacing the motherboard).

TIP

DECIPHERING THE LAYOUT

The manual that came with your motherboard probably has a schematic drawing that labels the major components of the motherboard. This can be very helpful when you're trying to determine things such as which IDE connector is the primary and which is the secondary or where the DIMM slots are.

Draw a map of the internals. On your map, note the position of the drives, which device plugs into what, where the cables run (what they go over or around), which slot each card is plugged into, and everything you see so you know how it all goes back together again. You might not know that the twisted red and blue wires are for the hard drive activity light, but if you know it connects to the two pins "over there" on the map, you'll be able to hook it back up correctly. Figure 3.5 shows a typical motherboard in a newer PC and the slots and connectors to which you connect the processor, RAM, sound cards, video cards, network cards, drives, and power supply. Your motherboard might vary somewhat, especially if you have an older system. But if you carefully note the location of each connection before disassembly, you'll be able to reassemble it. Also, before disconnecting each of the power plugs that connect your motherboard and drives to the power supply, be careful to note the position of the connectors. If any of the cables has a colored stripe (usually red) along one edge, be sure to note this when making your map so you can properly plug these back in when you are finished.

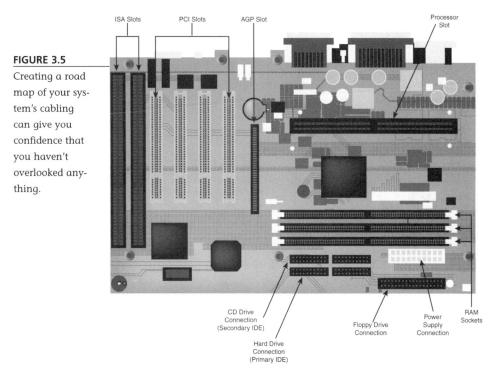

FIGURE 3.5

Creating a road map of your system's cabling can give you confidence that you haven't overlooked anything.

Noting All Connections

With some yellow stickies and ordinary cellophane tape, you can label and tag your computer's cards and cables as necessary while you work. Be sure to remove them all when you're done, though. Then, when you reassemble your system, you'll know that wire "A" connects to card "B" in the upper-right corner.

Tag each thing you unplug even if it's unrelated to what you're upgrading. Remember, space can be very cramped inside your system. For example, you might need to unplug the power connection and the controller cable for something such as the CD-ROM to get at the drive installed just above it in the chassis. Experience has taught us that it's easy to forget about things you disconnect while trying to get at the thing on which you want to work and on which you have your attention focused. If you forget to reconnect it, you'll power up your system after the upgrade only to find that something that was working before now appears broken. A yellow sticky on a loose power connector would have reminded you to reconnect the item.

Writing Down the Steps

Here's a trick that you should definitely use until you gain some experience with a particular hardware upgrade. Write down each thing you do, step by step. Say you're upgrading your old CD-ROM drive to a new CD-R/RW (Recordable/ReWritable) drive. If this is your first attempt at upgrading this particular component, take the time to write down each step as you complete it.

Roadmap to Your Upgrade

1. Disconnect power lead to CD drive. Label A.

2. Disconnect ribbon cable to CD. Red stripe on cable toward open side of case. Label B. Usually a thin wire is running from the CD drive to the sound card. Disconnect from the CD. Label C.

3. Remove four screws (two on each side) of drive bay bracket holding CD drive in case.

4. Slide CD drive out through front of case.

Now you've got a road map of the upgrade procedure. When you install the new CD-R/RW drive, you can simply check off the steps in reverse order (as appropriate). This can be a lifesaver, so you should take the necessary additional time to do this whenever you are performing an upgrade you're unfamiliar with or when working on a system that's new to you. Don't assume that every chassis is laid out the same way.

Working Inside the System Case

As we mentioned earlier (and will mention again), never work on an open computer chassis without first disconnecting the power cable from the system. Unplug it completely; don't just rely on switching off the power. The following sections discuss some other things you should keep in mind when working inside your computer.

No Jewelry

Take off any jewelry, including rings, watches, and bracelets. Don't wear loose clothing or dangling items such as ties or necklaces that can hang down or catch inside the case. Almost everything mounted on a circuit board has a sharp edge that can snag clothing or jewelry, not to mention the edges of the boards themselves.

Keep Track of Parts

This is a *must*—you have to keep track of every screw you remove from your system. *Every screw.* Keep count, just like medical surgeons do with sponges, so you know you've accounted for them all at the end of the operation, er, upgrade.

First, you must screw back whatever you take out. We've worked on computers that had the hard drive hanging by one lone remaining screw because the others had been lost at one time or another. Second, you don't want to have loose metal screws rolling around inside the computer chassis where they might become lodged across things that have current running through them. You also don't want them getting stuck in heat sink fans.

As you remove screws during an upgrade, place them in an ash tray, on a piece of doubled masking tape (which keeps them from rolling away), or in a small plastic film canister. The small boxes you get from the bank with a batch of checks make great containers for small parts, too.

If you do drop something into your system, be sure to retrieve it. But don't start fishing around inside the case with a magnet trying to remove a dropped screw. Magnets and computers are a huge incompatibility. You want to get a *parts grabber* (also known as a parts *retriever* or *holder*), which looks similar to a pencil. You push one end and a set of small wire claws pops out of the other end, enabling you to carefully snatch a small object out of the inner recesses of your system (see Figure 3.6).

Auto parts stores have longer articulated versions of these parts grabbers, but this is overkill for most computer users.

No Food or Drinks

Don't eat lunch while you're up to your elbows in the system case. If you need a cup of coffee, step away from your work area or leave the room entirely to avoid the temptation (and possible disaster). Ditto while you finish that ham on rye. You don't want to drop crumbs or liquid inside your computer case under any circumstances.

FIGURE 3.6

Picking up a fallen screw from an inaccessible cranny of your computer's insides is a snap with a parts retriever.

No Fast Moves

The working space inside your computer's chassis is very limited. The electronics parts are somewhat fragile, and sharp protrusions abound. Move around inside the case slowly and deliberately. Don't apply force—for example, to loosen a too-tight screw—unless you're properly balanced and can apply the force in a manner that won't cause a disaster if the screwdriver slips. A screwdriver scraping across your motherboard can ruin it in a heartbeat. Barking your knuckles on a drive cage is not much fun, either.

Don't force things in general, especially circuit boards. Some substantial pressure might be required to pop a board into or out of its slot, but be very careful not to twist the board or to apply pressure unevenly. It's important that you not crack the board you're installing or the motherboard that supports the slot into which you're plugging it. A circuit board is made of an epoxy material (which is somewhat brittle) to which various electrical gizmos are attached. These gizmos are all wired to each other by *traces* on the board. These traces look like spidery silver lines on some boards. If you crack a board by bending it, you can sever one of these traces and thus ruin the board.

Static Electricity and What to Do About It

Everyone's familiar with static electricity; you reach for a doorknob and just before you touch it, a spark leaps from you to the metal knob and you feel a small zap. This is called an *electrostatic discharge (ESD)*. An ESD is caused by your acquiring a surplus of electrons. Given a chance, nature likes to keep things balanced, so those electrons will leave you if they can by jumping to something else. Something conductive such as the doorknob or a computer circuit board or chip is attractive to the surplus electrons. Zap, indeed.

You must be grounded to not have a negative electrical charge when you work on your computer. When you're working on a computer, avoid those leather wingtips and don't shuffle your feet on the carpet. Try a pair of sneakers instead. Touch something that's grounded, but not the chassis of the computer on which you're working because after you unplug its power cable, it is no longer grounded.

An electrostatic discharge wrist strap is a handy thing to have if static electricity is a problem (see Figure 3.7). It consists of an attachment that makes contact with your wrist (with a conductor wire) and a cord you attach to something grounded. This enables any static buildup to flow from your wrist to

OFF THE WALL
CLEARING THE STATIC
    We once worked in a high-rise office building that caused ESD outbursts that were positively painful. It got to where you hated to open a door because you knew you were going to be shocked. We learned that if we laid the palm of our hand on the door for a moment before opening it, the door would gently draw off enough electrons so that we did not get shocked when we touched the doorknob. ■

ANOTHER FINE MESS
DANGER, HIGH VOLTAGE
    You acquire electrons by touching things. Dry atmospheric conditions increase your chance of acquiring electrons. Leather-soled shoes shuffling across a carpet are notorious for this, and you can produce quite a spark when you touch a conductive surface. It's best that this conductive surface *not* be inside your computer. That little static electricity zap you feel is caused by high-voltage electricity. No fooling, very high-voltage electricity. Several thousand volts is common; even the smallest spark requires 500 volts or so, which can ruin the delicate silicon chips found everywhere inside your PC. Rub a balloon on your head to the point where your hair starts standing on end and you'll be carrying a charge of tens of thousands of volts. This is not to be taken lightly when dealing with electronic components. ■

ground. The problem, of course, is finding a ground near to where you're working. Remember, the computer on which you're working isn't grounded after you unplug the power cable so it is not a candidate as a ground. We mention this again because it's a common mistake.

FIGURE 3.7

An ESD wrist strap is a sensible precaution against static electricity when working on your computer.

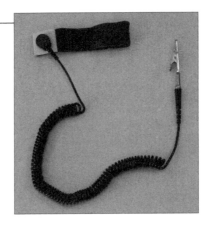

The best (albeit not cheap) solution we've come across is a *receptacle analyzer* carried by some electronics industry tool supply companies. It's a small gizmo that plugs into a three-prong wall outlet and lets you know whether you have a good ground. You plug your wrist strap into the analyzer, which is in turn plugged into the wall. It can feel a bit scary the first time you plug this wire hooked to your arm into something that's plugged into your wall outlet.

Tecra Tools sells a number of static defense tools, including the Stat Gard Receptacle Analyzer, wrist straps, static dissipating mats, and more. Their Web site is http://www.tecratools.com/ESD/ESD.html#ground.

If you think you'll be inside your machine enough to justify the $40–$50 expense, this is a good option. Otherwise, be very mindful about static, try to work in an uncarpeted area, and ground yourself to something before you even begin unpacking your upgrade components.

Required Tools

The good news is that unlike many do-it-yourself projects, you don't need to invest a fortune in tools to work on a computer. We'll discuss the types of tools you need in this section and conclude this chapter with a checklist of everything you'll need to tackle your upgrade tasks.

The System Journal

Here's a tool that is often over-looked but that can really come in handy. The *system journal* is simply a spiral notebook you keep next to your computer. You should write down everything out of the ordinary that happens to this computer. If Windows crashes, note the date, time, and what you were doing when it went kaput! If you hear a funny noise, note that, too.

By recording every crash, glitch, odd noise, and "hmmm, that was odd" incident all in one notebook, you can start to see patterns in the problems. Seeing the pattern is the first step toward solving a problem. You also can get a better warning of impending doom if the frequency of a given problem is increasing. This in turn helps you plan your upgrades and equipment replacements.

Also, you should use the journal to record every time you open the case, clean the computer, or upgrade a component. Note what you did to the system, when you did it, any problems you encountered, and how you resolved them. This can save you time on later upgrades by preventing you from having to figure out the same trick each time.

> ### PLAINSPEAKING
> #### THE RIGHT TOOL FOR THE JOB
>
> Only a few hand tools are needed to completely disassemble a computer right down to the bare metal chassis. Opening up the system case, which used to be a tiring undertaking, doesn't require any tools on many newer models. Although you don't need a garage full of tools, the tools you do need must be good ones (don't get a rusty, beat-up, old screwdriver from the kitchen junk drawer to tinker inside your system).
>
> Your tools should be clean and sized appropriately for the task at hand. The screws that hold your computer together are small; larger screwdrivers, or worn screwdrivers with rounded edges, can slip unexpectedly and damage your system or even your hand. ■

Screwdrivers

Your screwdrivers should have nice sharp edges so they'll grip the screw tightly. You'll need both Phillips and the regular slotted type. Make sure they fit the small screws that hold your system together—not too large, not too small. You don't want the screwdriver to slip and damage anything nearby. For the Phillips type, you should have a size #0 and a #1 and for the slotted type, a 1/8" and 3/16" will do.

We should mention a special type of screwdriver called a *Torx*, which has a tip in the shape of a six-pointed star (see Figure 3.8). Way back in the early days of the personal computer age, Compaq thought it would be a great idea if their systems used Torx screws, which made it nearly impossible for the average person to even open up the chassis without buying a special tool. What were they thinking? The good news is that it's uncommon nowadays to come across a situation in which a Torx driver is required (although it does happen from time to time). If you find you need a Torx and your local hardware store doesn't carry them, try an auto supply store.

FIGURE 3.8

Three types of screwdrivers are used when working on computers—the Phillips, the slotted, and the less common Torx.

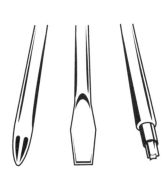

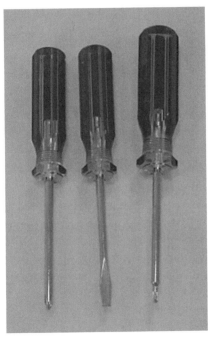

Nutdrivers

Many of the metal machine screws in your system have hexagonal heads on them with a slot for screwdriver use. The hex head of the screw enables you to use a nutdriver instead of a screwdriver to rotate the screw (see Figure 3.9).

A *nutdriver* is similar to the socket from a socket wrench that has been welded onto the end of a screwdriver handle. The nutdriver generally gives you a much better grip on the screw, especially if the slots in the screw are worn. You'll need a 3/16" and a 1/4" nutdriver in your toolkit.

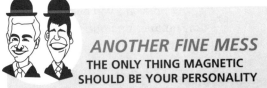

ANOTHER FINE MESS
THE ONLY THING MAGNETIC SHOULD BE YOUR PERSONALITY

Stay away from screwdrivers with magnetic tips. Yes, they are handy, but the risk of having magnetic fields moving around inside your computer is not worth the convenience. You risk damaging chips and data media, such as floppy disks, and your hard drive. ■

FIGURE 3.9

The nutdriver provides a solid grip and prevents the accidents that can occur when using a screwdriver.

Flashlight

Even if you heed our advice and work on your system up on a table with good lighting, you'll still need a bright flashlight. A good flashlight will provide directed light on the depths of the chassis.

Cable Ties

Computer cables (both internal and external) come in three types: too long, too short, and missing. If a cable is missing, the replacement will invariably be one of the other two types. It seems you're doomed to eventually wind up with most of your cables in the too long category.

Is a rat's nest of cables lurking behind your PC or PCs? If there is, here's how you can keep those cables organized and make it easier to connect, disconnect, access, and reposition your equipment.

Cable ties can help you here. You can get plastic-coated wire ties, but we prefer the Velcro or self-locking nylon cable ties (after they lock, they're locked forever) available for about 10 cents apiece in a variety of lengths and colors. You can find these at most computer and hardware stores.

After you've cinched the self-locking nylon ties tight, you'll have to snip them off with scissors or wire cutters. Still, they are the preferred method to keep your excess cables neatly organized inside your system. We also like them for tying off cable coils. On the other hand, Velcro ties are better for bundling several cables together (see Figure 3.10).

FIGURE 3.10

Nylon zip, Velcro, and plain twist ties can all help you deal with cable clutter.

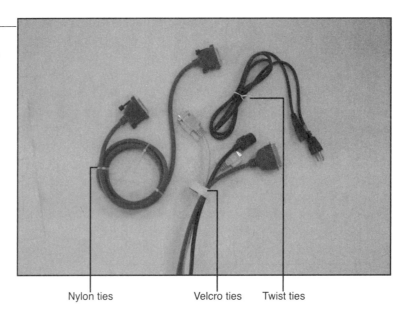

Nylon ties   Velcro ties   Twist ties

For keeping your cables neat and out from underfoot along the baseboard of your workspace, the ideal solution is a device that wraps the cables up but can also be easily opened and closed. Curtis cable organizers to the rescue.

Curtis makes a locking cable clip (part no. CO2) you can use to create a virtual conduit along the baseboard and perhaps at a few strategic locations on the back of a desk. Each clip has a one-inch, square, plastic plate mounted with a very strong self-adhesive so you can just peel and stick them. Position each clip properly the first time because they don't come off easily, and that's good! The front side of the plate sports a ratcheted ring you quickly can pop open, lock closed, loosen, or tighten. The ring diameter is slightly less than one inch. They come five in a box at $2.99 per box. We suggest you mount them twelve inches apart, closer in corners to minimize the tension on any given clip (see Figure 3.11). Keep extra cable neatly coiled and tied off at each end.

Check out these and other accessories at the Curtis Web site (http://www.curtis.com).

FIGURE 3.11

FIGURE 3.11

Putting Curtis
wall-mounted
locking cable
clips to good use
in one of our
offices.

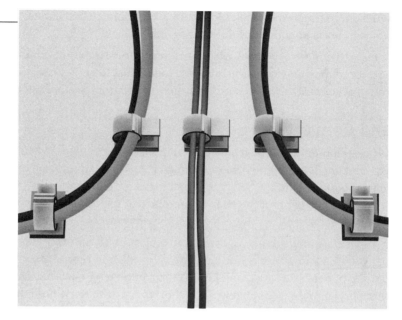

PC Toolkits

For less than $20 you can pick up a basic computer toolkit at most of the computer
superstores, such as CompUSA (see Figure 3.12). These usually come in a vinyl zip-
per case and contain the necessary sizes of Phillips and slotted screwdrivers, two nutdrivers, a pair of tweezers suitable for pulling jumper blocks and fishing loose screws
out of the computer case, and so on.

FIGURE 3.12

Even a basic kit
contains the
tools in the sizes
you'll need for
most upgrades.

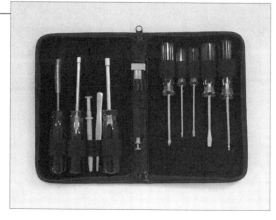

However, the toolkit might not have a three-claw parts grabber, which is so handy
that we recommend you either keep shopping until you find a kit that has one or

purchase one separately (refer to Figure 3.7). As mentioned earlier, you can find parts grabbers at your local auto parts store.

Some of the more expensive kits come with a wrist strap that grounds you against ESD. Don't buy an expensive 150-piece toolkit just to get a wrist strap, though. You can purchase ESD straps separately from any electronics supply store.

Splitters and Converters

We keep a number of miscellaneous but indispensable items in our tool bags. If all you're doing is swapping a sound card, you probably won't need any of these, but if you embark on upgrades of a more ambitious nature, chances are you'll need them. It's also a good bet that the nearest computer supply store will have closed five minutes before you realize you need one of these items.

A *Y-splitter* connects to one of the power cables inside your computer, effectively giving you an extra power connection. We've opened up computers, counted the unused power connectors, and found one available for our need—only to discover that particular unused cable was too short to reach the new hard drive. In such a case, you might be able to use a Y-splitter on one of the power cables closer to where you want power, thereby giving you an extra connector in the right place (see Figure 3.13).

FIGURE 3.13

Use a Y-splitter power connector to give yourself an extra power plug inside your PC.

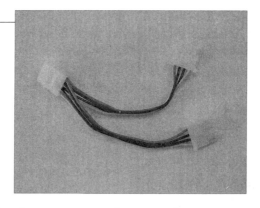

Another common snafu occurs when you want to plug a serial device into your computer's serial port. This shouldn't be a problem, except that the device has a cable that ends in a 25-pin D-Shell connector. The serial port on your computer is a 9-pin D-Shell receptacle. Argh! *Converter plugs* enable you to convert a 25-pin serial connector to a 9-pin serial connection or vice versa. Converters also exist to switch a 5-pin DIN keyboard plug into a smaller PS/2 connector. If you need to use an extension cable, you might run into a situation in which you need a *gender changer* to make a male plug into a female socket. You can get all these at computer or electronics supply stores (see Figure 3.14).

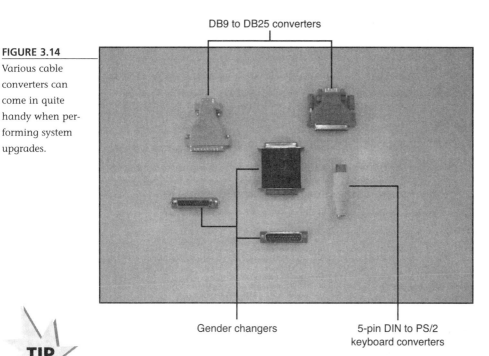

DB9 to DB25 converters

FIGURE 3.14

Various cable converters can come in quite handy when performing system upgrades.

Gender changers

5-pin DIN to PS/2 keyboard converters

TIP

WHERE'S AN EXTENSION CORD WHEN YOU NEED ONE?

If you fuss around with computers much, you probably have extra power cords lying around. They plug into a standard three-prong electrical outlet on one end and into a computer power connection at the other end. Said another way, one end of the cable is a male three-prong plug and the other end of the cable is a female three-prong plug. You need a converter that consists of a 6- to 8-inch length of cord that converts a power cable into an extension cord.

Tools Checklist

The following is a list of the things we recommend you have handy before you start upgrading your PC:

- Flashlight

- Nutdrivers (3/16" and 1/4")

- Screwdrivers (Phillips and slotted *without* magnetic tips)

- Tweezers (larger types suitable for picking up and holding machine screws, not the smaller type found in the medicine cabinet)

- ESD wrist strap or comparable ESD equipment (antistatic mat, sprays, and so on)

- Magnifying glass

- Cable ties

- Suitable container for holding screws and other small parts

- Electrical extension cord (three-prong)

- Extra PC power cable (and power cord–to–extension cord converter)

- An assortment of splitters and connectors depending on the upgrade project you're about to tackle

- The computer's system journal and NEAT box

Breaking Down Your Computer

If you've never worked on a computer before, it can be a bit intimidating the first time. The following are the basic steps you should perform (we're assuming here that this is your first time performing an upgrade):

First Timers

1. Label all the cables coming out of the back of your computer.

2. Label all the connectors to correspond to the attached cables.

3. Turn off the power.

4. Disconnect all cables plugged into your computer.

5. Move the system to an area where you can blow out the chassis. Remove the case cover and use a can of compressed air to thoroughly blow out the system.

6. Move the system to your prepared work area. You can move most systems with the cover off, but you must be very careful about bumping into things because all the delicate internal electronic components are exposed and unprotected. Replace the cover before moving the system if you are uneasy about this.

TIP

FINDING THE RIGHT JACK

As long as you're labeling things, here's a hot tip: The sound card on your system has several mini-plug connectors—one for your speakers, one for a microphone, and probably a line in and a line out. They might or might not be marked with cryptic icons or actual words etched in the shiny metal of the bracket end of the peripheral card, and these might be readable (in a strong light, with a magnifying glass, up on your work table). However, after you install the system and you have a handful of cables snaking this way and that, chances are good you'll be unable to read these default labels. Save yourself some headaches down the road and mark the back of your chassis (or the top or the side) and pencil in which connector is which. Then, when you're trying to plug in a microphone or headset, you'll know that the first plug on the left is the speaker, the second is the line in, the third is the microphone, and so on.

You're now ready to work on your upgrade. You should have a clean, uncluttered work area with adequate light and ventilation. When your upgrade is complete, replace the system and plug all the cables back in.

PART

THE CORE UPGRADES

4

UPGRADING THE BIOS

hen you hit that switch on your system, the BIOS is what grabs your computer by the neck, pours a hot cup of cyber-coffee down its throat, and gets it purring on all cylinders. The BIOS fires up the hardware and makes sure everything is okay before starting up the operating system. Keeping the hardware talking to the software is the job of the BIOS and new hardware might require a new BIOS. Beware, though; a BIOS upgrade is something you only undertake when you have a compelling reason to do so. It can be done, and sometimes has to be done, but it's not without risk. In this chapter, we'll show you how to keep the risk to a minimum.

Pre-Upgrade Checklist

1. Do your homework. Read this chapter completely and then study the instructions provided by your BIOS/motherboard manufacturer.

2. Determine whether your PC requires a BIOS upgrade.

3. Determine whether you can perform the upgrade.

4. Locate and download the required BIOS chip or flash upgrade file.

5. Back up everything: data, operating system, mission-critical applications, and BIOS settings.

6. Perform the upgrade.

7. Record all the new BIOS settings and store them in your NEAT box.

8. Update your inventory documentation to reflect the revised BIOS version number.

Reasons to Upgrade

The rule of thumb is to upgrade your computer's Basic Input and Output System (BIOS) only when you absolutely must. Don't run out and grab a later BIOS version just because one is available. Unless it gives you a fix or a feature you need, don't mess with it. This is one instance where the old *adage if it ain't broke, don't fix it* really applies.

What Is It I'm Upgrading Exactly?

The system BIOS is what is known in computer lingo as a *bootstrap* program that jumpstarts your PC and enables it to interact with the various hardware and peripherals attached to it, such as the system clock, keyboard, serial and parallel ports, hard drive(s), and so on. It's a set of built-in device drivers that provide the lowest-level access to your computer's hardware and is the program that actually loads the operating system. If you have a problem with your BIOS, you have real trouble indeed.

Remember, we're only talking about the system BIOS. This BIOS is stored in a read-only memory (ROM) chip on the motherboard of your computer (see Figure 4.1).

PLAINSPEAKING
THINK OF IT LIKE THIS

Think of your BIOS as your *hardware superintendent* that gets the call every time you flip on your computer's power switch. Picture a guy in a hard hat wearing a white lab coat and with a clipboard tucked under his arm. His job is to oversee the entire computer startup process. He ensures that the memory adds up and the hard disk is on the job, checking that each hardware item is present and accounted for and that it's primed with the proper settings.

If the BIOS is the superintendent, what the heck is the *CMOS*? These two terms are sometimes confused and mistakenly used as though they are interchangeable. If the BIOS is the guy in the hard hat then the CMOS is his clipboard where all the proper settings and specifications for each hardware device are recorded. We cover both terms in technical detail in this chapter, but if you're new to this, just think of the BIOS as the guy who makes sure the startup process works and the hardware is set up properly, and he gets the proper settings from his clipboard, the CMOS. ■

Other peripheral cards can contain their own BIOS program chips. A *device driver* is the software equivalent of a BIOS chip. The system BIOS starts first and fires off everything else.

TIP

RECOMMENDED GENERAL BIOS RESOURCES

If you want to know more about what makes the BIOS tick, check out these great Web sites:

- BIOS Setup Information Guide at `http://www.sysopt.com/bios.html`
- BIOS Survival Guide at `http://burks.bton.ac.uk/burks/pcinfo/hardware/bios_sg/bios_sg.htm`
- Tom's Hardware Guide on BIOS at `http://www.tomshardware.com/mainboard/99q1/990208/index.html`

FIGURE 4.1

The BIOS on this motherboard is permanently attached. Note its proximity to the replaceable CMOS battery.

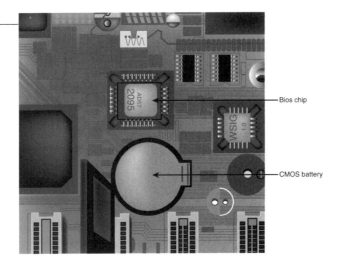

Bios chip

CMOS battery

And Why Do I Upgrade It?

Several situations can force you to upgrade your system's BIOS. Sometimes software will demand a BIOS upgrade. For example, when the Windows 98 operating system came out, it required a BIOS upgrade on some computers to work correctly.

More often, however, a BIOS upgrade is demanded by some new piece of hardware that must be active at bootup or by a feature your computer doesn't presently support. Occasionally, you might need a BIOS upgrade to fix some bug or glitch in your system. For example, some computers didn't support the date change to the year 2000 without first upgrading their BIOS.

Here's a classic hardware example of a system BIOS limitation requiring an upgrade. The

PLAINSPEAKING
SYSTEM BIOS, CARD BIOS, AND DEVICE DRIVERS

Remember, a BIOS is just a collection of device drivers coded into a ROM chip (also called *nonvolatile memory*). You're probably familiar with Windows device drivers, such as device drivers for your sound card and so on. Device drivers are the programs that make the hardware work. For equipment that can wait until the operating system is loaded, the more familiar device drivers stored on the hard disk and loaded by the operating system usually suffice. Some components, such as your graphics adapter card, have their own BIOS chips installed right on the card. One of the things the system BIOS does is look for cards that have their own BIOS routines and then load those drivers during the bootup process. This enables your system BIOS to not have to natively recognize the hundreds of different graphics cards out there; yet it still enables your video monitor to work before the operating system is loaded. ■

quantum leaps constantly being made in hard disk capacity often force a BIOS upgrade. The BIOS is the limiting factor in the size of a hard drive a computer can natively recognize. Whenever a major breakthrough in the size of hard drives has occurred, a system BIOS upgrade has been required to provide support for the new larger drives. For example, drives larger than 8.4GB have been supported only since 1998. So, a new piece of hardware can require that you upgrade your system BIOS for the new gizmo to work properly.

Your Current BIOS

The BIOS currently installed on your system was decided on by your motherboard manufacturer, so you need to know exactly what motherboard you have and what BIOS it is currently running. (You determined your motherboard model when you inventoried your system, as discussed in Chapter 2, "Preparing for an Upgrade.")

This is necessary because you need to get your BIOS upgrade from your motherboard manufacturer. Whereas only a handful of companies manufacture the majority of all BIOS programs (AMI, Award, Microid Research (MR), and Phoenix), each motherboard manufacturer licenses a particular version of the BIOS and then tweaks it for the specific motherboard on which it will be installed.

Help, I've Got a Clone Motherboard

If you buy a major brand-name computer, such as IBM or Compaq, chances are good that you'll get a readily identifiable motherboard with your system and a nice thick manual telling you all about it. However, if your computer is a no-name clone—in other words, not a major brand—determining exactly what motherboard you have inside the case might not be so easy.

If your system documentation is a bit on the inadequate side, even as to telling you what brand of motherboard you have, despair not. If the system has an Award or AMI BIOS, you often can backtrack the motherboard manufacturer from something called the BIOS *ID*.

You can get the BIOS ID in several ways. First, you can use any of a number of system analysis tools, such as the following:

- Sandra (discussed extensively in Chapter 2).

- Unicore BIOS Wizard (`http://www.unicore.com`), a freeware special-purpose utility that refers to the BIOS ID as the BIOS Signon.

- CTBIOS (provided by the German magazine *CT Magazine*) is another freebie that will give you the BIOS ID. The application is in German, but the ID is clearly labeled ID-String, so you won't have a language problem (see Figure 4.2). You'll find CTBIOS at this URL:

`ftp.heise.de/pub/ct/ctsi/ctbios13.zip`

FIGURE 4.2

The freebie CTBIOS utility shows you the ID, labeled ID-String.

Other system utilities also will do this; the important thing is just that you find this identifier. If you have a good eye and a fast hand, you can simply record this number from your computer screen as it appears (albeit briefly) during the bootup process. Here's the BIOS ID from an Award BIOS on one of our test computers:
`i440BX/ZX-977-2A69KPABC-00`

When the system boots up, this number appears briefly while the BIOS is loading. If you find that your ID number flashes by too quickly for you to write it down, try this trick. Hold down a key on your keyboard while booting the machine (or unplug your keyboard altogether before you boot up). This causes a keyboard error and the screen that prompts you to press F1 to continue should display your BIOS ID (usually in the lower-left corner) and give you all the time you need to write it down. You also can try pressing the Pause key to freeze the display while you record the BIOS ID. If you unplug your keyboard, power down before you reconnect it.

After you have the ID number, go over to the Motherboard HomeWorld Web site and use its search engine, nicknamed Spot, to search out your manufacturer:
`http://www.motherboards.org/spotbios.html`

It will give you advice on how to parse your ID string to find the motherboard identifier. Enter that and you should get back information that either clearly names your motherboard manufacturer or gives you enough information to puzzle it out. Consider what Spot returned in Figure 4.3.

FIGURE 4.3

Spot might name your motherboard or might just hint at it.

> **Search Results**
>
> Spot looked for **2A69KPABC** and decided that it smells just like something made by **epoxep61bxam2m** or **epoxep6zxb** or **epoxep6zxm** or **epoxepbx2** or **epoxepbx2p** or **epoxepbx3** or **epoxepbxca** or **epoxepbxt** or **epoxepzxa**
>
> **Search Results**
>
> in addition,
>
> Spot looked and looked for **2A69KPABC** and found these possible manufacturers:
>
> - *2A69KPABC* is made by **epoxep61bxam2m** or **epoxep6zxb** or **epoxep6zxm** or **epoxepbx2** or **epoxepbx2p** or **epoxepbx3** or **epoxepbxca** or **epoxepbxt** or **epoxepzxa**

From this information, we were able to determine that the motherboard manufacturer was EPoX by going to the manufacturers page (http://www.motherboards.org/manufact.html) and then jumping down to the Es (the motherboard manufacturers are listed alphabetically). From there, we were able to use the link provided to take us right to the EPoX Web site.

Manufacturer and Version Number

Determining the type of BIOS you have and its revision number can be a bit daunting, especially if you're trying to read it off the screen as it flashes by briefly during the bootup process. Unless you have a photographic eye or the patience to reboot your system as many times as necessary, forgo trying to get this information off the screen.

Instead, you can use a system analysis tool (again, such as Sandra or the Unicore BIOS

ANOTHER FINE MESS
NO ID CLUES FOR PHOENIX

If you have a Phoenix BIOS, you're completely out of luck if you can't figure out your motherboard manufacturer by other means (such as in the documentation or finding a label on the physical motherboard).

However, you might not be high and dry as far as getting a BIOS upgrade for your PC. Several firms, such as Micro Firmware, Inc. (http://www.firmware.com) and Unicore Software (http://www.unicore.com), sell BIOS upgrades for systems with obsolete motherboards and for motherboards whose manufacturers have gone out of business.

If you have a Phoenix BIOS, you can surf to the Unicore Web site and submit information about your system (processor, speed, BIOS version, and so on) and they will contact you with information about your options. Micro Firmware takes a hardware approach and doesn't try to upgrade your existing BIOS at all but instead sells you an add-in card with a BIOS on it that provides the upgraded features you're missing. Remember that an add-in card can have its own BIOS and these drivers get loaded during the boot process by the system BIOS. ■

Wizard) to access your system's BIOS information. But you can accomplish the same thing using the Windows Device Manager.

Get BIOS Information from Device Manager

1. On your Windows desktop, right-click the My Computer icon.

2. Select Properties from the pop-up menu to display the System Properties dialog box.

3. Click the Device Manager tab.

4. Click the Print button.

5. In the Print dialog box, select the System summary option and click OK to print the Resource Summary Report.

   At the top of the Resource Summary Report, you'll find your system's BIOS information, including the BIOS name, date, and version—which is everything you could want except the BIOS ID we discussed earlier (see Figure 4.4).

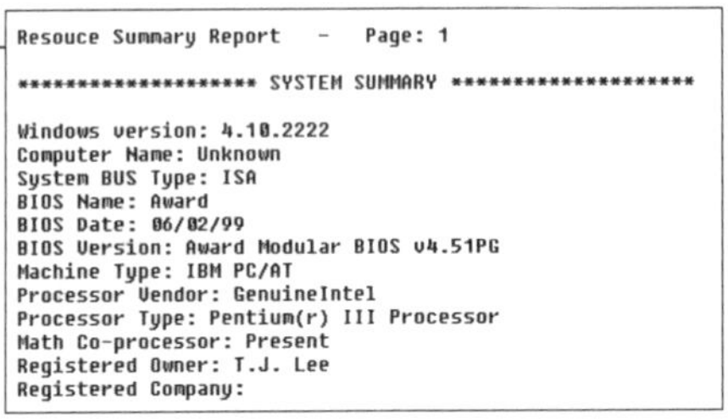

FIGURE 4.4

The Resource Summary Report is a fast way to get a printed copy of your BIOS information.

```
Resouce Summary Report   -   Page: 1

******************** SYSTEM SUMMARY ********************

Windows version: 4.10.2222
Computer Name: Unknown
System BUS Type: ISA
BIOS Name: Award
BIOS Date: 06/02/99
BIOS Version: Award Modular BIOS v4.51PG
Machine Type: IBM PC/AT
Processor Vendor: GenuineIntel
Processor Type: Pentium(r) III Processor
Math Co-processor: Present
Registered Owner: T.J. Lee
Registered Company:
```

KEEP SYSTEM INFORMATION HANDY AND UP TO DATE

It's a good idea to print out an All devices and system summary report from Device Manager, which provides you with a wealth of information about your system and the devices installed therein. Keep this report in your NEAT box and update it whenever you perform an upgrade on your system (see Figure 4.5).

FIGURE 4.5

The Print dialog box enables you to print either a System Summary Report or the more detailed All devices report.

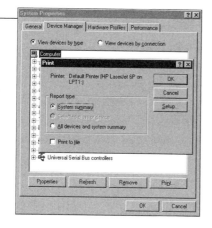

You also can get the BIOS information by entering the BIOS setup program. This utility enables you to change the BIOS settings stored in the CMOS (discussed in the next section). The process you use to access the BIOS setup utility differs depending on the BIOS manufacturer. For American Megatrends, Inc. (AMI) or an Award BIOS, you generally press the Delete key when you see the prompt flash on the screen during bootup (see Figure 4.6).

FIGURE 4.6

Watch carefully for the prompt that tells you what key(s) to press to access the BIOS Setup utility.

For systems using the Phoenix BIOS, you press F2 or Esc, or Ctrl+Alt+S for some earlier BIOS versions. Most of the later BIOS routines have a setup option that prevents the key combination to access the BIOS setup from being displayed. If you're not seeing the prompt during POST, your motherboard documentation should have the key access listed. On earlier systems, the BIOS setup key might be Del, Esc, Ctrl+Esc, or even Ctrl+Alt+Esc.

Record All Current CMOS Settings

CMOS stands for Complementary Metal-Oxide Semiconductor, and this chip is where the BIOS gets all its parameters and settings so it can recognize and work with the installed hardware. The CMOS stores information about what drives are installed, whether a floppy exists, whether the floppy should be checked at bootup, whether the CD-ROM should be considered a bootable device, the power management settings to use, and so on. Some upgrades require you to go into the CMOS and make changes to some of the settings.

The CMOS is capable of retaining these settings even when the PC is powered down. This is accomplished with a battery that maintains the settings when the computer is not running. PCs usually have thin, round power cells providing power to the CMOS; earlier models might even be outfitted with several AA pen-light batteries. It's important with these earlier systems that the batteries be properly maintained and not allowed to corrode or leak. Some systems have rechargeable nickel cadmium cells that get recharged whenever the PC is running. Some later motherboard designs even have a 10-year lithium cell epoxied right into the CMOS chip.

You need a record of all your current CMOS settings in your NEAT box in case you have problems and have to fall back on the fac-

ANOTHER FINE MESS
ALWAYS USE UPDATE BIOS DEFAULTS

You don't want to use any utilities that offer to automatically restore your old CMOS settings for you because the order or placement of the new settings (following the BIOS upgrade) might not match up to the old settings. Always choose Update BIOS Defaults in the CMOS after you update the BIOS. ■

ANOTHER FINE MESS
RESTORING THE CMOS TO ITS DEFAULT SETTINGS

You might need to restore your CMOS settings to their factory defaults if an errant setting causes problems with your system or if you get locked out of the BIOS setup utility. Most BIOS setup utilities enable you to password protect access to the BIOS setup. However, this can be a problem if you forget your password or you were not the person who originally assigned the password.

Check your motherboard documentation and always follow the instructions there for resetting the CMOS. A three-pin jumper block is usually adjacent to the CMOS battery on the motherboard. The two pins (usually pin 1 and pin 2) being jumped (also referred to as *shorted* because the jumper connects the pins being jumped and completes a circuit between them) keep the BIOS settings stored in the CMOS.

The following are the basic steps to reset the CMOS (check your motherboard manual for specific instructions for your system):

tory default settings to get things running again (we discuss the NEAT box in Chapter 3, "Things You Need"). Some of your hardware might not work properly with the default settings, so you'll want to be able to re-enter any changes you've made to the CMOS.

The simplest method to record all your CMOS settings is to either manually record them (using good old lead graphic technology as discussed in Chapter 2) or perform a series of screen dumps to your printer for all the settings.

TIP

HIGH PERFORMANCE
A number of advanced CMOS settings can affect the performance of your system. Some are obvious, but many are not. Before you go tinkering in the CMOS, keep in mind that unless you know what you're changing, you could make your system behave in unpredictable (which usually means unpleasant) ways. Be sure your technical knowledge is up to the task before you tweak obscure CMOS settings. A great site for the advanced user who wants to eke the last drop of performance from a computer is the System Optimization Information site at `http://www.sysopt.com/bios.html`.

If you do tweak an advanced CMOS setting and it causes a problem, try bypassing the extended CMOS settings by holding down the Ins key during bootup. This should get your system to boot to the point where you can go back into the BIOS setup and undo whatever mischief you caused.

Continued

1. Power down the system.

2. Pull the jumper from pins 1 and 2 and jump pin 2 to pin 3 (the pin that was unjumped). Figure 4.7 shows a typical CMOS reset jumper. Consult your motherboard manual for the exact location of the jumper (if your motherboard uses one).

3. Wait a minute or so and then replace the jumper in its original position.

4. Restart the system.

For some motherboards, you must go through a power cycle to reset the CMOS:

1. Power down the system.

2. Pull the jumper from pins 1 and 2 and jump pin 2 to pin 3 (the pin that was unjumped).

3. Power up the system (wait until the entire boot process is complete).

4. Power down the system.

5. Change the jumper back to its original position.

6. Power the system back up.

Again, it's important that you check the documentation for your specific motherboard, do what it instructs you to do, and be certain you have a record of what your current CMOS settings are so you can change those you need to after you've corrected the problem that caused you to reset them in the first place.

Never fool around with changing jumpers on a system that is running. In fact, as we've said before, you should never work inside the case of a running system. ▪

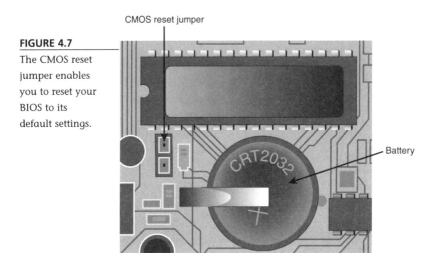

CMOS reset jumper

Battery

Performing the BIOS Upgrade

If you've done your homework to this point, you will have done the following things:

- Determined that your system needs a BIOS upgrade.

- Recorded all your BIOS model and version number information.

- Determined your motherboard manufacturer, model, and version number.

- Determined whether a BIOS upgrade is available for your motherboard.

- Downloaded the upgrade from the Internet or ordered it from the motherboard manufacturer.

- Recorded all your CMOS settings.

A BIOS upgrade involves locating the updated version of the BIOS for your specific motherboard and flashing the BIOS using a special piece of software that actually reprograms the BIOS chip on your computer. Earlier systems might not allow for this type of software upgrade, so you must physically replace the BIOS chip on the motherboard.

ANOTHER FINE MESS
IS THIS UPGRADE NECESSARY?
For systems that don't use the flash methodology, you must physically pull the BIOS chip from the motherboard and replace it with a newer upgraded chip. If this describes your system, you should consider purchasing a new system altogether (or at least a new motherboard) because you're getting close to the line of making upgrades to a system that really needs to be replaced. ■

Peripheral Card BIOS Upgrades

Occasionally, a BIOS upgrade might exist for some peripheral card, such as your video graphics adapter. These are usually flashable, so it's relatively easy to upgrade them when necessary, although, unless they're fixing a bug, most card manufacturers would rather you buy a new card than upgrade the existing one. Because each manufacturer's procedures are different, *always* follow the BIOS upgrade instructions that come with a particular card.

Step by Step—BIOS Chip

If, for whatever reason, you need to upgrade an older system by physically replacing the BIOS chip, the following are the steps you should perform. The process is relatively straightforward; the only tricky part is removing the old chip from its socket.

Replacing the BIOS Chip

1. Turn off the system, break it down, and move it to your work area.

2. Verify that the power cord has been disconnected.

3. Ensure you are grounded using an ESD wrist strap or other ESD methodology.

4. Open up the system and ensure you have a clear shot at the BIOS chip. You might have to remove cards or other internal devices to access the BIOS chip. Review the motherboard documentation to locate the BIOS chip if necessary.

5. Gently work the old BIOS chip out of its motherboard socket. Specialized tools called *chip pullers* can be used for this task, although we've had good results using a small, slot-bladed screwdriver to pry the chip loose. The goal is to work the chip out gently. The chip has two rows of pins down each of its long edges, and you want to work them out of the socket evenly without stressing the motherboard.

6. Replace the old BIOS chip with the new one, being careful not to bend any of the pins. Work it evenly into the motherboard socket without putting any significant pressure on the motherboard.

7. Close up the system (having first replaced anything you removed earlier to get to the BIOS chip, of course) and reinstall it in your workspace.

8. Power up the system and re-enter all the necessary CMOS information.

9. Shut down the system completely (meaning the power is off) and then reboot it (this is called a *cold boot*).

Step by Step—Flash

First and foremost, always follow the instructions provided by the manufacturers of the BIOS upgrade (usually the motherboard manufacturer) to the letter. The steps involved for a BIOS upgrade will vary from one manufacturer to another, so read any instructions carefully. Some motherboards, such as those from Intel, often require you to move a jumper to overwrite the BIOS. Others don't, so it's very important to do your homework for your particular motherboard.

That said, the process of flashing a BIOS to upgrade it will usually go something like this:

Flashing a BIOS

1. Download the BIOS upgrade from your motherboard manufacturer's Web site.

2. Extract this file into a separate directory. The upgrade file will most likely be a self-extracting file with an .exe extension. To extract it, simply run the file (double-click it in Windows Explorer). Carefully study any readme files contained therein for instructions.

3. Most BIOS upgrades want you to run the process from a disk you create and with which you boot your computer. The instructions might walk you through the process of creating a bootable 3 1/2-inch boot disk, or you might need to create one manually.

4. Some files must be copied to the boot disk (some files from the extracted download might exist that need to be further extracted at this point).

5. Boot your computer with the boot disk that now contains all the files necessary to flash your system with.

6. You'll probably see a menu generated by the boot floppy or a series of prompts to walk you through the flash process. Always select the option to save a backup copy of your current BIOS. In the event something goes wrong, you stand a good chance of recovering your system by using this backup.

   The update process is generally controlled by two components—the updater routine, which actually reprograms the BIOS chip, and a data fill, which contains the information used to update the BIOS.

Inherent Risks in BIOS Upgrades

The key to a successful BIOS upgrade is to not disturb the computer for the several minutes during which the BIOS chip is being reprogrammed. A power failure or a reboot during a flash upgrade can render a system completely unusable.

Should this happen, if the system will still boot to the point where it loads the flash BIOS boot disk you created, you can try rerunning the flash process. If you're unlucky and the system won't respond at all, you might be looking at a motherboard replacement because many newer boards have the BIOS chip soldered onto the board so they can't be popped out and replaced with a new BIOS chip.

If you are physically replacing a BIOS chip, you must remove the old chip without putting too much pressure on the motherboard because this can crack the epoxy and render the motherboard dysfunctional. When installing the new BIOS chip, be sure all the pins are straight and aligned correctly over the socket holes so you don't bend a pin while pushing the chip into the socket.

Upgrading the BIOS might or might not change the version number displayed by the system. However, if you enter the BIOS setup utility, the new version number might show up. Therefore, always ensure you record the upgrade and the new version number in your system journal, NEAT box, and inventory form. Save the flash BIOS boot disk you created for the upgrade and label it with the upgraded BIOS version and the date you performed the upgrade.

5

RAM

The single most useful upgrade you can perform on your computer is to add more and faster random access memory (RAM). You will experience faster performance and fewer problems with applications if you increase the memory in your computer.

Upgrade Checklist

1. Do your homework.

2. Determine whether your PC supports the quantity and type of RAM you are planning to upgrade with.

3. Determine whether you are comfortable performing the upgrade.

4. Purchase or acquire the necessary memory modules.

5. Organize your tools and workspace.

6. Back up everything: data, operating system, mission-critical applications, and BIOS settings. If you install memory and problems occur, you usually know it right away because your system won't function. But if problems develop after you've started using your computer, you could lose data as you work with it.

7. Install or replace the RAM.

8. Take good notes and permanently file them in your system log when finished.

9. Update your inventory documentation to reflect the newly added memory.

Memory Upgrade Payoff

A memory upgrade is one of the least expensive upgrades you can perform. Prices are around $2.00 per megabyte (MB) at the time of this writing. Memory chips have become a commodity, and although prices rise and fall, overall memory is cheap and provides one of the biggest returns for the money in terms of increased performance. Double or quadruple the RAM in an older system, say from 16 megabytes to 32 or 64 megabytes, and you'll hardly believe the speed increase.

Computers running different *operating systems (OSes)* have differing thresholds for minimum system RAM. See Table 5.1.

Table 5.1   Recommended Memory by Operating System

Operating System	Recommended Memory
Windows 95	32MB
Windows 98SE	64MB
Windows Millennium (Me)	64MB
Linux	64MB
Windows NT 4.0	96MB
Windows 2000 Professional	128MB
Windows 2000 Server	256MB

NOTE

MORE THAN ENOUGH MEMORY

Recommended memory will be more than the minimum required quoted in the OS's System Requirements documentation because you might actually want to run applications in addition to the operating system.

How you use your computer also dictates how much RAM is enough. If you run memory-intensive applications, such as Adobe Photoshop or CAD (computer-aided design) applications, you'll want even more.

Motherboard Form Factor

Adding memory is not as simple as picking up a few megabytes on the way home from the office and popping them into your system. First,

PLAINSPEAKING

MEMORY VERSUS STORAGE

It's easy to confuse computer memory, known as *RAM*, with computer storage (generally hard disk space) because both are measured in *megabytes*. But one important difference does exist. RAM is volatile in that what the computer loads into memory stays there only while the power is on or until the computer clears the memory to use it for something else. *Storage*—and we're talking about hard disk space in this context—is where the computer writes information that stays there even after the computer is shut down and the power is turned off.

Think of *memory* as the place where the computer does its thinking and calculations, and storage as the repository where it records the results. Files are opened from the hard disk and copied into RAM. Commands are executed, calculations are calculated, and answers arrived at all in RAM. If the power goes out, everything in RAM is gone in an instant. To be saved, the files must be closed and the information written to disk. ■

you must find out what type of memory your computer supports, starting with the type of memory modules you can plug into the motherboard.

Pull out your NEAT box (we discuss the NEAT box concept in Chapter 2, "Preparing for an Upgrade") and dig out the motherboard (aka mainboard) manual. You'll find memory information similar to the following:

```
"The mainboard supports (2)
168-pin DIMMs. The DIMMs can
be either EDO or SDRAM.C"
```

Or

```
"Mainboard supports 8MB to
256MB DIMM memory modules to
a maximum size of 768MB of
SDRAM. Supports only PC100
SDRAM DIMMs."
```

Don't panic. You'll have to get familiar with some basic vocabulary and acronyms to become memory savvy, but by the end of the chapter all this will make sense. Honest.

First, determine whether your PC uses SIMM, DIMM, or RIMM modules. Then, if you're upgrading an earlier system with SIMMs, you must further determine whether the SIMM sockets are 30-pin (about 3.5 inches long) or 72-pin (a tad over 4 inches long). DIMMs are 168-pin but are only about 1 inch longer than their 72-pin SIMM cousins. Again, your motherboard manual is the best place to look for this information.

If your system sports RIMMs, you won't have to spend any time wondering about what type of memory to install. RIMMs accept only Rambus DRAM (RDRAM). We'll cover all the major types of memory you can install on your system later in this chapter.

PLAINSPEAKING
SIMMS, DIMMS, AND RIMMS

Physical RAM comes packaged as a series of small chips soldered on a narrow strip of epoxy, called a *memory module*, that looks like a miniature peripheral card usually an inch or so high and three to four inches wide (see Figure 5.1). Similar to a peripheral card, it plugs into a slot on the motherboard. A number of special slots are specifically designed to accept memory modules. Different types of modules require different connector slots.

SIMMs (single inline memory modules) are found on 486 and the earlier Pentium computers. They can have 30 or 72 *pins*, which are the shiny metal connectors that run along the bottom edge of the module. They plug into slots having 30 or 72 connector receptacles.

DIMMs (double inline memory modules) are usually found on Pentium IIs and later systems. DIMMs fit in 168-pin slots.

RIMMs (Rambus inline memory modules) are a new and emerging technology presently found in only a few high-end systems and have 184-pin connectors. They are used exclusively for the new RDRAM (Rambus DRAM) type of memory.

You must find out which module type your system supports before you buy memory because the different types of modules are not interchangeable. ■

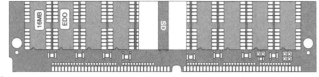

SIMM

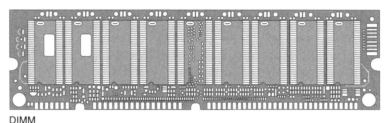

DIMM

RIMM

Memory Speed Ratings

After you know which type of
memory module your system
accepts, you must decide on
which type of memory you want to
install. A key factor in this decision
is the speed of the memory. The
rule of thumb is that faster memory is better than slower memory.

Memory used to be measured in
nanoseconds (and sometimes it
still is). But more often, it's being
measured and quoted in
megahertz.

PLAINSPEAKING
**TIME TO REPLACE THE
MOTHERBOARD**

If the PC you're thinking of upgrading doesn't have
memory module connectors but is of a vintage
where the individual memory chips get plugged
directly into sockets on the motherboard, stop
thinking *memory* upgrade and start thinking *motherboard* upgrade—it might even be time to start
looking at new systems. ■

A *nanosecond (ns)* is one one-billionth of a second. A *megahertz (MHz)* is a million
cycles per second. Don't bother memorizing that, just remember that the *lower* the
nanosecond rating, the faster the memory. The *higher* the megahertz rating, the
faster the memory. 100MHz is equal to 10ns.

When you see memory modules advertised as PC100 or PC133, they're talking about
speed ratings of 100MHz and 133MHz (10ns and 7.5ns), respectively.

If you're adding memory to a system (that is, you're *adding* to the memory already installed), you should match the speed of the existing memory chips. For example, if you have a machine with 4 memory module slots, and 2 are populated each with a 60ns 8MB SIMM, you'll want to populate the remaining 2 slots with 60ns memory as well. If you add faster memory modules to the existing modules, you won't get the benefit because all RAM will be accessed at the speed of the slowest memory installed.

If you're going to pull out all the old memory and replace everything, you can use faster memory—faster within the limits placed by your motherboard's design. Check your documentation to determine the fastest memory your system can handle.

Memory modules are grouped into what are called *banks* and are accessed by the motherboard accordingly. A bank corresponds to the data bus capacity of the system's microprocessor. SIMMs require you to group similar type and size of memory within a single bank for the memory to work properly. See Table 5.2.

Table 5.2 Grouping SIMMs into Memory Banks

System	30-Pin SIMMs per Bank	72-Pin SIMMs per Bank
32-bit (386DX, 486DX)	4	1
64-bit (Pentium and higher)	8	2

PLAINSPEAKING
PENTIUM AND CACHE LIMITATIONS

If you are upgrading a system running a Pentium processor (as opposed to a Pentium II or III), be aware that most Pentium systems have either a 256Kb or a 512Kb cache. With a 256Kb cache, upgrading beyond 64MB of memory does not usually provide any performance benefits and can actually slow the machine's responses. With a 512Kb cache, the maximum benefit limit moves up to 128MB. With a Pentium II, the sky is the limit because the cache is integrated into the processor. System cache and the effects on memory are discussed in more detail in Chapter 6, "CPU and Motherboard Upgrades." ■

You can't start popping in SIMMs of different sizes without regard to keeping the same size SIMMs in the same bank. Because of the forced groupings, you have a lot less flexibility in the amount of memory you'll be able to install. With 64-bit systems using DIMMs or RIMMs, the 64-bit width of the data bus matches the 64-bit width of the memory module, and each module is treated as its own bank.

In the next section, we discuss the various types of memory available to give you an idea of what you have to choose from when selecting memory for your RAM upgrade.

Types of Memory

Over the last few years, an explosive growth in the RAM industry has occurred with newer, better, and faster memory types appearing all the time. With more types of memory to choose from, it becomes more difficult to make a decision for the best type of RAM for your computer. In this section, we discuss the various types of memory that you're likely to run into and how to compare them.

But again, let us stress the importance of going with the memory type and speed recommended by your motherboard manufacturer.

ANOTHER FINE MESS
MOTHERBOARD UPGRADES AND RAM

If you're upgrading your system's motherboard to get a newer processor, be careful if you're trying to save a few bucks by figuring you'll just move the RAM chips from the old motherboard to your new motherboard. The faster processors available today demand the faster PC100 and PC133 RAM. Not only will you be better off getting newer and faster RAM for your new motherboard, the old RAM might not work in it at all. ■

The best type of RAM for your system is the one the motherboard designer had in mind. Add as much of that type of memory, using the fastest flavor of the same, that you can.

DRAM (dynamic random access memory) is the basic memory of PCs today. You'll also see it referred to as *FPM (fast page mode)* RAM. It's cheap and dense (you can pack a lot of memory into a small chip), but rather slow, especially compared to the processors on the market today. The slow nature of DRAM is what has spurred the development of a plethora of different flavors of RAM available for use in building and upgrading computers.

SRAM

SRAM (static RAM) is used for cache memory, not main system memory. However, because you hear this termed bantered about, you should know what it means. The *static* in SRAM means that once set, the memory does not need to be constantly refreshed as dynamic RAM does.

SRAM is much faster than DRAM, but it's also less dense than DRAM. SRAM is very expensive, so its implementation is limited to use as cache memory (discussed in Chapter 2).

EDO RAM

EDO RAM (extended data output RAM) was developed by Micron Technology for use in the first Pentium-class computers. To use EDO RAM, your motherboard's chipset must support it and accept SIMMs. It's faster than standard DRAM by 15%–20% and is a good choice for systems with a bus speed of up to 66MHz.

SDRAM

SDRAM (synchronous DRAM) is the current workhorse of PC memory. As with EDO memory, the motherboard chipset must support SDRAM and provide DIMM connector slots. SDRAM provides a 25% speed increase over the earlier EDO technology without any appreciable increase in cost, which is why it is used in so many systems. You'll see SDRAM DIMMs rated in speed terms of 66MHz, 100MHz, and 133MHz more often than the tradition nanoseconds metric. Use SDRAM that's rated at least as fast as the motherboard's bus speed. If the motherboard bus is 100MHz, you should install SDRAM that's rated 100MHz or PC100. The PC100 memory standard was devised by Intel and defines the specifications memory must meet to run in a system running a 100MHz bus speed.

You'll find SDRAM rated PC100 or PC133 for use in computers running 100MHz and 133MHz bus speeds. The Intel spec actually calls for the chips to run a tad faster than the bus. For example, to be certified PC100, SDRAM actually has to run at 125MHz to provide a margin of safety and ensure smooth operation at the 100MHz bus speed.

If you run memory that's faster than the motherboard speed, say by installing PC133 SDRAM in a 100MHz bus speed system, the memory will run at the slower 100MHz speed.

DDR SDRAM

DDR (double data rate) SDRAM is the next-generation SDRAM. Unfortunately, it is not backward compatible with motherboards designed for straight SDRAM, so upgrading to DDR means upgrading the motherboard as well. DDR SDRAM uses the same pin connector as plain SDRAM, although the memory modules are not interchangeable. You can't put DDR SDRAM on a motherboard unless it specifically supports it.

DDR SDRAM transfers data twice as fast as plain SDRAM, making it possible to double a data rate of 133MHz to 266MHz. This memory technology is just starting to gain popularity. You'll find video cards using this type of memory, and a number of motherboard and computer manufacturers are coming out with DDR support even though Intel is not endorsing this memory type. Intel favors RDRAM over DDR SDRAM.

RDRAM

Whereas DDR SDRAM is the evolution of SDRAM, RDRAM is a revolutionary new design for faster memory. RDRAM is a product of Rambus, Inc. Therefore, unlike SDRAM, it's a proprietary technology rather than an open standard.

Intel, the largest manufacturer of motherboards, has licensed this technology from Rambus, Inc., and is actively promoting it—so the outlook for long-term adoption is good. RDRAM uses a new type of connector called a RIMM, which uses 184 pins. It looks very similar to a DIMM, but the modules are not interchangeable. RIMMs add a new element in that current RIMMs run on 2.5 volts, but future specs call for modules that run on even lower voltages. As such, the RIMMs themselves have unique notches that control how they fit into a RIMM socket. This prevents the module from being installed backward or in motherboards designed for a voltage different from the memory module's rating.

Another departure from the SDRAM architecture requires all the RIMM sockets to make a complete circuit. Even if you install only one RDRAM memory module, you must populate the remaining, normally open, memory slots with what's called a *continuity module (C-RIMM)*. The C-RIMM does not provide any memory; it just enables the data to flow through all the RIMM connectors. A C-RIMM looks similar to a standard RIMM without any memory chips on it. C-RIMM continuity modules should be provided with the motherboard and also can be purchased separately from memory suppliers that are selling RIMM modules.

A straightforward progression of memory types has occurred up to, and including, the time SDRAM became the standard memory for personal computers. But with the advent of DDR SDRAM and RDRAM, a split has occurred, with no clear winner destined to become the next industry standard (see Figure 5.2). RDRAM has an advantage over DDR SDRAM in that it has faster theoretical limits than the DDR technology, and with processors in the 1GB+ range, this is significant. In the long run, though, RDRAM might overcome the problems it has with being extremely difficult and expensive to manufacture and become the next standard for memory type.

SLDRAM

SLDRAM (synchronous link DRAM) is a possible evolutionary successor to SDRAM. It's an open standard (nonproprietary) that theoretically could work with bus speeds in the 800MHz range.

SLDRAM, like DDR SDRAM, is backed by almost everyone in the memory business except for Intel. However, it has not appeared in motherboards to any great extent.

FIGURE 5.2

The progression of memory types was straightforward until the RDRAM/DDR DRAM split.

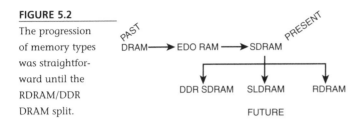

Adding Memory Modules

Memory can seem to be an enormously confusing swirl of weird acronyms, but it's pretty simple. You go with what the motherboard was designed for. You add as much as you can afford and need in order to run the operating system and applications you use. Generally speaking, the more you add, the better your system performs. After you determine which type of memory module you need, buy it and plug it into your system.

On the Mixing of Metals

Your motherboard determines more than just the type of memory you want to use. A potential problem with mixing tin and gold can occur.

When you start shopping for memory, you'll notice that most modules include information on whether they're gold or tin. For example, you might see a module described as the following:

`70ns EDO Tin - 4MB SIMM`

The metal type doesn't refer to how many copies they've sold but rather to the type of metal used to plate the module connectors.

Memory modules have a number of connectors, called pins, along the edge that insert into the connector slot on the motherboard. As discussed earlier, SIMMs come in either 30- or 72-pin modules; DIMMs are 168-pin modules; and RIMMs are 184-pin modules. These connectors are either plated with gold or tin. The memory module slots on the motherboard are also plated, and they, too, can be either gold or tin.

You'll be happier in the long run if you refrain from mixing different metals. Plugging a gold module into a tin slot or vice versa is inadvisable because a corrosive chemical process can increase the electrical resistance of the contact. Over time, parity errors can occur.

Tin on tin is okay, and gold on gold is fine, but mixing them is bad. Of course, it takes a long time for problems to happen, depending on a number of environmental factors. But do yourself a favor and match the metals.

Where to Get Memory

You can go to your computer's manufacturer to purchase upgrade memory or you can try some of the third-party memory suppliers on the Internet.

Crucial Technology, owned by Micro (the mail-order computer manufacturer), has a site set up to help you find the type of memory you need based on the type of computer you have. Its site is at the following address:

`http://www.crucial.com`

Kingston Technology is also a major supplier of memory modules and lets you search by manufacturer, model name, part number, or type of memory you're looking for. Its site is at the following address:

`http://www.kingston.com`

You also can get good deals on memory at the computer superstores, such as Fry's or CompUSA, or stores such as Best Buy. It's a lot cheaper, but it's no-frills and you don't usually get any installation instructions with the modules.

Installing Memory Modules

Although the same basic procedures apply in how you handle the memory modules, be they SIMM, DIMM, or RIMM, each type of module installs differently into its connectors.

Modules Install Differently

1. Be absolutely certain you're grounded against ESD. Static electricity and memory modules are two things you don't want in any proximity of one another. An ESD wrist strap, properly grounded, is the best way to guard against this.

2. Open up your system and locate the connectors where the memory modules will go. Remove any obstructions that interfere with clear access to the plug-in module connectors.

3. If you are replacing modules, carefully remove the old modules. This might involve releasing a locking clip at each end of the module slot. Note exactly how the old module came out of the slot—that is, which end of the module came from which end of the connector and which side was facing which way.

4. Remove the new module(s) from the antistatic wrap in which they invariably came. Do not touch the chips embedded on the module. Handle the module by only the edges. Pretend you don't want to leave any fingerprints.

5. Follow the installation instructions that accompany the new module (if any are provided) and insert the module into the connector slot.

Generally, SIMMs go into the connector slot at a 45-degree angle and then are pushed into an upright position perpendicular to the motherboard. SIMMs are notched on one end to ensure you insert them correctly into the slot. If you removed any modules in step 3, refer to how the old module lined up to the connector slot—which end was notched, and so on—to ensure you insert the new module properly. Figure 5.3 shows a motherboard with four SIMM slots.

DIMMs are notched in places along the connector edge—not on the ends like SIMMs—to ensure you get the new module into the slot facing the correct way. By looking at the DIMM and then along the connector (a flashlight helps), you'll see how to orient the DIMM. DIMMs generally go straight into the slot with release tabs on each end that level closed to hold the DIMM in place. Pushing these tabs away from the DIMM releases the module. You might want to lay a tower system on its side to insert and remove DIMMs; we've had them fall out of the system when releasing the tabs. Figure 5.4 shows a motherboard with three DIMMs.

Never force a module into a connector slot. Take your time and be sure the notches in the module line up with the corresponding spots in the connector slot. You should be able to hear or feel a click as the module is properly seated into the slot. Some SIMM connectors have locking clips that snap into place when the module is seated.

On some older systems, you have to go into the CMOS settings and then click Save new settings after upgrading. Some require you to tell the computer how much memory it now has. However, most systems will recognize the new memory when you boot it up.

FIGURE 5.3

Insert the SIMM at a slight angle and then tilt straight up. The clips on each end should lock into the notched slots on each end of the SIMM.

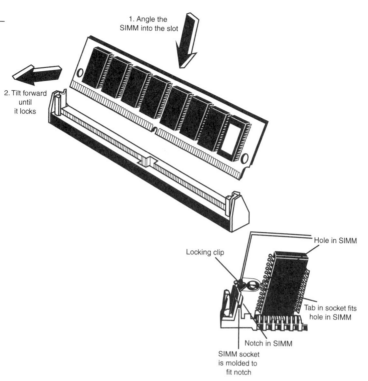

1. Angle the SIMM into the slot

2. Tilt forward until it locks

Hole in SIMM

Locking clip

Tab in socket fits hole in SIMM

Notch in SIMM

SIMM socket is molded to fit notch

FIGURE 5.4

DIMM and RIMM connectors go straight in and lock on each end with a tab. The tab locks the module in place, and pushing down on the tab at each end of the module ejects it from the slot.

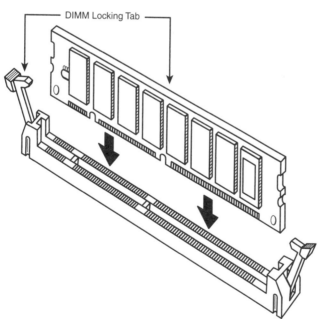

DIMM Locking Tab

TIP

HOW TO REMOVE A MODULE

If you've never removed a memory module, it can be a confusing process. Unlike peripheral cards that plug straight in and come straight out and are secured by a single bracket and screw, memory modules often have to be inserted at an angle and then be pushed in another direction until some clip-type connectors snap into place.

When removing modules to make way for new ones, read any installation instructions for the new modules carefully, and make sure you're grounded against ESD. To remove the old modules, just reverse the instructions for inserting the new ones.

If the new modules didn't come with instructions, take your time and study the connector slots that contain the old modules carefully. You might have to release clips or tabs at each end of the module and then work the module straight out (in the case of DIMMs) or tilt the module to an angle and then pull it out (in the case of SIMMs).

6

CPU AND MOTHERBOARD UPGRADES

In Chapter 2, "Preparing for an Upgrade," you saw the plethora of CPUs from AMD and Intel that have resulted in many upgrade options for systems. Although computers continue to get cheaper on the whole, you can still save some money and protect your investment in peripherals by swapping out a CPU or the entire motherboard for a new model. It's not something to be undertaken lightly, but with care and planning it's not an impossible task.

Preliminary Upgrade Checklist

1. Read Chapter 2, "Preparing for an Upgrade." Get up to speed on buses, slots, sockets, L1 versus L2 caches, and related information pertaining to motherboards and CPUs.

2. Read Chapter 4, "Upgrading the BIOS," to ensure you can identify your current motherboard by manufacturer, make, and model.

3. Read Chapter 5, "RAM," and know the differences between SIMMs, DIMMs, and RIMMs.

4. Determine whether you'll upgrade just the CPU or both the CPU and motherboard.

5. Research and determine the upgrade components you'll need.

6. Determine whether you can perform the upgrade.

7. Purchase or acquire the component(s).

8. Organize your tools and workspace. See Chapter 3, "Things You Need."

9. Back up all data and mission-critical applications you want saved. Upgrading a motherboard can require reformatting your hard disk and reinstalling your operating system. This is very important (as you'll see later).

10. Test your startup disk.

11. Perform the upgrade.

12. Take good notes, and permanently file them in your system log when finished.

13. Update your inventory documentation to reflect the upgraded or newly added component.

Caveats and Admonishments

The *motherboard* (also referred to as the *system board* or *main board*) and *central processing unit (CPU)* are the most important components that make up your computer. The motherboard provides the throne and ancillary support mechanisms, called the *chipset*, that enable the CPU to control the processing of information on your computer. These two components define the speed at which your computer operates, the bus on which all peripheral cards are attached to your system, the ports for USB and FireWire devices, the keyboard, and the mouse—in short, the motherboard *is the computer* for all intents and purposes (see Figure 6.1).

FIGURE 6.1

Be sure you're familiar with the layout and parts that make up the motherboard before you attempt to upgrade one.

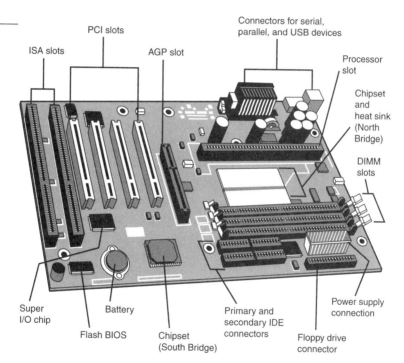

What You're Getting Into

As you'll see in this chapter, installing a new motherboard is one of the more advanced exercises in computer upgrading. For one thing, you must practically uninstall every other component in your system just to get at the old motherboard to remove it and install the new one. That means you run the risk of tweaking, dropping, misplacing, or losing nearly every screw, adapter card, cable, and connector in the system. In addition, you also run the risk of cracking the new motherboard by applying too much pressure or applying it unevenly when you mount the motherboard in the chassis. It can be stressful.

A very real possibility also exists that, even though you think you'll just swap out the old motherboard for a new one and be up and running in an hour at most, you'll actually be down a day or two and then wind up having to reformat your hard disk and reinstall your operating system. Ouch! Even the guys in the lab coats that build systems for a living end up having to go the scorched earth route on one out of four motherboard upgrades. The old operating system is chock-full of drivers for the *old* motherboard, and sometimes you just can't get it to believe things have changed.

As such, don't rush into a motherboard upgrade without some serious consideration.

Just the CPU or the Whole Motherboard?

A given motherboard is usually rated to accept not just one but several different CPUs. For example, an ASUS K7V motherboard can accept CPUs (AMD's Athlon series) from 550MHz all the way up to 1GB MHz chips. By just upgrading the CPU, you could nearly double the speed of the processor.

ANOTHER FINE MESS
IS IT ROCKET SCIENCE?

It's difficult to walk the line between giving you a clear warning about the rather technically involved aspects of motherboard upgrade and just scaring you silly and making you think you'd be insane to even attempt the upgrade. You do have to know what you're getting involved in, but it's not rocket science by a long shot—and not nearly as scary as upgrading a BIOS.

Our first motherboard "upgrade" was thrust upon us when a new system we purchased (longer ago than we care to think about) showed up with a DOA (dead-on-arrival) motherboard. The manufacturer eagerly overnighted us a replacement motherboard but could not have a technician out for several days. We desperately needed to get this system working, so we figured we'd give it a shot ourselves.

It was this exercise that taught us the value of labeling, diagramming, and writing down the steps that we flogged to death in Chapter 3. Lots of cleared space to set things as they came out of the system helped, as well. With patience, planning, and a willingness to go hands-on, you, too, can replace a motherboard. However, we know this exercise is not for everyone. If upgrading your video card gave you palpitations, you might want to find a good, dependable clone shop to upgrade your motherboard for you. ▪

To determine what your processor upgrade possibilities are, you need to know the exact manufacturer of your motherboard as well as the specific make and model. If you don't have the documentation that came with your system's motherboard, you'll have to do some sleuthing. Determining manufacturers was discussed in Chapter 4 because you must know the same information when seeking a BIOS upgrade. After you know the manufacturer, go to its Web site, look up the specifications for your motherboard, and see which CPUs your board is rated to accept. A BIOS upgrade might be required, as well.

ANOTHER FINE MESS
BEWARE OF CUSTOM MOTHERBOARDS

Note that some of the advice in this section isn't as applicable to some of the systems from the major PC manufacturers (Dell, HP, Compaq, and so on) because they tend to use motherboards that have been customized to the point of being proprietary. As a colleague of ours is fond of saying, "Proprietary systems … bad!"

Often, major PC manufacturers use custom motherboards designed to fit in unique cases, making them difficult or impossible to upgrade with off-the-shelf motherboards. Be sure you know whether the motherboard in your PC is an industry standard form factor, such as ATX, or whether you're at the mercy of the manufacturer when it comes to upgrades. ■

If you upgrade just the CPU, you keep all your current peripherals, although you might still need to uninstall components to make removing the current CPU and installing the new one possible.

Is Upgrade the Right Decision?

Think that the first thing to decide is the make and model motherboard you should get? Buzzt! Choosing the right motherboard is important, no doubt about it. But what you first have to give careful consideration to is whether upgrading is the right decision at all. First, take a long, hard look at your existing system—the one you're planning to upgrade.

If you've got an old 486 and decide that all you need is a new motherboard with a speed demon CPU, think again. Remember the old joke about the guy who takes his old clunker into the automotive repair shop to get an oil change? The service rep takes one look at the car and says, "Buddy, keep the oil and change the car." Thinking you can take an aged computer and breathe new life into it with a quick motherboard upgrade might be a matter of, "Hey, keep the keyboard and change the computer."

It all depends on which type of components you have in your existing system. As a worst-case scenario, consider that old 486 just mentioned. You could drop a new, high-powered motherboard into it, but the power supply is going to be woefully underpowered for the new CPU. You'll need an AGP (accelerated graphics port) adapter to take advantage of the improved video slot on the new motherboard. Clearly, a better decision in this example would be to purchase a new system or build one yourself from the ground up. Consider the following before making your upgrade or new system decision:

■ Make sure your computer chassis accepts the form factor of the new motherboard you're considering.

■ Check the wattage rating on your power supply and make sure it's adequate for the CPU, combined with the peripherals, you'll be hooking up to the system. A discussion of how to determine how much power a system draws is in Chapter 10, "Adding Power Protection."

■ Determine whether your adapter cards (sound, video, network, SCSI controllers, and so on) will migrate comfortably to the new motherboard's slots.

■ Determine whether your current system's RAM will transfer to the new motherboard. This will depend on the type of memory modules your current system has and the type of memory slots on the new motherboard (see Chapter 5 for more on SIMMs, DIMMs, and RIMMs).

■ Consider whether your current case can hold not only the new motherboard's form factor, but the additional drives, cards, and so on that the new board will enable you to install. If it won't, you'll quickly run into a situation in which you'll want some nifty new upgrade, but it won't fit in the case. If the case is this limited, it's time to bite the bullet and buy a new PC.

Motherboard Design Decisions

If you've got a degree in computer science and another in electrical engineering, by all means, pick any motherboard that suits your fancy. You can always whip out a soldering iron if things aren't what they should be. For the rest of us, go with a brand name, from a company that has a good reputation. That's not always easy to do because of the speed at which things move in the computer business. But some motherboard manufacturers have been around long enough to be considered "brand names," and you can trust them to make good on claims and replace boards that have problems.

The following manufacturers are all highly thought of: Abit, ASUS, BIOSTAR, EpOX, Gigabyte, Intel, Micro-Star (MSI), Supermicro, and Tyan. However, as we said, the speed at which computer companies come and go—especially in the hardware components end of things—is breathtaking. By the time you read this, there might well be new stars in the motherboard business worthy of consideration.

Know what you need, what you desire, and the difference between the two so you know where you can compromise. Start by deciding on the CPU chip you want to power your system. That means either Intel (http://www.intel.com) or AMD (http://www.amd.com), and starting with their current product offerings is a good idea. The type of CPU will narrow down the choice of motherboard to just those models that accommodate the CPU you want to drive it. After you have decided on a particular CPU, start thinking about all the other aspects of the motherboard you must make decisions about.

Do you want all PCI slots or do you need an ISA slot or two for some legacy add-in cards? Know the difference between an AGP (accelerated graphics port) slot and an AMR (audio modem riser) slot. The AGP is found on newer motherboards and dedicates a slot for graphics cards that take advantage of the better video possible using this slot. The AMR is found on motherboards made for low-cost systems so a combo modem/sound card can be plugged in, saving the manufacturer a few beans when producing mass-market machines. Chances are very good you won't be thrilled with a combo modem/sound card and will wind up adding a dedicated card for each into the system. Therefore, you'd be better off not having an AMR slot on your motherboard in the first place.

This means you must do your homework, or ask a knowledgeable friend or clone shop (and hope they've done their homework). Read all the reviews you can find on the Web about motherboards to get an idea of what's available and to start to narrow your selection. The best recommendations therefore come from people who have installed and are using a given product. You can get feedback on CPUs and motherboards on several forums dedicated to those topics. Go to http://www.deja.com/usenet and search on "motherboard;" you'll find several forums discussing this topic. AMD hosts a message board at http://amdzone.pcstats.com/, and Intel hosts one at http://www.intel.com/newsgroups/moboindex.htm. In fact, most of the motherboard manufacturers have some type of message board on their sites.

Intel keeps threatening to close their motherboard forums, so keep that in mind (although they were still running at the time of this writing).

MOTHERBOARD AND CPU RESOURCE

Check out Tom's Hardware Mainboard Guide site for lots of current information on motherboards:

`http://www.tomshardware.com/mainboard/index.html`

You'll also want to bookmark the Motherboard Homeworld site, which is a tremendous resource for motherboard information, including a listing of all major motherboard manufacturers and their contact information (including Web site URLs):

`http://motherboards.org/`

After you have looked over the current offerings in new motherboards, read the reviews, asked some questions or lurked on the forums (as in to monitor the traffic on message boards to glean advice without actually participating in the conversation) for a while, and have an inkling as to which features you want on your new motherboard, check out MOBOT at

`http://iceberg.pchomeworld.com/cgi-win/MoBotGen/MoBot.asp`

MOBOT is a nifty Web page on the Motherboard Homeworld site that lets you enter your criteria and then makes recommendations for the make and model motherboard that best suits your needs. You enter information such as the following:

- **Platform**—This is the type of socket or slot design you want (more on this in a later section).

- **L2 Cache**—This specifies the size of the L2 memory cache you want.

- **Form Factor**—Motherboards come in several shapes, called the *form factor*, and you should ensure that you get a motherboard that fits into your system's chassis. Form factors are discussed in the next section of this chapter.

- **Manufacturer**—Remember to get a brand-name motherboard.

- **Processor Type**—Whatever you can buy today will be eclipsed by an announcement of a newer and faster CPU tomorrow. That's just the nature of the beast. If you wait to get the latest and greatest, you'll forever be waiting.

- **Chipset**—This is a set of chips that controls how the motherboard interacts with all the things attached to the computer; think of a central nervous system for your PC and that's what a chipset is all about. The following sites contain what you need to know to get up to speed on chipsets:

```
http://www6.tomshardware.com/howto/00q2/000412/index-04.html
http://motherboards.org/chipset.html
```

- **Expansion Slots**—Pick your type and quantity: AGP, PCI, ISA, VLB (VESA local bus), or EISA (see Chapter 2 for more on the various types of slots available for PCs).

- **Memory**—This is how much RAM and which type of modules you want: SIMM, DIMM, or RIMM (see Chapter 5 for more on RAM and module types).

- **Onboard**—This section is where you make your wish list for onboard options (also discussed in more detail in a later section of this chapter). Things such as onboard audio or SCSI can be built into the motherboard and thereby save you from having to add a card to handle that option.

If you're not sure what to select in a given category you can select Any, which broadens your search criteria.

Don't overlook compatibility with the software you're going to run on the computer, primarily the operating system. Hardware development often outstrips software advancements, and you don't want to get too far ahead of the programs you need to run on your computer. Ask around and make sure the OS you plan to run is compatible with the motherboard you're thinking of upgrading to, especially the CPU chip.

Form Factors

PC motherboards are not completely interchangeable among the various types of system cases you can have. You might think that motherboard form factors are divided along the same lines as system cases—that is, desktop, low-profile desktop, tower, mid-tower, mini-tower, and the like—but you'd be wrong. Various form factors sometimes require a particular case, but so many chassis manufacturers exist that you can't count on a given type of case taking a particular form factor for a motherboard. What's more, a given chassis might be drilled to accept several different motherboard form factors.

Always make sure you know what the form factor is of the motherboard you are upgrading before you choose a replacement board. Be sure you get a motherboard of a form factor type that will fit your chassis.

A number of form factor types are available: AT; Baby AT; LPX; NLX; WTX; the ATX line, including ATX, mini-ATX, micro-ATX, flex-ATX; and dozens of specialty designs and proprietary boards such as those found in laptop systems.

AT and Baby AT

Unless you're updating a truly ancient system (386–486 vintage), you're probably not dealing with a system requiring an AT form factor. This is a good thing because the design of these boards makes them difficult to work with. The Baby AT form factor is still used for a number of older Pentium CPU models, but it too is considered an obsolete design.

To tell whether you're dealing with an older form factor, check the placement of the CPU. Often, the CPU is located on the motherboard where it interferes with full-length peripheral cards fitting in the system. Usually, a number of ISA slots are on the board (most newer form factors sport only 1 or 2 for backward-compatibility or no ISA slots at all). Finally, input/output ports (serial, parallel, mouse, and so on) are not mounted on the motherboard but are connected to it via small cables running to cutouts in the chassis.

LPX and NLX

The LPX design has a riser card that mounts perpendicularly to the motherboard (usually in the center), and the expansion slots are found on this card. This means that peripheral cards wind up mounted parallel in a stacked layout above the motherboard. This enables the motherboard to be smaller in overall area—in effect, using a high-rise design to take the slots up and off the motherboard.

The problem with LPX systems is that, because of the way the original LPX design was implemented by various manufacturers, LPX motherboards might not be interchangeable across different system manufacturers. If you have an LPX form factor board in the system you're trying to upgrade, be sure that your replacement board will fit the chassis. The LPX design was very popular with low-cost, mass-marketed systems sold through retail outlets. An LPX system has expansion card slots parallel to the motherboard and a single row of input/output ports mounted directly on the motherboard.

The NLX form factor is a more standardized designed that has replaced the older LPX form factor and also uses the riser card to hold the expansion slots. The riser, in the case of the NLX, however, is located along the side of the motherboard. In fact, the motherboard plugs into the riser instead of the reverse, as is the case for the LPX. The riser card mounts separately in the case so the motherboard can be removed from the system, leaving all the peripheral cards untouched (see Figure 6.2).

FIGURE 6.2

An NLX motherboard plugs into the slot riser, giving it a very distinct look.

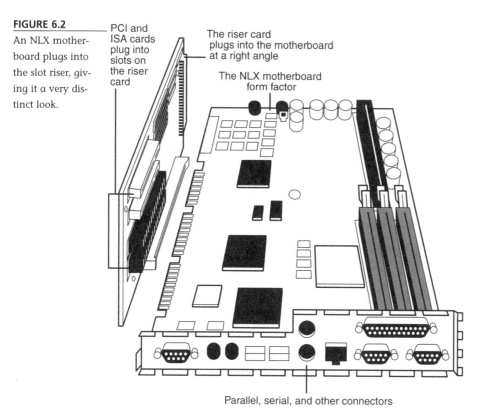

PCI and ISA cards plug into slots on the riser card

The riser card plugs into the motherboard at a right angle

The NLX motherboard form factor

Parallel, serial, and other connectors

NLX systems also have expansion card slots parallel to the motherboard and a single or double row of input/output ports mounted directly on the motherboard.

Both form factors are used extensively in small-footprint desktop systems, although occasionally you'll find one in one of the smaller tower designs.

WTX

This is a new form factor that will be used for multiprocessor servers or higher-end workstations. These will be very large motherboards and will require a specialized chassis that provides access for such a large board, as well as larger power supplies to handle the demands of this type of system.

ATX Form Factors

The ATX form factor, which includes (from largest to smallest) the ATX, mini-ATX, micro-ATX, and flex-ATX, is the most popular of the current designs and probably is what you'll be upgrading to.

The ATX corrected the problems that plagued the Baby AT design and has proven to be very popular. Most chassis that use the ATX form factor accept all variations, meaning that even in a larger case, you could mount a smaller micro-ATX form factor motherboard.

Options on Board

Motherboards are being manufactured with features that were once found only in peripheral cards. You can find motherboards with video capabilities built in, which means you can forego adding a graphics card to your system. The downside, of course, is that you might not like the video quality of the chips on the motherboard and wind up adding a killer graphics adapter anyway. The same applies to SCSI, network, and audio built into the motherboard.

Motherboards with several built-in features are the NLX form factor designs. Because the NLX is a design that limits the number of available expansion slots, the options built into the motherboard make sense. It also lets a manufacturer make a slightly less expensive system because it doesn't have to provide (or install) core features, such as video, as separate peripheral cards.

Keep in mind that although you might be very happy with a motherboard's built-in audio or video, a new and improved peripheral card coming on the market might require you to perform another upgrade. This upgrade can become more complicated because you now must disable a function built into the motherboard so you can go back to a separate add-in card. A failure in a built-in option can require you to replace the entire motherboard instead of just popping out a peripheral card. Consider carefully before deciding on a new motherboard that has many built-in options.

CPU Sockets and Slots

In Chapter 2, the various methodologies of connecting a CPU to your motherboard were discussed as part of inventorying your current system's components. Intel uses numbered sockets (1, 2, 3, 4, 5, 7, 8, and PGA-370) and slots (1 and 2) that go on a motherboard and that receive the CPU chip itself. AMD uses a slightly different type of slot (A or B) for its processors to plug into a motherboard. AMD uses Socket A for its new Duron processors.

ASSORTED SLOTS AND SOCKETS

The following Motherboard Homeworld page has a well-organized table full of data on current and future connection types, plus write-ups on each one (below the table), complete with pictures of many of the slot and socket types:

`http://www.motherboards.org/sockets.html`

Slots are just that—slots very much like those you plug your peripheral cards into, although these are a bit longer. The CPU chip, mated with monster heat sinks and cooling fan(s), makes up the large package that gets plugged into the slot. A motherboard can come with the CPU already installed, or the CPU might come separately (which is often the case with slot-type motherboards). If that's the case, you'll have to install the CPU onto the motherboard.

The CPU module plugs into the slot just as add-in cards plug into their slots on the motherboard, only with a lot more care. Study the documentation carefully before trying to install the CPU, and make sure you understand the proper orientation of the CPU module on the motherboard. You should also ensure that any locking clips are released before you plug in the CPU module. Likewise, make sure the locking clips are firmly secured and that the module is properly seated in the slot as per the documentation.

Slot-type processors are secured to the motherboard using a retention mechanism that mounts perpendicularly to your motherboard and then holds the processor firmly in the slot. The retention mechanism is specific to the motherboard, so be sure you read the instructions that came with both your motherboard and processor. A typical retention mechanism is shown in Figure 6.3.

After the retention mechanism is installed, mount the heat sink and fan to the processor as directed in the manual for your specific processor. Then, mount the processor in the retention mechanism (see Figure 6.4).

FIGURE 6.3

The retention mechanism mounts to the motherboard with plastic fasteners; the processor is held in place by the retention brackets.

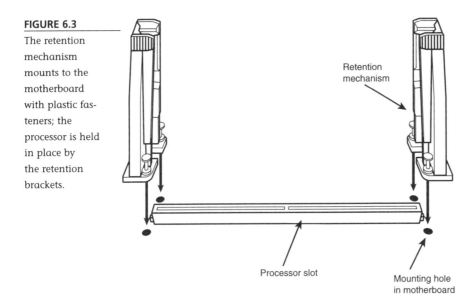

Retention mechanism

Processor slot

Mounting hole in motherboard

FIGURE 6.4

CPU modules with heat sinks and fans attached are huge and require gentle care to be properly seated and locked onto the motherboard.

Insert the processor (with fan and heat sink attached) into the slot with firm, controlled pressure

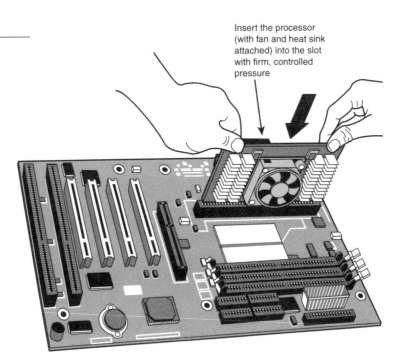

Sockets accept CPUs that are generally large, square chips with several small pins sticking out of one side (see Figure 6.5). These pins must match up with the holes in the socket on the motherboard. Most newer sockets are of the type called *zero insertion force (ZIF)*, meaning you unlock a release lever, align the pins on the chip with those of the socket, and just set the chip in place. Then, the lever is locked and the CPU chip is held firmly in place. As we mentioned back in Chapter 2, the ZIF socket is not "zero force" when it comes to getting the locking lever released and locked back down. Be sure you study the documentation that comes with your motherboard and that you understand how the locking mechanism works before you try to install the CPU.

FIGURE 6.5

Socketed processors are seated in a socket and secured with a lever. The heat sink and fan are then mounted on top of the processor.

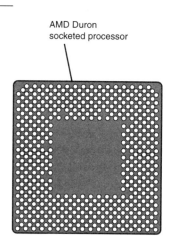

AMD Duron socketed processor

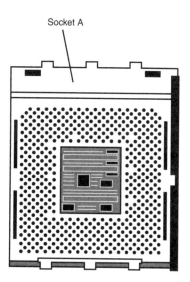

Socket A

Both Intel and AMD often manufacture a given type of CPU in both slot and socket configurations. Currently, a shift back to sockets has been seen (notably the Socket 7 and 370 from Intel and the Socket A from AMD). This is because they're usually a bit cheaper; the CPUs run a tad cooler; and, with the CPU installed, they often take up less physical room than the slot-mounted CPU module. Often an advantage also exists in the size of the cache and the speed at which it runs with a socket CPU.

Depending on how and where you purchase the CPU module/chip, it might come already installed on the motherboard as we mentioned, or you might have to not only install it, but mount the heat sinks and fans on the CPU chip yourself. This is especially true if you purchase what some resellers call an *OEM version*, which is a cheaper but stripped-down CPU product that might not even come with documentation. Watch out for this if you have a choice between an OEM version and the retail version (what Intel refers to as *boxed processors*). OEM versions usually have a very short warranty compared to retail versions. This is definitely not the place to start trying to save a few extra bucks, unless you are very, very knowledgeable about what you're up to and have built systems before.

You must know exactly what you're getting. Be absolutely sure you understand everything that will be required of you to complete the setup and installation of both the CPU and your motherboard before you decide on a vendor and a particular model.

The Mammoth Motherboard Upgrade Checklist

This section is broken down into three parts: what to do before you actually start the upgrade, the upgrade itself, and what to do to get your system working again after the upgrade. Be sure to read through everything before you decide whether you're up to performing a motherboard upgrade yourself.

Allow yourself plenty of time to perform this upgrade and find a time and place of relative peace and serenity. It won't benefit you to have phone calls, interruptions, screaming kids, or a lot of traffic through your work area when you're performing this type of upgrade. Prepare your work area, make sure you're grounded against ESD, and ensure you have the tools discussed in Chapter 3.

Another thing to consider before you start is the technical support offered by the retailer you purchased your CPU and motherboard from. Will telephone technical support be available during the time you'll be performing the upgrade? If the retailer offers technical support only via its Web site or email, how will you contact the retailer if you need help and the only computer you have is in pieces all around you? Take time zones into account, as well—it never fails that we need technical support at 4:00 p.m., only to belatedly realize that phone support closed at 5:00 p.m. in a time zone that's three hours ahead of the one we're in.

Upgrading the CPU Checklist

Changing out one CPU for another is less complicated than changing out the entire motherboard, but not by much. Take your time and go through the process step by methodical step:

Upgrading the CPU

1. Review all the materials that came with your CPU.

2. Make sure that, if your CPU upgrades requires a BIOS upgrade, you have the necessary files and disks prepared before starting your upgrade. See Chapter 4. Make note of all your CMOS settings in case you need to reset any of them after the upgrade.

3. Unpack the new CPU and ensure everything you'll need is included (in other words, that nothing is missing or that you weren't sent the wrong part). Install on the CPU any required heat sinks and fans. Again, most retail CPUs will come with this already installed, whereas OEM versions probably won't.

4. Shut down and disconnect your system (see Chapter 3's section "Breaking Down Your Computer").

5. Open up the chassis and carefully remove any components you have to in order to provide unobstructed access to the CPU. Label anything you need to so you can be assured of getting the component reinstalled after the upgrade is complete.

6. Depending on the type of socket or slot, you can reuse the cooling fan on the current processor. Unclip the fan from the CPU and set it aside (you might or might not have to unplug the fan from its power and motherboard connectors to do this). Figure 6.6 shows the basic anatomy of a processor, its socket, and the heat sink and fan assembly.

7. Disconnect the old CPU from its socket or slot (depending on the motherboard design). ZIF connectors require you to move the lever laterally (which usually requires firm, steady pressure) and then upward 90 degrees, which releases the CPU from the socket (see Figure 6.7). Slots have retaining mechanisms that you'll have to release before the CPU module can be removed. Some slots have clips you have to push as you pull the module out of the slot.

FIGURE 6.6

Remove heat sinks carefully because you might be able to reuse them, depending on the type of socket and system being upgraded.

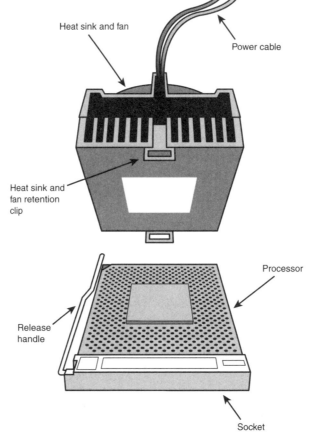

Heat sink and fan

Power cable

Heat sink and fan retention clip

Processor

Release handle

Socket

FIGURE 6.7

Raise the ZIF socket lever to release the CPU; after the lever is raised, lift the CPU out gently with your fingers and place it inside a static bag.

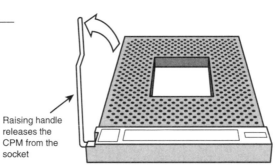

Raising handle releases the CPM from the socket

8. Install the new CPU into the socket or slot. This should be the reverse procedure you just used on the old CPU. Be sure socket-type CPU chips have their pins properly aligned with the holes on the socket. Place the CPU in the socket and lock it in with the ZIF lever. Slots are usually notched, so you can't insert them in backward, but consult the documentation that came with your CPU to ensure you are inserting it correctly. Socket processors usually have the pin arrays in two of the corners angled in a such a manner to make improper insertion difficult (see Figure 6.8).

FIGURE 6.8

Always be sure you line up the processor (a socket-type shown here) for proper insertion.

The pins on the bottom side of the processor line up with the pin holes in the socket

Lower the lever once the CPU is installed

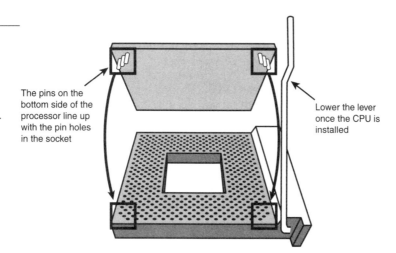

9. Reattach the CPU fan and heat sink using the clips supplied with the unit (see Figure 6.9).

10. Plug the fan's power cable back into your motherboard; the location of the power supply connector on the motherboard varies from manufacturer to manufacturer, but it's always located near the processor socket.

FIGURE 6.9

The fan and heat sink clip directly to the processor socket.

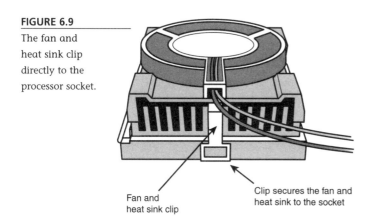

Fan and heat sink clip

Clip secures the fan and heat sink to the socket

11. You usually have to change jumper settings on the motherboard, depending on the chip upgrade you're performing. Again, check that documentation and make sure all jumpers are set correctly.

12. Reinstall any components you had to remove to gain unobstructed access to the slot/socket.

13. At this point, you should be ready to reboot your system. If a BIOS upgrade is necessary for this CPU upgrade, you'll have to do that. After everything is done, go into your CMOS and see whether the settings match those you noted in step 2.

Pre–Motherboard Upgrade Checklist

Assuming you have access to only one system—the computer you're upgrading—you should perform everything you need to *before* you unplug the computer to remove the old motherboard:

- Make sure you've checked the motherboard manufacturer's Web site for any bulletins about your board.

- Check the online documentation and compare it to the printed documentation that came with your board (the Web site might have updated material). Print out any relevant information.

- Download any updates to the BIOS or drivers for your new motherboard (if available).

- Print out the Hardware Central Web page that tells you what the BIOS beep codes mean. When your system starts up, the BIOS runs a self-diagnostic and communicates the results by beeping. This can come in handy after your upgrade is complete and you restart your system the first time. The Web page is at

  http://www.hardwarecentral.com/hardwarecentral/tutorials/13/1/

- Copy any downloaded files you might need to a 3.5" floppy disk. Your hard disk might not be available for some time after you start the upgrade.

- Prepare your work area before unpacking the new motherboard and CPU. A clean, well-prepared work area is a must. Because you'll be uninstalling so many of your system's components to get at the motherboard, be sure you have plenty of space to set things where they won't get in the way.

■ Unpack the new motherboard and ensure that everything you need is included and that you've been sent the correct model (before breaking down your old system). Handle the board with great care and only when you are properly grounded against ESD.

■ Compare the motherboard with its schematic in the documentation. Verify that all jumpers are set correctly for your desired configuration (especially jumpers that reset the CMOS because powering up a system with the CMOS jumpers "shorted" can damage the motherboard). These are usually set correctly by the reseller/manufacturer, but it doesn't hurt to check them.

■ Install the CPU on the motherboard if necessary (sometimes the CPU comes mounted on the motherboard, but sometimes it arrives packaged separately). Refer to the documentation that comes with your CPU/motherboard and follow any instructions provided for setting up the motherboard.

■ If you have purchased RAM chips for the new motherboard, install them now. If you're migrating the memory modules from the old motherboard, you'll do that later in the upgrade process.

Motherboard Upgrade Checklist

First and foremost, you should study the documentation that comes with your motherboard and do what the manufacturer recommends. The steps here cover the general steps necessary to install a motherboard, but every motherboard upgrade is a journey unto itself. Therefore, read and carefully follow the instructions from the manufacturer:

Upgrading the Motherboard

1. Review all the materials that came with your motherboard. Okay, we said that about a zillion times and you're tired of hearing it. But sure as shooting, some new wrinkle will be introduced between the time we write this and the time you read it, and that might be some new, critical hoop that you have to jump through—so RTFM (read the *fine* manual), okay?

2. Make note of all your current system's CMOS settings so you can compare them to the post-upgrade settings. This assumes you are not also replacing everything else in your computer, as well as the motherboard, which would render the old CMOS settings of no importance.

3. Shut down and disconnect your system (see Chapter 3's section "Breaking Down Your Computer").

4. Open the chassis and carefully remove all the peripheral cards from the old motherboard. If you are migrating the RAM modules from the old motherboard to the new, remove them at this time and install them on the new motherboard. Label anything and everything you need to so you can be assured of getting the component reinstalled after the upgrade is complete.

5. Disconnect all the cables that attach to the motherboard. This includes the primary and secondary IDE drive cables, the floppy cable, the thin cables that connect to the power switch, the reset switch, the LED lights on the front of the system case, the speaker, the hard disk activity LED, and so on. Keep in mind that you'll need to reattach all these to the new motherboard, so labeling is a must.

6. Unplug the main power supply plug from the motherboard. This is the 20-pin (assuming you're working with an ATX form factor) connector on the bundle of wires from the system power supply to the motherboard.

7. Carefully unscrew the old motherboard from the chassis. Save the screws. The old motherboard might have plastic *standoffs*, which are fasteners that snap into or onto the motherboard and then into holes or depressions in the chassis (see Figure 6.10). They should not hinder the removal of the old motherboard, but you might have to jiggle the board (carefully, of course) a bit to dislodge them from the chassis because they sometimes clip into slots in the chassis.

ANOTHER FINE MESS
BEWARE OF THE BABY AT POWER CONNECTORS

Hopefully, you won't be upgrading to a Baby AT form factor motherboard (which is a bit long in the tooth and out of date). But, should you ever find yourself in a situation in which you're dealing with one, beware of the power connector.

The Baby AT has a dual-plug power connector. Two plugs bring the wires from the power supply to the motherboard connector, and they plug in side by side. Without any safeguards to prevent you from plugging them in backward, which can destroy the motherboard, the instant power is applied and also creates a substantial fire hazard.

The two plugs should be connected to the motherboard so that the black cables on each plug are next to each other. ∎

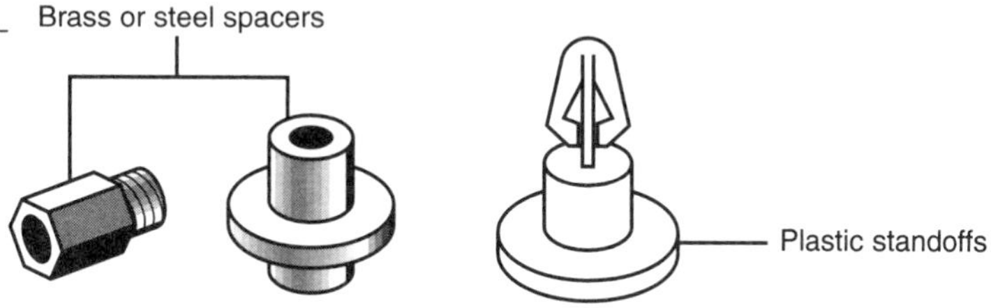

FIGURE 6.10

Plastic or brass standoffs are fitted into the chassis (or motherboard tray if your case includes it), and the motherboard is fastened to them.

Brass or steel spacers

Plastic standoffs

FIGURE 6.10

Plastic or brass standoffs are fitted into the chassis (or motherboard tray if your case includes it), and the motherboard is fastened to them.

8. Remove the old motherboard from the chassis.

9. Determine which holes in your system chassis will be used to secure the new motherboard. It might not be the same holes as the old motherboard used if you are changing form factors, say from an ATX to a micro-ATX.

10. Your new motherboard will have some sort of spacers to keep it from touching the chassis. It might use the plastic standoffs discussed in step 7, or it might use hexagon-shaped brass or steel pins as spacers (refer to Figure 6.9). These are special fasteners that screw into the chassis but in turn accept a screw in the middle of the hex head. The motherboard sits on top of the spacers and is screwed into the hex spacers.

   Attach the spacers either to the motherboard (if using the plastic type) or screw the spacers into the chassis, first ensuring you're screwing them into the holes in the chassis that line up with the mounting screw holes on the motherboard. These screw holes on the motherboard should have (nonconductive) metal rings around them. If they don't then you probably received a number of small plastic washers to insulate the screws from the motherboard. Be sure to use them.

   Insert the new motherboard into the chassis. Be sure you have the orientation correct because you don't want to mount it upside down. Keeping the motherboard flat and, without warping it or putting too much pressure on any one point on the board, screw the motherboard to the system chassis. The board should be supported in each corner as well as the interior portions of the motherboard.

11. Reconnect the main power supply plug to the motherboard that you removed in step 6.

12. Reconnect the cables you removed in step 5.

13. Reinstall all the peripheral cards removed in step 4.

14. Take a break and then double-check every connection in the system. You shouldn't have any loose wires or spare parts (unless you are not migrating all your peripheral cards to the new motherboard, of course).

Making the Upgraded System Operational

The motherboard is now upgraded. From a hardware standpoint, you're finished, but your system is not yet up and running. What's more, even if the system fires up without problems after you hit the power button, you still haven't gotten Windows to agree to recognize your new hardware and give you access to your hard disk. But you are close.

What's left is first seeing whether you hooked everything up correctly from a mechanical hardware standpoint. Second, and more importantly from most users' viewpoint, is trying to see whether you can get Windows to recognize your new motherboard so you can actually use your new motherboard with your old operating system, applications, and—most important of all—your old data.

Restarting the Computer

Close up your system. Connect the monitor, keyboard, mouse, and power cord and turn it on. If the hardware spirits decide to smile upon you, you'll hear a single beep (assuming an AMD BIOS).

If you hear more than one, thing's aren't so good. The AMD BIOS emits beeps as part of a self-diagnostic routine (the Phoenix BIOS uses a series of beeps to convey similar information). If you hear more than one beep, use the listing of beep codes you printed out from the Hardware Central Web site, as discussed in the "Pre–Motherboard Upgrade Checklist" section earlier in this chapter (you did print that out, didn't you?).

If the system starts but you get an error message onscreen, you might have to reset some of your CMOS values. In step 2 of the previous section, you recorded all the preupgrade CMOS settings. Boot the system and go into the CMOS settings to see whether any of the settings are incorrect, given your hardware.

At this point, if you're still having problems setting the hardware to boot properly, you might need to find out how good your vendor's technical support is. However, if your system boots properly but your operating system is giving you problems, that's another story.

Restarting the Windows Operating System

You might fire up your newly upgraded system and have Windows load, recognize that there's a new motherboard, and proceed to start detecting your new hardware and loading drivers. All is right in the world.

Then again, Windows might pitch a fit and your computer might start having problems. This is where things get dicey; no one we know has found the magic bullet that works in every situation and lets you recover from Windows' refusal to peaceably live with the new motherboard.

What has to happen is that Windows has to be enticed to go out and redetect all your installed hardware. If Windows decides to do this on its own, it will detect something, install a driver, want to reboot, then detect some more, reboot, and on and on—making you think it's going to reboot forever. Let it. Don't try to skip the reboots, thinking you install all the drivers and then just reboot at the end. According to those who claim to understand the workings of Windows (and how toothpaste makers manage to get three colors of toothpaste in the same tube), Windows cannot properly detect some hardware unless some other hardware has been detected and installed and rebooted first.

If Windows doesn't decide to do the detecting for you, you can try the following, but we're not guaranteeing this will work in all cases. We've been told by our favorite clone shop gurus that even they wind up having to reformat and reinstall Windows on one out of four systems in which they've upgraded the motherboard. The reinstalling Windows part isn't bad, but reformatting the drive creates a huge headache.

Restarting the System

1. Boot Windows up into Safe Mode (boot the system and when you see the text "Starting Windows" appear, press F8; then select the third option, "Safe Mode," from the Startup menu).

2. Go into Device Manager (right click the My Computer icon and choose properties; then click the Device Manager tab).

3. Remove "any device associated with the motherboard."

   This is where it gets tricky, as you might expect. Which devices are associated with the motherboard? USB controllers? Hard disk controllers? Everything under the System devices branch? You could just remove everything and let Windows do what it can to sort things out—sort of a scorched-earth approach.

4. Shut down Windows and power off the system.

5. Reboot the computer using your startup disk.

6. Reinstall Windows from the Windows CD using this command-line string:

   `d:setup /p f`

   In this code, *d:* is the CD-ROM drive. The `setup` command is followed by a space, a forward slash (/), the letter *p*, another space, and the letter *f*. Next, press Enter.

   This forces your hardware to be redetected during the Windows reinstall. Again, reboot as often as Windows requires.

The last step is to reformat your hard drive and reinstall your operating system to get Windows to properly recognize your hardware. That's why back in the section "Preliminary Upgrade Checklist," at the beginning of this chapter, we told you to back up all data and mission-critical applications you want saved. If you must resort to a reformat and reinstall of Windows, you'll need this backup so you can restore the software you need to get your system back up and running.

7

UPGRADING THE HARD DISK

You can't be too thin, too rich, or have too much hard disk space. Personal computers have come a long way from the 10MB hard drive upgrades that first came out for the original IBM PC. New drives are measured in gigabytes; yet just like closet space, it seems you're always running out of room. This is partly caused by applications becoming easier to use, which results in our using more of them. Another cause is the plethora of programs, many of them free, that can be downloaded from the Internet.

Upgrade Checklist

1. Do your homework. You must know the specs of your new disk and whether it's compatible with your system's hard disk controller.

2. Determine whether your PC BIOS supports the size of the drive you're going to add.

3. Determine whether you can perform the upgrade.

4. Purchase or acquire the drive. If you're adding a SCSI drive, you will need to add a SCSI controller card if you don't already have one.

5. Organize your tools and workspace.

6. Back up everything: data, operating system, mission-critical applications, and BIOS information.

7. Test your startup disk.

8. Perform the upgrade.

9. Take good notes, and permanently file them in your system log when finished.

10. Update your inventory documentation to reflect the upgraded or newly added component.

SCSI Versus EIDE

The first hurdle to jump in performing a hard drive upgrade is deciding on the type of drive to which you want to upgrade. *Type* means the type of interface between the physical hard drive and the computer. This interface is also known as the hard disk *controller*. Your choices for most computers are between small computer system interface (SCSI, which is pronounced *scuzzy*) and enhanced integrated drive electronics (EIDE).

Most people go with whichever drive type their computer already supports. So, if they have currently have an EIDE controller, they upgrade to another EIDE drive. Or, if they have a SCSI controller, they upgrade to another SCSI drive.

Keep in mind that almost all systems today come with EIDE on the motherboard. So, unless you or the previous owner had SCSI installed, your system is already EIDE. Because systems come with EIDE installed, staying with EIDE is cheaper than switching to SCSI. This is due to SCSI requiring you to install a SCSI controller in addition to buying SCSI drives, which are marginally more expensive than similar EIDE drives. SCSI drives do have better performance, meaning they transfer data more quickly, and you can install more drives on SCSI than on EIDE. However, with 20-gigabyte EIDE drives common, this is not a huge consideration anymore.

Aside from cost and performance, the physical hard drives for either SCSI or IDE are identical except for some circuitry on the drive itself that lets the drive talk to either the EIDE or SCSI controller. However, no dual drives exist that can be used for either EIDE or SCSI. You have to make sure you buy a drive that works with the type of controller you plan on using.

EIDE

EIDE is cheap and relatively easy to work with. Most computers support two IDE channels. Each channel can then support up to two IDE devices, so you're limited to a total of four devices. Devices can be hard drives, CD or DVD drives, scanners, Zip (and other removable media) drives, and tape backup devices.

Adding a second hard drive to a system can breathe new life into your computer. Hard drive space is cheap when figured by the megabyte, and adding a second drive is a fairly easy procedure.

PLAINSPEAKING
A TECHNOLOGY BY ANY OTHER NAME

Western Digital, a maker of hard drives, owns the terms "IDE" and "Enhanced IDE," so other hard drive manufacturers have taken to referring to their IDE drives by the standard name *ATA (Advanced Technology Attachment)* interface. When shopping for hard drives, just remember that IDE and ATA are equivalent terms. EIDE, the "enhanced" version of IDE, and IDE, the standard that preceded it, are also used interchangeably, which is not technically correct. Given that EIDE is now the standard, when we say "IDE," we're really referring to EIDE. ■

EIDE Controller

You'll find that most motherboards have an EIDE controller built right into the motherboard itself. This eliminates the need to add a separate controller card for the hard drive. In general, this makes EIDE a cheaper upgrade decision than SCSI.

A number of different flavors of IDE and EIDE have existed over the years. Table 7.1 shows how these versions have progressed. Note that the maximum transfer speed shown is the *theoretical* maximum speed. It wasn't until ATA-4 that drives actually started attaining the speeds the EIDE bus is capable of. ATA-2 drives, for example, rarely attained even an 8MB/second transfer speed. ATA-3 offered only minor improvements in power management and nothing in the way of increased speed.

Table 7.1 A Confusing Plethora of EIDE Standards and Street Names

Specification	What It's Called on the Street	Maximum Transfer Speed	Total Devices Supported
ATA 1	IDE	8.3MB/second	2
ATA 2	EIDE Fast ATA, Fast ATA-2	16.6MB/second	4
ATA 3	ATA-3	16.6MB/second	4
ATA 4	EIDE Ultra-33, ATA/33	33.3MB/second	4
ATA 5	EIDE Ultra-66 ATA/66	66.6MB/second	4
ATA 6	EIDE Ultra-100 ATA/100	100.0MB/second	4

The main limitation is that you can have only two EIDE *channels*—referred to as *primary* and *secondary*—with each channel using a single IRQ and only two devices attached to each channel (see Table 7.2). This makes the effective limit for EIDE four devices in your system.

Table 7.2 Only Four EIDE Devices Are Supported by a PC

Channel	IRQ	Number of Devices
Port 1 (Primary)	14	2 (Master/Slave)
Port 2 (Secondary)	15	2 (Master/Slave)

NOTE

CONNECT TWO DEVICES TO ONE

See the section "Get the Jump on Jumpers" later in this chapter for more information on connecting two devices to one IDE channel.

ATA is also forward- and backward-compatible. You can attach a slower disk on a faster controller and vice versa. But the slowest device will dictate your speed and throughput.

If your system board does not have a built-in EIDE controller that supports ATA-4 or higher speeds, you can add a controller card (much as you would add a SCSI controller card). This takes up a slot on your PCI bus, but we've seen cards advertised that purport to add four EIDE channels—effectively raising the number of devices to eight, which doubles the standard limitation.

NOTE

EIDE CONTROLLER CARDS AND RAID

You can use an EIDE add-in controller to support a redundant arrays of independent disks (RAID) setup in which data is written across multiple drives. *Striping* data is spread across multiple drives to improve performance, whereas RAID *mirroring* creates a copy of all data on another drive to give you a constant backup. You can configure a RAID setup in multiple ways using combinations of striping and mirroring. RAID is beyond the scope of this book and is not for the novice or faint of heart. However, we wanted to mention it as an option. For more information on RAID take a look here:

`http://www6.tomshardware.com/storage/00q1/000329/fastrak66-03.html`

Although this adds to the cost of your upgrade, these cards have a street price that's only about one-third the cost of a SCSI controller.

The fact that the EIDE controller is built into the motherboard and the fact that ATA drives are cheaper than the equivalent SCSI drive makes EIDE the most economical way to go when planning an upgrade. The key consideration is the total number of devices you'll be adding to the system.

IDE Cable

As discussed, an IDE channel supports two devices. The first drive is drive 0 (zero) and is called the *master* drive. The second drive is drive 1 and is called the *slave*. ATA hard drives usually have a jumper or jumpers that must be set to designate a drive as master or slave. Carefully check the documentation that comes with your drive to ensure it is configured correctly. The same holds true when installing ATA devices other than hard disks, such as CD-ROM, CD-R/RW, or DVD devices. The first device (device 1) is always the master, and the second device (device 2) connected is the slave.

EIDE devices connect to the EIDE controller (usually a connector on the motherboard) using a flat ribbon cable. If you're connecting both a master and a slave device, make sure your cable has a total of three connectors (one for the controller connection on the motherboard and one each for the two devices). Oddly enough, if your system came with only a single EIDE drive installed, the cable used may connect only a single device to the controller. Often, you'll have to upgrade the cable when adding a second drive (see Figure 7.1).

FIGURE 7.1
Standard IDE cable showing the pin 1 stripe and the master (drive 0) and slave (drive 1) connectors.

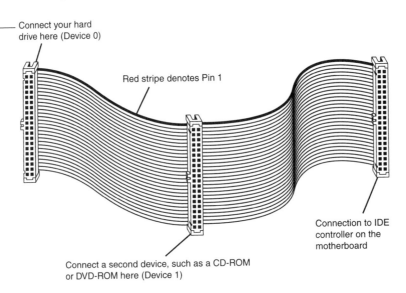

Connect your hard drive here (Device 0)

Red stripe denotes Pin 1

Connection to IDE controller on the motherboard

Connect a second device, such as a CD-ROM or DVD-ROM here (Device 1)

TIP

CABLE CONUNDRUM

IDE/EIDE cables are flat, 40-pin cables. But the ATA-4 specification allows for an optional cable (called an 80-wire/40-pin cable) that has improved shielding to reduce signal noise and improve the transfer rate. ATA-5 and above *require* this type of cable, so be sure you have the proper cabling on hand before you start your upgrade.

The 80-wire cables will work with the older drives; therefore, if you have to buy a cable, get the newer 80-wire version. The cables look the same, so make sure you are getting what you need when buying a cable. Some manufacturers are making the connector that plugs into the EIDE controller connection blue instead of black or platinum, making it easier to identify these cables.

When the cable connectors are color-coded, the blue connects the controller, whereas the black connector designates the master device. Additionally, the gray is for the slave device when cable select is used.

Get the Jump on Jumpers

Jumpers control whether your IDE devices are identified as master or slave devices. Setting the jumpers on an ATA drive or device can seem confusing at first glance, but it's really not difficult. Four jumper possibilities exist, controlled by adding or removing (or moving) jumper shunts on a set of jumper pins:

- **A single drive on the channel**—This usually requires a specific jumper setting to let the controller know that only one drive is available with which to communicate.

- **Two drives, where this device is the master**—The jumper setting lets the controller know two drives exist and this one is the master.

- **Two drives, where this device is the slave**

- **Cable select**—This setting lets the cable used to connect the drives determine which is the master and which is the slave. This is a special setting used by all and devices.

Even though only four settings are possible, the way the jumpers are set depends on the make and model of the drive itself. The *jumper block* consists of a number of wire pins on the EIDE drive usually—but not always—between the IDE connector and the power connector (see Figure 7.2).

Jumper *shunts* are small, plastic rectangles that you slide over two of the pins in the jumper block. This shunt makes the two pins into a circuit; in effect the pins now are in electrical contact with each other. Which pins are jumpered (connected by the shunt) tells the drive whether it is master, slave, or cable select.

Check your documentation carefully to see how your drive should be jumpered for your configuration.

FIGURE 7.2

By placing the jumper shunts over the correct sets of pins, you can configure the drive to be master, slave, or cable select. See your drive manual or markings on the drive case itself for placement of the jumper shunt (placement varies from drive to drive).

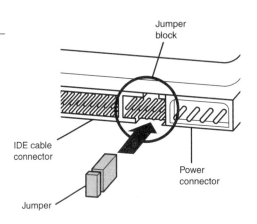

Jumper block

IDE cable connector

Power connector

Jumper

TIP

JAVA APPLET IS AVAILABLE TO VIEW

A very handy Java applet, which you can view, is in your browser, and it visually shows you the jumper settings for a number of drives:

`http://www.ontrack.com/JumperViewer/`

Click the Start Ontrack Jumper Viewer link. (Your browser must support Java for you to access this; Java is supported by all recent versions of Netscape Navigator and Microsoft Internet Explorer.)

You can use the cable select setting (sometimes marked as CS or CSEL) if the computer system supports it (cable select was first defined in the ATA-2 specification), the devices on the channel support it, and you have an EIDE cable that is wired for it. The cable select setting designates the drive to be master or slave, depending on where on the EIDE cable it's connected. If two devices are on the same channel and you want to set one to cable select, both must be set to cable select.

You run into problems if you jumper two drives on the same channel to be cable select but use a regular EIDE cable. In this case, both drives are recognized as master and conflicts occur. However, you can use a cable select cable and jumper the drives to be master and slave, and everything will work without problems. For this reason, most of the systems we've seen rely on jumper settings as master/slave, and cable select is not used that often.

Always check the manufacturer's documentation or Web site for the correct jumper settings. You'll find links to a number of hard drive manufacturers at `http://www.itechs-systems.com/pages/dmj.htm`.

SCSI Drives

SCSI has two benefits over EIDE. First, it offers better performance in data transfer rates. Second, you can connect more SCSI devices to a single controller, which uses only a single IRQ. In a typical environment, the performance of a single hard disk won't improve much from the SCSI interface. Rather, the power of SCSI is that several devices can use the bus at the same time, and not use the bus when they don't need it. Therefore, the best benefits from SCSI result when several devices are all used on the same bus.

SCSI supports command queuing, such that up to 256 commands for an individual device can be queued up for processing, letting the device work away while other devices use the SCSI bus. Again, you don't see any performance improvements if you are using only a single device. However, with multitasking operating systems, such as Windows NT or Windows 2000, running multiple devices you see a significant improvement.

Generally, a SCSI drive costs more than a similarly sized EIDE drive, and you have to factor in the cost of a SCSI controller. Although motherboards are available with an integrated SCSI controller, they are not common and usually cost more than those with the ubiquitous EIDE controllers built into most motherboards. In most cases, you must have (or purchase) a SCSI adapter card (controller) that then must be plugged into a free slot in your computer.

SCSI Adapter Card

A number of flavors of SCSI technology are available. Some flavors of SCSI support eight physical devices and some support sixteen. Each device in the "chain" is assigned a unique number so the controller can identify all the devices attached to the SCSI bus. One of the biggest benefits of going the SCSI route is that the SCSI controller card uses only one IRQ. The card then controls the additional devices, thereby reducing the total number of IRQs necessary to support the individual pieces of hardware attached to the computer.

Typical SCSI devices include hard drives, of course, but also CD-ROM drives, CD-R/RW drives, scanners, Iomega Zip (and other removable) drives, DVDs, and tape backup devices.

If you're upgrading both the controller and hard disk, be sure to get a disk drive that supports the type of card you're installing. If you already have a SCSI controller, you need to know which flavor of the various SCSI standards it supports so you can purchase the correct drive. Table 7.3 lists the SCSI standards.

SCSI drives are backward- and forward-compatible to the extent allowed by the cabling standards. What this means is that you could connect a newer SCSI hard drive that supports a higher data transfer speed to an older SCSI controller card and it would work. But the drive would function at the slower speed of the controller card, and you'd lose the feature benefit of having a higher-speed drive. Conversely, you could install a high-end SCSI controller and connect an older, slower SCSI device. Mixing older with newer SCSI devices isn't easy because the cables used to connect the devices keep changing along with the standards.

PLAINSPEAKING
HOW MANY DEVICES?

How many devices a given SCSI controller can work with is confusing because of the way things are numbered when working with this drive type. As we've said, you can attach up to 7 SCSI devices to some SCSI controllers, and 15 to others. But we've also said that some flavors of SCSI support a total of 8–16 devices. This apparent discrepancy is because the SCSI adapter card counts for 1 of the supported "devices." After you pop the card into the chassis, you can connect 7–15 *other* devices.

It gets even more confusing when you consider how SCSI devices are numbered. A system using narrow SCSI can have devices 0–7, for a total of 8 devices. But remember, 1 of these devices is the SCSI controller card. The card is usually set to an ID of 7. Wide SCSI supports devices numbered 0–15, for a total of 16 devices—with the card usually set to 16. ■

PLAINSPEAKING
SCSI SPEED MISCONCEPTIONS

A common misconception is that if you add a slower device (slower than the transfer rates the controller is capable of) then every device on the bus must run at the slower speed. This is not true. The SCSI controller "speaks" to each SCSI device at the speed set for that device in the BIOS. Each device then operates at its own speed, so a device operating slower than the fastest speed the controller is capable of does not slow down all the devices connected to the SCSI bus. ■

Table 7.3   A Confusing Plethora of SCSI Standards and Street Names

Specification	What It's Called on the Street	Maximum Transfer Speed	Total Devices Supported
SCSI-1	SCSI	5MB/second	8
SCSI-2	Fast SCSI or Fast Narrow	10MB/second	8
SCSI-2	Fast Wide SCSI	20MB/second	16
SCSI-3	Ultra SCSI, or SCSI-3, or Fast-20, or Ultra Narrow	20MB/second	8
SCSI-3	Ultra 2 or Fast-40	40MB/second	8
SCSI-3	Wide Ultra SCSI or Fast Wide	40MB/second	16
SCSI-3	Wide Ultra 2	80MB/second	16
SCSI-3	Ultra 3	80MB/second	8
SCSI-3	Wide Ultra 3 or Ultra 160	160MB/second	16
SCSI-3	Ultra 320	320MB/second	16

SCSI-1 devices use a 25-pin cable; SCSI-2 and some SCSI-3 devices use a 50-pin cable; and a 68-pin cable connection indicates a SCSI-3 device. Converters exist that, for example, enable you to connect a 50-pin device to a 68-pin controller connector. Some SCSI cards can have both a 50- and 68-pin internal connector (*internal* means connectors on the card for connecting devices inside the computer chassis). Only one connector will be on the back of the card for connecting external devices.

Keep in mind that you are generally better off using the type of devices dictated by the type of controller you are using. This might require you to upgrade your SCSI controller, as well as your hard drive, so you can enjoy the added benefits of increased speed and throughput.

The capability to connect multiple devices to a single SCSI controller card, and to have multiple controller cards installed in a single PC (each card consuming only one precious IRQ), makes SCSI a serious contender for situations in which you've installed a number of devices. The cost of the SCSI card is justified when you allocate it across all the devices you can connect to it. However, if you are going to install only a hard drive or two, the cost of the card combined with the premium you pay for the drives make EIDE a more economical upgrade.

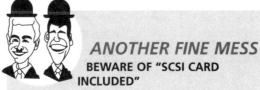

ANOTHER FINE MESS
BEWARE OF "SCSI CARD INCLUDED"

You'll find that when you purchase some SCSI devices (such as a scanner), it comes with a SCSI card—sort of like the free prize in a cereal box. However, if you think you can start hooking up multiple SCSI devices to it, think again. Most of these "included with" cards do not allow you to connect anything but the device they came with. ■

SCSI ID Settings

Each SCSI device must have a unique ID number. Setting the ID number usually involves setting jumpers on the device itself, although some devices can be set via software (see Figure 7.3). A *jumper block* is a group of wire pins. A jumper *shunt* is a small, plastic rectangle that you slide over two of the pins in the jumper block. This shunt makes the two pins into a circuit; in effect, the pins now are in electrical contact with each other. Always check the documentation to determine how the ID number is set and whether the device has a preferred number. Figure 7.3 shows a typical jumper block found on the back side of a SCSI device. Although the jumper settings shown here are common, you should check the documentation that came with your specific drive for the exact placement of the jumper shunt for each SCSI ID.

FIGURE 7.3

Setting a SCSI ID on most drives involves setting jumper shunts on the correct pins on a specific jumper block.

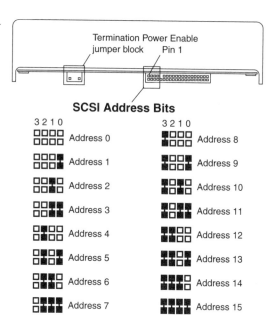

Daisy-Chaining SCSI Devices

SCSI devices connect in a daisy-chain, one device connecting to the next device, which in turn connects to the next device, and so on, starting with the SCSI controller card.

A ribbon cable attaches to the internal connector on the card (inside your computer's chassis) and runs to the first device in the chain. The cable can have multiple connectors along its length, and all the internal devices connect to the cable (see Figure 7.4).

FIGURE 7.4

An internal SCSI ribbon can have several connectors. It has to snake its way through your PC's innards, connecting to each SCSI device installed inside the chassis.

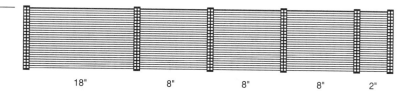

Having a cable with enough connectors is important to enable you to attach all your internal devices. Your SCSI controller card also has a connector on the back of the card to which you can attach an external cable for running to external SCSI devices. Most external SCSI devices have two connectors on them: one to which the cable from the existing chain can connect, and a second connector for attaching the next device in the chain.

A SCSI chain must be terminated at the two extreme ends of the chain. A SCSI terminator can be a physical termination device plugged into the unused connector on the last device in the chain. Or, as is more common, you can enable termination of the last device via a jumper, switch setting, or software command.

The most common configuration is a SCSI card attached to a number of internal devices. In this case, the card itself is at one end of the chain and must be terminated. If you have devices connected to a SCSI adapter card via the internal connection and the external connection, the card is inside the chain and is not to be terminated. Instead, the last internal device connected to the chain and the last external device connected to the chain are each terminated.

Each SCSI device has its own unique ID number. The controller card is usually the highest number supported to avoid accidental conflicts. The first device is ID 0, and each added device in the chain is usually incremented by one. Some devices are manually configured via jumpers or switches, whereas some support being dynamically assigned values at bootup by the controller card.

External Hard Drives (USB/FireWire)

A growing trend is externally installed hard drives using the newer FireWire and USB connectors. There's a lot to be said for the ease of installation with these type of external hard drives. You plug the drive into an available port on the back of the computer, and the operating system (hopefully) recognizes the new hardware and installs the proper drivers.

PLAINSPEAKING
TYPES OF TERMINATION
A number of types of SCSI terminators exist, which you must use depending on the configuration and type of SCSI controller you're using. For example, a passive terminator is used for SCSI-1 or slow SCSI-2, whereas active terminators are using for Fast SCSI devices. In addition, feed-through terminators are available for special termination cases. The important thing is to read the documentation that comes with your SCSI controller and the device that will be terminated. Always use the recommended type of terminator. ■

The big caveat, of course, is that the system on which you're going to install this type of drive must support the type of connection required by the drive. Not only that, but the operating system must recognize the technology as well. For example, Windows NT does not natively support USB.

These external drives are a traditional drive mounted in a plastic case. The trick is that the interface uses either USB or FireWire to talk to the operating system. Given that a hard disk is still at the core of things, you have to handle these types of drives as carefully as you would an internally mounted drive.

For ease of installation, use—and most of all—portability you can't beat external USB/FireWire drives.

USB External Drives

With some model USB drives, you don't have to worry about external power supplies or cords because the drive draws power over the USB connection. Others require an external AC power connection to run the drive and cooling fans in the drive's external chassis. Another nice feature is that the drive is easily portable between systems and the drive is *hot-swappable*, meaning it can be plugged in and unplugged from a running system.

The downside is the relatively slow transfer rate of 1.5 megabytes per second when compared to the 60MB–100MB per second transfer rates attainable under EIDE and SCSI. You'll also pay a bit more per megabyte of storage compared to traditional EIDE and SCSI.

FireWire External Drives

FireWire drives also can run off the FireWire port connection for power. FireWire, in addition, delivers faster transfer rates than USB with drives offering 15 megabytes per second. Still, this is way below what you'll get from EIDE or SCSI.

Similar to USB, external FireWire drives are hot-swappable, which is an amazingly handy thing if you have to share gigabytes of information between systems that are not networked. It's also handy if you want to grab your hard drive and take it home so you can continue to work there with access to all your data.

FireWire ports are not found as widely, even on new systems, as the ubiquitous USB port. However, FireWire adapter cards are available that plug into a PCI slot, which will add two FireWire ports to your system for well under $100.

Installing an Internal Hard Drive

Installing an internal hard drive is not difficult if you prepare properly. In fact, the preparation is more involved than actually connecting the physical drive to your system.

Handling Tips for Any Drive

Unlike peripheral cards, motherboards, and the like, a hard drive has a number of moving parts that include bearings, platters, and servo arms that actuate the read/write heads over the rapidly spinning platters. (Modern drive platters spin at anywhere between 5,400rpm and 10,000rpm or more, where *rpm* means revolutions per minute and translates to a range of 90–167 revolutions per second.) The heads and the platters must line up perfectly. This makes a hard drive particularly sensitive to sudden jolts and strong vibrations. The drive, like other components discussed in Chapter 3, "Things You Need," can also be damaged by electrostatic discharge (ESD). Follow these tips when upgrading a hard drive:

- *Always prepare your work area before removing the new drive from any shock absorbing packaging materials.* Avoid physically jarring the drive. A clean, well-prepared work area can help avoid any possibility that the drive might accidentally be dropped or knocked over. Never set a drive on its edge because just falling over on its top or bottom can damage it.

- *Handle the drive with care and only when you are properly grounded against ESD.* When you remove the drive from its antistatic plastic, you can set the drive on the bag prior to mounting it in the system chassis.

- *Avoid touching the circuit board usually affixed to the bottom of the drive.*

- *Study the documentation that accompanies the drive so you can set any jumpers necessary for your particular needs and installation.* If the drive does not come with documentation (and we've run into mail-order drives that didn't), check the manufacturer's Web site. Many times all the documentation, manuals, and installation guides are available on the Web.

  The Tech Page has a database of the specifications for more than 2,000 drives and is a good place to look if you can't find the documentation for the drive you're installing:

  `http://www.thetechpage.com/cgi-bin/default.cgi`

- *While the drive is out and before you install it, write down any and all part, model, and serial numbers that are visible on the drive.* Be sure to put these in your NEAT box.

Mounting Brackets and Screws

Newer system chassis have 3 1/2-inch drive bays for mounting narrow drives without having to fuss with mounting brackets. But some drive bays in your system can be a full 5.25 inches across (see Figure 7.5). If you need to mount a 3 1/2-inch drive in a 5 1/4-inch bay, you'll need mounting accessories that might not come with your drive. It's these sorts of surprises that make installing drives difficult.

FIGURE 7.5

This system has both a 5.25-inch cage and a 3.5-inch cage for mounting drives.

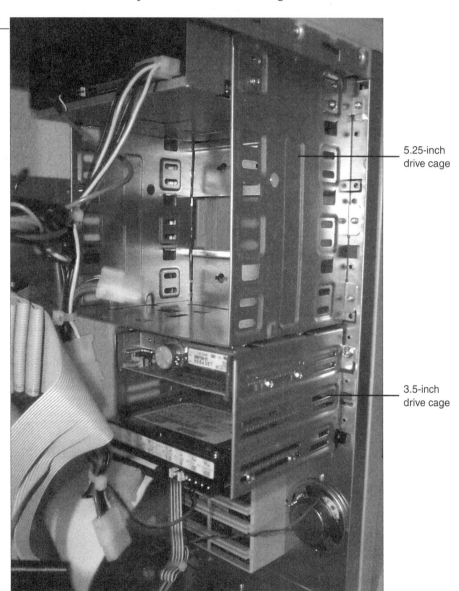

5.25-inch drive cage

3.5-inch drive cage

If the drive you are installing is narrower than the drive bay's metal cage to which the drive must be attached, you'll have to attach a mounting bracket or a set of drive rails. Mounting brackets are metal boxes open on each end and one side, and they attach to each side of the drive (see Figure 7.6). The brackets, or *rails* as they are sometimes referred to, are then screwed to the drive bay cage securing the hard drive in place.

FIGURE 7.6

Brackets let you mount a 3.5-inch–wide drive inside a full-size drive bay.

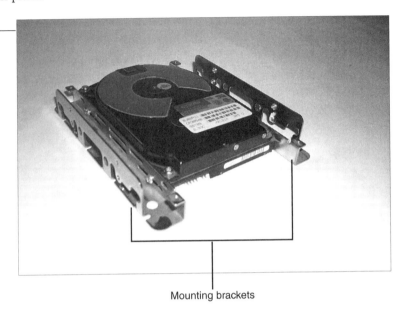

Mounting brackets

Note that the screws that secure the drive to the cage, or the mounting bracket, actually screw into the side of the drive itself. This means you can't just grab any screw that fits without considering how long it is. Using a screw that penetrates too far into the drive can cause damage. Be sure to check the documentation to see which screws should be used to mount the drive. Two screws on each side of the drive or mounting bracket should be adequate. Depending on the system you're upgrading, the drive might go into the system from inside the chassis (see Figure 7.7).

FIGURE 7.7

Here, a 3 1/2-inch drive fits into the drive cage from inside the system chassis.

More often, the drive will be inserted into the chassis from the front of the system. This is accomplished by first opening the system chassis and choosing a slot in the drive bay to hold the drive. You must then remove a plastic cover, called a *bezel*, from the front panel of the computer (see Figure 7.8).

FIGURE 7.8

Bezels can cover both the 5.25-inch and 3.5-inch slots in the front of the computer and can be popped in and out by carefully pulling a middle edge and bowing the bezel outward in the middle.

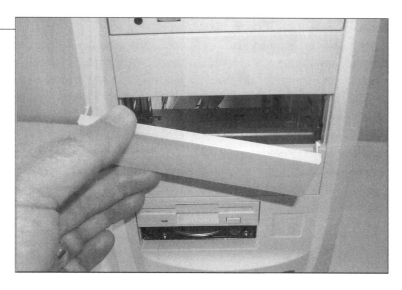

Be mindful of airflow around the drive when selecting the bay in your chassis in which you'll install the drive. Unfortunately, the length of the connector cable and the available bays sometimes dictate where you'll install it. The more airflow, the better to keep your drive from overheating (drives that spin at 7,200rpm and higher generate a substantial amount of heat). Running a drive too hot can shorten its useful life.

TIP

CHASSIS FEATURES

Some chassis feature a removable drive cage that enables you to slide the cage out of the chassis, mount the drive or drives, and then slide it back into the case. This is very nice if working space inside the PC is limited or if you have big hands.

Ribbon Cables and Pin 1

Drives might or might not come with the proper cables necessary to connect them to your controller. The general rule of cables (too short, too long, or missing) is modified when dealing with internal drive cables. Internal drive cables are either too short or don't have enough connectors. Make sure you have the proper ribbon cable for the drive you are installing, that it is long enough, and that it has the necessary number of connectors to attach to all the target devices.

Before mounting the drive in the system chassis, take a close look at the connector on the drive where the ribbon cable will attach the drive to the controller. Drives have one end of the connector marked as "Pin 1." With a felt-tip marker, put an X or other mark somewhere on the drive where you can easily see it when looking at the connector end of the drive (as it will appear after you've mounted the drive in the system chassis). Even though newer equipment is keyed so that you cannot plug the ribbon cable into the drive incorrectly, it's a good idea to double-check.

You don't want to plug the ribbon cable into the drive connector backward. Avoid this by lining up the red stripe that runs along one edge of the ribbon cable with pin 1 on the drive connector. The same rule applies to the connector on the motherboard (EIDE) or the controller card (SCSI). This also applies to both SCSI and ATA drives (see Figure 7.9).

FIGURE 7.9
Line up the pins with the connector carefully and gently rock the connector back and forth to get a solid seat.

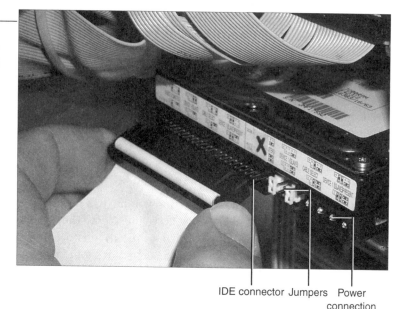

IDE connector   Jumpers   Power connection

Power Connection

Plugging in the power lead is easy (assuming you have a free power connector) because both the power lead coming from the power supply and the power receptacle on the drive itself are notched, making it impossible to insert it incorrectly (see Figure 7.10). Grasp the lead firmly and work it into the receptacle all the way. Again, as with the ribbon cable, a side-to-side rocking motion with gentle but firm pressure works best.

FIGURE 7.10
Plug in the power lead with gentle but firm pressure and make sure it is fully seated in the receptacle.

If you're short of free power leads inside your chassis, you can use a Y-splitter (discussed back in Chapter 3; see Figure 3.14) so you can plug in your drive.

Cylinders, Heads, Sectors, and Mode

Newer BIOSs support automatic drive typing and can usually figure out what they need to know about your new drive. However, you should record the values for the number of cylinders, heads, sectors, and the mode to use for this drive in your NEAT box or even on a note taped inside the system cover of your computer. You don't have to understand the difference between a cylinder and a sector as long as you record the values correctly.

Should the BIOS lose this information and you have to manually enter this data, it's handy to have recorded it in a readily accessible place. The first three values (cylinders, heads, and sectors) tell the BIOS what it needs to know about the physical size of the disk. The mode is the addressing scheme that should be used—Cylinder Head Sector (CHS) or Logical Block Addressing (LBA). This information is usually found in the documentation accompanying your drive, or it might be printed on the physical drive itself.

Hard Drive Installation Checklist

Here are the steps to follow when installing/upgrading a hard drive.

WORKING ON THE HARD DRIVE

1. If you're upgrading the hard drive that the computer will boot from when the system is started, you must have prepared, and tested, a bootable 3 1/2-inch disk that contains the files you'll need to format the new drive and that includes drivers for your CD-ROM drive. A Windows 98 or Windows Me (Millennium Edition) start disk will boot the system and give you the option of starting your PC with or without CD-ROM support. Be sure to choose "with CD-ROM support" so you can install Windows from your CD on the new drive.

   It's tricky to get a boot disk with CD support for Windows 95 systems. However, a Windows 98 or Windows Me boot disk will boot a Windows 95 machine with CD support. This is a nifty trick if you're working on a Windows 95 system and can get a Windows 98 or Windows Me startup disk.

2. Review the materials that came with the drive you are installing. If you have little in the way of documentation, visit the drive manufacturer's Web site

and print out any information you'll need regarding installation instructions, jumper settings, and cable requirements. (This assumes you have only the one system and, while installing the drive, you'll not have any way to access information on the Internet.)

3. Shut down and disconnect your system (see Chapter 3's section "Breaking Down Your Computer").

4. Open up the chassis and determine where you will mount the drive. If you are replacing a drive, the easiest location will no doubt be the one the current drive is occupying. If you are adding a drive to the system, check the existing ribbon connector and determine whether it has enough connections (and is long enough) to accommodate the new drive. Obtain a ribbon cable upgrade, if necessary, as well as any drive mounting accessories that might be required. (See "Mounting Brackets and Screws" earlier in this chapter.)

5. If you're replacing an EIDE drive, ensure the drive is jumpered the same as the existing drive (master or slave). If you are adding another drive, make sure it is set to master or slave as necessary, depending on how you want the drives configured. You might have to reset the jumper on the existing drive, as well. (See "IDE Cable" earlier in this chapter.)

   If you're replacing an existing SCSI drive, determine the current drive's ID number. Jumper the replacement drive to use the same ID. If this is an additional drive, set the ID to an unused ID number. (See "SCSI ID Settings" earlier in this chapter.)

6. If this is a drive replacement, remove the old drive from the system. Remove the bezel, if necessary, to remove the drive through the front of the system case.

7. Install the new drive in the appropriate drive bay, securing the drive to the cage using the proper length screws as recommended by the manufacturer.

8. Start your computer with your 3 1/2-inch bootable disk (if you've upgraded the boot hard drive) and go into the CMOS. Check to see that the drive was autodetected properly and that the installed drive has been correctly identified. Manually enter the correct cylinders, heads, sectors, and mode information, if necessary.

9. Partition and format the drive as discussed in the next section.

FDISK and Formatting the New Drive

A hard disk comes from the factory *low-level* formatted, meaning the disk has been divided into tracks and sectors. You must partition the drive, set an active partition from which the system will attempt to boot, create extended partitions, and format the drive (high-level) so you can copy data and install programs to the drive. This is known as *high-level* formatting.

In working with drives at this level, you must understand how drives are numbered and lettered by the operating system. The first physical drive is drive 1, and the primary partition on it is drive letter C (usually the active partition) on that physical drive. (For the purposes of this discussion, drive 1 will be the boot drive and C will be the primary active partition. Other configurations are beyond the scope of this book.)

Each physical drive must have a primary partition that has the same drive letter designation as the physical drive. You can also create an *extended* partition that can then have a number of logical drive letters assigned within it.

For example, drive 1 has a primary, active partition—C—and an extended partition that is then divided into two logical drives—D and E. The purpose of creating logical drives on an extended partition is to organize your data and programs on separate partitions, with each acting like a separate drive and having its own drive letter. You might put programs on D and data on E while keeping the operating system on C. What's important to remember is that C, D, and E are all on physical drive 1. Partitioning is something you can do to organize your drive; you decide how much of the gross disk space is allocated to each partition. However, you can still have a single drive 1 with the entire drive formatted as C.

If you're working with a Windows 95 machine, you must be aware of the limitations of the FAT file system, as opposed to FAT32. With FAT32, the individual cluster size on a partition is smaller, making the drive more efficient in storing information. It also lets the drive function with fewer (larger) partitions. The original Windows 95 supported only FAT; it wasn't until OSR2 (OEM Service Release 2, the second version of Windows 95) that FAT32 was supported. If you're still running a Windows 95 system, we recommend upgrading the operating system to Windows 98 Second Edition or Windows Me.

Preparing the Primary Drive

If you're upgrading your primary hard drive, the drive that boots up your computer, you must have a working 3 1/2-inch boot disk so you can start your system and prepare your new drive for installation of your operating system, programs, and data.

Install the drive as discussed in the previous section and then boot your computer with your start disk. At the A: prompt, type **FDISK** and press Enter. If you're configuring a drive larger than 512MB (and drives smaller than 2GB are rare these days), you'll be prompted about whether you want to enable large drive support. Assuming you're going to be installing Windows 98 and using FAT32, click Y(es). See Figure 7.11.

FIGURE 7.11

Be sure to enable large disk support if you're running FAT32.

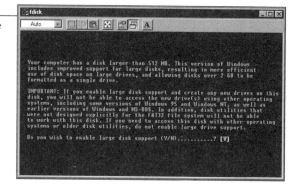

After you've dealt with large disk support, the main FDISK menu appears. You must first create a primary partition on your drive (option 1); then you set that partition as active (option 2). It's important to note that the first line under the menu title, FDISK Options, shows you the drive on which you are currently working (see Figure 7.12). From FDISK's perspective, the first physical drive is numbered 1, and subsequent drives are numbered 2, 3, 4, and so on. *Always be aware of which drive you are working on because FDISK is a powerful utility and can wipe out all the data on a given partition in an instant.* Take your time when using this utility. In fact, we recommend you unplug the phone, put the dog outside, and do some Zen breathing exercises before using FDISK. Option 5 lets you select the drive with which you want to work.

FIGURE 7.12

Select the menu option you want by typing the item's number and pressing Enter.

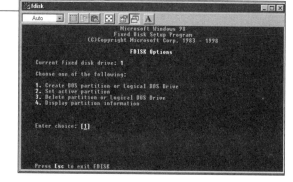

Option 1, Create DOS Partition or Logical DOS Drive, takes you to a secondary menu (see Figure 7.13). From this menu you can create a primary partition, an extended partition, or logical drives within an extended partition.

After the drive has been partitioned, you must format each partition in the drive. You do this using the FORMAT command with each drive letter you're using. To format the primary partition on drive 1, you would type **FORMAT C:** /**S** from the A: prompt.

The /S switch tells the FORMAT command to transfer the system files necessary to boot this partition from the boot floppy to the hard disk. You can perform this system file transfer to a primary partition that has already been formatted by using the command SYS *x*:\, where *x* is the drive letter of the primary drive. This is useful if you need to make a disk originally installed as a second drive the primary boot drive.

For other partitions on the new drive, you just issue the command FORMAT *x*: from the A: prompt, where *x* is the drive letter.

CAUTION

SPECIFY THE CORRECT DRIVE
Be careful to specify the correct drive because a format operation will wipe out any existing data on the drive.

After all the partitions are formatted and the system files transferred, the drive is bootable.

Preparing a Second Hard Drive

As mentioned earlier, the first physical drive is drive 1. Add a second physical and that new physical drive becomes drive 2. This second physical drive will be recognized by your system as the D drive. This has some significant ramifications.

For example, under Windows 95 or 98, say on drive 1 you have the primary/active C partition drive, as well as D and E created as logical drives within an extended partition. When you add drive 2, it becomes the D drive and all the logical drive letters on drive 1 get bumped. The D and E logical drives become E and F. Any logical drives created on drive 2's extended partition would then start with letter G. Yes, it's confusing, but you can't do anything about it. Add a third drive and it becomes E and all the logical drives get reshuffled again. Under Windows NT or 2000, this is fortunately not the case and you can assign drive letters to partitions manually through the operating system. If you have PartitionMagic, it comes with a utility called DriveMapper that lets you assign drive letters under Windows 95 or 98.

You would use FDISK on this second physical drive to create a primary partition and any extended partitions you wanted. Only the primary partition on the first drive needs to be made active.

Partition Tricks

A physical drive. must have at least a single primary partition, and it can (but doesn't have to) take up the entire drive. (We're talking about drives you can actually buy and install, not theoretical terabyte-size monster drives.) As discussed in the previous section, a drive is given a letter by the system and that letter is used for the primary partition on that drive. Extended partitions can be created and subdivided into logical drives, with each logical drive often referred to as a partition.

The main reasons to divide a drive into multiple partitions are to better organize the data and programs that reside there and to reduce the cluster size. A *cluster* is the smallest amount of disk space to which a file or portion thereof can be allocated. The larger the cluster size, the more wasted space on a drive. A file or part of a file might not take up all the space within a single cluster, with the remaining portion going unused. Multiply this by thousands of files, and you can have tens and even hundreds of megabytes of unused wasted space on a large hard drive, all depending on the partition's cluster size.

Smaller partitions often allow for smaller cluster sizes. To fine-tune disk usage and partition size, we use and recommend a partitioning utility by PowerQuest called PartitionMagic (http://www.powerquest.com/partitionmagic/index.html). It's not the only partition utility on the market, but it's the one we have extensive experience with.

With PartitionMagic, you can repartition a disk that already has data on it, resize partitions, and create new ones (assuming enough empty space exists for this to happen). You can also convert back and forth between a variety of file systems, say from FAT16 to FAT32 or to NTFS (Windows NT File System) or the Linux file system. It also can format a partition much more quickly than the DOS-based FORMAT utility.

PartitionMagic also helps you optimize the partition size so you lose the least amount of space due to cluster allocation waste. In addition, it comes with some utilities of its own that can help you move your data into your new drive, as discussed in the next section..

Moving into a New Drive

If the purpose of your disk upgrade is to replace an old drive with a new hard disk, you'll want to move all your data and programs to the new drive from the old one before removing the old drive entirely from the system. This means first installing the new drive as a second drive and copying the contents from the old to the new.

Migrating Hard Drive Contents

1. Install the new physical drive as drive 2.

2. Create a primary partition and (if desired) an extended partition on drive 2.

3. Format drive 2's primary partition with the system files using the command FORMAT D: /S, or if the drive has already been formatted, use the command SYS D: on drive 2.

4. Format any extended partition's logical drives on drive 2.

5. Boot the system normally and then copy the contents of drive 1 to drive 2. Methods to accomplish this are discussed in the next section.

6. Replace the old drive with the new drive. Change the SCSI ID or the EIDE master/slave jumper as necessary.

7. Restart the system using your bootable 3 1/2-inch disk and use FDISK to make the primary partition on the new drive active.

8. Restart the system, booting off the new drive.

The trick is getting all the files copied. Prior to Windows 95, this was a fairly simple process; however, with hidden files and folders and the like, it has become more complicated.

Cloning the Original Information

Xcopy32 (the enhanced version of the old DOS workhorse utility Xcopy), which comes with Windows 9x and Windows Me, can be used to copy a drive's contents from one disk to another. The command is
XCOPY32 C:*.* D: /E/C/H/R/K

In this command, C: is the old drive and D: is the new drive. The /E switch tells Xcopy32 to include all subdirectories, including empty ones. The /C switch tells it to continue copying even after an error, whereas /H tells it to copy hidden and system files. /R tells it to overwrite read-only files (which isn't necessary because you've just formatted the replacement disk but would be required if you performed this action multiple times on the same group of files), and the /K switch tells it to copy each file's attributes as well.

The result is that you end up with a copy of most of the files on your hard disk. Files in use at the time Xcopy32 is run won't be copied, such as the Windows swap file, but you'll get the bulk of the critical files. It's time-consuming, you must be sure you enter all the switches correctly. In addition, you have to do this for each logical drive on the physical disk to a corresponding partition on the destination disk. This approach also forces you to have identical partition structures on both drives.

Drive Cloning

Although Xcopy32 works, it is a slow process, must be repeated for each logical drive, and is prone to typographic errors when entering the command in a DOS window.

Another alternative is use a third-party utility, such as DriveCopy from PowerQuest (http://www.powerquest.com/drivecopy/index.html) or Ghost from Symantec (http://www.symantec.com/sabu/ghost/ghost_personal/).

These cloning utilities perform a sector-by-sector copy from one drive to the other, essentially cloning the drive instead of copying the files one by one. Both programs copy an entire hard disk in one fell swoop, and both are faster and less subject to error overall than the Xcopy32 method.

TIP

XCOPY FOR ALL OCCASIONS

There's a great article by M. David Stone on the uses of Xcopy to back up the contents of one drive onto another. It was written for Windows 95 but applies to later versions. See it online at http://www.primeconsulting.com/articles/wuon/v1i1pg5.htm.

Floppy Drive Replacements

One of the key steps in replacing the primary hard drive in a computer involves being able to boot the system from a 3 1/2-inch disk, which means the floppy drive must be in working condition.

If you're like us, you hardly ever use your floppy drive, let alone boot your system off one. Therefore, it's critical that you have a working, up-to-date start disk and that the floppy drive itself is in good working condition.

With disuse, the floppy drive is subject to dust contamination; therefore, you should test your floppy drive's condition before relying on it to boot your computer. Should your floppy drive go bad, swapping it out for a new drive is simple. The basic procedure is identical to replacing a hard drive. Unplug the old, plug in the new, and restart the system.

Note that the power connector for the floppy is smaller than that for an internal drive (hard drive, CD, or DVD) and is shaped differently (see Figure 7.14).

FIGURE 7.14

The power supply connector for a floppy drive is shown here above a standard power connector for an internal drive.

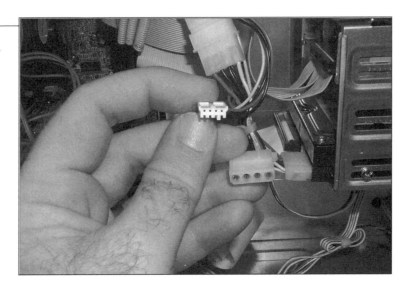

The flat ribbon cable for a floppy drive is unique in that a portion of the cable is twisted 180 degrees to the rest of the cable (see Figure 7.15).

Should you find that you need to replace your floppy drive, you can use the standard 3 1/2-inch 1.44MB floppy drive. You also might consider one of the higher-capacity drives, such as the Imation LS-120 SuperDisk (http://www.superdisk.com). A SuperDisk drive looks just like a regular 1.44MB floppy but will read and write both 1.44MB and 120MB floppy disks.

FIGURE 7.15

A floppy cable is a flat ribbon cable, but a portion of the cable is twisted 180 degrees.

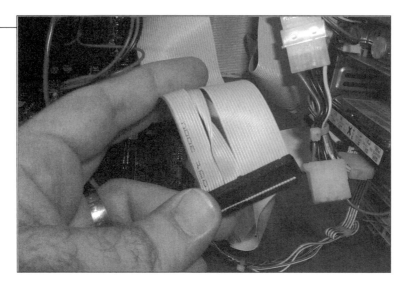

UPGRADING AN INTERNET CONNECTION

The Internet is your gateway to information; people; and a wide variety of important services, such as shopping, banking, travel, and entertainment. Streaming video and audio, whiteboarding, videoconferencing, and other dense real-time multimedia applications are exploding on the Internet. You can no longer afford to lag behind with a form of access that requires connecting repeatedly during the course of the day and that pokes along at 1/20 or less of the bandwidth of DSL and cable. In this chapter, you'll learn how to join the high-speed access party.

Upgrade Checklist

1. Do your homework.

2. Determine whether your PC supports the planned upgrade.

3. Determine whether you can perform the upgrade.

4. Order the access service.

5. Back up everything: data, operating system, mission-critical applications, and BIOS.

6. Test your startup disk.

7. Perform the upgrade.

8. Take good notes, and permanently file them in your system log when you're finished.

9. Update your inventory documentation to reflect the upgraded or newly added component.

Dial-Up Connections

According to The Yankee Group, residential, high-speed Internet access in the U.S. will be in demand by 3.3 million subscribers in the year 2000, with a predicted 16.6 million subscribers by 2004. Get ready to catch the wave.

We assume that many of you are currently using a dial-up modem to connect to the Internet at somewhere between 28.8 and 56.6Kbps. Also, most PCs leave the factory with dial-up networking (DUN) connectivity built in, if not already installed. So, although we won't spend any time on the issue of upgrading from an Internet-less PC to one using dial-up connectivity, here are some resources you will find useful on the topic of DUN:

■ **Windows 98 Dial-Up Networking Troubleshooter**—To use this tool, select Start, Help, click the Search tab, type `dial-up networking`, and press Enter. Next, choose the Dial-Up Networking Troubleshooter topic and click Display. Follow the instructions from there, as shown in Figure 8.1.

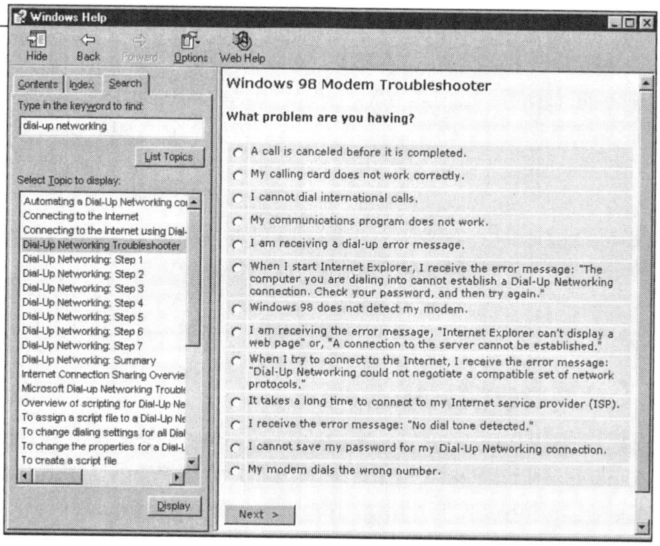

FIGURE 8.1

The Windows 98 Dial-Up Networking Troubleshooter, similar to a mini-expert system, walks you through a series of intelligent questions to help you unravel dial-up connectivity problems.

■ **56K.com**—Although initially founded to support various 56K modem standards, Les Jones has expanded his site to cover many other types of Internet access. Go to `http://56k.com`.

■ **Microsoft Knowledge Base article "Description of Internet Connection Sharing"**—Go to `http://support.microsoft.com/support/kb/articles/q234/8/15.asp`, which includes a description of ICS, in addition to links to other popular Knowledge Base articles on ICS.

■ **Tim Higgins's Sharing Your Internet Connection page**—Go to `http://www.timhiggins.com/ppd/sharing.htm`.

■ **Microsoft's public newsgroups**—Microsoft's public news server's address is `msnews.microsoft.com`. This server uses the NNTP protocol. Hundreds of newsgroups are supported, and they are moderated by Microsoft MVPs (Most

Valued Professionals), folks who have proven they really know the topic(s) for which they earned the MVP moniker. Check out `microsoft.public.win98.comm.dun` and `microsoft.public.win98.comm.modem` in particular.

- **WinFiles.com Windows 95/98 dial-up networking tools**—Go to `http://winfiles.cnet.com/apps/98/dialup-misc.html`.

- **NewApps.com's dial-up networking tools**—Go to `http://www.newapps.com/appstopics/Win_95_Dial-up_Networking_Tools_-_Misc.html`.

- **Freeware32.com's dial-up networking section**—Go to `http://freeware32.efront.com/file/dialup1.htm`.

TIP

EXTERNAL MODEMS ARE A MUST

If you're connecting to the Internet using a modem, always use an external model. To heck with the integration pedants who scoff at cables and devices that protrude from your PC. When it comes to system and modem troubleshooting, an external modem can't be beat. If we had a dollar for every time we had saved ourselves considerable frustration by simply turning an external modem's power switch off and back on instead of rebooting the PC, we'd be filthy rich and retired in the Caribbean by now.

High-Speed Connections

In this book, we consider any type of Internet connection that provides downstream bandwidth *greater than* 128Kbps to be high-speed. Of course, what's high-speed today will seem laughably lethargic tomorrow, but for now it's a practical demarcation. In Table 8.1, we review modern access technologies and compare them to the aging but dogged standards (see the first and second row) of 56Kbps dial-up and 128Kbps ISDN. In the sections that follow, we describe in more detail each technology and how to go about upgrading it.

Table 8.1 Comparison of High-Speed Internet Connections

Type of Connection[3]	Downstream Bandwidth (Kbps)[1]	Upstream Bandwidth (Kbps)[1]	Install Cost[6]	Equipment Cost[7]	Monthly Cost[5]
56K dial-up[2]	56	34	$38[8]	$147[9]	$22[10]
ISDN[2]	64–128	64–128	$100–$300*	$200–$350	$19–$50*

Type of Connection[3]	Downstream Bandwidth (Kbps)[1]	Upstream Bandwidth (Kbps)[1]	Install Cost[6]	Equipment Cost[7]	Monthly Cost[5]
Cable	384–36,000[11]	128–4,000	up to $175*	Up to $349[12]*	$39–$49*
DirecPC	400	34	$300[13]	$215–$240[14]	$132[15]
DSL[4]	128–6,100	16–1,544	$100–$500*	Modem up to $610*	$39–$840*
DSL (Lee's actual)[4]	768	128	$150[16]	$25–$50[17]	$55[18]
DSL (T.J.'s actual)[4]	988	93	$199	$25–$50[19]	$59[20]

1. For ease of comparison, all bandwidth values are shown in Kbps; to convert to Mbps, divide by 1,000; for example, a downstream rate for DSL shown as 6,100Kbps is equal to 6.1Mbps.

2. The 56K dial-up and ISDN rows are shown for comparison purposes only (56Kbps and 128Kbps are not considered high-speed connections in this analysis).

3. The types are shown in alphabetical order.

4. The DSL rows show potential downstream rates for xDSL types except RADSL, UDSL, and VDSL, which are not readily available at this time (UDSL is only a proposal).

5. In the Monthly Cost column, prices exclude the cost of an ISP unless otherwise noted.

6. In the Install Cost column, we use a value of your time at $75.00/hour; see footnotes for specific time estimates when you would be performing a self-install.

7. Your costs may vary either due to regional factors or for purely competitive reasons, so carefully research all potential access service providers in your area.

8. We estimate this installation will take one-half hour.

9. Equipment: modem. On April 2, 2000, the three top-selling 56K external modems at NECX Direct had an average price of $147 ($84.95, $241.95, and $113.95).

10. The cost of a basic-service residential phone line in Hermosa Beach, California, is $21.95/month.

11. In the real world where the rubber meets the road, high-end cable downstream bandwidth is around 4Mbps. The 36Mbps value cited here is not currently implemented in any consumer market; it would require a sophisticated modulation technique called quadrature amplitude modulation (QAM).

12. Equipment: (1) NIC; (2) lease/buy a modem.

13. We estimate this installation will take four hours.

14. Equipment: (1) NIC @ $25–$50; (2) satellite dish, modem, and software @ $150; (3) DIY install kit @ $40. Based on information from InfoDish at http://www.infodish.com. Hughes says you can either go to a local dealer or buy direct online (see http://www.direcpc.com/consumer/buy/usa.html#direct). A PC Connection sales representative told us (April 2, 2000) that they no longer support the Hughes DirecPC product line and steered us to "any local retailer." The link to CDW data for Hughes appears permanently dysfunctional, and Hughes is not listed on CDW's Shop By Brand page.

15. DirecPC service plan pricing: $20/month for 25 hours, $35/month for 100 hours, or $110/month for 200 hours. The table shows the cost of the 200-hour plan at $110 plus the cost of the phone line at $22. For more information, see `http://www.direcpc.com/consumer/cost/cost.html`.

16. We estimate this installation will take two hours in a self-install scenario. (This is how long it took Lee to perform his DSL setup using GTE's self-install kit.)

17. Equipment: (1) NIC @ $25–$50; (2) free modem.

18. GTE's Bronze+ program (768/128Kbps) is $32.50, plus the cost of the phone line @ $22.

19. Equipment: (1) NIC @ $25–$50; (2) modem included in the installation fee.

20. PacBell's basic DSL program (1500/128Kbps) is $39.95, plus the cost of the phone line @ $19.

* Source: PC Magazine, April 22, 1999.

Cable

If your local cable TV provider supports Internet connectivity, great; if not, move along to another section because there's nothing you can do to get your provider to move any more quickly. Well, you could write some letters and beg, but market forces of epic proportions are at work here, so if a connection isn't available in your area today, select another technology that is available for you today.

An Internet connection between your PC and your cable provider is relatively simple. You install a network interface card and connect it to a cable modem. Cable providers typically offer either internal PCI-based modems or external USB-based modems. The cable modem connects to your local neighborhood's cable TV network (officially called a *hybrid fiber/coax (HFC)* network). From there, signals travel upstream and eventually wind their way to your cable company's plant and then on to the Internet. You might have heard that a cable connection "gets slower" when more of your neighbors use the Internet at a particular time. That's true, and it's due to the nature of the cable TV network. It's called a *broadband* network, in which all the bandwidth is divided among the number of currently active nodes (your PC represents one such node).

Leggo My PC!

Many of our professional colleagues were very early adopters of cable and DSL access, bless them. We've heard only horror stories from them, primarily about botched installations. The common theme was, "Don't let a provider's technician touch your PC. Sign a waiver if you have to; just don't let an outsider touch your PC." The logic being that the technician who rolls on out to your home or office might not yet be well trained in PCs and Internet connectivity. If they are, that's great, but what if they aren't? It'll be too late after you figure that out. We'll grant you that the situation can vary wildly among providers, and certainly from one technician to another. However, in the meantime, the caveat remains: Get a self-install kit if at all possible.

See the section "Order and Installation Checklist" later in this chapter for instructions on how to go about ordering, installing, configuring, optimizing, and testing a high-speed Internet connection.

Table 8.2 summarizes the pros and cons of cable for Internet access.

Table 8.2 Cable Internet Connection Pros and Cons

Pros/Cons (+/-)	Cable
+	You are always connected.
+	Your phone line isn't tied up while you're online (which it is for dial-up but not DSL).
-	You are sharing bandwidth with the other cable customers in your neighborhood, so if that network is busy, your bandwidth suffers.
-	As of the time of this writing, you don't have a choice as to your ISP; it's your CATV provider.

Here are some good online resources on cable connectivity:

- **Cable Modem Help (**`http://www.cablemodemhelp.com`**)**—A great collection of FAQs that you can search or browse by category in a list format. The site also offers a mailing list.

- **Cable Modem Info Center (**`http://www.cabledatacomnews.com`**)**—Includes white papers, an info center, FAQs, ISP and integrator lists, links, market statistics, and more.

- **CATV CyberLab (**`http://www.catv.org`**)**—"An ongoing market research study conducted by GecKo Research & Publishing" that aims to provide free market intelligence and news about the cable industry.

- **Rolf Östergaard's Cable-Modems.Org site (**`http://www.cable-modems.org`**)**—Offers a tutorial, FAQs, articles, suggested books, a modem photo gallery, and tools.

- `comp.dcom.modems.cable`—A public newsgroup.

- **56K.com**—Located at `http://56k.com`.

Digital Subscriber Line (DSL)

DSL is your best bet for a low-cost, convenient, always-on connection. Your first step along the DSL path is to call your local telephone company's DSL Internet connectivity division and request a line test. The result of the test (which might take several days or even longer) is a formal declaration by the phone company of whether or not your phone number is eligible for DSL. The test should be free. If you're eligible, continue by following the steps outlined in the upcoming section, "Order and Installation Checklist."

NOTE

CABLE ACCESS PREDICTED TO DECLINE FROM 80% TO 42% PENETRATION IN FIVE YEARS

In a previously cited study by The Yankee Group, research shows that out of a U.S. installed base of 1.4 million customers, about 80% were using cable modems to connect to the Internet. But the study predicts cable dropping to 42% by the end of 2004 in response to fierce competition by the telcos and their DSL offerings.

DSL uses existing telephone wiring to transmit digital signals from your PC to the telephone company. This use of a digital signal puts the "digital" in "DSL." Remember that "modem" is shorthand for "modulator/demodulator." With a traditional dial-up modem, digital signals from your PC are converted to analog for transmission along the phone line in audio form; and incoming downstream signals get converted by the modem from analog back to digital for the PC to process. Although you'll often see the term "DSL modem," it really isn't a modem—it's a terminal adapter; no digital-to-analog conversion is taking place. The same technical note applies to the phrase "cable modem." The device does provide signal modulation/demodulation functions, but it also acts as a hub, an encryptor, a network bridge, and a tuner, among others. Throughout this book, we use the terms "DSL modem" and "cable modem" for convenience.

Check Your DSL Eligibility

Browse to the 2Wire DSL Resource Center at http://www.2wire.com and click the 2Wire DSL Lookup link. Enter your phone number and address, and the site reports whether your local phone company has DSL equipment installed in your area. Enter your address and it will even tell you how far you are from the nearest Central Office. The site also provides a breakdown by various DSL types; quick facts about DSL connections; how DSL compares to other access technologies such as ISDN, cable, and satellite access; and a comprehensive glossary of telecommunications terms. If this service indicates you that don't appear to be eligible, you should still confirm this with your phone company.

Table 8.3 summarizes the pros and cons of a DSL connection.

Table 8.3   DSL Internet Connection Pros and Cons

Pros/Cons (+/-)	DSL
+	You are always connected.
+	You are not sharing bandwidth with anyone else.
+	A single phone line using DSL can provide simultaneous voice and data transmission. This is more than just a convenience; it enables you to eliminate a superfluous second phone line.
-	Although copper phone wire is ubiquitous in this country, you must be within approximately 20,000 feet (3.8 miles) of the nearest phone company Central Office (CO) to be eligible for this service. The farther you are "as the wire goes" from the CO, the slower your speed will be.

Here are some good online resources about DSL access:

- **The DSLReports site** (`http://www.dslreports.com`)—Offers message boards, free tests and tools, speed tweaks, and a plentiful set of FAQs. We discuss this robust site throughout this chapter.

- **The ADSL Forum site** (`http://www.adsl.com`)—Includes FAQs, technical and market information, vendor lists, a press room, an events calendar, and a members-only section.

- `comp.dcom.xdsl`—A public newsgroup.

- **Paradyne Corporation's** *The DSL Sourcebook, 2nd Edition* (`http://www.paradyne.com/sourcebook_offer/`)—Available in PDF format for downloading and viewing offline and as HTML for online viewing. It is a technical treatise on DSL; its coverage ranges from the copper wire infrastructure on up to emerging services and applications for DSL.

- **56K.com**—Located at `http://56k.com`.

Our DSL Order Fiascoes

We both had difficulties ordering DSL. What saved us was our diligence in following our own guidelines for dealing with technical support (see Chapter 24, "Dealing with Technical Support").

T.J. got stuck in the infamous "a week or 10 days" whirlpool with his telco PacBell. Whenever someone tells you "a week or 10 days," what they usually leave out is that it's a week or 10 days—from whenever you ask. After several weeks hanging out in the whirlpool, he got a scheduled install date. Then, disaster struck. PacBell called to tell him that DSL won't work reliably in his area and they're checking into alternatives and he should hear from them, oh, in a week or 10 days. Half an hour later he got a call from the DSL field technician who told him he's on his way over to perform the install. Alice, having fallen through the looking-glass, could not have been more confused. The technician showed up and the actual install was anticlimatic. He fiddled with the wall plug so that one phone line ran to the terminal adapter (DSL modem) and one to an actual phone; T.J. added a second network interface card himself; they plugged everything in; and there he was, on the Internet—no dialing; just an addictive "always on" connection. It was two months from T.J.'s initial order to the real thing.

Lee's trek into the miasma of DSL began officially on March 22, 1999. It took a total of 16 phone calls (totaling 2.5 hours) over a 1-year period to get the service instantiated. (For about 3 or 4 months during the summer of 1999, Lee gave up on GTE and DSL altogether in disgust, but then started the campaign up again in the fall.)

GTE didn't keep its promise to follow up in 4 to 7 business days regarding the result of a free line test; instead it took them 10 weeks. (Note: He's only 1,000 feet from the Central Office; it's literally 20 houses down the block.) During the fall, GTE's DSL division sent him email about a free modem and installation. On the first call he made about that offer, the representative told him DSL was not available for his line. He used the tried-and-true technique of calling back a second time, got a different rep, and was told he *did* qualify. The order was officially underway, but he'd have to wait 4 to 6 weeks to get an installation appointment.

Two months later, a field engineer left voice mail instructing him to call a special phone number and cite a reference number. When he called this number, he heard a conversation among some GTE representatives, but they couldn't hear him. He was silently—and unwillingly—eavesdropping on a conference call about an irate customer's DSL problems. This is a true story!

Long story short, after several more calls and transfers, Earl (not his real name) answered, listened patiently to Lee's whole story, apologized, and promised to set things right. And he did, by offering the option of a field rep or a self-install kit through the mail. Lee chose the latter, and the self-install kit arrived on March 7, 2000. For Lee, installing the kit and activating the DSL service was as anticlimactic as it was for T.J. But they'll both tell you that there's no turning back.

To read all the gory details (many we omitted here in the interest of space), T.J. and Lee's *The Naked PC* articles on their DSL order fiascoes are available at these pages:

- *Digital Subscriber Line: It Rocks!*
  (http://www.thenakedpc.com/articles/v02/21/0221-02.html)

- *Digital Subscriber Line: The Horror, Part 1* (http://www.thenakedpc.com/
  articles/v03/06/0306-03.html)

- *Digital Subscriber Line: The Ecstasy, Part 2* (http://www.thenakedpc.com/
  articles/v03/07/0307-02.html)

DirecPC

With DirecPC access, your PC communicates upstream via a traditional phone line using analog signals and a dial-up modem. Your upstream requests eventually wind their way to the DirecPC satellite, which beams the data down where it is picked up by your satellite dish. If you're interested in this service, continue by following the steps outlined in the upcoming section, "Order and Installation Checklist."

Table 8.4 summarizes the pros and cons of a DirecPC connection.

Table 8.4   DirecPC Internet Connection Pros and Cons

Pros/Cons (+/-)	DirecPC
+	Might be the only high-speed, downstream game in town in some areas.
+	You are not sharing bandwidth with anyone else.
+	You are always connected for downstream (note that you are not always connected for upstream, which uses standard dial-up).
-	You must have an unobstructed line of sight to the south.
-	Fair Access Policy (FAP). This is a highly controversial choke-collar placed on subscribers. FAP's purported purpose is to "prevent abusive consumption of bandwidth by a handful of users" by monitoring downstream activity and comparing it to metrics established by what Hughes calls a "historical, statistical analysis of its user base." We cringe at the very idea. Traffic on the DirecPC public newsgroup is strongly opposed to the FAP.
-	The installation can be very technical, tedious, and somewhat physical. For example, the itemized list of a DirecPC Installation Kit: (1) 25 ft. cable with Weatherproof F type connectors; (1) 75 ft. cable with Weatherproof F type connectors; (1) 30 ft. #8 type grounding wire; (8) cable clips; (1) tube of silicon sealant; (1) compass; (6) alligator clips; (1) ground clamp; (1) single coax ground clamp; (1) hex nut 1/4-20 CF; (1) washer 1/4 external tooth; and (1) die cut corrugated container.
-	A Pentium 200 processor is required.
-	You're usually paying for two services: the DirecPC connection for downstream and another ISP for your upstream dial-up connection.

Here are some good online resources on the subject of DirecPC:

- `alt.satellite.direcpc`—A public newsgroup. (Warning: Many of this group's frequent participants are profoundly upset with Hughes and will go to great lengths to convince you not to buy DirecPC or its related products/services. You might encounter some colorful, emotionally charged language here.)

- `http://www.direcpc.com` **and** `http://www.direcduo.com`—These sites provide the manufacturer's point of view from DirecPC and DirecDuo, respectively.

- **The Unofficial DirecPC page** (`http://www.wojo.com/direcpc/`)—Describes itself as "the good, the bad, and the ugly about Hughes Networks DirecPC and DirecDuo." The site includes tips and tricks, FAQs, software, speed reports, and links.

- **56K.com**—Located at `http://56k.com`.

Order and Installation Checklist

Regardless of whether you order DSL, cable, or DirecPC service, the following checklist will help you complete the ordering and installation process:

1. Place the order.

   When you place your order, taking good notes is the key. For more information about dealing with technical support or customer service personnel over the phone, see Chapter 24.

2. Diligently track the order.

   Get a due date for everything the service provider is going to do, and follow up on them regularly.

3. Study your provider's system requirements, and meet them.

4. Record your current access settings.

   One simple way to record your current access settings is to store screen shots in a word processing document. Create a new WordPad or Word document, run through your dial-up connectoid's Properties dialog box, take screen shots of each tab in the dialog box (Alt+Print Scrn copies the desktop's current window to the Clipboard), and paste each shot into the document one after the other. Repeat the process for your email client settings and your modem settings. Save the document in a safe place; in our office, we use a path and filename structure like this: `D:\Data\Configuration\<PC name>\<PC name> <description>.doc`—for example, `D:\Data\Configuration\UFO\UFO GTE Connectoid Settings.doc`.

5. Make a full data backup.

6. (Optional) Clone your production partition.

   For more information on cloning partitions, see Chapter 22, "Managing Disk Partitions."

7. Disable Internet Connection Sharing if it's installed and enabled.

   If your Windows operating system supports ICS and it is currently installed and enabled, we recommend you temporarily disable it before setting up your new Internet connection—just to minimize the number of possible conflicts. To temporarily disable ICS on the Connection Sharing computer (also known as the host computer), do the following: Start Control Panel, run the Internet Connections applet, click the Connections tab, click the Sharing button, clear the Enable Internet Connection Sharing checkbox, click OK, and click OK again.

8. Endure your provider's onsite install, or perform a self-install.

9. Uninstall any superfluous dial-up devices.

10. Test and optimize your connection.

    The exact names of the specific settings you'll need to calibrate vary from one browser or email client to another. However, you'll need to make these changes only once. You must tell your browser to never dial a connection and your email client to use the LAN to connect. Do the following:

    ▪ In Microsoft Internet Explorer 5, choose Tools, Internet Options, Connections, Never Dial a Connection, OK.

    ▪ In Outlook 98/2000, choose Tools, Services, select your Internet email account, Properties, Connection, Connect Using My Local Area Network (LAN), OK. Then, close and restart Outlook.

    See this chapter's "Measuring Your True Connection Speed" section for information on testing and improving your high-speed connection.

11. Install and test a personal firewall.

    A high-speed connection usually—but not always—gives you a static IP address. This makes you more of a target for hackers, necessitating a firewall. (We recommend a firewall for anyone, whether your IP address is static or dynamic, and regardless of your connection type or speed.) For more information on personal firewalls, see this chapter's section "Protecting Your PC with a Personal Firewall."

12. Cancel any superfluous phone lines.

13. (Optional) If a week goes by with satisfactory performance, you can delete the clone of your production partition.

Measuring Your True Connection Speed

Your downstream channel's theoretical maximum bandwidth is one thing, and its effective bandwidth is another. If you want to see exactly how fast—or slow—your connection really is, here's how to do so:

1. Look at your service agreement and see which downstream rate you're paying for.

2. Don't use a Web browser to test download throughput; use an FTP client instead.

   Due to the very nature of the HTTP protocol, a Web browser doesn't maintain a continuous connection throughout the entire process of downloading a file. You should use an FTP client for this test (this is true for any large file downloads). Free FTP clients are ubiquitous. Try DaveCentral (`http://www.davecentral.com`) or Freeware 32.com (`http://freeware32.efront.com`).

TIP

WHO YOU GONNA FTP? WS_FTP PRO!

We have been using Ipswitch, Inc.'s WS_FTP Pro FTP client for years, and recommend it highly. You can download a full-featured evaluation copy (30-day trial period) from `http://www.ipswitch.com`. After that, if you're as happy as we predict you'll be, it's a worthwhile $30 (street).

3. Download a medium-size file or larger; that is, at least 5MB.

4. If your ISP sports an anonymous FTP site, it contains at least one large file you can download, and it's not too many hops away, this might be an ideal testing ground. Otherwise, you'll need to poke around until you find a reasonably "local" FTP server that isn't throttled down, and conduct your tests with it consistently.

5. Perform more than one download test.

   For a reasonable average (note we didn't say *reliable*, just *reasonable*), download the exact same file from the same FTP site three times. Perform one download during peak hours, the second during off-peak hours that same day, and then the third on the next day during peak hours. Then, average the three.

An excellent tool is available on the DSLReports Web site for testing your connection's speed both upstream and downstream. (Thanks to *The Naked PC* subscriber Jerry Newman for pointing us to this Web site.) Furthermore, this site contains plentiful, well-documented tips on how to optimize your settings.

DSLreports' speed test link is at `http://www.dslreports.com/doconcern`, as shown in Figure 8.2.

FIGURE 8.2

The DSLreports speed test reports upstream and downstream bandwidth.

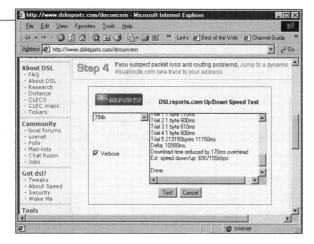

The tips link is at `http://www.dslreports.com/tweaks` (in the Jump to control, select your operating system and then click the Show button).

After performing the tests countless times on multiple DSL connections, and reading and applying the tweaks, we recommend you follow these steps:

1. Because this involves updating your Registry, all the usual caveats about editing the Registry apply. Before doing anything else, you should check whether your system is already optimized in regard to the Registry DefaultRcvWindow setting. Click Start, choose Run, type **regedit**, and press Enter. Then, browse to the key `HKEY_LOCAL_MACHINE\System\CurrentControlSet\Services\VxD\MSTCP` and see whether a value named `DefaultRcvWindow` exists. If not, your system is not yet optimized; if such a key does exist, note its setting, but leave it alone for now. Close the Registry Editor.

2. Close all running applications.

3. Start your browser and clear its cache. For Internet Explorer 5, select Tools, Internet Options, click the Delete Files button, and then click OK.

4. Close your browser and then reopen it to the speed test link.

5. Follow their steps 1–4 (use the Verbose test mode), remember to select the nearest download speed from the speed drop-down control, click the Test button, and wait for the test to finish. When we initially tested this tool, it took about 30 seconds on a 768/128Kbps downstream/upstream DSL connection.

Our first-time, unoptimized test results were 391/121Kbps (downstream/upstream). That was 50% slower on the downstream side than what one of us was paying for, and certainly suboptimal. So, we followed their suggestions about the `DefaultRcvWindow` setting.

6. They provide ready-to-go REG files that will do the work for you. See the table in the middle of the Windows tweaks page. We used the Medium (32KB) REG file for Windows 98—`Rwin98-m.reg`. The Registry hack involves simply increasing your PC's TCP receive window. This parameter tells the sender (an upstream source such as a Web or FTP server) how many bytes it can send to the receiver (your PC) before requiring an acknowledgment; the larger the TCP receive window value, the faster your downstream speed, to a point.

7. After you download the REG file, just double-click it and when prompted with `Are you sure you want to add the information in <path>\<filename>.reg to the registry?`, click Yes. Figure 8.3 shows the affected portion of the Registry.

FIGURE 8.3

The Registry's `DefaultRcvWind ow` value belongs to the key `HKEY_LOCAL_MAC HINE\System\ CurrentControl Set\Services\ VxD\MSTCP`.

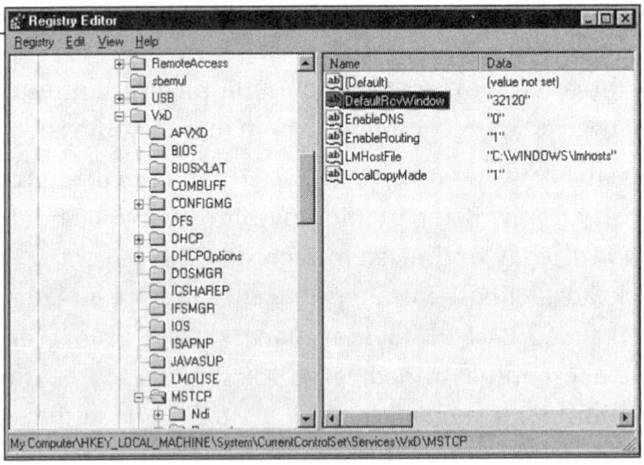

8. Restart your PC. *This is critical!*

9. If you really want to be meticulous, clear your browser's cache and restart it clean (as described earlier). Now go to the speed test link and perform the test again.

Our second-time test results were 624/82Kbps. On the downstream side, that's a 1.6× improvement. As the famous *Top Gun* line goes, "I feel the need, the

need for speed!" We continued to run the tests daily
by removing the
`DefaultRcvWindow` value,
rebooting, retesting, then
applying the
`DefaultRcvWindow` setting
again, rebooting, retesting...
you get the picture. Our
results consistently averaged
680Kbps downstream opti-
mized and around 390Kbps
unoptimized. We also cross-
checked the DSLreports test
results by downloading the
same large file with an FTP
client, as described earlier.

ANOTHER FINE MESS
**MICROSOFT KNOWLEDGE BASE
ARTICLE ABOUT ICS AND HIGH-
BANDWIDTH DEVICES**

Microsoft has published a useful article titled "Slow
Transfer Rates with ICS and High-Bandwidth
Devices"
(`http://support.microsoft.com/support/
kb/articles/q230/1/16.asp`). In effect, it sug-
gests a Registry hack in a case in which an ICS host
PC is experiencing slow transfer rates. The hack is to
delete the value `HKEY_LOCAL_MACHINE\System\
CurrentControlSet\Services\ICSharing\
Settings\General\InternetMTU`, but only if it
is *not* a dial-up connection. ■

Protecting Your PC with a Personal Firewall

You should be running a personal firewall no matter how you connect to the
Internet. Until now, you might have felt that because your ISP assigns you an IP
address dynamically and that address changes from one connection session to
another, you're safe from outside attack. Wrong. While it's technically true that an
attacker's assault on any PC is easier if the target PC's IP address is static (the same
from one connection to another), the sophistication and volume of these assaults is
growing at an astounding rate. You would be imprudent to not protect yourself.

Think of it this way: Unless you live in a remote, rural area or a very small and
insular town, you don't leave your car or home unlocked. Why leave your PC
unlocked every time you connect to the Internet? We predict—along with plenty of
other pundits lined up around the block—that personal firewall software will be
built right in to future operating systems. Furthermore, we predict that a personal
firewall utility will be configured out of the box to be very aggressive (as in, protecting your PC), just as any modern antivirus application's options are set aggressively
right out of the box.

In the meantime, several popular products are available, as of the time of this writing, that will do a good job protecting your PC while you're connected to the
Internet.

TIP

EXCUSE ME, BUT YOUR PORT 139 IS WIDE OPEN

By following these steps, you can test for and, if necessary, close any access the Internet has to your PC's shared devices (hard disks and printers). A port is the final recipient to which an Internet packet is addressed, but the recipient isn't a person—it's a service. Frequently provided services, such as FTP, SMTP email, Web (HTTP), NetBIOS session, and so forth, each have standard numbers; for example, a NetBIOS session port is usually port 139. For more information about ports, see `http://grc.com/su-ports.htm`.

1. Visit Steve Gibson's Shields UP! Web page at `http://grc.com`. Click the Shields UP! link and click the Test My Shields! button. When that test is complete, click the Probe My Ports! button. You might be shocked to see that your PC's bathrobe is open.

2. If the tests find any open holes in your PC's security space, the accompanying commentary will include recommendations on what to do. In particular, we strongly encourage you to read Steve's quintessential guides to proper network component configuration—*Network Bondage* (`http://grc.com/su-bondage.htm`) and *Network Discipline for Windows 9x* (`http://grc.com/su-rebinding9x.htm`). A page for Windows NT users is also available. Steve's thorough, friendly advice on proper network component settings can't be beat.

   The most common PC security gaffe is to leave network services (such as file and printer sharing, client for Microsoft networks, and so on) turned on for one or more of your TCP/IP protocol instances, thereby exposing all your shared devices to anyone who can figure out your PC's IP address. If you think that password-securing your shared devices is adequate, think again. A determined hacker will brute-force crack your passwords. Why put yourself at risk when following Steve's recommendations is so well-documented, and when running a personal firewall is so easy?

3. If your PC's port 139 is open, here's how to minimize external access to your shared devices, short of installing a personal firewall (more on that subject later in this chapter). *Remember, this is documented for you in Steve's detailed FAQ, so we're boiling this way down here and urge you to study his FAQ first.* Note that our minimalist steps assume you've already installed NetBEUI and that you are not using TCP/IP for a local area network; again, please read Steve's FAQ before proceeding.

4. Right-click the Network Neighborhood desktop icon and choose Properties.

5. Locate and select the TCP/IP protocol instance that's bound to the network card to which your high-speed modem connects. In Figure 8.4, the Linksys LNE100TX Fast Ethernet Adapter is connected to the high-speed modem; the `TCP/IP ->` segment indicates the binding between TCP/IP and the network card.

FIGURE 8.4

Use the Network
dialog box to
identify the
TCP/IP-to-
network adapter
binding (the
same network
card to which
your high-speed
modem is con-
nected).

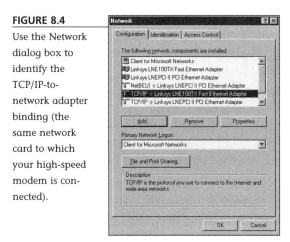

6. Click the Properties button, click the Bindings tab, and ensure that none of the network component checkboxes are checked for this TCP/IP protocol instance (see Figure
8.5). Repeat this process of clearing *all* network component bindings from *all* other
TCP/IP instances listed in Network Neighborhood. When you're finished, click Yes at
the prompt to restart your computer.

FIGURE 8.5

Clear all the net-
work compo-
nents from the
TCP/IP protocol's
bindings.

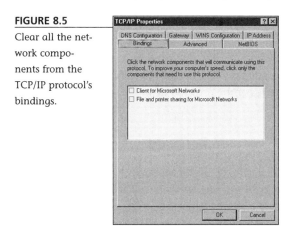

7. Return to the Shields UP! page and test your PC's vulnerability again. At this point,
your shared devices should no longer be accessible to the outside world. Nonetheless,
we strongly recommend you next install a personal firewall.

ZoneAlarm 2.0

Zone Labs' ZoneAlarm is free for personal and nonprofit use; business and professional customers pay an incredibly reasonable $19.95. You can download it at `http://www.zonealarm.com`. Don't shy away because it's free. This is an excellent program, and we highly recommend it.

When you install it, ZoneAlarm goes to work on your behalf right away. It automatically blocks all attempts by outside forces to connect to your PC. It also blocks all attempts by applications running on your own PC to communicate—without your knowledge—over the Internet or over your local network (if you have one). This includes blocking your cable neighbors' access to any shared devices on your network.

When it detects suspicious incoming or outbound traffic, ZoneAlarm displays a message box with the application's filename and which resource it is attempting to access (local network or Internet), and gives you several options (see Figure 8.6). Clicking the Yes button enables this particular stream of traffic to proceed, and clicking No stops it cold. If you want ZoneAlarm to remember to handle this event for this particular application the same way every time it occurs, check the handy Remember the Answer Each Time I Use This Program checkbox. Note that the Remember checkbox is not turned on by default; otherwise, you might unintentionally turn off onscreen notification of other suspicious traffic from this same application. This is an example of savvy customer-based thinking on Zone Labs' part.

In the course of a routine day, you probably use all the applications that require Internet access, at which point ZoneAlarm will be configured for ongoing use. You might be surprised by how many tools you use that involve accessing the Internet! Any other applications you use less often can be granted access (or not) on a case-by-case basis.

TIP

LOGGING INTRUDER ALERTS

ZoneAlarm versions prior to 2.1.7 do not support alert logging; version 2.1.7 and beyond does. However, ZoneAlarm doesn't turn on logging by default. You definitely want this feature on, so click the Alerts button and then check the Log alerts to a text file checkbox. Also note that the log file has a nonstandard extension of .txt; most log files have a .log extension. Look for the file `C:\Windows\Internet Logs\ZALog.txt`.

FIGURE 8.6

ZoneAlarm's "traffic sniffer" message box gives you a range of options for handling suspicious inbound or outbound traffic. Here it captured the first instance of Norton AntiVirus Live Update, which we added to this PC's "good guys" list.

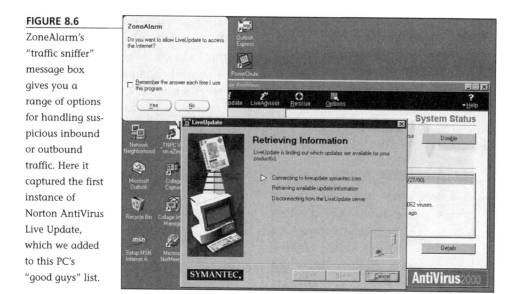

Figure 8.7 shows how ZoneAlarm reacts to an intruder.

FIGURE 8.7

ZoneAlarm's intruder alert message box tells you which of your ports was assaulted, the originating IP address, and the time of the intrusion.

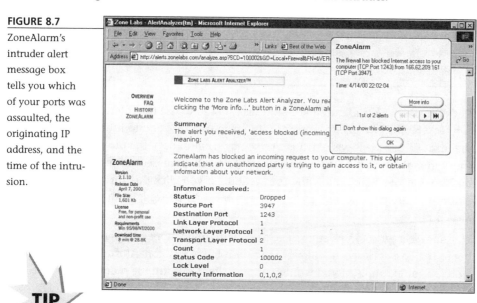

TIP

START OUT CAUTIOUS

When you first configure ZoneAlarm, we recommend you *not* ask it to remember the settings for a specific application. Instead, let it alert you to every infraction so you can observe all your applications' patterns. After a few days, you'll have enough information to properly judge whether it's okay to permanently set an application to connect to the Internet without alerting you each time.

If you want to open up the hood and configure ZoneAlarm directly, double-click its icon in the system tray. We leave it to the reader to explore the plethora of settings and choices. Programs is the most important feature to be aware of. (This is where you can review and change the settings you implement when responding to ZoneAlarm's message box alerts.) We feel all the other settings are appropriate for use without modification, although of course, we encourage you to use your own discretion. As you can see in Figure 8.8, ZoneAlarm has a somewhat unusual user interface.

FIGURE 8.8

ZoneAlarm's Programs panel gives you complete control over each application's access to the Internet.

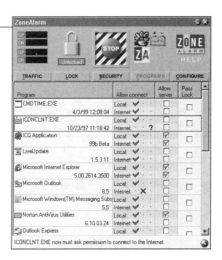

Click Programs to configure the programs allowed to use the Internet. The Allow connect column reveals two rows of settings marked Local and Internet. If you click the first of three positions (each is marked by a small dot), the program places a check to indicate "allow the connection." If you click the second position, it places an X to indicate "don't allow the connection." If you click the third position, it places a ? here to indicate "ask user every time." As we said, it's an unusual interface, but it works.

The Allow server settings let you decide which applications can perform server functions. The Pass lock setting allows a program to bypass ZoneAlarm's Automatic Lock feature—for example, if you wanted an FTP client to continue a download even though you activated the lock.

NOTE

OTHER PERSONAL FIREWALLS

We unhesitatingly recommend ZoneAlarm as a personal firewall, but other competitors do exist. If you're curious, check out Norton Internet Security 2000 (http://www.symantec.com) and BlackICE Defender (http://www.networkice.com).

9

ADDING A NETWORK

Somewhere in the neighborhood of 15–20 million homes in the United States have more than one PC, primed for a networking solution. Not to mention the millions of PCs in small businesses everywhere. (There were 460 million PCs in use worldwide in 1998.) We are fast becoming a multi-PC culture, and easy interoperability between them will eventually be built in and taken for granted just like a phone's dial tone. In the meantime, you'll have to build your own local area network and in so doing choose among competing architectures. But the upside is that you'll be able to share printers, files, and Internet access among several PCs.

Upgrade Checklist

1. Do your homework.

2. Determine whether your PC supports the planned upgrade.

3. Determine whether you can perform the upgrade.

4. Purchase or acquire the component.

5. Organize your tools and workspace. See Chapter 3, "Things You Need."

6. If you're installing a peripheral card to instantiate your network, back up everything: data, operating system, mission-critical applications, and BIOS settings. Otherwise, skip this step.

7. If you're installing a peripheral card to instantiate your network, test your startup disk. Otherwise, skip this step.

8. Perform the upgrade.

9. Take good notes, and permanently file them in your system log when you're finished.

10. Update your inventory documentation to reflect the upgraded or newly added component.

Network Architectures

Network architectures come in five flavors:

- Direct cable connection

- Ethernet

- Phone-line

- Power-line

- Wireless

Table 9.1 outlines how each of these LAN architectures compare on several key dimensions. No one implementation is the clear winner for every situation; instead, you must evaluate the physical environment in which your LAN will operate, whether you own or rent the space, how long you plan to operate there, and what your LAN expansion plans are. Later in this section, we cover each of these five implementations in detail.

Table 9.1   Comparison of Networking Architectures

	Direct Cable[1]	**Ethernet**	**Phone-Line**	**Power-Line**	**HomeRF**[2]
Transmission rate (Mbps)	12 (USB)[3]	10, 100, 1000	1 (HomePNA 1.0), 10 (HomePNA 2.0)	0.350	1.6
Transmission distance (feet)[4]	16 (USB)	328 (twisted-pair) 607 (coax)[5]	500 (varies by vendor)[6]	Varies	150[7]
Physical impact[8]	None	Potentially high	Potentially high if you don't have phone jacks where all the PCs are	None	None
Cost (2 PCs)	$80[9]	$113[10]	$100[11]	$80[12]	$238[13]
Ease of install[14,15]	Very easy	Moderately	Moderately difficult	Moderately easy	Varies from moderately easy to moderately difficult

Table 9.1 continued

	Direct Cable[1]	Ethernet	Phone-Line	Power-Line	HomeRF[2]
Other impacts[16]	USB not supported by WinNT 4, so would have to use parallel or serial	n/a	None	Operation of home appliances (for example, dishwasher or clothes washer) can interfere with the LAN; might not work with all AC outlets	Doesn't support WinNT 4 or Win2000[17]

1. For connecting a maximum of two PCs.

2. Later in this chapter, we cover other wireless solutions, including IEEE 802.11 and Bluetooth, that on some dimensions have slightly different specifications than HomeRF.

3. For comparison: 1.2Mbps (parallel) versus .1152Mbps, which is 115.2Kbps (serial).

4. Maximum.

5. This cell contains values for standard (10Mbps) Ethernet and does not reflect values for 100Mbps or 1000Mbps (1GB) Ethernet.

6. For Tut Systems' HR1000T HomeRun Adapter, the limit is a maximum distance of 500 feet (152 meters) between the two farthest nodes on the LAN.

7. HomeRF Working Group states "range up to 50 meters."

8. Impact on your home/office/SOHO environment; for example, holes in walls for cables and outlets.

9. Belkin USB Direct Connect (p/n F5U104) at `http://catalog.belkin.com/IWCatProductPage.process?Product_ID=20963`.

10. Linksys EtherFast Switched 10/100 Network in a Box (p/n FESWSK5): one 5-port 10/100 switch, two 10/100 NICs, two twisted-pair cables, and software (see `http://www.linksys.com/products/product.asp?prid=15&grid=12`); priced at $112.99 on 7/2/2000 at PC Zone.

11. D-Link DHN-910 10Mb Home Phoneline Network In A Box: two PCI 10Mb home phone-line adapters, two phone-line cables, and software (see `http://www.dlink.com/products/kits/dhn910/`); priced at $99.99 on 7/2/2000 at Egghead.com.

12. Intelogis PassPort Network Plug-in Kit (p/n 01010): two PC adapters, one printer adapter, all necessary software, and two parallel cables for your computers (use your printer's existing cable for the printer adapter); priced at $79.95 on 7/3/2000 at PC Connection.

13. Two Intel AnyPoint Wireless USB Model 1.6Mbps units (p/n APRW1USB) at $119 each MSRP.

14. *Installation considerations: hardware, nondriver software, and drivers.*

15. *Five-point scale: very easy, moderately easy; average; moderately difficult; very difficult.*

16. *Topology's impact on other aspects of your operation (for example, power-line network throughput degraded when you use your dishwasher).*

17. *At the time of this writing, wireless networking support is not available for Windows 2000, although support might exist by the time you read this.*

Direct Cable Connection

You can quickly connect two PCs using a simple *direct cable connection,* and you won't have to open up their cases (see Figure 9.1). The special type of cable you use is called a *null modem* cable and can be either serial or parallel (parallel is faster). (Officially speaking, this type of cross-over cable is called *null modem* if it's serial and *parallel data-transfer* if it's parallel.) The cable is half of the equation; the other half is the Windows 9x Direct Cable Connection feature built into the operating system.

NOTE

WINDOWS NT AND DIRECT CABLE CONNECTION

Unlike Windows 95 and 98, Windows NT does not include the Direct Cable Connection feature. However, the Microsoft Knowledge Base article "Connecting Windows NT to Windows 95 with a Null-Modem Cable" describes how to connect a Windows 95 PC to a Windows NT PC. You can connect them so that WinNT is the host and Win95 is the guest, or so that Win95 is the host and WinNT is the guest. For more information, see
`http://support.microsoft.com/support/kb/articles/Q142/0/65.asp`.

FIGURE 9.1

A Belkin Pro
Series Direct
Cable
Connection for
Windows 95, 98,
and 2000
(shown here is a
parallel model).
(Photo courtesy
of Belkin)

Note that this solution can connect a maximum of two PCs. One is designated the *host* and one the *guest.* A common scenario is for the host PC to be a home/home office PC and the guest PC to be a laptop you bring home from work.

Setting up this feature is relatively painless. To start the Direct Cable Connection Wizard, select Start, Programs, Accessories, Communications, Direct Cable Connection, and follow the Wizard's instructions. (If that command isn't available, you must install it on both PCs: Use Control Panel's Add/Remove Programs applet, go into Windows Setup, select Communications, Details, choose Direct Cable Connection, and click OK twice.)

Getting the Right Cable for a Direct Cable Connection

Microsoft's Knowledge Base article "Cables That Are Compatible with Direct Cable Connection" (`http://support.microsoft.com/support/kb/articles/Q142/3/24.asp`) can help you determine exactly which type of cable will meet your needs. If you're into IR (infrared) technology, you can connect two IR-equipped PCs without a cable. Aside from the ports themselves, you'll need a clear line of sight between the two PCs, and you must keep them within a few feet of each other.

Direct Cable Connections enable the guest PC to see and interact with any resources the host has shared via the file/print sharing protocol. If the host PC is connected to a network, the guest PC will be capable of accessing that network.

LINKING TWO PCS VIA USB

Various vendors market USB-based products that connect two PCs without quite as much fuss as Direct Cable Connection. Naturally, both PCs must support USB and have at least one free USB port. These connections typically provide data transfer rates near USB's maximum of 12Mbps, are by definition hot-swappable, support drag-and-drop, and can print remote files. For example, check out USBgear's USB PC to PC Link at `http://www.usbgear.com/usa/view_detail.cfm?id=101`, as shown in Figure 9.2. Xircom also offers a USBnet solution at `http://www.xircom.com/cda/page/0,1298,0-0-1_1-178,00.html`.

You'll recall that serial runs at a glacial 115.2Kbps, parallel at 1.2Mbps, and USB at 12Mbps (refer to Table 9.1), so if you must choose a PC-to-PC, non-networked cable solution, we recommend the USB link variety over Direct Cable Connection.

FIGURE 9.2

USBgear's USB
PC to PC Link
product.

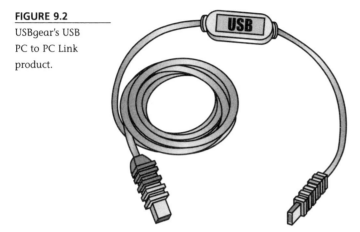

Ethernet Networking

Ethernet was developed in 1976 by Xerox, DEC, and Intel. *Ethernet* devices transmit data in bundles called *packets*. A packet includes the actual data plus a header and a footer to identify the source and destination PCs' addresses and a special value (the *cyclic redundancy check*) used by the destination PC to determine whether the packet was damaged somehow during transmission. A PC in an Ethernet network listens to the data traffic on the cable and waits until it senses an opening; then it begins transmitting. When two PCs on the network transmit data at the same time and their data collides—as happens on occasion—they wait a random amount of time (called the *backoff interval*) before trying to send again, thereby avoiding a collision. Additional backoff algorithms take over if a subsequent collision occurs.

For those of you interested in the formal definition, this is from the Federal Standard 1037C:

> "A standard protocol (IEEE 802.3) for a 10-Mb/s baseband local area network (LAN) bus using carrier-sense multiple access with collision detection (CSMA/CD) as the access method, implemented at the Physical Layer in the ISO Open Systems Interconnection—Reference Model, establishing the physical characteristics of a CSMA/CD network. Note 1: Ethernet is a standard for using various transmission media, such as coaxial cables, unshielded twisted pairs, and optical fibers. Note 2: The IEEE-802.3 standard is based on a proprietary product with a similar name."

Translation: *Baseband* means the wires carry only one signal at a time instead of multiple signals simultaneously. The value 10Mbps indicates Ethernet's standard transmission speed—10 million bits per second. *CSMA/CD* describes a particular algorithm used to deal with the statistically inevitable collisions that occur when multiple devices try to use the medium (wire) at the same time; in short, devices that sense a collision each wait a random amount of time before sending the signal again. The *ISO Open Systems Interconnection—Reference Model* is a model of precisely how disparate devices or systems can interconnect and network with each other.

NOTE

THE ISO OPEN SYSTEMS INTERCONNECTION—REFERENCE MODEL
For more information about the ISO Open Systems Interconnection—Reference Model, see `http://www.iso.ch/cate/3510001.html` and search on the phrase "reference model."

NOTE

THE IEEE 802 STANDARDS FOR LOCAL AREA NETWORKS
For more information about IEEE 802, see `http://standards.ieee.org/index.html` and the numeric cross-listing at `http://standards.ieee.org/catalog/numeric.html`. You must pay to get access to this standards information.

To connect two or more PCs into an Ethernet local area network, you must install one network interface card (NIC) in each PC. This means opening up the chassis.

What's more, you'll probably need to spend some time tweaking each PC's networking protocols (more on this later in the chapter).

Here are our NIC recommendations:

- Avoid nameless clone card manufacturers. They might be a few bucks cheaper, but clone cards and their drivers are not as reliable as those made by market leaders such as 3Com, Intel, LinkSys, NetGear, and Xircom.

- Get auto-sensing 10/100 cards (more on that later).

ANOTHER FINE MESS
THE COAX CONUNDRUM

Connecting computers with coaxial cable is cheaper because you don't need a hub or switch, but coax does have its drawbacks. Using coax, you must daisy-chain your machines such that computer A is cabled to computer B, which is cabled to computer C, and so on. A break anywhere in the chain breaks the entire network. Coax cable is not as easy to work with as twisted-pair because coax is thicker, it's stiffer, and you have to close any open connections with a terminator. We prefer twisted-pair cables and hubs/switches because adding and disconnecting systems from your network is easier. But if you're hooking up only two PCs on an Ethernet LAN, coax is a cheap way to go. ■

■ You need only one port, so after you've chosen between twisted-pair or coax, don't bother getting multiport cards.

■ Get PCI cards unless you have legacy PCs with only ISA slots.

After installing the NICs, you'll need the necessary cabling (we suggest you use twisted-pair wire and not coaxial cable) to connect all the PCs. You'll also need a special black-box device called a *hub*, or a slightly smarter device called a *switch*.

Let's get back to the subject of wiring for a moment. *10BASE-T* refers to a specific (and quite common) Ethernet implementation that uses a particular type of cable, specifically, twisted-pair. 10BASE-T has a maximum run length of 100 meters (about 328 feet) and uses a connector called an *RJ-45 connector* (see Figure 9.3). This cable is also referred to as *Category 5* (or Cat-5) cable, and can be used for LAN implementations other than 10BASE-T. The original type of twisted-pair Ethernet cable is called *Category 3*, but because it has a maximum throughput of 16Mbps, it's not suitable for use in a Fast Ethernet setting.

FIGURE 9.3

The RJ-45 (left) connector looks just like the connector on your telephone, but it is slightly larger, thereby making it impossible to mistakenly plug an RJ-11 (right) or RJ-45 into the wrong connector.

RJ-45

RJ-11

If you're going to use coaxial cable for an Ethernet LAN, most likely you'll use RG-58 A/U cable. This cable has a maximum run length of 185 meters (about 607 feet) and connects via a BNC push-and-twist connector. With coax, you don't need a hub because you can connect multiple PCs—one PC to the next—via BNC

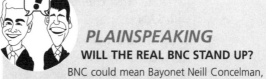

PLAINSPEAKING
WILL THE REAL BNC STAND UP?
BNC could mean Bayonet Neill Concelman, the inventor of the connector. Or perhaps British Naval Connector, or maybe Bayonet Nut Connector, or do you favor Barrel Nut Connector? ■

T-connectors. At the two "ends" of the chain, one of the arms of each end-point T-connector is a metal plug that terminates/sinks the signal.

The device that gathers all these cables together into a central location, and passes signals among PCs on a LAN, is a hub. Each PC's network cable connects to a port on the hub. Think of it as a central switching station, like a train yard. But hubs are dumb, effectively just signal splitters. Switches go hubs one better by separating traffic on each port and knowing—to a limited degree—which packets should be sent to a specific port. This dramatically reduces signal collisions, and thereby dramatically increases the throughput (read: speed) of your LAN. Until recently, smart devices called switches were priced out of the home, SOHO, and small business markets, but now a switch is so affordable that we recommend you get a switch and not a hub.

PLAINSPEAKING
FAST (AND REALLY FAST) ETHERNET

The standard Ethernet (10Mbps) is being supplanted by Fast Ethernet (also called 100BASE-T). Fast Ethernet supports a transmission rate of 100Mbps, which is 10 times faster than its predecessor. Although most newly manufactured network adapters sold today can operate at either 10Mbps or 100Mbps, some relics that work only at 10Mbps still exist. When you buy a NIC, be sure to get one that can run at either 10Mbps or 100Mbps to maximize your investment.

Actually, there's no such moniker as *Really Fast Ethernet*. We're jokingly referring to Gigabit Ethernet that runs at 1 gigabit (1,000 megabits) per second. ∎

Phone-Line Networking

A phone-line network uses existing phone-line wiring in your home or office as the carrier for the network traffic, and uses the existing telephone wall jacks as its ports. A PCI adapter card in each PC includes the necessary jacks. After you install the card and the attendant drivers, you plug it into a phone jack and the PC is connected to other computers similarly plugged into the same phone line that supports your LAN.

The standards body for phone-line networking is the Home Phone-line Networking Alliance (HomePNA). This is a nonprofit association of industry leaders who share the goal of a single, unified phone-line networking industry standard. HomePNA has recently released a new 2.0 standard with a throughput of 10Mbps (the same as standard Ethernet), which is 10 times the 1Mbps throughput of HomePNA 1.0. Version 2.0 is completely backward-compatible, so your investment in any existing HomePNA 1.0 equipment is protected.

Power-Line Networking

A power-line network uses the wire carrying the 110-volt AC (alternating current) pulsing through your home or office's power lines as the carrier for network traffic. You don't have to open the chassis to install a power-line network. Instead, each PC requires a *module*, as does your printer. A module plugs directly into an electrical wall outlet and connects to your PC's parallel port. On the other hand, when connecting a printer, the module plugs into the printer's parallel cable connection. Certain appliances can interfere with this solution's operation—for example, ceiling fans, dishwashers, and clothes washers. Field reports indicate that not all outlets work with the modules. After the modules are connected, you install a special software program on the computers you are networking, which enables the modules to recognize each other automatically. From the software, you control which local resources you want to make available to other machines on your network, and also control your security settings.

Wireless Networking

Right now, the wireless networking arena is a jungle of hyperbole and competing standards. If you choose to implement a wireless network today, it's still in the pioneering "arrows in your back" phase, so be prepared for a bumpy ride. Give it another year for one (or possibly two) clear winners to emerge.

All wireless networking implementations today use radio frequency (RF) as the propagation medium. Think of it this way: With a wired network, wires carry the signal (copper twisted-pair, coax, or fiber-optic) and with a wireless RF network, the air carries the signal. (Technically, we all know that the atmosphere's molecules don't actually carry the signal; it's an electromagnetic wave phenomenon, but it's a convenient representation nonetheless.)

HomeRF is a wireless technology designed specifically for the home environment. Its primary use is to provide data networking and connections between a variety of devices: PCs, cordless phones, and broadband cable/DSL modems among others. Although HomeRF and Bluetooth share the same frequency spectrum of 2.4GHz, their proponents say they don't interfere with each other. (It's 2.45GHz to be precise, and this band is referred to by the regulatory bodies and wireless engineers as the *ISM*, or *Industrial-Scientific-Medical* band.) HomeRF provides 150 feet of connectivity, has a transmission rate of 1.6Mbps, and operates at 2.4GHz.

Bluetooth is a wireless technology designed to provide short-range connections (30 feet, compared to HomeRF's 150-foot range) between mobile devices, as well as to the Internet through black-box Internet bridges. Bluetooth supports 30 feet of connectivity, has a transmission rate of 725Kbps, and uses the 2.4 GHz band.

IEEE 802.11 defines the standard for wireless Ethernet. This technology provides high-speed wireless networking for laptop and desktop computers, as well as a wide range of mobile computing devices. IEEE 802.11 provides 150 feet of connectivity, runs at 11Mbps, and operates at 2.4GHz.

Conclusion

We began this chapter by saying that to build your own LAN you must choose among competing architectures and factor in your physical environment, whether you own or rent, how long you're staying, and your expansion plans. In this section, we provide an executive summary of each architecture, and situations in which they do (or don't) make sense. Your mileage might vary.

- **Direct cable connection**

  - The best choice if you're on a severe shoestring budget and have only two *reasonably adjacent* PCs to connect.

  - Can be as slow as molasses in winter if you're using a serial cable, so if you must go this route, get a USB PC-to-PC cable.

- **Ethernet network**

  - The worldwide corporate standard.

  - The fastest of all the architectures.

  - You must install a network adapter, and it might require some tweaking of network protocols. (For USB-enabled PCs, USB-to-Ethernet adapters are available that eliminate the need to physically install a NIC in the PC.)

  - Likely to continue as a standard bearer well into the future.

  - Not an option if PCs are widely dispersed *and* you can't afford to punch holes in walls, install jacks, and run conduit (or if you can't perform tenant improvements due to lease restrictions, in which case perhaps it's time to move into a leased space that's prewired for Ethernet).

  - Works great if the PCs are all in the same room or you can sneak the wiring along the baseboard to the room next door.

  - Suitable for sharing a high-speed Internet connection.

  - We recommend Ethernet above all others, unless you have special environmental constraints.

■ **Phone-line network**

- ■ High convenience factor; however, phone jacks aren't as ubiquitous as the phone-line networking manufacturers would have you believe.

- ■ Under HomePNA 1.0, a phone-line network is s-l-o-w, but with the advent of HomePNA 2.0 (10Mbps), it's on par with standard Ethernet.

- ■ Suitable for sharing a high-speed Internet connection.

- ■ A common implementation is when your PCs are on different floors.

■ **Power-line network**

- ■ High convenience factor, but awkward and problematic in the real world.

- ■ S-l-o-w.

- ■ Not suitable for sharing a high-speed Internet connection.

- ■ We don't recommend that you waste any time on this technology at present.

■ **Wireless network**

- ■ An emerging set of technologies is competing vehemently for market leadership; there might be more than one winner here (our prediction: wireless Ethernet and Bluetooth).

- ■ All three standards employ the same 2.4GHz frequency used by microwave ovens, cordless phones, baby monitors, garage door openers, and wireless speakers. This potential for device conflicts can pose a risk to the acceptance of wireless by the general public.

- ■ Suitable for sharing a high-speed Internet connection.

- ■ Can transmit non–line-of-sight; for example, through a briefcase, wall, or floor.

- ■ Currently only of interest (and value) to folks who literally want to be able to roam around their home/office environment with a laptop and retain a LAN/Internet connection. It's very cool and exciting, but it's still for pioneers only.

NETWORK KITS

If you have two PCs and don't have any immediate plans to expand your PC count, take a look at the numerous kits available from vendors in every networking architecture category. A kit should contain everything you need to connect two PCs: connection hardware (NICs, power-line adapters, and so on), cables, interoperability software (if required), Internet connection sharing software, and robust documentation.

Creating Your Network

These are the general steps you should follow when creating your network. Note that because so many architectures are available to choose from, we have generalized our steps accordingly. At some points in this checklist, you'll be relying on the hardware manufacturer's documentation:

1. Install the network hardware exactly as instructed by the manufacturer.

2. The manufacturer's instructions might already include this step as a longer series of steps, but just in case … if you're required to open your PC's case, be sure to perform a backup first and test your startup disk (see the "Upgrade Checklist" at the beginning of this chapter).

3. After you have all the PCs set, if they're powered down, power them all up and confirm that they boot properly.

4. Test that each PC can see every other PC in the network. If one or more PCs doesn't see the others, the troubleshooting steps you follow will depend on the architecture you've chosen, so refer to the manufacturer's instructions.

   If you're using wired Ethernet and want to optimize your network protocol settings, as we did in Chapter 8, "Upgrading an Internet Connection," we strongly encourage you to read Steve Gibson's quintessential and thorough guide to proper network component configuration, "Network Bondage" (http://grc.com/su-bondage.htm), and "Network Discipline for Windows 9x" (http://grc.com/su-rebinding9x.htm). A page is also available for Windows NT users.

5. If the PCs see each other, set the appropriate file and printer sharing levels.

6. After your file and printer sharing parameters are set, perform a test print operation from a PC without the network's printer attached to it. Then, perform several file transfer tests. We recommend you transfer a large file, at least

10MB, and perform a stopwatch test to verify you're getting the expected throughput.

CAUTION

MAXIMUM THEORETICAL THROUGHPUT VERSUS THE REAL THING
When you perform your file transfer test, calculate the actual transfer rate in Mbps (megabits per second). Then, compare that rate to the theoretical rate of your network's technology. You might be shocked to see the difference between theory and where the rubber meets the road.

Windows and Internet Connection Sharing

Are you running Windows 98 SE, Windows Millennium, or Windows 2000 on at least one PC? If you are, and you're running a local area network to which that PC is connected, and you're willing to have that PC act as the Connection Sharing PC (also called the *host* and the *gateway*) by installing Internet Connection Sharing (ICS), then all the other PCs on your network (called *clients*) can share the host's Internet connection. (Note that we use the term *gateway* loosely and it shouldn't be confused with an actual gateway, say for an ISP.) This is true regardless of the connection type—dial-up, ISDN, DSL, or cable—and is a major benefit of Windows 98 SE versus Windows 98. As a practical matter, the impact on the ICS host is minimal and hidden in the background (more on this in a moment), with one exception: Whenever the host is turned off, the other PCs on the network don't have Internet access.

Only the host must be running Windows 98 SE, Millennium, or Windows 2000. ICS supports clients that run Windows 95, 98, 98 SE, Millennium, NT 4.0, and 2000, as well as non-Windows clients that are TCP/IP-enabled (such as MacOS and flavors of UNIX), all without any other software. As you'll see in a moment, setting up a client is easy. You run a single EXE program via disk, via CD-R/CD-RW, or across the LAN; this program is provided when you set up ICS on the host. For those of you who play games over the Internet or who need Point-to-Point Tunneling Protocol (PPTP) and virtual private network (VPN) to access your company's network, ICS fully supports these activities.

NOTE

ICS IS IN THE BOX
ICS is a built-in component of Windows 98 SE, Windows Me, and Windows 2000. You can't download it as an added component.

Here are the steps we recommend you follow when installing ICS on the host and client PCs. This list assumes your network is already set up and functioning properly:

1. Remove any unnecessary dial-up devices.

   In Chapter 8, we provide a checklist for installing a high-speed connection. One of the steps is to uninstall any superfluous dial-up devices. If you haven't already done so, we suggest you do this both for the host and the client PCs, assuming one or more of them have any such devices still installed.

2. Clean up the host PC's network and security settings.

   In Chapter 8, we also discuss Internet access and security issues. Please ensure that you've taken all the necessary precautions outlined therein, including cleaning up your host PC's TCP/IP protocol instance bindings and settings, removing any unused protocols, and then installing a personal firewall.

3. Repeat step 2 for your client PCs.

4. If your host PC doesn't have TCP/IP installed, install it now.

   In a nutshell: Right-click the desktop's Network Neighborhood icon, click the Configuration tab (if it isn't already on top), click the Add button, select Protocol, click Add, select Microsoft from the Manufacturers list, select TCP/IP from the Network Protocols list, click OK twice, insert your Windows 98 CD if prompted, and then let the system reboot. For more detailed instructions, see the list of resources at the end of this section. You should test your Internet connection now before installing Internet Connection Sharing.

5. Install ICS on the host PC.

   Start Control Panel, run the Add/Remove Programs applet, click the Windows Setup tab, select the Internet Tools component, click the Details button, check the Internet Connection Sharing checkbox, and then click OK twice. This starts the Internet Connection Sharing Wizard, as shown in Figure 9.4. Following the Wizard's steps takes very little time (pick a network adapter for use as your Internet connection, create a Client Configuration Disk, and then choose to restart).

6. Configure ICS to display its icon in the host PC's taskbar.

   After your PC has restarted, you won't notice any change on your desktop. For some odd reason, ICS doesn't automatically put its icon in the system tray, so here's how to do that. From Control Panel, run the Internet Options applet, click the Connections tab, click the Sharing button in the Local Area Network (LAN) settings frame, check the Show Icon in Taskbar checkbox (see Figure 9.5), and click OK twice.

FIGURE 9.4

The Internet Connection Sharing Wizard makes it extremely easy to install ICS on the host PC.

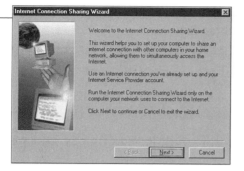

FIGURE 9.5

A well-hidden checkbox is the only way to get the ICS icon to appear in the host PC's system tray.

7. Set up each client PC to use ICS.

   One of the byproducts of running the Internet Connection Sharing Wizard is a 3 1/2-inch disk, but you won't find any Microsoft documentation on precisely what to do with it. When you look at the disk's contents, you'll see two files: `Icsclset.exe` and `Readme.txt`. The Readme file has no client install instructions, either. We never had any success using the disk, so because the client PCs are on the network, we simply used the copy of `Icsclset.exe` that ICS installs in the host PC's C:\Windows\System folder. When you run this file on a client PC, it starts the Browser Connection Setup Wizard and in less than five seconds you'll be done with the Wizard and able to connect your client PC's browser to the Internet through the host PC. Try it!

NOTE

PROBLEMS?

If you have a connection problem at this point, consult the resources listed at the end of this section.

8. Optimize the connectivity speed for the host and client PCs using the `DefaultRcvWindow` Registry value.

   Chapter 8 describes how to do this for high-speed access connections. Note that you should tweak client PCs as well as the host PC.

9. Optimize the host PC's bandwidth—if it's not a dial-up connection—by deleting the Registry's `InternetMTU` value.

   The Microsoft Knowledge Base article "Slow Transfer Rates with ICS and High-Bandwidth Devices" (`http://support.microsoft.com/support/kb/articles/q230/1/16.asp`) describes how to overcome suboptimal downloads in some circumstances, *but only if the host is not using a dial-up connection.*

Online Resources

Here is a list of online resources for a variety of networking and related topics:

- **Glossary of telecommunications terms**—Located at `http://www.its.bldrdoc.gov/fs-1037/`. This document is the hypertext version of Federal Standard 1037C, *Glossary of Telecommunication Terms*, 1996.

- **HomePlug Powerline Alliance**—Located at `http://www.homeplug.com`. It promotes open specifications for high-speed home power-line networking products and counts 13 member firms. Big-name members include 3Com, Cisco, Compaq, Intel, Motorola, and Texas Instruments.

- **HomePNA**—Located at `http://www.homepna.org`. See especially "Which technologies have been selected by the Alliance?" and "How does home phone-line networking work?"

- **Intel's AnyPoint Interactive Product Selector**—Available by browsing to `http://www.intel.com/anypoint/`; then, look for the "Interactive Product Selector" link.

- `comp.dcom.lans.ethernet`—This newsgroup's FAQ is an excellent resource.

- **The HomeRF Working Group**—Located at `http://www.homerf.org`. It promotes open specifications for wireless digital communication between PCs and other consumer electronic devices in the home. Members include 3Com, Compaq, Dolby, Hitachi-Maxell, HP, IBM, Intel, Matsushita, Microsoft, Motorola, Philips, Radio Shack, Samsung, Sharp, and Texas Instruments, with more than 90 members total (note the high-profile consumer electronics firms).

The HomeRF Working Group has developed and promotes a wireless communications protocol for data and voice called the Shared Wireless Access Protocol (SWAP).

- **The Official Bluetooth SIG Web site**—Located at
  `http://www.bluetooth.com`. Options include FAQs (brief), news, product information, an event calendar, a press room, and more for SIG members.

- **The Wireless LAN Association (WLANA)**—Located at
  `http://www.wlana.com`. The site maintains an events calendar, a suggested reading list, links to various industry articles, and a discussion forum.

- **"Windows 98 Second Edition—Connection Sharing"**—Located at
  `http://www.thenakedpc.com/articles/v02/14/0214-02.html`.

- **"Security Features of Internet Connection Sharing"**—Located at
  `http://support.microsoft.com/support/kb/articles/q241/5/70.asp`.

- **"Slow Transfer Rates with ICS and High-Bandwidth Devices"**—
  Located at
  `http://support.microsoft.com/support/kb/articles/q230/1/16.asp`.

- **"How to Troubleshoot Internet Connection Sharing Problems"**—
  Located at
  `http://support.microsoft.com/support/kb/articles/q238/1/35.asp`.

- **"TCP/IP Must Be Bound to All Adapters Connecting ICS Host to LAN"**—Located at
  `http://support.microsoft.com/support/kb/articles/q230/0/70.asp`.

- **Tim Higgins' Sharing Your Internet Connection site**—Located at
  `http://www.timhiggins.com/ppd/sharing.htm`.

- **"Your site doesn't talk about ICS (Microsoft's Internet Connection Sharing) or NAT (Internet Network Address Translation), could you say something about them?"**—This FAQ is available at
  `http://grc.com/faq-shieldsup.htm#NAT`.

PART **III**

UPGRADES TO CONSIDER

10

ADDING POWER PROTECTION

Protect the delicate silicon and electronic parts of your computer from the ravages of rampant electrical spikes and low voltage dips. The excellent benefit/cost ratio of uninterruptible power supplies (UPSs) makes them a very desirable, if not mandatory, upgrade.

Upgrade Checklist

1. Do your homework.

2. Determine whether the power protection you're adding is sufficient for the equipment you're trying to protect.

3. Purchase or acquire the surge suppressor or UPS device.

4. Organize the area where the device will be installed.

5. Read any documentation carefully. UPS devices usually require that you connect the battery and then charge the system for a number of hours before using them. Pay special attention to any safety precautions and labels.

6. Take good notes and permanently file them in your system log when finished.

7. Update your inventory documentation to reflect the upgraded or newly added component.

Determining Your Power Protection Needs

How much power do you need to run all the equipment you have? If you don't have any idea whatsoever then join the club. Seldom does anyone think about how much power something draws when they buy it. You just bring it home, uncrate it, plug it in, and never give it another thought. If you don't have any free electrical outlets, you plug in another power strip and off you go.

But it does make a difference. Every electrical doohickey you buy draws a specific amount of power, usually measured in watts. In grade school, we all learned the dangers of plugging too many appliances into a single outlet, but with power strips it's easy to plug way too many things into a single outlet. In one of our offices, every time we brought in something new that required plugging in, we had to first determine what could be unplugged.

Not only is there an issue with how much power your electronics are drawing, but with the quality of the power that's coming out of the wall. Is the ground leg grounded properly? Can the power provide enough wattage for all the goodies you have running? Are there significant fluctuations?

Clean Versus Dirty Power

Ever been working on your computer and suddenly it decides to reboot itself? The lights in the room don't go out, so you know a power failure didn't occur. The most likely culprit is a drop in power below the threshold of the minimum current the power supply wants. The radio might keep playing and lights don't even flicker, but the system reboots anyway.

Power supplies are designed to shut down or reset the system if the power drops below a certain point (and you just blamed it on Windows, didn't you?).

Therefore, low power is bad just as too much power is bad. Low-power brownouts, called *sags*, are sometimes unavoidable. They're sometimes planned by your local power utility to deal with high demand caused by extremely hot summer days when everyone cranks up their air conditioning. The power company will reduce power in selected areas, shifting the brownout around to cut down on overall demand.

Even more dangerous to your equipment is a sudden jump in power, which is called a *spike*. Any fluctuation, surges, spikes, or drops in power can cause problems. What you want is clean (no noise or interference), steady, stable power.

Another issue is that of line *noise*. Electrical noise on power lines can be caused by electromagnetic interference (EMI), radio-frequency interference (RFI), or inductive

ANOTHER FINE MESS
UNDERPOWERED POWER SUPPLIES

Another thing to remember when considering power is to ensure your PC's power supply is adequate for any internal upgrades you'll be adding to the system. An older system with a power supply in the 200-watt to 230-watt range that has a card in every slot and multiple drives might be seriously underpowered. Although the power supply itself can be upgraded, you might want to consider a new system case with a new motherboard and power supply. Current systems come with 300-watt power supplies as standard and some high-end systems can have a 425-watt or higher power supply. ■

loads placed on the circuit by motors or other electrical devices. Electrical wire acts just like an antenna and can pick up interference from a number of sources, such as fluorescent light fixtures, telephone lines, radio signals, and so on.

Grounding Is Essential

The power supply in your PC offers protection against some types of power problems. The higher the quality of the power supply, the better protection it supplies. Most people are also aware that they should use surge suppressors for added protection against sudden power surges and spikes.

But for any power protection schemes to work adequately, you *must* have properly grounded electrical outlets providing the AC power at the wall. Never, ever, use an adapter that enables you to plug a three-prong plug into a two-prong receptacle (see Figure 10.1).

FIGURE 10.1

Never use a three-prong power adapter to plug a three-prong plug into a two-prong outlet.

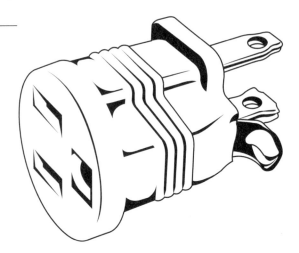

Don't assume that because your outlets have three-prong receptacles, the ground leg is properly grounded. Get an outlet tester at a hardware store or consult with an electrician about the outlets where you'll plug in your equipment. Outlet testers are inexpensive and easy to use. Plug one into your outlet and it'll display colored lights indicating whether the outlet is properly grounded and whether the hot and neutral wires are correctly connected. You must have a good ground or your power protection equipment won't have anywhere to shunt power spikes.

Power Company Problems

If you suspect your power is not all it could be, you're probably right. We've seen problems come right from the power company on what should have been clean, isolated circuits. The power can be good at the pole where it enters the building but bad at the wall, which indicates a problem with the internal wiring or with how the wall plug was installed. When in doubt, call your power company to have your lines tested or bring in a qualified electrician, or do both.

Protecting All Entry Points into Your PC

Upgrading power protection is useless if you don't protect all the entry points into your computer (besides the electrical plug). If lightning misses the power transformer but instead strikes the telephone pole outside your house, you'll have a bolt of electricity running down the cord that leads from the phone jack in the wall directly into your modem, which goes directly into your system.

If you have multiple machines networked and are using an active hub, the hub is plugged into the wall and your computer is plugged into the hub. Don't miss this often-overlooked entry point. A power surge into the hub can spike the network connections and dump a huge jolt into your network card, which is in turn plugged directly into your computer's motherboard (see Figure 10.2).

FIGURE 10.2

An electrical surge or spike can find its way into your computer in more than one way.

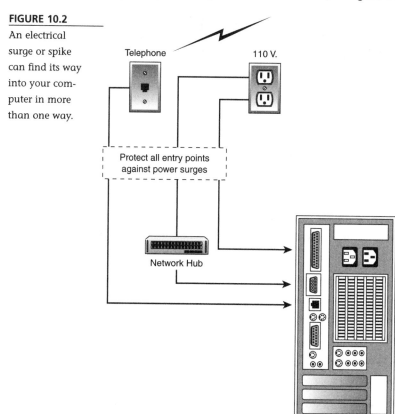

Telephone

110 V.

Protect all entry points against power surges

Network Hub

Protecting your computer with the most sophisticated equipment available does you no good whatsoever if you leave other entry points unguarded. Protect all entry points where a power spike can get in and fry the delicate electronic components that comprise your system.

Surge Suppressors

Everyone who has ever purchased or installed a computer is familiar with the first line of defense against power surges, the surge suppressor (see Figure 10.3). A surge suppressor sits between the wall outlet and your computer. If a spike occurs on the power line, the surge suppressor is supposed to shunt it harmlessly to the ground, thereby preventing it from ever reaching your system. The suppressor usually gives up the ghost when this happens, sacrificing itself to protect your computer.

FIGURE 10.3

A typical eight-outlet surge suppressor with reset button.

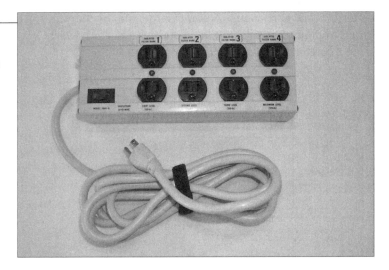

Most users plug in a surge suppressor and promptly forget about it, assuming it will do its job forever. Wrong. Very wrong, as you'll see. Surge suppressors have definite limitations that you must understand to better protect your computer.

Why Surges Occur

Power surges can be caused by a number of things, the most spectacular being when lightning strikes a power line and sends a huge jolt of electricity into the power grid.

Another source of surges is, oddly enough, caused by a power outage. When the power goes out, a great many electrical appliances and motors that were happily chugging along are suddenly without juice. But they also are left switched on.

When the power is restored, the power company must take into account all the things that are still switched on and that will instantly start consuming power as soon as some electrons come down the wire. Therefore, they up the amperage to kick-start all the appliances that were left on when the lights went out. This is a man-made surge.

When the lights go out, it's a good idea to go around and switch off everything that was running. This protects the motors and electrical components from the restart surge. If you're having a lightning storm, it's prudent to unplug your electrical appliances, especially computers, from the wall outlets. This guarantees complete protection from a lightning strike to a nearby power pole.

Surge Suppressor Limitations

First, the cheaper surge suppressors don't offer much more in the way of protection than what's built into modern power supplies. They're rated to stop spikes up to only 5–6 kiloamps. This offers protection from spikes that might occur when the power company boosts the current when restoring power after an outage. But if lightning strikes your power lines, it can generate a spike from 50 to 500 kiloamps and blast through a surge suppressor, frying your system before the suppressor can commit suicide and protect your computer.

Second, most suppressors use a technology based on metal-oxide varistors (MOVs) called *shunt* or *parallel* mode. MOVs sit across the hot wire and the ground wire, and under normal conditions do not conduct electricity. At higher voltages they become conductive and shunt the electricity to the ground wire. In effect, they short the circuit when a surge or spike comes along.

The problem with this technology is that MOVs wear out with use. The normal power fluctuations that occur in power lines can render the MOVs completely useless over time. Few suppressors come equipped with warning lights or any indicator to let you know when the MOVs go bad (and these warning lights might not be all that reliable, either).

Last, surge suppressors do nothing about line noise. Again, line noise results from static and interference caused by electromagnetic interference (EMI), radio-frequency interference (RFI), or inductive loads caused by machinery (usually electrical motors).

Because surge suppressor are the type of protection that most people use (offering less protection the longer you use them), why is it that more computers don't get fried? The answer is that the majority of computer users don't experience regular lightning strikes, power outages, surges, or brownouts.

Some surge suppressors don't rely on MOVs—for example, the products made by ZeroSurge (`www.zerosurge.com/index.html`).

That said, we are not suggesting you should forego power protection. Quite the opposite; we strongly favor power protection and think it makes a very good upgrade investment. A surge suppressor that does not rely on MOVs, and meets Underwriters Laboratories' revised Standard for TVSS (Transient Voltage Surge Suppressor) products, UL 1449, is a good choice.

Nevertheless, given how UPS prices have dropped in recent years, we recommend you go with a UPS whenever possible.

Uninterruptible Power Supply

Better by far than a surge suppressor is an uninterruptible power supply (UPS) device. More expensive than the typical power strip–type surge suppressor, they also provide the best protection for your computer.

As the name implies, they provide "uninterruptible" power. If the power at the wall suddenly fails, the electrical devices plugged into the UPS keep right on running oblivious to the power blackout. A good UPS must provide three very important functions: conditioned power, battery backup, and automatic system shutdown.

STANDBY VERSUS UNINTERRUPTIBLE

Be sure you're getting a real *uninterruptible* power supply. A standby power supply is not the same thing as a true UPS, and the cheaper units provide no power conditioning at all. A *standby power supply (SPS)* waits until the power drops and then steps in and switches you to the backup battery. A lot can go wrong during the instant that the standby unit switches to battery power. Avoid any device that includes a switch time in its specifications. In such a case, you're getting an SPS, not a UPS.

Conditioned Line Power

UPS devices filter out any line noise that might be present, which provides what is called *conditioned* power. In addition to filtering line noise, conditioning includes dealing with surges, sags (brownouts), and spikes. This is the most important feature a UPS provides—a steady stream of safe, clean, conditioned power to your computer and peripherals.

It's capable of doing this because, when connected to a UPS, your computer is not running on power from the wall at all. The UPS draws power from the wall to keep its battery charged. Anything plugged into the UPS runs off the battery. The battery's 12-volt DC power is converted to 110 volts and fed to your computer. All the noise, sags, and surges are handled by the UPS while constant power is delivered from the battery.

Battery Backup

The battery is the heart of a UPS device. Its purpose is to provide power constantly to the system being protected. In the event that outside power is shut off, it keeps everything running for some number of minutes, giving you time to save all your files and shut down the system.

UPS devices are not usually designed to give you hours of computing time, but rather just enough time to shut down the system after the power fails (although for enough money you can buy one measured in hours). Minutes are usually all that are required; you only need to save your files and exit your operating system to avoid data loss in the event of a power failure.

You should never have any open and unsaved files if you're not seated at your system, anyway. If you haven't already, make it a habit to save anything that's open before you get out of our your chair and leave your system unattended. Closing your files is not a bad idea, either, if others have access to your keyboard when you're away.

UPS devices, similar to the surge suppressor strips discussed earlier, have a number of outlets on them for you to plug in the equipment you want protected. But not all plugs are created equal. For example, the last UPS we installed (an APC BP500U; see Figure 10.4) has a total of seven outlets. But only four provide backup power from the battery; the other three outlets provide only surge suppression. Study the UPS plug labels carefully when you set it up.

Although we'd like to think that these surge-only plugs are conditioned, that would be wishful thinking. Don't count on any outlets not backed up by the battery to provide you with conditioned power. Unless it is clearly stated to the contrary, you can assume that any surge-only plugs are relying on MOVs for spike protection.

Orderly System Shutdown

A UPS device serves two primary purposes. First, it conditions the power going to your most critical electronic components, usually the computer and the monitor. Second, it provides you with power in the event the current from the wall is cut off. It doesn't provide unlimited power to keep banging away on the keyboard by candlelight, but provides a few minutes in which you can save your open files, perform a normal system shutdown, and turn off the system.

FIGURE 10.4

Note the four conditioned plugs on the left and the three surge-only plugs on the right. This unit also provides a USB interface to automatically shut down the computer when power shuts off.

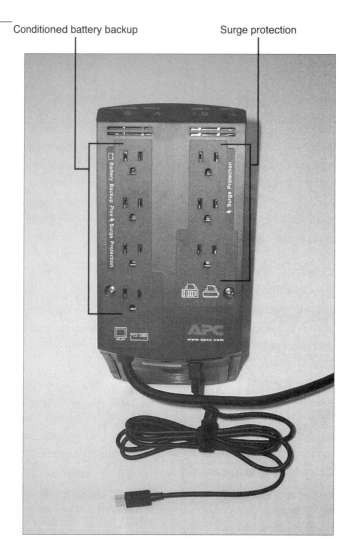

Conditioned battery backup

Surge protection

This second feature does you little good if you're not at your keyboard when the lights go out. Eventually, the battery in the UPS runs out of juice and your system goes off as if you had pulled the plug out of the wall. Unsaved work is gone in a heartbeat. To prevent you from having to stay chained to your desk, many UPS models come with software that runs on the computer and monitors the UPS. This software runs in the background, and when the battery level reaches a critical low point, it leaps into action and does what you would do if you were sitting at the keyboard, which is shut down the system. Here are the features common to most UPS devices that provide monitoring software:

- Save open files in running applications

- Close running applications

- Instruct the operating system to shut down

- Turn off the UPS device

These are nifty features, to be sure. But despite the broad claims, you must understand the limitations of monitoring software.

Knowing what commands are necessary to save files and close applications means the software must have a good understanding of the operating system that's running. Therefore, most UPS monitoring software is designed for a specific operating system. If it works with Windows 98, don't expect it to know what to do with Linux. Be sure you get the right monitoring software for your operating system. Tripp Lite has software available that works with equipment from a number of different UPS manufacturers and supports a plethora of different operating systems. Check it out at `http://www.tripplite.com/software/index.html`.

TIP

DOES IT REALLY CLOSE APPLICATIONS?

No. Monitoring software, such as Power Management Extensions from APC, does not actually perform a File, Exit on each running application. Rather, it talks to the operating system and gets it to shut them down. Anything not meeting the standards for the operating system won't close properly.

You run into the same problems with individual applications. Windows software of this type can shut down the major Microsoft Office applications, such as Word and Excel, but you can't be sure it can deal with everything you run on your system.

Files are indeed saved—providing, of course, that they have been saved at least once already and have a valid filename. Most monitoring software finds that naming a newly created document is beyond its capabilities. APC's Power Management Extensions (see Figure 10.5), for example, won't save a PowerPoint presentation file if it contains embedded objects, nor can it handle a file created in Word 95 if it's opened in Word 97. If you leave an application in a state in which an internal dialog box is onscreen, any open files might not be saved.

Another factor is the time required to save the open files. By the time the software goes into automatic shutdown mode, typically only a handful of minutes are left. If the system is trying to save that Great American Novel you've written and left open and unsaved on your system, the system might not have enough time. At some critical point, the monitoring software says "to heck with it" and tells the operating system to shut down and forget the unsaved files.

UPS monitoring
software usually
adds a panel to
the Power
Management
dialog box
(accessed via
Start, Settings,
Control Panel,
Power
Management).

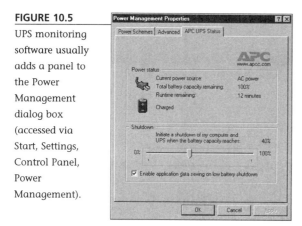

Despite the limitations, monitoring software provides a nice protection layer and
can deal with many of the issues involved with an orderly system shutdown.

Choosing a UPS

To choose a UPS device, you must calculate the total amount of power (in watts)
that your system and any additional peripherals you'll be plugging into it will draw.
This is not as straightforward as it might sound.

Your system's power supply will be rated in watts. For example, 486 cases usually
come with a 200-watt to 230-watt power supply. Newer systems (with ATX form-
factor motherboards) have 250-watt to 300-watt power supplies. This is the maximum amount of power the system can draw without blowing a fuse. That assumes
every slot is being used and at least two or three drives are installed (in addition to
the floppy drive).

You also need to take into account any peripherals you want to keep running if the
power fails. It would be difficult to do anything with your system if, for example, the
power goes out, the PC keeps on running, but the monitor shuts off. Ditto if you are
running your monitor/mouse/keyboard through a power-switching device. Things
such as speakers, printers, and modems might not need to be provided with backup
power depending on the nature of the work you do on your computer.

The problem with adding all the wattages each device could draw is that you wind
up getting more protection than you need. Most devices rarely draw the maximum
for which they are rated; usually a margin of safety is built in. What's wrong with
overprotection? It's a matter of cost. Going from a 300-watt UPS to a 900-watt UPS
can triple the price. When you get to the 1,500-watt level, you're talking the price of
a new computer.

One of the top vendors providing UPS devices, American Power Conversion (www.apcc.com/products/ups.cfm), provides a Web-based form that helps you calculate the unit you'll need to protect the equipment you have (see Figure 10.6). You'll find it at http://www.apcc.com/sizing/.

FIGURE 10.6

After you complete the form, the calculator recommends specific models of UPS devices.

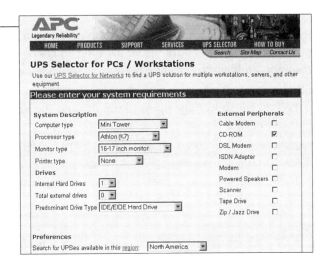

Keep in mind that this is only a guideline. Remember, you're using the calculator of a company that has a vested interest in selling you products. It's a bit like asking an eager salesperson, "Gee, I don't know, what do you think I need?"

But overall we feel that the form does a good job in making the right recommendations. You should do your homework and know the following information:

- Computer type (form factor: desktop, mini-tower, and so on).

- Processor type (PIII, K7, and so on).

- Monitor (size in inches).

- How many internal hard drives and which type of drive controller (IDE, SCSI, and so on).

- Geographical region in which the system will be used (North America and so on).

- Percentage to allow for future expansion; this is tricky because the calculator does not assume a fully loaded system. Therefore, you should allow for any upgrades you're planning in the future that would fill a bus slot or otherwise increase the load.

- Runtime (usually measured in minutes). How long the system must run on battery power before you can save your files and shut it down.

■ Voltage used where the UPS will be plugged in (for example, 120 volts for North America).

■ Whether you want unattended shutdown capability (recommended).

■ Whether you'll want backup power for a printer.

Trying to add backup power for a printer can triple the wattage-output requirement for a UPS device. Consider long and hard before deciding you need to run a printer for a few minutes during a blackout because it's a very costly decision.

The two factors that have the most impact on the cost of a UPS are the amount of output it generates (how much wattage it has to supply) and the length of time the UPS has to provide power in a blackout.

Another major vender supplying UPS devices is Tripp Lite Power Protection (`www.tripplite.com/products/home_office.htm`). Its site promises a calculator form will be available soon, but it was not in operation at the time of this writing.

Installing a UPS

When installing a UPS, it's important to pick a good spot for it to sit. This should be out of the way of traffic and where you won't be kicking it under your desk. It's also a good idea to put something sturdy under it so it doesn't snuggle down into the plush pile carpeting and overheat. You'll also want to install it hours before you'll need to use it to give the battery time to charge.

Install UPS Early

1. Unpack your UPS and carefully review the documentation that accompanies it.

2. Follow the instructions and carefully open the battery compartment. UPS devices are shipped from the factory with the battery *disconnected.*

3. Connect the hot lead to the battery per the instructions that come with the unit. This usually involves slipping a colored wire onto a post connection (see Figure 10.7).

4. Replace the battery and reseal the battery compartment. Ensure no wires are crimped or caught in the compartment cover.

5. Position the UPS unit and plug it into an outside AC power source (usually a wall outlet). Do not plug the UPS into a surge suppressor, power strip, or another UPS. Plug it directly into an outlet where you're getting power directly from your power utility.

FIGURE 10.7

The battery must
be connected
before you can
use the UPS.
Never work on
the UPS device
unless it is
unplugged from
the wall.

FIGURE 10.7

The battery must be connected before you can use the UPS. Never work on the UPS device unless it is unplugged from the wall.

6. A warning indicator light usually will tell you whether the outlet it's plugged into is wired incorrectly (this happens more often than you might think). If this lights up, consult an electrician.

7. Switch on the UPS. Generally, a self-test routine is triggered and the results are indicated by colored LED lights. If everything checks out okay, let the battery charge the recommended length of time.

8. Plug in your equipment—keeping in mind that some of the UPS' receptacles might not provide conditioned power backed up by the battery.

9. Most units enable the filtering of electrical spikes from your telephone line going into your modem or DSL router. This is an often-overlooked point of entry for spikes (see Figure 10.8).

ANOTHER FINE MESS
GENERATORS AND UPS DEVICES DON'T MIX

Never power a UPS device from a fuel-powered generator. Gas and diesel generators generate power, but severe output voltage distortion, er, when supplying nonlinear loads... look, we have it on good authority that it's a bad thing. If you want the electrical engineer explanation, check out the white paper *Using UPS with AC Generators* from the APC technical support site at

`http://159.215.19.5/KBASEWB2.NSF/Tnotes +External/911D4E82949685DB8525672300568 CB8` ■

FIGURE 10.8

Most UPS (and higher-end surge suppressors) offer filtering for your telephone line. Some models filter your network connections as well.

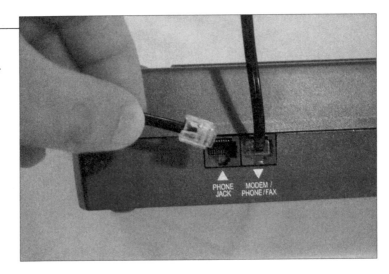

OFF THE WALL
INSTALLATION DON'TS

A UPS device generally runs hotter than a straight surge suppressor power strip. Keep this in mind when you install a UPS and avoid sticking it under the desk or putting it in the corner where the wild dust bunnies roam. You want some decent ventilation so it can dissipate heat. In addition, clean it regularly so an insulating blanket of dust does not cover it. You also want to avoid direct sunlight on this device, as well as your computer case and the picture tube of your monitor. ■

TIP

SYSTEM SETUP

For tips and tricks galore on general personal computer setup, see *The Unofficial Guide to PCs*, Chapter 4, by T.J. Lee, Lee Hudspeth, and Dan Butler (ISBN: 0-7897-1797-2).

ANOTHER FINE MESS
PROBLEMS WITH POWER BLOCKS

Many computer peripherals run on direct current (DC); heck, your computer itself runs on DC voltage. Their electrical cords have bulbous *converter bricks* on the end, ranging in size from roughly a pack of playing cards to a can of soup. When plugging these bricks into a power strip, UPS, or even the wall, it's easy to cover up a plug and effectively limit the number of devices you can plug in. You'd think that the converter would be built into the device itself, wouldn't you? Or, at the very least, a 12-inch pigtail cord should be between the brick and the receptacle plug. What we'd really like to see are more power strips and UPS devices in which the receptacles are rotated 90 degrees so a converter brick won't hang over the adjacent plug. If you run into this problem, you can find short extension cords (three-wire grounded) at most home warehouse stores—sometimes 2 feet or shorter in length. Plugging the extension cord into the brick gives you a plug that won't eat up additional plugs. ■

11

ADDING USB COMPATIBILITY

I f you have the need for a new peripheral that is external and operates at low to medium speed (USB operates at 1.5 megabytes/sec, or 12 megabits/sec), give serious consideration to buying a USB version of that peripheral. Another key advantage to using USB peripherals is that they are hot-swappable. This is a benefit not only if you and your officemates often swap equipment or you move around and thus tote portable peripherals with you, it's also a benefit for a stationary PC user: With USB you don't have to power down your PC to attach a new peripheral.

Upgrade Checklist

1. Do your homework.

2. Determine whether your PC supports the planned upgrade.

3. Determine whether you can perform the upgrade.

4. Purchase or acquire the component.

5. Organize your tools and workspace. See Chapter 3, "Things You Need."

6. If you're installing a USB host controller to a PCI slot, back up everything: data, operating system, mission-critical applications, and BIOS. Otherwise, skip this step.

7. If you're installing a USB host controller to a PCI slot, test your startup disk. Otherwise, skip this step.

8. Perform the upgrade.

9. Take good notes, and permanently file them in your system log when you're finished.

10. Update your inventory documentation to reflect the upgraded or newly added component.

The Universal Serial Bus

The primary focus of this chapter is on upgrading a PC that supports USB but has no USB ports, and on attaching USB peripherals. USB has moved from a grassroots bus to mainstream. According to *PC Data*, the majority of top-selling peripherals in the following product categories were USB-enabled: keyboards, mice, digital joysticks, floppy drives, digital speakers, and low-end printers (based on U.S. retail sales figures for 1999).

It's getting harder and harder to find a PC hardware category that doesn't support USB. Take a look at any retailer's Web site on any given day and you'll see plenty of USB compatibility coverage. This following is not intended as a comprehensive list:

- Digital cameras (still and video)

- CD-R/RW drives

- Hard disk drives

- Iomega Zip drives

- Castlewood Orb drives

- Floppy drives

- Superdisk (LS-120) drives

- Cartridge tape drives

- Iomega Jaz drives

- PDA (personal digital assistant) adapters, cradles, and synchronization devices

- A wide variety of USB-to-whatever protocol adapters/converters

- Networking hardware (adapters, hubs, and network bridges)

- Digital voice recorders

- Input devices (joysticks, mice, and keyboards)

- Modems

- Printers

- Scanners

- Speakers

SEE ALSO

➤ *For details on the history and architecture of the USB bus, see Chapter 2, "Preparing for an Upgrade," page 23*

Here is a quick recap of USB's main features:

- Medium-speed serial bus (1.5 megabytes/sec)

NOTE

USB 2.0 SPRINTING AHEAD?

In April 2000, the USB 2.0 Promoter Group announced a new version of USB that offers a significant increase in bandwidth: from USB 1.1's speed of 1.5 megabytes/sec to version 2.0's maximum of 60 megabytes/sec. (For comparison, recall that FireWire runs at 25 megabytes/sec and PCI at 132 megabytes/sec.) Of course, whenever you read press releases or specifications for USB, you'll always see the units that use the "largest" numbers: For version 1.1, they'll use the 12 megabits/sec value instead of the equivalent—but "smaller-looking"—value of 1.5 megabytes/sec. We prefer to remember the values in their megabytes/sec form, but whichever you prefer, just remember when comparing a bus or device's purported throughput to always do so in the same units. To convert from bits/second to bytes/second, divide the bits/sec rating by 8.

Note that USB 2.0 is designed to be fully forward- and backward-compatible with existing USB systems. The Group states that a full retail ramp-up of USB 2.0 will occur in 2001.

- Supports up to 127 devices (theoretically)

- Supports Plug and Play

- Supports hot-swapping

- Provides low levels of power to devices over the bus (can eliminate bulky power bricks and cables in some cases)

- Does not require an IRQ for each device on the bus

- No peripheral cards required

- Supported by Windows 95 B (OEM Service Release 2) and Windows 95 C, but *not* supported by earlier versions of Window 95

TIP

WINDOWS 95 AND USB SUPPORT

It can be troublesome to get your hands on a copy of Windows 95 B or C, and then find that the prospect of an operating system upgrade is about as exciting as a root canal. After all, you've got productive work to do. Because you'd have to perform the upgrade anyway (from a pre-B version of Windows 95), you're much better off upgrading to Windows 98 SE, Windows Millennium (Me), or Windows 2000. By doing this, you'll get all the benefits of those newer operating systems, including USB support.

- Supported by Windows 98, Windows Me, and Windows 2000

- *Not* supported by Windows NT 3.x and 4.x

TIP

USBREADY WILL ASSESS YOUR PC'S USB STATUS

Intel has written a free USB evaluation utility called USBReady. Go get it at
`http://www.usb.org/data/usbready.exe`. See Figures 2.21 and 2.22 in Chapter 2,
"Preparing for an Upgrade."

Adding a USB Host Controller

Before jumping into adding a USB controller, first perform a visual inspection of
your machine to see whether you already have USB ports. Figure 11.1 shows what
a PC's USB ports look like. The USB A-male connector that plugs in to the port is
shown in Figure 11.4. Note that some manufacturers include USB ports on the front
of PCs as well as on the back. If you do have USB ports, you can skip the following
material on adding a USB host controller.

FIGURE 11.1

Two USB ports,
shown here on
the back of a PC
adjacent to the
serial and paral-
lel ports. (Photo
courtesy of USB
Implementers
Forum)

A USB host controller is a peripheral card with two or more USB ports (usually either
two or four), as shown in Figure 11.2. You also might see these referred to as *USB
upgrade cards*. You can use a USB host controller in two scenarios. First, you can use
it to add USB ports to a PC that currently has none. As described in Chapter 2, a PC's
USB capabilities are bred into its South Bridge chipset. You can check that chipset's
documentation to determine whether it supports USB (even though no physical ports
are supplied), or you can run Intel's free USB evaluation utility USBReady
(`http://www.usb.org/data/usbready.exe`).

FIGURE 11.2

The Belkin USB BusPort is a host controller that adds two USB ports via a PCI card.

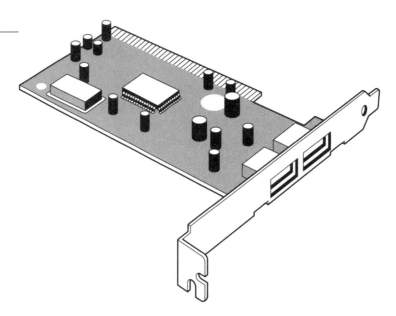

Secondly, you can use a USB host controller to add more USB ports to a PC that already has ports, although in this case you will be using a PCI slot. If you need more USB ports but don't want to give up a slot, or don't have one to sacrifice, you need a hub (more on this in a moment). These upgrade cards are readily available from manufacturers such as Belkin (http://www.belkin.com) and Xircom (http://www.xircom.com).

TIP

USE ALLUSB'S PRODUCT CATEGORY LISTINGS TO LOCATE A USB UPGRADE CARD

Go to http://www.allusb.com/products.html, select Cards: PCI in the Product Listings drop-down control, and you'll see an extensive listing of relevant products.

Here are the steps for adding a USB host controller:

1. Shut down and disconnect your system (see Chapter 3's section "Breaking Down Your Computer").

2. As usual, when working inside the case, discharge all static electricity and wear an ESD wrist strap.

3. Install the USB host controller card in accordance with the manufacturer's instructions.

4. Use Device Manager to validate that the card is functioning properly as far as Windows is concerned.

5. With the PC powered up, plug in a USB peripheral and let hot-swappability and PnP work their magic.

Here's what happens when you connect a USB device to a USB-compatible system:

1. If the PC hasn't "seen" this device before, Windows runs the New Hardware Found applet that identifies the device, builds a Driver Info Database, and then prompts you to insert your operating system's master CD (in some cases you might want to insert a CD that contains more recent drivers; your mileage may vary). That's it—no rebooting required.

2. If the device has been installed on this PC before, when you connect the device, literally nothing happens overtly; the device simply becomes available and functions normally.

PLAINSPEAKING
USB POWER CONSIDERATIONS

Because USB distributes power across the bus, low-power devices such as mice and keyboards don't require their own power cables and the nuisance of a brick plugged into an AC outlet. If you need a USB hub, carefully choose the right model depending on your incremental peripheral device power requirements. Add up the power needs of the devices that will be plugged into the hub and make sure the hub supplies adequate power of its own to handle these devices, instead of relying on the bus for power (in which case it is called an *unpowered* hub). For example, a Belkin DockStation (p/n F5U120-PC) is a powered hub and provides 500mA (milliamperes) of current to downstream USB devices. A low-power USB device such as a mouse usually operates at or below 100mA, whereas a high-power USB device operates in the range 100mA–500mA.

To see how much power your attached devices are drawing, use Microsoft's free USB Viewer utility, as shown in Figure 11.3. The trick is that you first must install the Windows Resource Kit: Insert your Win98 CD; from the \tools\reskit folder, double-click Setup.exe; and then follow the instructions from there. Or, you can just run `\tools\reskit\diagnose\usbview.exe`. ∎

Follow these very simple rules when dealing with USB peripheral cables:

■ A standard USB cable has an A-male connector at one end and a B-male connector at the other. The A-male connector plugs into the host PC's USB port or a hub's port. The B-male connector plugs into the peripheral device itself (although most lightweight peripherals have the cable molded into the peripheral itself to avoid signal degradation and awkward ergonomics, and to eliminate the port connection as a point of failure). As you can see in Figure 11.4, the two connector types are shaped differently to avoid connection errors.

FIGURE 11.3

Microsoft's free USB Viewer tool provides a somewhat arcane look at the devices on a PC's USB bus.

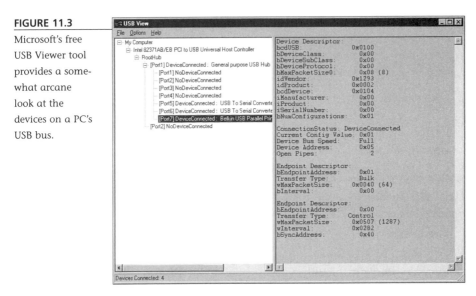

FIGURE 11.4

A USB A-male connector and a USB B-male connector. (Photo courtesy of allUSB.com)

- Don't buy or use a cable longer than 5 meters (16.4 feet).

- If, for some reason, you need a run longer than 5 meters, use an Active Extension Cable or hubs. This can provide a maximum run of 25 meters (82 feet).

  An Active Extension Cable is a 5-meter cable with a built-in 1-port hub. It includes a chip that buffers the signals in accordance with USB specifications (see Figure 11.5). You can daisy-chain 4 Active Extension Cables plus 1, 5-meter peripheral cable, yielding the maximum supported run of 25 meters.

- Plenty of USB devices conveniently contain a built-in hub; this is true of most USB keyboards (two ports is the most common configuration). You can plug other low-power devices, such as a mouse or joystick, right into the keyboard's open USB ports. Next time you buy a system (or a new keyboard), be sure to specify a USB model.

FIGURE 11.5

A-TEN's USB
Active Extension
Cable.

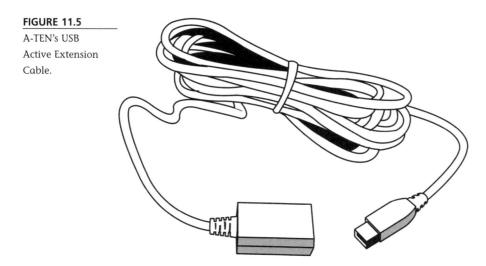

Online Resources

Several excellent USB online resources are available that can help you learn more about the bus or locate products and cables:

■ **AllUSB**—Located at `http://www.allusb.com`; includes USB FAQs, extensive product listings (by well-organized categories), hot product information and press releases, a company index, and a news library.

■ **Belkin's USB Wizard**—Located at `http://catalog.belkin.com/templates/catalog/config/usb/usbconfig.tem`; helps you either select which device(s)—and how many—you want to connect to your PC using any of Belkin's USB products, or select the Belkin USB device you want to add to your PC (see Figure 11.6).

■ **USB Implementers Forum (USB-IF)**—Located at `http://www.usb.org`; offers an extensive set of FAQs, press material, and developer resources. It also has a database of USB products that the Forum lists as having "passed a series of tests defined by the creators of USB." (Note: The USB-IF tests only the products made by its member companies.) The USB-IF was established in 1996 when Intel, aided by six other companies (Compaq, Digital, IBM, Microsoft, NEC, and Northern Telecom), created the USB bus.

■ **USB Workshop**—Located at `http://www.usbworkshop.com`; has news, FAQs, a products database, hardware reviews, and user-based forums.

FIGURE 11.6

Belkin's USB
Wizard can help
you determine
which of its USB
products is right
for your needs.

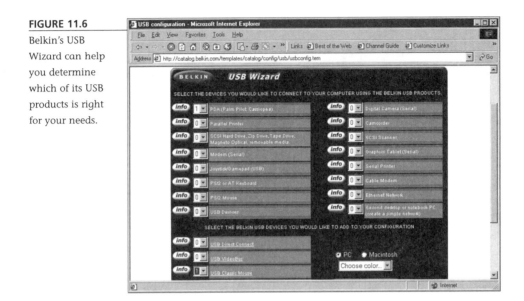

PART **IV**

UPGRADING PERIPHERALS

MONITOR AND GRAPHIC CARD UPGRADES

12

*I*f you're befuddled by terms such as dot pitch, aperture grills, dot masks, digital versus analog, then pull up a chair. In this chapter, you'll get up to speed on the terminology and learn what you need to know to make a good monitor upgrade decision. You'll also learn that the monitor is only half the equation when trying to upgrade your graphics. Your monitor (and the graphics card that drives it) is the one part of your system you'll be staring at more than any other, and a bad decision is not only disappointing, it can cause eyestrain and other physical problems. This is an area where doing your research and homework really counts.

Upgrade Checklist

1. Do your homework. A bad upgrade decision will be apparent every time you switch on your system.

2. Determine whether your PC graphics card supports the planned monitor upgrade or vice versa.

3. Determine whether you can perform the upgrade.

4. Purchase or acquire the monitor and graphics card.

5. Organize your tools and workspace.

6. Perform the upgrade.

7. Take good notes, and permanently file them in your system log when finished.

8. Update your inventory documentation to reflect the upgraded or newly added component.

Selecting a CRT Monitor

In this section, the focus is on the physical monitor and all the bells and whistles that are important in making a solid upgrade decision. But the monitor, although the most visually impressive component, is half of the parts equation that ultimately creates the images you see when you switch on your computer. The monitor must work correctly with your graphics adapter, which translates the signals from the computer into images displayed on your screen.

You don't necessarily need to get a degree in monitor engineering to make a wise selection in choosing a replacement or upgrade for your existing monitor. But you do have to know some of the terms used in describing the features of a monitor and how to compare these features between various manufacturers.

Monitors fall into roughly two categories: *CRT (cathode-ray tube)* monitors, which offer the best bang for the buck, and the more expensive *LCD (liquid crystal display)* monitors. Relatively cheap, CRTs offer large-size screens, but they're very bulky, consuming huge amounts of desk space, and putting out a lot of waste heat. LCD displays run more coolly and take up much less physical space but are very expensive and not as flexible in handling various resolutions. And the right resolution is the key to monitor nirvana.

Resolution

To be happy with your monitor, you must choose the right size screen area given the physical space with you have to work and the resolution your eyes prefer. Because your monitor is going to sit about 22 inches from the tip of your nose and is your focal point whenever you're using your computer, you must factor in your physical comfort to a practical extent when considering a monitor upgrade.

To understand what *resolution* is all about, a quick discussion of how a monitor works is in order.

The inside of the monitor screen is made up of tiny thingies called *phosphor dots.* When phosphor dots are hit by a stream of electrons, the dots glow. Three colors of dots are used—red, green, and blue—and they're usually arranged in triangular patterns. A single pixel (a *pixel* is the smallest resolvable area of an image) is made up of a number of phosphor dots.

Pixels are what is referred to when discussing screen resolutions. For example, 800×600 (Super VGA resolution) means the screen resolves to 800 pixels across and 600 pixels high. By changing the number of phosphor dots that make up a single pixel, a monitor can display images at various resolutions.

However, different size monitors have a fixed number of phosphor dots. This means that enough physical phosphor dots might not be present to create enough pixels to support a given resolution. For example, you can't generate a resolution of 1,280×1,024 on a 14-inch monitor. Then again, you really wouldn't want to because, as you increase the resolution, the individual objects (icons, text, windows, and so on) that make up the image get smaller; therefore, you need a larger screen area to keep things readable. 1,280×1,024 on a 14-inch monitor would create an image with objects so small that it would be impractical. Table 12.1 shows our recommended resolutions for various screen sizes.

Table 12.1 Recommended Screen Sizes and Resolutions

CRT Size	Resolution	Comments
15-inch	800×600	Approximately 25% more viewable area than a 14-inch CRT
17-inch	1,024×768	Approximately 30% more viewable area than a 15-inch CRT
19-inch	1,280×1,024	Approximately 35% more viewable area than a 17-inch CRT
21-inch	1,208×1,024 or 1,600×1,200	Approximately 60% more viewable area than a 17-inch CRT

The 17-inch monitor is really the smallest screen size you should consider. If you have a vision problem, you can drop the resolution down one level, sacrificing onscreen area for increased image size.

TIP

DON'T ASSUME ANY MONITOR = ANY RESOLUTION
As we mentioned, a limit exists to the number of physical phosphors that can exist on the inside of a CRT. But monitors in the 17-inch and larger category often support multiple resolutions. It differs from monitor to monitor, though, so don't assume you can run a given monitor at a given resolution. Always check a monitor's minimum and maximum resolutions supported for that particular unit. The graphics adapter you install in your system can also impact the resolutions you can display onscreen as well as the size of the fonts displayed at any given resolution.

How do you determine which resolution works best for you? This is a tricky problem because we all have different vision qualities. The best way to determine which resolution works best for you is to try various monitors running at different resolutions. This might mean sitting down at a friend's or associate's computer, or spending some time in a local computer superstore staring at the monitors on display. Take your time and remember you'll have to live with your resolution decision—so get something that won't make your eyes start planning a mutiny.

At What Resolution Is This Monitor Running?

To see at which resolution a monitor is running, do the following:

1. Right-click an empty area of the Windows desktop; then select Properties from the pop-up menu.

2. Click the Settings tab in the Display Properties dialog box.

3. Two-thirds of the way down on the right is the Screen area setting. Below the adjustment slider is the current setting. You can change the setting by moving the slider to switch to a higher (more) or lower (less) resolution.

Mask and the Dot Pitch

A *mask* focuses the electrons being streamed through the CRT onto the phosphor dots. The glass tube in your monitor looks sort of like a funnel with the small end at the back of the monitor and the large end at the front. A number of electron guns sit at the back and blast electrons onto the larger screen end of the tube. A mask sits between the electron guns and the phosphor dots to better direct the electrons onto the phosphors.

Three types of masks are commonly available in CRT monitors today: the *shadow* mask (which comes in two separate flavors, classic and asymmetrical), the *aperture* grille (also known as a *stripe* mask), and the *slot* mask.

The aperture grille is held in place by fine wires, and you can actually see these wires if you look at the monitor very closely. This really bothers some people, but others don't really notice the wires.

What makes the mask important is the effect the mask can have on something called *dot pitch*. The dot pitch is the distance (in millimeters) between a phosphor dot of one color and the next phosphor dot of the same color. This distance is measured diagonally for shadow masks and horizontally for aperture grille and slot masks. This makes a straight comparison between the dot pitch numbers difficult when comparing a monitors using different types of masks. Better to first decide on the general type of mask you prefer based on color and sharpness; then you can compare apples to apples.

Aperture grille and slot mask are considered to provide brighter images with richer, more saturated colors. Therefore, they're good for working with pictures and photographs. Shadow masks generally provide a crisper, sharper image, giving you sharper text and line art (see Table 12.2).

Table 12.2   Choosing the Correct Mask

Mask Type	Pro	Con	Recommended Dot Pitch
Aperture grille/stripe	Brighter image, better colors	Thin lines on the inside of the monitor might be visible	.25mm or less
Slot	Brighter image, better colors	None	.25mm or less
Shadow (classic and asymmetrical)	Crisper image, sharper definition	None	.28mm or less

The rule of thumb is the smaller the dot pitch, the better the image. For either flavor of shadow mask, don't get anything over a .28mm dot pitch. For aperture grille/stripe or slot masks, CRTs don't get anything with a dot pitch larger than .25mm.

Displayable Screen Size

Just because a monitor says it's a 17- or 19-inch monitor (indicating the diagonal measurement of the screen) doesn't mean the viewable area of the screen will measure 17 or 19 inches. You must know which tricks CRT manufacturers employ to make you think you're getting a great deal on a bigger monitor than you're actually getting.

First, the monitor size is actually the diagonal measurement of the actual cathode ray tube that sits inside the monitor housing. Tubes come in various sizes and— more importantly—shapes. CRTs are classified as *spherical* (hardly used any more), *flat squared*, or *flat*. The spherical and flat squared tubes are convex at the display end of the tube, with flat squared being much less convex than spherical tubes. The more convex, the more distorted the image is around the edges of the screen. Flat tubes are just that: flat. They actually appear concave the first time you sit down in front of one of them. In addition, they have next to no distortion around the edges of the tube (providing more viewable screen area).

The less distortion, the more practical viewable screen area a given tube has and the closer you get to actually receiving the promised number of inches the manufacturer claims for a given monitor. But, you'll never get the full CRT size no matter what type of tube you get. The plastic shell of the monitor itself covers a portion of the physical tube, eating up an inch or more of the viewable area.

Some manufacturers have started listing the viewable screen area along with the size of the CRT, but even then you have to be careful in relying on the numbers. That's because depending on the monitor, the video card, video drivers, and resolution at which you want to work might not be optimal if you expand the image to the extreme physical limits of the viewable area. An image so expanded might appear curved or otherwise distorted.

ANOTHER FINE MESS
A 20-INCH MONITOR IN A 19-INCH BAG

A while back, some unscrupulous monitor manufacturers were selling 19-inch monitors that had a larger viewable area than their competitors' 19-inch models. They did this by taking cheap, 20-inch spherical CRTs and selling them as 19-inch monitors. This made it appear as though consumers were getting a better deal than a similar 19-inch flat square or flat CRT monitor. The reality was they got an inferior image due to the convex qualities of the spherical tube. ■

Refresh and Scan Rates

The electron guns shoot the electrons through the mask, and they cause the phosphors to glow. But this glow slowly fades, and the gun must constantly sweep the flow of electrons across the phosphors to keep them glowing and to adjust for changes in the image as you use the computer. This gives us two additional measurements to consider when selecting monitors: the refresh and scan rates.

The *refresh rate* is an overall measurement of how often the phosphor dots are made to glow. The *scan rate* is a measure of how many times per second the electron beam starts on the next row of phosphor dots. Between the two ratings, the refresh rate is the more important and the one you'll see quoted by monitor manufacturers.

ANOTHER FINE MESS
INTERLACED MONITORS

It's unlikely you'll run into a new interlaced monitor these days. *Interlacing* was something that was used to try to get early monitor prices down by sacrificing image quality. However, you'll still see present-day monitors advertised as "noninterlaced," so a brief discussion of what interlacing is all about is warranted.

Old monitors used to use a trick whereby instead of refreshing each line of phosphors, they refreshed only every other line. This enabled a faster overall refresh rate but with a very noticeable flicker to the screen as the electron gun in the CRT swept over the phosphors. Avoid an interlaced monitor for the insidiously inferior thing it is. ■

The faster the refresh and the scan rates, the less flicker you'll perceive on your monitor's screen. Refresh rates are quoted in *Hertz (Hz)*, which means cycles per second. For a resolution of 1,024×768, you want a refresh rate of 85Hz or higher. For 1,280×1,024 or higher, you want a refresh rate in the low 70s or higher.

Footprint

When planning on your monitor upgrade, don't neglect *all* the physical dimensions of your prospective new monitor—including the fact that monitors weigh about the same as boat anchors. A 21-inch monitor requires a very solid surface to sit on given its substantial relationship with gravity.

Don't overlook the vertical clearance you'll need, either. A shelf over your desk might limit the size monitor you can upgrade to. A huge amount of waste heat is also produced by a CRT. You might not be able to cook TV dinners on top of the monitor, but you'll want to have adequate vertical and side clearance for proper ventilation. In many offices, monitors take the place of space heaters.

Also, consider the depth of the monitor. A typical 17-inch monitor is also 17 inches deep. If your desk it not very deep or if it's placed up against a wall or other obstacle, every inch of viewable screen area moves the display surface one inch closer to your nose. By the time you've wrestled a 21-inch monitor onto the corner of your desk, it might be 5 inches from where you normally sit at the keyboard. This will cause you no end of ergonomic problems as you try to back away from the screen to view it comfortably.

TIP

THE SHORT NECK CRT

If you're pressed for space consider a *short neck* CRT monitor. These use a truncated CRT that's not as deep as regular tubes, moving the electron guns closer to the front of the tube screen. This makes it possible to build a 17- or 19-inch monitor that's only 15 inches deep.

The Facts About LCD Monitors

Make no mistake, LCD monitors, or *panels* as they're called, are the coming thing in computer screens. LCD stands for Liquid Crystal Display and has come a long way from its debut in digital watches. When we talk about LCD monitors for computers, we're including LED (light-emitting diodes) and LEP (light-emitting polymer) technologies, as well. It all boils down to a computer screen that has some serious advantages over CRT-based monitors.

The question is when will all these advantages outweigh the disadvantages and make you want to upgrade to this technology? The single biggest drawback is the cost because, given the current manufacturing constraints, they are not just expensive, they are *hideously* expensive.

Another issue with LCDs revolves around the graphics cards used in most computers today. LCDs are digital devices, and the average graphics card puts out an analog signal. Some LCDs force you to use a proprietary digital graphics adapter, whereas others are ready plug-in replacements for CRTs and convert the analog signal to digital at the panel. Also, graphics card manufacturers are starting to come out with adapters that allow either an analog or digital video device to be plugged in.

Resolution

LCDs provide a super crisp and sharp image, and the better ones provide more saturated color than their CRT counterparts. This is because of the different method in which the LCD displays an image. There is no CRT, meaning that no curved surface exists to cause distortion. In addition, no electron guns exist, hence no stream of electrons to get out of alignment and cause image problems.

The pixels in an LCD are made up of what are called *cells*, which are either on or off. The color goes right to the edge of the cell, which abuts the cell next to it. Therefore, no unlighted area exists, as it does with the space between phosphor dots in a CRT. So, you can get a sharper, more defined image with an LCD.

A fixed number of cells exists across and down the panel, making up the maximum resolution the panel can display. This maximum resolution setting on an LCD is important because, when you try to view images at lesser resolutions, things can start to get weird.

For example, consider an LCD with a maximum resolution of 1,024×768. Switch from the maximum resolution to 800×600 and some LCDs try to do what a CRT does—to expand the image so that 800 pixels display across the entire width of the viewable screen area. This expands objects displayed within the image. The problem with LCDs is in the geometry of the cells. To do this, the panel has to start grouping cells together to create larger pixels, and the image can distort as the panel starts to double up on cells. This can result in aliased objects with jagged edges and make for a very poor image overall.

Newer LCDs work around this problem by simply using less of the screen space to display the image. The result is very different from what you'd expect with a traditional CRT and again is caused by the difference in how the two technologies work. Keeping with our example of an LCD that is 1,024×768, instead of trying to stretch the image so 800 pixels extend across the 1,024 cells that make up the width of the screen, the panel just uses 800 of the total number of the cells across and 600 cells down in which to display the image. Instead of objects getting larger to fill the image across and down the entire viewable area of the screen, the image is just displayed using less screen space. This avoids the need to alias the objects and no distortion occurs. This can be a bit of a shock, especially if you're playing a computer game that switches resolutions. Suddenly, your gaming experience is reduced to a smaller image taking up only a portion of the screen.

ANOTHER FINE MESS
DEAD CELLS

One of the things that contributes to the high cost of LCD panels is the difficulty in manufacturing them. One of the biggest quality control problems is with bad cells. Rarely does a single panel not contain several cells permanently switched off, which creates a dark point, or permanently switched on, which creates a bright point. Some manufacturers consider up to six bad cells an acceptable quality level, but some users have very little tolerance for *any* bad cells, saying even one can be a huge distraction. And when you're paying such a huge premium over a traditional CRT, it's tough to justify getting a screen that's not perfect. If you go for an LCD, be sure you know how many bad cells the manufacturer thinks is acceptable because they won't replace a screen if it's within their established limits. ■

Mask and the Dot Pitch

These things, while vital considerations when considering CRT monitor upgrades, have no equivalent in LCD. This is because of the way the cells work without all the baggage of electron beams and focusing devices within a cathode-ray tube.

Displayable Screen Size

As we discussed earlier in this chapter, a CRT's size and its viewable area are two different things. The fundamental differences between a glass CRT and an LCD panel's cells mean that, unlike the CRT, the LCD has no lost viewable screen area around the edges of the monitor housing. This means that comparing screen sizes between LCDs and CRTs using just the manufacturer's ratings is difficult.

For example, you'd think that a 17-inch CRT would give you more screen than a 15-inch LCD, but you'd be wrong. A 15-inch LCD gives you approximately the same viewable screen area as a 17-inch CRT (see Table 12.3).

Table 12.3 LCD and CRT Equivalent Sizes

CRT Size (Manufacturer's Rating)	LCD (Manufacturer's Rating)	Recommended Resolutions
17-inch	15-inch	1024×768
21-inch	18-inch	1280×1024

Refresh and Scan Rates

You need a fast refresh rate for a CRT or the screen will perceptibly flicker as the electron beam sweeps the phosphor dots. LCD screens don't flicker because the individual cells are controlled electrically and are either on or off. They don't fade and then get refreshed periodically, at least not in the manner of CRTs.

When the image changes, an LCD screen does get refreshed in that some cells are turned off, whereas others are turned on to cause the image on the LCD screen to change. This means that a refresh rate is listed for a given LCD, but it does not need to be as fast as a CRT rate. LCDs in the 50Hz–60Hz range are acceptable, at least for computer software applications. Slower refresh rates on LCDs are a problem, however, if you plan to watch a lot of full-motion video. If you want to get an LCD and watch DVD movies on your computer, you'll definitely want to give the panel you're contemplating a screen test to see whether the refresh rate causes more flicker than you can stand.

NOTE

FLICKER FASTER THAN THE HUMAN EYE

CRTs always flicker. It's inherent in their design. The electron guns blaze away, sweeping over the phosphor dots from side to side, top to bottom, one line at a time. Mere human eyes cannot perceive any flicker if the refresh rate is fast enough. The image appears to be solid without any jittering or movement. But the flicker is there. If you've ever seen a running computer monitor captured on a television broadcast, you have probably noticed that the image on the monitor not only flickered, it positively danced and rolled. If you saw the monitor with your eyes, you'd most likely not have noticed any flicker, but the television set you were watching uses a different scan rate than the computer monitor. This difference makes the computer screen look like it's having convulsions when seen on the TV.

Footprint

This is where the LCD beats the CRT hands down. Flat-panel LCDs are just that, flat. The screen is only a few inches thick and takes up 75%–90% less physical volume than a comparably sized CRT. LCDs weigh a lot less than CRTs, too—usually along the lines of 80% less depending on the models involved.

You can mount flat panels on the wall, but we've never seen this done effectively. It's important that your computer screen be at the correct angle and placement so that you are looking just slightly down at it. And it has to be far enough away from your nose that you can easily focus your eyes on it. Most people don't have desks positioned so that the wall is just the right distance and angle for a computer screen.

Because they're light and not bulky, moving and adjusting the LCD to a good viewing position is easy, and LCDs put out very little heat and none of the radiation that a CRT is capable of emitting. This makes LCDs friendly to the work environment and very energy efficient.

Unique LCD Issues

The analog-to-digital conversion issue is a problem if you're upgrading to an LCD panel. LCDs are digital devices, and as we said earlier, most computer graphics adapters output only analog signals.

Conversion between analog and digital can cause problems and result in pixel jitter where the image jumps as the screen redraws to follow the changes. This is more of a problem where a lot of movement and redrawing is done onscreen. You can also run into aliasing problems and image patterns (called *moiré*) appearing—all of which make for a poor image.

It's interesting to note that the computer is sending digital signals to the graphics card, which converts the native digital signals to analog for display on a CRT. Most of the LCD panels currently available on the market must then convert it back to digital. Not only does this degrade the signal, but it adds to the cost of the panel.

The alternative is to go with an LCD panel that uses a dedicated digital graphics adapter or one that supports dual digital/analog connectors.

Installing a Monitor

Installing a monitor is one of the easiest tasks in all of PC-dom. Unpack it, plug in two cables (video and power) (because it's all external, the PC case doesn't have to come off), and you get to play around with dozens of neat little settings such as picture rotation, color temperature, side curvature, and so forth. Basically, if you're a knob-twiddler, you'll love it. It's all fun and games unless you wind up staring at a solid black screen. However, you must perform a few steps, if that occurs to try to correct any problems.

Unpacking and Positioning the Monitor

Open the box that contains the monitor. This is the most fragile component of your system, so take the appropriate care removing it from the box. Even a 15" monitor is bulkier and heavier than you would think. Be aware of its uneven weight because it is much heavier toward the screen end of the unit than to the back.

Get someone to help you uncrate the monitor and set it in position. Wrestling a 21" monitor can easily throw out your back (something we can attest to, unfortunately). Be careful. It will be tightly wedged into the box, braced with Styrofoam blocks at the front and back. After the monitor is clear of the box, you must get those blocks off; don't trust them to stay braced after the monitor is out of the box. If you set the rig down at this point, it might well tip right over. Crash. You'll need one of those nice, clean flat surfaces we've touted throughout this book to set it on. If the PC's chassis is not going to sit under the monitor, get the monitor positioned where it will live after everything is connected. If you are installing a desktop chassis and plan on setting the monitor on it, ensure that it can take the weight of a 19" or larger monitor.

Put the Styrofoam blocks back into the shipping box, along with any other extra packing material and flotsam. Close up the box and move it out of the assembly area. Get all the documentation and accompanying disks into your NEAT box. The less clutter, the better.

NOTE

THE NEAT BOX

We discussed the NEAT box back in Chapter 3. *NEAT* stands for **n**ew computer **e**mergency catch**a**ll **t**runk and can be anything from an old shoebox to a large plastic trash bag. We favor the plastic box type (available at most office supply stores), about 12 inches wide, 16 inches long, and 8 inches deep. Into your NEAT box goes everything that accompanies each component of your system. Manuals, install disks, specification sheets, instructions, CD-ROMs, licenses, invoices, packing slips, spare parts, screws, twist ties, cables, connectors—everything. A NEAT box ensures that you have to search for things in only one place.

An often overlooked factor in a monitor's performance (or your perception thereof) is its physical positioning. First, don't put your monitor where direct sunlight hits it (especially the screen). A monitor puts out enough heat on its own, so you don't want to cook it further. Direct solar radiation can damage the phosphors in the CRT, so no direct sunshine on the screen.

Second, orient it properly in relation to where and how you sit. Configure it so you look slightly down at the screen; this helps avoid neck strain. You want to be looking at the monitor and the keyboard without a significant or repetitive raising or lowering of your head. It's common to try to set the monitor so that it's at eye level or even higher, but from experience, we've found this configuration fatiguing over time.

SAVE THAT BOX

Save the monitor's box. If you have to ship it back to the retailer (or manufacturer), you'll want to use the original box and packing materials it came in. We suggest saving the box for at least 30 days after you get everything working, and longer if you have the available storage room.

Adjusting the Image

Monitor ease of use and adjustment is another often-overlooked feature. You might find a monitor that meets all your requirements, but don't forget that after you plug it in, you're going to have to adjust its brightness, contrast, color settings, horizontal and vertical alignment, side curvature (geometry), and so on. Granted, you probably have to do this only once, but if the controls are awkward to use, it could take hours instead of minutes.

ADJUSTING THE PICTURE

You won't be adjusting your monitor very often, but when you need to do so you'd better be able to remember how. Monitors vary widely in how their controls are designed, where they are located, and whether they are physical or software-based. We suggest you jot down notes on the process, unless your monitor manual has very good instructions or the controls are extraordinarily intuitive.

IN THE EYE OF THE BEHOLDER

If you're buying a monitor from a retail store, make sure you understand how the controls work by actually trying them out in the store. We've found that dedicated buttons on (or inside) the monitor that control its settings are preferable to complex, onscreen menus; in the latter design you must make selection after selection using only a few keys that do various things depending on which menu you're viewing. It makes our eyes cross. But this is very subjective, and we know others in our field who think menus are easier. We must admit the software-based controls are, well, cooler.

DON'T TOUCH THAT SCREEN!

We cringe whenever we see someone else's monitor with <shudder> fingerprints on it. Folks, please don't touch your screen. Let's face it, our fingers (epidermis, in general) contain oils and dirt that adhere to the monitor's surface. Over time, numerous fingerprints will produce a smeared image. Then, you'll have to clean the surface. Second, a trivial bad habit can escalate to a serious bad habit. We're talking about touching a screen with an object such as a pen, pencil, or ruler, an act that can put a permanent—and very annoying—scratch on the screen surface. If you can train yourself not to touch a screen with your finger(s), it's much less likely you'll do so with a hard, sharp object.

As for cleaning the screen, there's just one rule: *Use the cleaning technique and solution recommended by the manufacturer*. That means no home-brew cleaning solution, no special cloths you buy mail order or while standing in line at the 7-Eleven, no way. You're not dealing with a plain glass window. Often, the monitor screen surface has an antireflective coating that ammonia- or alcohol-based cleaners can damage. Open the user's guide, read the paragraph on cleaning the screen's surface, and do exactly what it says.

Connecting the Monitor to the PC

If all goes according to plan, this should take all of about five minutes.

Five Minutes to Connect!

1. Before disconnecting your old monitor, go into Device Manager (right-click My Computer, select Properties, and click the Device Manager tab) and note what Windows has as the current monitor and driver (if not generic Plug and Play). This way, if you have to put the old monitor back on the system, you'll know what settings to use.

2. As usual, power everything down and disconnect all cables.

3. Be sure the monitor's power switch is in the off position.

4. Connect the monitor's power cord to its receptacle at the back of the monitor.

5. Connect the monitor's power cord to a power outlet (we recommend a filtered outlet on your UPS as discussed back in Chapter 10, "Adding Power Protection").

6. Connect the monitor's video cable to your graphics card's port connector.

7. Turn on the monitor, turn on your PC, and if all goes well, as Windows is beginning to display its desktop, the Add New Hardware Wizard will take over. These are the steps. (Note that your mileage might vary depending on the exact model you're installing, the exact version/upgrade of Windows, and your system configuration.)

The wizard's first panel reports, This wizard searches for new drivers for: Plug and Play Monitor. Click the Next button.

The next panel gives you two options: Search for the Best Driver for Your Device. (Recommended), or Display a List of All the Drivers in a Specific Location, so you can select the driver you want. We advise you to use the first option, and (as you'll see in a moment) when prompted, tell Windows to also include the monitor's install disk (or CD) in its search. Click the Next button.

The next panel tells you Windows will search for new drivers in its driver database on your hard drive, and in any of the following selected locations. Click Next to start the search. The checkboxes are as follows: Floppy Disk Drives, CD-ROM Drive, Microsoft Windows Update, and Specify a Location. Select the appropriate box(es) for your situation; then click Next.

The next panel reports Windows has found an updated driver for this device, and also some other drivers that should work with this device. What do you want to install? You'll see two options: The Updated Driver (Recommended) <device name>, and One of the Other Drivers. Select the first option, unless there is a special circumstance afoot. Then, click the Next button.

Windows tells you it's ready to install it and show the physical location of the new driver. Click Next; shortly thereafter Windows reports that it has finished installing the driver. Click the Finish button.

8. Customize your monitor's various settings, such as picture rotation, color temperature, side curvature, and so on.

9. Use Device Manager to verify that the monitor is functioning properly as far as Windows is concerned (in other words, no error or warning icons appear), as shown in Figure 12.1.

10. Test your monitor's performance.

One quick way to do this is with some free online tools provided by ZDNet's Virtual Lab. Point your browser to http://www.zdnet.com/vlabs/index.html and follow the instructions for testing your monitor. These tests include a master test pattern, color scales test, extreme grayscale with color bars test, horizontal resolution test, and a crosshatch and dot test (see Figure 12.2).

FIGURE 12.1

Windows' Device Manager shows that the newly installed Sony monitor is functioning properly.

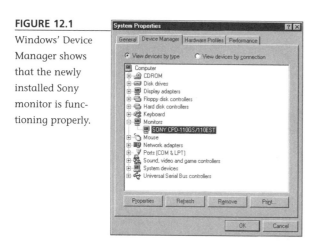

FIGURE 12.2

This is ZDNet's free online master test pattern (one of several available at this Web site) that can help you evaluate your monitor's performance.

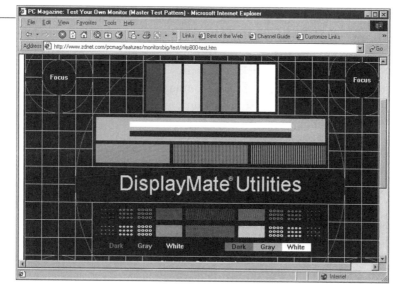

Two Monitors Better Than One?

Windows 98 and Windows 2000 support the use of multiple monitors. If you're upgrading to a new monitor and graphics card, you might want to consider installing them along with the old card and monitor and using dual monitors (see Figure 12.3).

The graphics adapters must be PCI or AGP cards (either multiple PCIs or 1 AGP and the rest PCI), one for each monitor. We've not seen any motherboards with multiple AGP slots so far. The real trick is that not all graphics adapters will let you set up this multiple-monitor trick. It's actually the graphics card driver that determines whether a given video card can handle the needs of multiple monitors. A Microsoft Knowledge Base article on what cards are supported is available at `http://support.microsoft.com/support/kb/articles/Q182/7/08.ASP`

The problem is that it's not updated often enough for new cards, so you might just have to install the cards you have and see whether it's going to work.

One monitor (usually the first monitor installed) is the primary monitor, and the rest are extended areas of your Windows desktop. If you're using an AGP system, check the BIOS to see whether you can designate that slot as your primary video. If the BIOS does not, uninstall your AGP video card, install a video card in slot 1 of the PCI bus, and get that card working. Windows will default that card at the primary video slot. Then, reinstall the AGP card (or a second PCI card if you are upgrading a strictly PCI system).

In the Display Properties dialog box (right-click the desktop, choose Properties, and click the Setting tab), you'll see two monitors represented (see Figure 12.4).

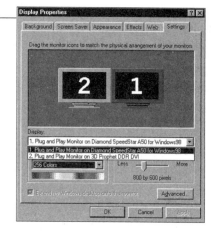

FIGURE 12.4

Set the resolution and color options for each of the two monitors (they don't have to be set the same, but it's usually easier if they are).

Your mouse recognizes the dual screens as one large Windows desktop, and if you scroll off the edge of one monitor, it shows up at the edge of the next monitor.

You'll find a very detailed How-To article on setting up dual monitors under Windows 98 on the ZDNet site:

`http://home.zdnet.com/zdhelp/howto_help/jeffknows/jk020399/jk020399a.html`

Troubleshooting Monitor Problems

When you boot your system, if you get a black screen (no picture), here are the troubleshooting steps to follow.

Black Screen Help

1. *Remember that upgrading a graphics card and a monitor simultaneously is not advisable.* That will make it much harder to pinpoint the culprit component if something goes wrong.

2. Verify that the monitor's power cord is securely seated at the back of the monitor and is plugged in to a power outlet.

3. Verify that the monitor's power cord is connected to a functioning power outlet.

   This doesn't mean simply checking that it is plugged in. Here's the test: Is what it's plugged into working? If it's plugged directly into the wall, verify that the circuit is live by plugging in any small appliance (a desk lamp works fine for us). If the monitor is plugged into a UPS or a power strip, verify that the UPS or strip is turned on and supplying power; do this by plugging in any small appliance. Naturally, if you're not getting power to the UPS, power strip, or the circuit servicing them, you'll need to contact an electrician.

4. Verify that the monitor's power switch is in the on position. This is difficult if it's a push-button switch. If this is the case, make sure you press the button firmly.

5. Verify that the monitor's video cable is connected securely to your graphics card's port connector.

6. Find the brightness and contrast controls on the monitor (these are usually thumbwheel-type controls) and try adjusting them both. It's possible that they've gotten turned all the way down and are displaying a black image.

7. Because this book is about upgrades, it's reasonable for us to assume that immediately before you connected the new monitor to your graphics card that you disconnected an old—but fully functional—monitor. However, because assumptions can be trouble themselves, let's cover all the possibilities.

   If you have another monitor handy that is known to be good, connect it back up and see what happens. If, after a boot, it displays your Windows desktop correctly, the new monitor is DOA (dead on arrival). If that known-to-be-good monitor is black upon bootup, you have a dysfunctional graphics card or at the very least a bad graphics card port connector—which are effectively one and the same problem (no video). (Another possibility is that some very unlikely events have conspired to really ruin your day, because it is probable but not likely that both the graphics card and the monitor simultaneously decided to collaborate and play dead.) You'll have to put in a known-to-be-good graphics card and retest the new monitor.

   It's possible that you have in your possession only the new monitor; in the case where the upgrade is prompted by the old monitor dying on you. So, with no other monitor available, you have no choice but to transport the monitor to another location that has a PC you can test it on. It's a hassle. So, if this is out of the question, you'll need to contact the manufacturer's technical support or customer service group for their policy.

8. Study your monitor's user's guide; look for a troubleshooting section.

   If the monitor reports an onscreen message (usually in huge block letters) such as NO INPUT SIGNAL when you power it on (followed by the PC), it can't see a signal from the graphics card. If the video cable is securely connected to the graphics card, open the PC's case and verify that the graphics card is firmly seated in its slot (if, *immediately* prior to this moment in time, an old monitor was connected and functioning, skip this step and instead consider the new monitor as DOA).

If the monitor reports a different onscreen message, check the user's guide.

9. Study your user's guide for a self-test or self-diagnosis feature.

For example, on a Sony, the self-diagnosis feature works like this: The screen will be blank and the power indicator will light up solid green or flash orange (indicating power-saving mode). If it's green, power down the PC, turn off the monitor and then turn it back on, press and hold the + button (on the front panel) for two seconds. If three colored bars appear—red, green, and blue—the monitor is working properly, so the problem is presumably with the PC. If it flashes orange, turn off the monitor and then turn it back on. If the power indicator lights green, the monitor is working properly. If the power indicator is still flashing orange, the monitor is dysfunctional, so call technical support.

TIP

WHAT'S NEW AND WHAT'S OLD, A CATCH-22

Believe it or not, with some monitors, you might not get any picture even if everything is configured perfectly. This can happen under Windows 9x for particular monitor models, and the only workaround is to reconnect the old monitor, install the new monitor's setup disk, and select the new monitor by name from the manufacturer's list of monitors. Basically, you're installing the new monitor's driver before the new monitor is actually connected to your PC. But this is a field-tested technique. Go figure.

10. Call the manufacturer's technical support group and have them walk you through their paces. If you're lucky, the situation is correctable right there over the phone. Otherwise, you'll be returning the monitor on a Returned Merchandise Authorization (RMA). See Chapter 24, "Dealing with Technical Support," for more information.

Upgrading Graphics Adapters

A monitor upgrade should always go hand in hand with graphics adapter (also known as graphics card or video card) considerations. A bad choice on either end results in a less-than-satisfying viewing experience.

At the minimum, you need a card that supports the resolution you want to run on the monitor. You can have a monitor that supports a resolution higher than the maximum supported by the card, which is a limiting factor in what you can display.

You also must consider all the bells and whistles you can get on a graphics adapter; these depend on the type of features you want supported on your system. Some higher-end cards come with large amounts of very fast memory to make full-motion graphics found in computer games flow smoothly. Some cards take the output from a DVD drive and pipe it to an external television connected to the card.

TIP

GETTING THE RIGHT GRAPHICS ADAPTER

You can get a plethora of features in a graphics adapter. Do you need a video-in socket so you can dump VHS video to your computer for editing? How about a connection for an S3 video output so you can plug a television directly into your computer to output DVD movies to your TV?

To find the right graphics adapter card, you're going to have to do some homework and determine which features you require. A number of information sites are on the Web that can get you up to speed in a hurry.

The PC Technology Guide provides a great tutorial on what makes a graphics card tick and covers all the terms with which you'll need to be familiar:

http://www.pctechguide.com/05graphics.htm

Sharky Extreme has the latest reviews of the hot graphics card, especially those that PC gamers will be interested in:

www.sharkyextreme.com

You'll also find detailed information on video adapters at Tom's Hardware Guide site:

www.tomshardware.com

As with most upgrades, the more features you try to utilize, the more time you can expect to spend fussing with the upgrade to get everything working correctly.

PCI Versus AGP

You can still get graphics cards for either the PCI bus or the AGP (Accelerated Graphics Port) bus. If your motherboard has an AGP slot, we recommend you go with an AGP card for improved video performance. If you're running an older motherboard that doesn't have an AGP slot, go with a PCI card with an adequate amount of onboard memory (more on memory issues shortly).

2D Versus 3D Versus Combo Cards

It used to be that you had to decide between a 2D (2-dimension) card, which is good for text and Windows application graphics, and a 3D (3-dimension) card, which is optimized for computer games and the heavy demands of moving video and graphics.

If you wanted to upgrade your graphics adapter, you usually just added a 3D card to your system in addition to your existing 2D card. The monitor plugged into the 3D card, and the 3D card in turn plugged into the 2D card. If you're upgrading an older system, don't be surprised if two cards are installed in this configuration. When combo cards that offered both 2D and 3D graphics on the same card came out, they did a fair job on the 2D side, but were weak for 3D-intensive work.

The good news is that the current crop of graphics cards have both 2D and 3D capabilities and do a very nice job with both. The high-end cards also host a plethora of new video features, as well. Just be sure you're not getting an older card that supports only 2D.

Higher-end cards boast of "turbo-boosted 3D in high resolutions" and "per-pixel shading." You'll pay a premium price for increased features and performance, but you'll notice the benefits of leading-edge features only if you play the most graphics-intensive computer games and simulations, or do high-end graphics design work. If all you want to do is work on a spreadsheet or type in your word processor, you can do without these features and save yourself some money.

Video Memory

Graphics adapters need quick access to system memory, which is one of the speed bottlenecks that the dedicated AGP slot addresses. However, you'll also find that video cards carry their own onboard memory. The general rule is the more memory, the better the card can shuffle the images displayed onscreen, producing a noticeable improvement in performance.

You need a minimum of 4MB onboard memory to run 1,024×768 or lower resolutions with 16 million colors. Double this to 8MB if you want higher resolutions.

If you want more bells and whistles, such as TV, HDTV output, or digital (DVI) output, on your card, get something with 64MB of RAM or more. Video cards usually carry the faster types of RAM, such as DDR SDRAM memory (see Chapter 5, "RAM," for more on RAM types). Therefore, you'll pay more but get faster performance than with conventional SDRAM memory. Cards such as the GeForce line from Hercules (http://www.hercules.com/) or the Voodoo line from 3Dfx (http://www.3dfx.com/) usually contain the latest state-of-the-art features. However, you'll pay five times or more than for cards that would handle the needs of a typical Windows user.

Installing a Graphics Card

Follow these steps to install a new graphics card:

Preparing to Install a Graphics Card

1. Before removing your old graphics card, go into Device Manager (right-click My Computer, select Properties, and click the Device Manager tab) and note what Windows has as the current graphics card and driver. This way, if you have to put the card back on the system, you'll know what settings to use.

2. Shut down and disconnect your system (see Chapter 3's section "Breaking Down Your Computer").

3. As usual, when working inside the case, discharge all static electricity and wear an ESD wrist strap.

4. Carefully remove the old graphics card and set it aside in an antistatic bag (if you have one) for safekeeping. After you install the upgrade card, you can put the old one in the bag your new one came in.

5. Install the new graphics card in accordance with the manufacturer's instructions. For best performance, you should get a graphics card that goes in your system's AGP slot (available on Pentium II motherboards and higher). See Figure 12.5.

FIGURE 12.5

Seat the graphics adapter carefully in the AGP slot as shown here.

If you are installing a PCI graphics card, insert it into an available PCI slot.

If you're not replacing an existing card, you'll have to remove the slot cover from the chassis. This cover is removed to allow the connectors on the card to extrude through to the back of the system so you can connect your monitor cable to the card.

After it's installed, be sure you secure the card to the chassis (see Figure 12.6).

FIGURE 12.6

Adapter cards must be secured to the chassis via a screw where the bracket fits to the back panel of the system.

6. Connect the monitor's video cable to your graphics card's port connector. This is the 15-pin female D-shell connector that protrudes from the back of your system.

7. Turn on the monitor, turn on your PC, and if all goes well, as Windows is beginning to display its desktop, the Add New Hardware Wizard will take over. For more information, see the section "Connecting the Monitor to the PC" earlier in this chapter.

8. Depending on your graphics card manufacturer, you might be automatically prompted to install a set of graphic display tools to enhance your graphics card's performance or extend its capabilities. We suggest you do install these tools. If not prompted, follow your graphics card's installation instructions for installing these tools. Customize these tools' settings to your liking, as shown in Figure 12.7.

FIGURE 12.7

The Diamond
InControl Tools
98 Properties
dialog box gives
you access to
this utility's fea-
tures.

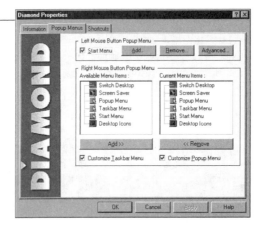

9. Use Device Manager to validate that the graphics card (display adapter) is functioning properly as far as Windows is concerned. Beware: If you're running the older Windows 95, it does not always know what to make of an AGP graphics card and you might see an error icon indicating a conflict in Device Manager (a red X through the device icon) or a warning icon (an exclamation point in a yellow circle). Assuming your monitor/graphics card is working properly, you don't have to worry about this.

TIP

KEEPING GRAPHICS CARDS COOL

As mentioned earlier, graphics adapters carry their own onboard memory—sometimes a lot more memory, as in 64 megabytes or more. This can make a graphics card run very hot, so it's common to find heat sinks and fans mounted on them.

If your motherboard sports only a single AGP slot then you don't have much choice of where to mount the card. But, if you have a choice, keep this heat aspect in mind. Try to keep an empty slot on each side of the card to allow for better heat dissipation.

Troubleshooting Graphics Card Problems

Troubleshooting a new graphics card installation (assumes a working monitor) involves the following:

1. *Remember that upgrading a graphics card and a monitor simultaneously is not advisable.* That will make it much harder to pinpoint the culprit component if something goes wrong.

2. Follow the appropriate steps in the section "Troubleshooting Monitor Problems" to ensure the monitor is not at fault.

3. Power down the PC and monitor; disconnect all power cables; open the PC case; and verify that the graphics card is properly and securely seated and that it is installed in the proper slot. Even though it shouldn't be possible to install an AGP card in a PCI slot and vice versa, you should verify that the card is in the proper type slot.

4. If you're using a PCI graphics card, try the card in a different PCI slot.

5. If you're working on a system with multiple graphics cards, remove all but the graphics card you're trying to troubleshoot.

6. Although this usually is not applicable to new cards, you can try cleaning the connectors on the card. Remove the card from its slot and carefully and gently clean the edge connectors with a clean dry cloth. This removes any oil from your hands that might have gotten on the edge connector. If the edge connectors aren't shiny, you can take a new #2 pencil and use the eraser to clean the edge connectors. Be very careful to remove any eraser leavings from the card before reinstallation. Reseat the card.

7. Try the card in another PC.

8. Study your card's user's guide; look for a troubleshooting section.

9. Call the manufacturer's technical support group and have them walk you through their paces.

13

PRINTER
UPGRADES

What's to know about upgrading a printer? You plug it in and you're done, right? Wrong. Although upgrading your printer is a fairly straightforward procedure, it is not something you want to jump into without proper consideration.

Upgrade Checklist

1. Do your homework.

2. Determine whether your PC supports the type of connection required for this printer.

3. Determine whether you can perform the upgrade. This boils down to being able to plug in the necessary cables and set up the printer itself. Setting up some printers is more complicated than you might think, so study the documentation that accompanies the printer carefully.

4. Purchase or acquire the printer.

5. Organize any necessary tools and the installation space.

6. Make sure you have all printer documentation and driver/software disks in your NEAT box.

7. Perform the upgrade.

8. Take good notes and permanently file them in your system log when finished.

9. Update your inventory documentation to reflect the upgraded or newly added component.

General Considerations

One of the key steps in ensuring the success of any upgrade is to understand what you want to accomplish. This ensures you get the correct upgrade and don't spend unnecessary time and effort, only to wind up with the same problem you tried to resolve.

Printers appear to be a fairly straightforward type of upgrade in that they are easily installed. But getting the right printer for your needs is not nearly as simple as connecting it to your computer.

Resolution and Speed

First, let's define some terms so that you're comparing apples to apples when deciding on a printer resolution. At the low end, you'll find printers rated for 600 dots per inch (dpi).

At the mid- to high-end are 1200dpi printers. 1200dpi is rapidly replacing 600dpi as the standard and provides not twice the resolution of a 600dpi printer but four times the resolution with 1.44 million dots per square inch. This gets you very close to the quality range you'd get from a commercial service bureau's commercial typesetting equipment, which is typically 1200dpi–2400dpi.

Inkjet printers come in resolutions from a low of 600dpi ×300dpi to a high of 1440dpi×720dpi. When comparing different resolution printers, it might be helpful to multiply the down and across dpi numbers and compare the total number of dots per square inch that each printer can generate.

At the same resolution, a laser printer will always provide a sharper image than an inkjet because of differences in the technology. Ink sprayed on a piece of paper will spread a tad and be absorbed into the paper to some extent, thereby softening the edges and giving it a blurry look when compared to the laser printer's sharper edges.

The key to selecting the proper resolution is to think through the types of images you'll be printing. If you are going to print photographs, you'll want all the dots per inch you can afford. If you are printing graphics, such as bar charts and line-drawn figures, you don't need as much resolution to create quality output.

PLAINSPEAKING
DPI

The basis of offset printing (in which an image is offset to a piece of paper) is how the human eye interprets a series of teensy-weensy dots on a printed page as actually an image of something.

Printers (both laser and inkjet models) print by applying a series of tiny dots on a piece of paper. The smaller the dots and the more dots in a given area on the page, the better the picture will look. This is called *resolution* and is measured in dots per square inch.

When you see a printer quoted as 600dpi, where only the one number is presented, you can usually assume that this means the resolution is 600×600 dots per inch. 600 dots down a one-inch square and 600 dots across for a total of 360,000 dots in all. However, you'd be well advised to verify this because a printer that calls itself 600dpi but is only 600×300 is not going to have anywhere near the quality of a 600dpi×600dpi printer. ∎

You also must consider speed as an issue. Again, the type of printing you'll do will have a big impact. If you print reams of pages that you need in a hurry after you click the Print button, you'll want a faster printer. Conversely, if you print only occasionally and can wait to pick up the printed pages, speed is less of a concern.

The more speed and the more resolution, the more the printer will cost. Resolution provides sharper images, and speed will keep your printer from becoming a bottleneck in production. But it all weighs heavily against your printing requirements.

Paper Stock and Envelopes

When choosing a printer upgrade, give careful consideration to the type of paper you'll be using. You can't run heavy card stock through some printers. Therefore, if you need to print specialty items, ensure that the printer is rated to handle that paper weight. Special finishes on paper stock can cause you some problems, as well.

Another factor to consider is the printer's minimum and maximum paper sizes. If you need to run 11×17 sheets (or larger tabloid sizes), be sure that's supported in the printer specifications. If you need to run paper smaller than 8.5×11, ensure that it can handle that as well.

You generally can run heavier stock through a printer that allows a straight pass through—that is, where the paper enters the printer and comes straight out the back without having to do any s turns or 180-degree rollovers.

Most printers can deal with an envelope or two, but if your printing chores include printing dozens of envelopes, you'll want to look into a feeder attachment that can run stacks of envelopes automatically. If you're planning to run mail merges in which you first print a form letter, then an envelope, then the next form letter, and so on, you'd better check with the manufacturer. Most printers—even with an envelope feeder—won't do this gracefully, if at all. You usually have to print the letters, print the envelopes, and then manually collate everything. For big merge jobs, a service bureau still makes good sense.

TIP

WHEN IN DOUBT

If you're not sure whether the printer to which you want to upgrade can handle a particular paper stock, take a few sheets down to your local computer superstore and have the salesperson convince you by printing a few copies on your sample paper. Seeing is believing.

Memory

Just as with computer memory, the axiom *more is better* applies to printer memory, too. If you print complex graphics, your print jobs will execute more quickly with more RAM. Without enough memory, the printer might balk altogether at your print job, leaving you with partially printed graphics or without hard copy of your photos or drawings.

Printers now come standard with 4MB of RAM and up, although you'll still find models sporting 2MB. Memory is cheap, and you can add it later if you need more—up to the printer's maximum capacity. Find out how many available memory slots the printer has and whether you can add standard SIMMs or DIMMs (see Figure 13.1). These plug into the printer just as they do on your motherboard.

SEE ALSO

➤ *For more details on upgrading memory modules, see "Installing Memory Modules," page 131*

And like the motherboard, you can use only the type of module and memory supported by the printer, so check the specifications carefully when making your upgrade purchases.

FIGURE 13.1

Accessing the memory slots can involve removing a side panel or cover from the printer.

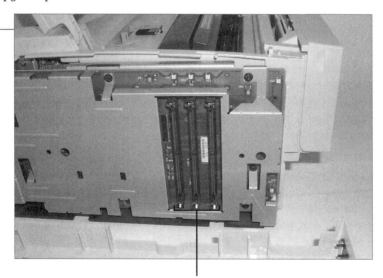

Memory slots

If you must add proprietary memory modules sold only by the printer manufacturer, expect to pay a huge premium for additional RAM.

Connection

Consider how you'll be connecting the printer to your computer. For most of us, it's usually a standard Centronics parallel connection between the printer and the parallel port on the back of our system chassis. But even that is not as simple as it once was.

In the beginning there was the standard parallel port, and it was slow. That led to the development of the *enhanced parallel port (EPP)*. It was developed by a consortium of Intel, Xircom, and Zenith Data Systems to try to improve the throughput and performance of the standard port while maintaining compatibility with the earlier version.

ANOTHER FINE MESS

DON'T FORGET THE CABLE

Most printers now support EPC and provide fast throughput between the printer and the computer—providing you have the right cable. Forget about using that old Centronics cable that you've been using since the 1980s. What most people don't realize is that the printer cable used to connect the printer to the computer must also support EPC. Cables that have this capability usually call themselves *IEEE 1284* cables. If a cable says that it's only bidirectional, beware! It might support only the earlier EPP standard. Be sure you're getting the correct cable; otherwise, you won't be able to utilize the faster printer speed you paid for. What makes this difficult is that all printer cables look alike. No easy way exists to tell an IEEE 1284 cable from a plain Centronics printer cable. ■

The EPP was then superceded by the IEEE 1284 bidirectional parallel port specification called the *enhanced capabilities port (ECP)*. Windows 98 and Windows 2000 natively support ECP. If you're connecting a printer to your computer, you definitely want a printer that supports EPC.

Newer printers often come equipped with USB connections, which enables you to plug them into your system via a USB port (see Figure 13.2). This frees up the parallel port for other devices, such as a scanner or digital camera. You also can get adapter cables that enable you to plug a printer not equipped for USB into a computer's USB port (supporting the IEEE 1284 standard). These have a standard Centronics interface on one end and a USB connector on the other. This gives you some flexibility, depending on what your connection needs are.

You also might want to consider a printer that has a built-in network connection. The printer plugs into your network just like a PC and becomes a shared resource to all the computers. Several models we've worked with come with a 10BASE-T Ethernet interface as standard equipment.

FIGURE 13.2

The USB ports on your computer are small, non-descript slots usually placed side by side.

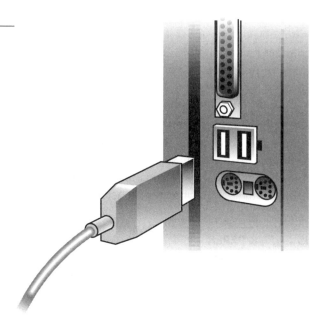

Consumables

Most people forget to calculate the cost of consumables as part of their homework when deciding on a printer upgrade. Your old printer might use toner cartridges that cost $50 new, and you might be able to get recycles for $20. But that new printer you just brought home uses only toner cartridges that cost $120 new and doesn't have recycles available for it yet.

Color inkjet printers are cheap (available for under $100), but the ink and special paper they favor can run you over 10 times the cost of a color laser printer's consumables, which is not to say that running a color laser is cheap. Toner cartridges for a color laser can run from $30 to over $100 depending on color and rated number of copies or impressions (how much it will print) per cartridge. And you won't be getting away with only one toner cartridge, either. Most color lasers (the good ones, anyway) need four: black, magenta, cyan, and yellow. Steer clear of any that try to get by with three colors. They mix magenta, cyan, and yellow to make an ersatz black, and the quality is poor at best.

TIP

TONER ON THE CHEAP

When choosing a printer model for your upgrade, it's a good money-saving idea to check with your local or online print toner cartridge recyclers to see whether they supply recycled toner cartridges for the model you have in mind. Recycled toner cartridges, from a reputable retailer, can save you a fortune over the life of a printer. Sometimes issues arise with the manufacturer's warranty if you use recycled cartridges, so read the fine print carefully.

Calculating consumable costs is easier if you know approximately how many pages you typically print per month and (if you print color) how many of those pages are printed in color. If you print with a color inkjet, you'll get better results with special, coated paper designed for that purpose. This paper does not absorb the ink into the paper itself, which results in a noticeably sharper image. The tradeoff is that it can cost up to four times more than traditional paper.

Some manufacturers quote an average price for consumables. When comparing printers, ensure that the assumptions about average pages per month or per year are really comparable and that they're using the same assumed page coverage in terms of ink (the percentage of the page that is actually being printed upon).

TIP

LASER VERSUS COPIER PAPER

The only difference between copier paper and paper sold specifically for laser printers is that laser paper costs more and is just a bit whiter. The whiter paper makes the text and graphics printed by a laser printer look better than it really is by increasing the contrast between the dark printing and the white background. It's really an optical illusion. For internal documents, you can save some money by buying the cheaper copier paper.

Color

We're at the beginning of the color age as the cost of really good color printers is starting to edge under the $1,000 price point. Within the next five years, color printers will be as ubiquitous as the familiar black-and-white laser printers are now.

TIP

BECOME A COLOR PRINTER GURU

If you really want to become the office color printer guru, you need to get a copy of M. David Stone's book *The Underground Guide to Color Printers* (Addison-Wesley, ISBN: 0-201-48378-5). It's not a new book, but it covers the nuts and bolts of color printing in witty, concise, and understandable prose, penned by one of the premier computer writers in the business.

A number of color printer technologies currently are available. Some melt wax pellets; others use a film ribbon (much like the old dot-matrix printers of yesteryear). Some of the new thermal wax transfer printers create stunning output, but as prices on color lasers and color inkjets hit the floor, your only solid choices are color inkjet or color laser technology.

Laser Printers

Lasers provide the best-looking print output for the lowest per-page cost of all the alternative types of printers available. Although you can use an inkjet printer and get passable results, the cost per page and the lack of quality are both good arguments for using a laser printer.

Color printers are indeed all the rage, but color lasers haven't come down much below the $2,000 level. On the other hand, a black-and-white laser can be had for several hundred dollars. This makes black-and-white the only choice for many users.

If you need high-quality color output, a color laser might be the way to go. You'll be amazed at the quality you can get from a color laser. The biggest compromise will be with speed.

It takes four times as long to print color because each color must be printed in a separate operation. This makes the paper feeding and printing mechanism more complex—hence, the higher cost. Still, prices for color lasers are steadily dropping so this might become a very attractive upgrade.

PLAINSPEAKING
IT'S ALL IN THE DOTS

A laser works by melting tiny bits of plastic toner onto paper at relatively high temperatures (200–300 degrees Fahrenheit). This process works great for solid print objects. such as letters and lines, but when you start dealing with graphics and photographs, solid black won't work. It's a neat trick to create the effect of shading and halftones when all you can do is melt a bit of plastic on a piece of paper.

Laser printers solve the problem the same way commercial lithographers do on printing presses. They print dots. If you want gray, you print a smattering of dots, which enables the white of the paper to show through and give the effect of gray. Black dots of varying sizes result in different shades of gray.

Color laser printing also borrows from commercial printing in that it renders color pictures as a series of overlaid dots. Commercial lithography uses a four-color printing press to print a color photo. A color laser printer has four separate toner cartridges. To create a color image, a piece of paper has to be printed on four times; that is, it must actually pass through the internal workings of the printer four times. In each individual pass, a different color is printed on the page. For photographs in which the colors are *mixed*, a series of dots is printed in one color. Then, the next color is added as another series of dots in the next pass. Different colors and effects are achieved by controlling the size and placement of the dots. ∎

LED Printers

The light-emitting diode (LED) page printer is an odd duck among printers. It is basically a laser printer without the laser (see Figure 13.3).

FIGURE 13.3

LED technology enables light to go directly from the LED array to the drum, passing through a focusing lens in a more straightforward path than a laser printer.

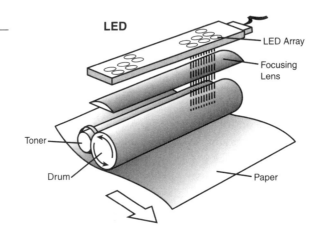

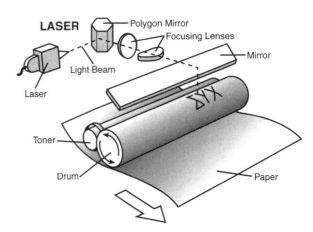

These printers, similar to lasers, use a rotating drum and fuse toner to the pages as a copier does. In addition, they crank out pages that are impossible to discern from those printed on a true laser. The difference is that they use light from an array of LEDs, focused through a lens, to create the image instead of a laser beam. Without drawing any schematics, suffice it to say that this way of doing things isn't particularly better or worse that using a laser—it's just different.

LED printers have been around a long time but have never really challenged the laser for market dominance. That said, no compelling reason exists to not consider an LED over a laser printer. Make your comparisons based on the other criteria discussed in this chapter, and if the LED is the better buy, go for it.

Actually, one difference does exist that might make the LED a better choice, and that is when considering color printers. As discussed in the previous section, a color laser has four toner cartridges (black, cyan, magenta, and yellow). This is what makes a color laser print a page so slowly; the page has to reverse direction and go back the other way, then reverse again, and so on.

Because of the nature of the LED printer's design, it can lay down all four colors on the drum and print the page in a single pass. This makes an LED printer as fast as a black-and-white printer—considerably faster than a color laser printer.

Inkjet Printers

Inkjet printers can be found for well under $100, which makes them a very attractive way to upgrade to color. However, while the price of the printer is extremely cheap when compared to color lasers, the cost in consumables is much higher.

Avoid the few inkjet models that put all the colors of ink into a single reservoir container. You want to be able to add ink cartridges for each color separately because you'll always run out of yellow long before cyan and magenta. The cost of ink on a per-page basis compared to color laser toner can run 10 times higher or more. Additionally, inkjet quality suffers greatly when printing on standard paper, so for good inkjet output you need a special, coated paper stock that sells for a premium.

If your color printing needs are relatively light, you can add a color inkjet to your system and use it in conjunction with your black-and-white laser.

ANOTHER FINE MESS
LED REGISTRATION PROBLEMS

When laying down multiple toner colors, in effect layers, it is critical that each color be in the absolute correct position relative to the other colors being applied and to the page itself. The need to exactly position each layer of color is called *registration*. The only problem that we've seen with color LED technology is a tendency for the registration to be a bit off. It's not a glaring problem, but it can cause problems, depending on the type of color printing you do. Be careful to test any color LED printer and ensure that the registration is within the limits dictated by your needs. ■

ANOTHER FINE MESS
USE THE RIGHT SWITCH

We see numerous inkjet printer problems caused by plugging in the printer to a surge or power strip and using the switch on the strip instead of on the printer to turn the printer on and off. When you shut off the power via the printer's built-in switch, the printer controls the head placement for a normal shutdown and parks the ink cartridges in a manner that should increase their useful life and prevent printing problems. When you bypass the printer's power switch, this parking won't occur. If you upgrade to an inkjet printer, always use the printer's power switch. ■

Printer/Copier/Fax/Scanner Devices

A long time ago (in the Neolithic age, going by Internet years), we read an article by Lincoln Specter about a dream machine he thought would make a great product. It combined several office machines that all used similar technologies into a single unit that he called a *skippy* (no idea why he called it that but it serves as a better handle than "multifunction print/scan/fax/copier devices" or "hydra").

The skippy could print like a regular printer. Adding a scanner module made sense because a printer plus a scanner made the skippy a copier. Add a modem and the skippy could double as a fax machine. You would end up with a 4-in-1 wonder machine that you can now purchase down at your local computer superstore.

The allure of this upgrade is that you get a lot of functions in a single machine that takes up about the same space as a laser printer. The cost of a skippy device is much less than the cumulative prices of all the standalone components you'd have to purchase to get the same set of functions.

There are, of course, a number of tradeoffs:

- Not all skippies include all four features. Some dump the fax capabilities and some don't function as a copier.

- Resolutions are often limited and less than you'd get in a standalone device.

- A failure in any one function usually renders the entire skippy useless until fixed.

- The cost of consumables can be higher than standalone devices.

- If you later want to upgrade any one component, you have to replace the entire skippy or you wind up having multiple devices—a skippy and a new, redundant standalone scanner, for example.

Despite the drawbacks, the low cost makes a skippy a very attractive upgrade. Just be very sure to check the feature set carefully before purchasing. Try to get as much resolution as possible in the skippy components where you need them. For example, if you do color scanning then pay close attention to the resolutions supported. Look for a skippy that lets you do things such as fax and copy even if the PC to which it's connected is turned off.

Troubleshooting Printer Upgrades

A printer upgrade generally goes smoothly. It's a three-step process:

1. Set up the printer.

2. Connect the printer to the computer using the proper cable.

3. Install the proper printer driver.

Because there doesn't seem to be much involved with printer installs, there's a temptation to take shortcuts, not bother to read the installation instructions provided by the manufacturer, just hook it up, and start printing. This is what causes most problems.

Unpacking and Setting Up

It is very important that you uncrate your new printer carefully and read the unpacking instructions the manufacturer provides. Printers are shipped with numerous clips, restraining brackets, and in some cases plain old tape to keep parts from moving around during shipping. If you try running your printer without removing all these packaging devices, you run the risk of seriously damaging the printer.

Removing all this stuff requires you to open up the printer and fiddle around in the bowels of the machine. Treat this like surgery. Be sure you have clean hands, free of any Styrofoam pieces that like to cling to you. You don't want to introduce any foreign materials to the inside of the printer chassis.

Printers have their own central processors and RAM and are, in fact, specialized computers in their own right. Treat them with the same care as you would your PC when opening up the chassis.

Cables

Ensure that you have the proper cables on hand before you install your printer upgrade. Printers often don't come with the cables necessary to connect them to your computer, which can be a major shocker when you're trying to get your printer installed because you need to get a critical report printed out in a hurry.

Parallel cables top out at about 10 feet in length with most of them being only 6 feet, so the location of the printer becomes a consideration. This is a limitation of parallel connections. Serial printer connections don't suffer from this problem, so distance between the printer and the computer if you're connecting via a serial cable is not as critical. When installing the printer, ensure that the cables are connected to the proper ports and that they are securely seated.

Drivers

When you physically connect your printer to your computer, you'll need to install the required printer driver. In Windows 98 and Windows Millennium, perform the following steps:

Install the Printer Driver

1. Double-click the My Computer icon.

2. Open the Printer folder.

3. Double-click the Add Printer icon to start the Add Printer Wizard.

4. Follow the instructions to install your specific printer. See Figure 13.4.

FIGURE 13.4

In the Add Printer Wizard, you can install any of a number of drivers that ship with Windows. If the printer manufacturer supplied a driver, click the Have Disk button.

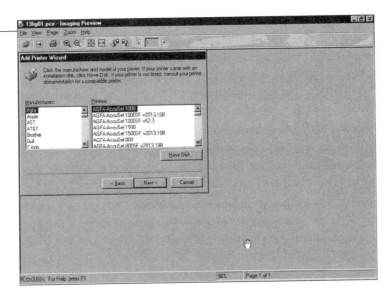

If the printer you are installing connects with the printer via a USB port, as soon as you plug it in you'll be prompted to install the new hardware. An updated driver is almost certainly available on the Internet for the printer you are installing—newer than even the one that comes on the disk shipped with the printer. To find an updated printer driver, you can start by going to the manufacturer's Web site and searching for drivers. However, we like to start at the Printer Drivers and Plotter Drivers page on the Drivers HeadQuarters site at `http://www.drivershq.com/List/indexprinters.html`. They have links that will take you directly to the printer driver pages of every printer you're likely to encounter.

TIP

SAME PRINTER, DIFFERENT FLAVORS

From our newsletter, *The Naked PC*, comes this outstanding tip for quickly changing the settings on your printer. Install the same printer driver using the Add Printer Wizard, giving each install a different name. Then, select each printer as it appears in the Printer folder, right-click it, and select the Properties option. Change the properties for the printer so you can have one printer driver set up for duplex, another for printing watermarks, and so on.

Figure 13.5 shows some of the options you can change for each of the printer configurations.

FIGURE 13.5

Printers come with a dizzying array of options these days. You can create multiple printer installs, each with a different set of selected options.

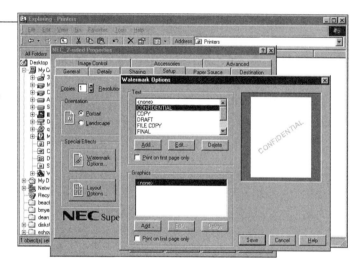

14

SPEAKER UPGRADES

*T*he sound quality of PC games and educational software is improving by the minute. Demand is skyrocketing for streaming audio used in a variety of contexts: Internet radio, Internet telephony, Internet TV, and Internet videoconferencing. College students aren't the only ones downloading MP3 files en masse, cutting and playing their own CDs on their computers, and basically using their PCs as a proxy stereo system. And don't forget about DVDs for home theater movie viewing and immersive 3D audio games.

With a burgeoning range of audio-enhanced (and enhancing) applications, you'll eventually have to upgrade the cheap speakers that came with your PC as an afterthought. Otherwise, you're likely to be listening to teeth-gritting sounds emanating from those tinny, little paper cones of a quality reminiscent of your first car's AM radio speaker.

Upgrade Checklist

1. Do your homework.

   This includes plenty of A-B testing in your local audio retailer's listening room. Don't forget to take your favorite audio CDs.

2. Determine whether your current sound card and listening room support the planned upgrade.

3. Determine whether you can perform the upgrade.

4. Purchase or acquire the component.

5. Organize your tools and workspace.

   See Chapter 3, "Things You Need."

6. Perform the upgrade.

7. Take good notes, and permanently file them in your system log when you're finished.

8. Update your inventory documentation to reflect the upgraded or newly added component.

How Do Humans Hear?

Selecting the right speakers for you and your ears is a very subjective process. Before we can get very far, we need to understand a modicum about how humans hear and the vocabulary used when discussing sound and speakers.

The first term to understand is *frequency*, also called *pitch*. The typical frequency range of human hearing is between 20 and 20,000Hz. The Hz unit in this context measures how many pulses—that's the frequency—of compressed air are passing across the eardrum every second. Fewer pulses is a lower frequency (pitch), such as the low notes on a piano or the rumbling of a kettle drum. More pulses is a higher frequency (pitch), such as the upper register of a violin or piccolo. These pulses are called *sound waves*.

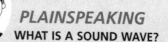

PLAINSPEAKING
WHAT IS A SOUND WAVE?

A drumstick hits the surface of a kettle drum. The kinetic energy of the stick striking the drum skin causes the drum skin to vibrate. The first vibration releases energy into the nearby air, causing those air molecules to move faster than they were moving before, and faster than the air molecules farther away from the drum skin are moving. This increased motion of the air is a localized compression (increased air pressure), and it moves outward away from the drum skin in all directions like a wave. Thus, the expression *sound wave*. ■

The next relevant term is *amplitude*, also called *volume*. The energy level of a sound wave is its amplitude—that is, how loud it is.

The human ear also processes sound waves based on their duration. As sound waves pass through the ear, sound-receptor cells (also called *hair cells* because of their physical appearance; see Figure 14.1) respond to the energy attributes of the sound waves—frequency, amplitude, and duration—and trigger nerve signals that eventually enter the brain and produce the hearing experience. The hair cells reside in the inner ear's cochlea, which is a snail-shaped structure.

FIGURE 14.1

A hair cell shown highly magnified. Movements in the cilia at the tip of the cell cause electrical signals that are transmitted to the brain for processing. (Photograph courtesy of Dr. David P. Corey, Massachusetts General Hospital)

A loudspeaker produces sound by moving a cone in a dynamic cone speaker, or an ultra-thin plastic diaphragm (in an electrostatic speaker) that in turn creates sound waves that approximate the original sound. In fact, it's the degree to which a speaker re-creates a recorded sonic event's original sound waves that determines how realistic you think the reproduction is (the quality of the original recording is equally important).

How Roomy Is Your Listening Room?

While you read this section, it will be helpful to be seated at your PC. If that's not practical, just picture that environment in your mind's eye. Look at the space surrounding your PC to try to imagine where you would put a new set of speakers (perhaps just a stereo pair, perhaps more components such as a subwoofer or even a 5.1 system's six speakers). Consider the following questions:

NOTE

THIS ISN'T AN AUDIOPHILE EXPERIMENT!

An entire audiophile culture exists surrounding (no pun intended) listening rooms, and rightfully so. In that context, a listening room is a specialized space intended to not get in the way of the ideal, perfect rendering of a recording. Here we're using the term to describe where you sit when listening to sounds emanating from your PC.

■ **How big is the room?**—A smaller room won't need speakers with as much wattage as a larger room. You can always get speakers with more wattage than the room can handle, but that would make sense only if you know you're going to move to a larger room in the near future or you want to risk going deaf.

■ **Which objects are located directly between you and your current speakers, and where you would posi-**

PLAINSPEAKING
WHAT DID YOU SAY?
"There are only 16,000 hair cells in a human cochlea, compared to some 100 million photoreceptors in the retina of the eye, and they are extremely vulnerable. Life in a high-decibel society of pounding jackhammers, screeching subway cars, and heavy metal rock music can take a devastating toll on them. But whatever the cause—overexposure to loud noises, disease, heredity, or aging—people tend to lose 40 percent of their hair cells by the age of 65. And once destroyed, these cells do not regenerate." (Goldberg, Jeff. *The Quivering Bundles That Let Us Hear.* Howard Hughes Medical Institute, 1997.) ■

tion your new speakers?—If you want a more faithful, optimal listening space, you should relocate any such objects.

■ **What other objects or surfaces in the room might reflect or absorb sound from your speakers?**—For the best sound, you should position the speakers, yourself, and other large objects so that there is an open space encircling you and your speakers. In general, absorbent objects are okay (they can help dampen reverberation) as long as they aren't in the listener's line-of-hearing. Watch out for objects that resonate at certain frequencies, causing a rattling or excessively boomy sound; for example, a loosely hung sliding glass closet door frame. Hard surfaces near the speakers, the listener, or both can cause "room clutter," which means a poor *stereo image*.

TAKE IT FROM THE DOLBY MASTERS

The folks at Dolby Laboratories, Inc. provide a free PDF document titled "Surround Sound for Games and PCs" (`http://www.dolby.com/multi/i.br.9811.surrsoundbooklet.pdf`). This document includes numerous tips and diagrams about optimal speaker placement.

Analyzing Your Listening Room

ETF 5.0 by ETF Acoustic Ltd. is a Windows-based listening room analysis tool. Gordon Brockhouse (News Editor, *Audio Ideas Guide*) reviews version 4.0 of this product at `http://www.audio-ideas.com/reviews/etf.html`. Version 5.0 retails for $149.95, but as Gordon points out, "...you don't have to spend a nickel to obtain one of ETF 4.0's great benefits: an education. Together, the superb manual and extensive help files provide a mini-course on room acoustics and their effect on sound quality. A trial version, available free of charge from ETF's Web site (`http://www.etfacoustic.com`), includes this material, plus a 'crippled' version." Version 5.0 also has a free demo version. Take a tip from us: Downloading and studying the user guide is worthwhile—if for nothing other than learning the "mirror trick" to help properly position absorbent material to control sound reflection problems.

■ **Where are your ears positioned relative to your speakers?**—Picture a straight line drawn from the speaker closest to your right ear to that same ear, and a straight line from the speaker closest to your left ear to that ear. (Remember that ideally the space between those lines should be empty.) For nonsurround setups, try to position your speakers and your chair so that your ears are horizontally level with the speakers' tweeters.

NOTE

POSITIONING SURROUND SPEAKERS

According to Cambridge SoundWorks, "All surround speakers sound best placed well above ear level and to the left and right of the listener (even though surround speakers are often referred to as the 'rear' speakers)."

■ **Does the room have one or more doors, windows, or other "exit points" for sound waves?**—Consider whether these exits are usually open or closed, and what kinds of outside noises are impinging on your room. Also consider the reverse; what's sonic bliss to you—at any decibel level—might be anathema to your cohabitants.

Your listening room's layout dictates your choice of a speaker form factor. That is, whether to choose bookshelf (small rooms), center channel (game and movie enthusiasts), floor-standing (audio enthusiasts), home theater (movie enthusiasts), or surround speakers (game and movie enthusiasts). As discussed in the next section "What Do You Listen To?" the listening environment also dictates how much power (wattage) you want your speakers to handle.

What Do You Listen To?

If you use your speakers primarily for a specific type of listening, that will directly impact your upgrade decision. Consider these types of listening preferences and the recommended speaker configuration for each. Note that we include a "general use" category where you'll let your own subjective needs and preferences be your guide.

■ **Games**—The most important audio attribute for good gaming is "sound positioning" (okay, okay, volume counts, too). This means the capability of the PC's sound system to simulate a three-dimensional (3D) audio environment that matches what's displayed onscreen. For example, you're in a cave being chased by a slavering monster; when you close your eyes, you want to hear the reverberations of a cave environment and your brain to think that the scrabbling sound of the monster's claws on stone are behind you and slightly to the right, exactly where the game software has the monster positioned.

The current competing approaches to 3D audio are EAX (Creative Labs) and A3D (Aureal).

EAX (Environmental Audio eXtensions) is based on a simulation technique and requires that you use a four-speaker configuration.

A3D involves creating a physical model of the acoustic environment being represented. This is a much more tedious approach than that used by EAX, but expert listeners agree that A3D provides a more accurate 3D audio experience. Reviewers use terms such as *immersive* for A3D versus *canned* for EAX.

■ **Music**—When listening to music, the key is an accurate and undistorted reproduction of the original recording. We're culturally accustomed to listening to music in an audience/artist arrangement where the performer(s) is in front of us, often on a stage. Although music-lovers and audiophiles have certainly dabbled in a variety of surround sound technologies over the years, the preferred speaker configuration for listening to music continues to be a pair of stereo loudspeakers (maximum power coupled with maximum efficiency, relative to other speaker configurations). However, with the convergence of high fidelity, home theater, and PC sound systems, this is a rapidly changing market, so shop carefully and let your ears be your guide.

NOTE

A SIDEBAR FOR AUDIOPHILES AND PC MUSICIANS

We don't have room here to delve into all the intriguing new technologies that are springing up from the kaleidoscopic merging of the PC, consumer audio/video, home theater, and music/recording industries. Nor do we have room to explore the high-end audio components that intrigue us and our audiophile and musician friends. But for those readers who want to learn more about such components, check out the resources listed at the end of this chapter.

■ **Movies**—The main audio goal for movie enthusiasts, like gamers, is to create an immersive sonic environment. In this case, a Dolby Digital 5.1 channel system hits the mark.

A Dolby Digital 5.1 channel system is composed of five main channels carried by one speaker per channel (three speakers for left, center, and right screen; and two speakers for left and right surround), plus one subwoofer for the supplemental bass. Many audio/video components already include a Dolby Digital 5.1 decoder, so don't assume that a speaker system marked as "DD 5.1" includes one. To recap, the "5" in "5.1" refers to the five channels carried by the five nonsubwoofer speakers and the "1" refers to the one subwoofer channel. (Note: These configurations are referred to variously as "Dolby Digital 5.1 channel system," "Dolby Digital 5.1 speaker system," or just "DD 5.1.")

NOTE

LEXICON BLUES

The folks at Dolby Laboratories, Inc. state that the ".1" in 5.1 refers to the fact that the low-frequency effects (LFE) channel that is pumped to a system's subwoofer carries only about one-tenth of a regular channel's bandwidth. (A subwoofer typically has a frequency response of 20Hz–200Hz, and 200Hz is one-tenth of 20,000Hz, which is the upper limit

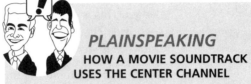

PLAINSPEAKING

HOW A MOVIE SOUNDTRACK USES THE CENTER CHANNEL

According to a Cambridge SoundWorks FAQ, "In most movie soundtracks, the vast majority of sound is contained in the center channel. In addition to dialogue, there are special effects and music coming from the center channel. The sound quality of the center channel is a big factor in how a home theater system performs." ■

of human hearing). The etymology of these arcane terms is a murky business at best, so now you know two possible meanings.

You also will encounter surround sound 4.1 configurations, made up of four speakers plus one subwoofer, with a 5.1 setup's center speaker being emulated through the two front speakers.

■ **General use**—This is not as difficult a category to configure as you might think. If you run your PC under a variety of audio formats, the key question is, "What type of listening is predominant for this PC?" Answer that question objectively, then select the best speakers for that particular category, and enjoy.

Match Your Speakers and Your Sound Card

PC speakers can perform only as well as the sound card and amplifier that are sending them signals. However, it's far better to have a budget sound card and great speakers than a great sound card and budget speakers. That's because the speakers are the last link in the chain between your PC and your ears.

When shopping for a new sound card or speakers, you're bound to run across this acronym: S/PDIF (or SP-DIF). This acronym stands for "Sony/Philips Digital InterFace," a widely recognized standard for passing a digital signal between consumer electronics components. The interface provides a digital audio data stream that can be piped directly to digital recording devices, such as Digital Audio Tape (DAT); digital playback devices, such as a digital signal-ready amplifier; or digital speakers. The audio signal remains entirely digital until the last possible moment in the audio signal chain. This yields a cleaner signal because digital processing and interconnections along the signal's path don't add any noise. The only limiting factors are the quality of the digital-to-analog converters used at the end of the path and the quality of the original recording.

TIP

FOR SPEAKER SYSTEMS SPORTING THE LABEL "DIGITAL," ALWAYS CHECK FOR AN S/PDIF DIGITAL INPUT PORT

Some manufacturers bill a particular speaker model as "true Dolby Digital 5.1 surround sound," but omit an S/PDIF digital input port. As always, do your homework.

TIP

DO YOURSELF A FAVOR; AVOID UNAMPLIFIED SPEAKERS

Even if you're in the "general use" listening category, you owe it to yourself to get some speakers with punch. This means avoiding unamplified speakers altogether. Please. While we're setting ground rules, if you're budget-conscious to a fault, get a speaker set with an aggregate power rating of at least 30 watts. The moderately budget-conscious among you should target a minimum of 60–80 watts.

Setting a Budget

To set a budget, you need to know your listening room's characteristics and limitations, your preferred sound source(s), your sound card's capabilities, and whether you plan on keeping your new speakers for a long time or just until you can afford some real thumpers. Pick a quiet, uncrowded weekday, collect your favorite demo tracks and DVDs, head over to your audio retailer's listening room, and listen.

Perform A-B tests by switching between a pair of speakers during a demo track. Compare at least five sets of speakers. Take your time narrowing down your candidates. Take notes about which speaker systems you like or don't like, and note their retail prices. Next, check out what other consumers had to say about the candidates on AudioREVIEW.com (see the resource listing at the end of this chapter), and then go shopping online for some good deals. Don't forget auction sites, such as eBay (http://www.ebay.com), and meta-auction sites, such as Auction Rover (http://www.auctionrover.com).

Audio expert reviews of specific speakers and sound cards can be helpful because you probably don't have the extensive array of test equipment they do (we certainly don't), or their breadth of listening experience. That said, although you certainly can learn much from these reviews, always let your own ears be your final guide.

TIP

AUCTION ROVER MAKES COMPARISON SHOPPING EASIER

Auction Rover has a handy InstantSearch feature that lets you narrow your feature preferences in a variety of complex ways—for example, by price (range), speaker type, maximum power rating (range), driver size (inches), subwoofer watts (range), warranty, manufacturer, and merchant.

Keep the Volume Low at First

When you install your new speakers, before they are connected up to a power source, turn any and all volume potentiometers completely down to zero/off. Then, when you boot the PC, if everything comes up okay, turn the volume potentiometer up ever so slightly and test the speakers from a variety of audio sources. Then, naturally, CRANK IT!

NOTE

SPECIFICATIONS

A plethora of specifications and ratings exist for a speaker system, but the most important are frequency response, RMS power, signal-to-noise ratio, driver size, magnetic shielding, and must-have features (more on this in a moment).

Frequency response, simply put, is the frequency range a particular piece of equipment or speaker can accurately reproduce. As you'll recall from the "How Do Humans Hear?" section, the human hearing frequency range is 20Hz–20,000Hz.

RMS (root mean square) is a mathematical technique for averaging numbers. When used to measure a component's power in watts, it is a de facto standard for evaluating and comparing the power-handling characteristics of audio equipment. You'll often see this specification referred to as *total audio output*. Roughly put, more is better.

The *signal-to-noise ratio* (S/N ratio) is the ratio of signal level to noise level, expressed in decibels.

Driver size measures the diameter of a speaker's driver. As with power, in rough terms, a bigger number is better.

Magnetic shielding is simple: Get it. Otherwise, your speakers can interfere with your monitor's display if they are too close together.

The interesting thing about must-have features is that one person's must-have is another's ho-hum. Case in point, the Altec Lansing ADA880R Dolby Digital Speaker System—a 4.1

multimedia desktop set—has what we consider to be an indispensable feature. It automatically detects the signal source and adjusts its five speakers accordingly for Dolby Digital, Dolby Pro Logic, or plain vanilla stereo. See what we mean? Either this immediately makes you salivate, or you were yawning two sentences ago. Regardless, look carefully at a speaker system's total feature set and determine exactly which compelling, must-have features it has, or doesn't.

USB AND DIGITAL SOUND

Some speakers now offer USB support as an alternative to traditional PC audio system designs. In the traditional analog design, a sound card takes the digital data stream from a source (such as a CD-ROM drive playing an audio CD) and converts it to analog, at which time there is plenty of opportunity for electromagnetic interference (noise) to be added to the signal. So, by the time the signal reaches the speakers, it has likely been rendered noisier. Using the USB port to transmit digital data directly from the audio source bypasses the potentially noisy PC box and sound card. The digital signal must still be converted to analog, but not until the last possible moment when it reaches the USB speaker system's digital-to-analog converter (DAC) and amplifier. Barring problems or flaws in the DAC and amplifier, this signal should be virtually free of distortion.

USB speakers enable you to eliminate a sound card, which frees up an IRQ. But it's unclear how well these types of speakers will work with other USB devices, so be sure you do plenty of research before trying out this new technology.

Online Resources

You're bound to learn something about speakers, audio equipment, and the latest in consumer electronics by browsing these pages:

- **AudioREVIEW.com**—Catalogs audio component reviews by consumers, ranks components using these consumer ratings (a five-star scale), and includes graphic displays of rankings sorted by name or rating. Located at `http://www.audioreview.com`. This site rocks. For speaker reviews, go to `http://www.audioreview.com/reviews/Speaker/`.

- **Dolby Laboratories, Inc.'s Technical Information page**—Located at `http://www.dolby.com/tech/`. It's full of exquisitely written descriptions (at a variety of levels of engineering depth) of topics such as Dolby Digital (AC-3), Dolby Surround, Dolby Surround Pro Logic, Film Sound, and more. See `http://www.dolby.com/tech/l.br.9901.DDFAQ.html` for Dolby Digital FAQs.

■ **DVD Review's Lingo page**—Contains a glossary of jargon that will appeal to DVD and video/film buffs at `http://www.dvdreview.com/html/lingo.shtml`.

■ *Sound On Sound* **magazine's high-tech music recording glossary**—Located at `http://www.sospubs.co.uk/sos/regular_htm/glossary.htm`.

■ *The Absolute Sound* **magazine**—Calls itself "the high end journal of audio and music." Read for yourself at `http://www.theabsolutesound.com`.

■ **The Audio Revolution's Features How-To page**—Located at `http://www.audiorevolution.com/equip/features.html`; contains links to an audio test disc, room tuning recommendations, the best DVD demo films, and their commentary on the best-sounding demo tracks of all time.

■ **Deras' well-informed, hip appraisal of the hardware, software, and subculture of the PC musician**—Bookmark this site (`http://pc-musician.com`) even if you don't lay down your own tracks. It's chock-full of content relevant to anyone interested in PC audio.

PART V

ADDING THE EXTRAS

15

ADDING A CD-RECORDABLE OR CD-REWRITABLE DRIVE

Today, a CD drive that can record to either CD-Recordable (CD-R) discs or CD-Rewritable (CD-RW) discs is as indispensable as a good Internet connection. These drives can conveniently perform countless tasks for you. You can use these drives to do the following:

- Make backup copies of your favorite audio CDs

- Create audio CDs from your favorite MP3 tracks

- Make backup copies of your primary application CDs. Distribute large files (say, anything over 5MB), via a medium such as the 3 1/2-inch floppy drive

- Create your very own virtual PC on a single disc

- Back up data or an entire partition (operating system and all) to one or more discs

- Archive data or a partition

- Use a CD-R/RW drive as a dynamic storage medium (essentially, treat it as if it were another hard disk)

- Use a CD-RW as a digital camera accessory

Adding a CD-RW as a second CD-ROM drive is the most common configuration. We'll explore many of these technologies in this chapter.

Upgrade Checklist

1. Do your homework.

2. Determine whether your PC supports the planned upgrade.

3. Determine whether you can perform the upgrade.

4. Purchase or acquire the component.

5. Organize your tools and workspace. See Chapter 3, "Things You Need."

6. Back up everything: data, operating system, mission-critical applications, and BIOS.

7. Test your startup disk.

8. Perform the upgrade.

9. Take good notes, and permanently file them in your system log when you're finished.

10. Update your inventory documentation to reflect the upgraded or newly added component.

Burning Your Own CDs

You can create (*burn*) two types of CD discs. *CD-Recordable (CD-R)* discs, after being "closed" by your premastering software, can't be written to again. A disc is closed when (1) you manually tell the software to close the disc; (2) automatically when the current recording session is closed; or (3) by the software when the disc becomes full. You can create multiple sessions on a CD-R disc at different times as long as you close only the session and leave the disc itself "open" (up to the pragmatic limit of the disc becoming physically full).

CD-Rewritable (CD-RW) discs, on the other hand, can be written to repeatedly (in practice, up to 1,000 times), either in small increments or as complete volumes (more on this later in the chapter).

CD-R drives and the associated disc media appeared first because recordable disc (write-once) technology was easier to implement. Today, we don't see much benefit to buying a drive that isn't capable of both recording and rewriting. To get the real benefit from this technology, you should get a recorder that can write to CD-RW discs.

Selecting a Drive

You must consider several important factors when selecting a CD-R/RW drive. We cover them in this section.

Speed

Because a CD-R/RW drive's main purpose is to record, not play back (although it certainly can play back CDs), let's focus on its recording speed as the most important speed-based feature.

The speed at which first-generation audio CDs are recorded is 150KB/second, equivalent to 9MB/minute (this is also the rate at which an audio CD is played back). At 150KB/second (often called *1x speed* or *single speed*), it takes 74 minutes to burn 650MB of data—the maximum amount supported by the vast majority of CDs today (although 80-minute, 700MB capacity CDs are increasingly common). Table 15.1 shows the increases in efficiency from the first-generation systems to those that today can write at a blazing 12x speed. (Note: What we think of as blazing today will, of course, be pokey next year, if not tomorrow.)

Table 15.1   CD-R/RW Drive Record Speeds in Kilobytes/Second and Megabytes/Minute

Record Speed	KB/Second	MB/Minute	Minutes (Approx.) to Burn 650MB
1x	150	9	72
2x	300	18	36

Table 15.1 continued

Record Speed	KB/Second	MB/Minute	Minutes (Approx.) to Burn 650MB
4x	600	36	18
6x	900	54	12
8x	1200	72	9
12x	1800	108	6

NOTE

A CD-RW DRIVE'S RECORDING SPEED FOR A CD-RW IS USUALLY HALF THAT OF RECORDING A CD-R DISC
When evaluating a CD-RW drive, be sure to note its maximum-rated recording speed for a CD-R as opposed to a CD-RW. Typically, the recording speed for a CD-RW will be about half that of a CD-R. For example, at the time of this writing the Creative Labs CD-RW Blaster 8432's specifications state, "Maximum recording rate of 1,200KB/second (8x) for CD-R and 600KB/second (4x) for CD-RW."

Data Buffer

Having a large data buffer on the drive itself helps prevent buffer underruns. Of the 17 CD-RW drives reviewed in depth by *PC Magazine*'s March 1, 2000 issue, the average buffer size was 2.6MB. Of the 17 drives reviewed, only 1 had a 1MB buffer; 10 had a 2MB buffer (59% of the group); and 6 had 4MB. Get a drive with the largest data buffer you can afford.

PLAINSPEAKING
WHAT IS A BUFFER UNDERRUN?
While the disc is being written, the CD-R/RW drive fetches new data from its onboard buffer. A *buffer underrun* occurs when the buffer becomes empty unexpectedly. This can occur because the system can't get data from the source CD-ROM, hard drive, tape drive, or other source drive to the CD-R/RW drive's buffer quickly enough, for whatever reason. At that point, the destination disc is still spinning but no data is available to write; therefore, you get an instant coaster. Actually, if you are recording a multisession disc, all might not be lost. If adequate space remains on the disc, you might be able to close that session and optionally start a new one. However, the success of such a recovery is not guaranteed, so it's best to take the precautions outlined in this chapter's sidebar "Dealing with CD-R/RW Recording Problems" than ever waste time with a buffer underrun. ■

WHAT IS BURN-PROOF?

This is a term trademarked by Sanyo; *BURN* stands for Buffer Under RuN. It's an intriguing technology that appears to prevent buffer underruns and enables you to multitask your PC while burning a disc. For more information on BURN-Proof, see `http://www.burn-proof.com`, `http://www.cdrinfo.com/hardware/sanyobp900/index.shtml`, and `http://www.cdrinfo.com/hardware/sanyo-crdbp2/index.shtml`.

Bus

The most common bus used today for CD-R/RW drives is the IDE bus. Although this is a relatively low-cost bus configuration that doesn't take up a peripheral slot (it does take up either a master or slave position on one of your PC's two IDE channels), the nature of the IDE bus is such that in certain circumstances the data being sent to the CD-R/RW drive can be interrupted. Even if the interruption is only temporary, in the case of a CD-R, you'll get a coaster instead of the desired data on the disc (more on buffer underruns later in the chapter). It's especially important that you install a CD-R/RW drive on the secondary IDE channel (the channel on which your hard drive is not installed) to avoid some of these device-conflict interruptions, as described later in this chapter.

The most reliable bus architecture for a CD-R/RW drive is SCSI. Some CD-R/RW drives come with their own SCSI adapter, but some don't. In either case, although you will pay a premium for a SCSI version, the reliability during the operation of burning a CD-R/RW disc is vastly greater than an IDE counterpart. Furthermore, you'll be able to daisy-chain additional devices on the SCSI bus without the need for any additional IRQs, and all those devices benefit from the SCSI bus's superior architecture and speed potential. Setting up a SCSI adapter and its devices can be a bit more work than simply installing a CD-R/RW drive on the IDE bus, but for readers of this book, the difference should be negligible.

GET A SCSI ADAPTER THAT'S DESIGNED FOR WRITING CD-R/RW DISCS

A proper adapter card is a must. A SCSI adapter not designed to specifically handle a CD-R/RW will result in buffer underruns.

ACCESSING YOUR SCSI CD-ROM DRIVE FROM A BOOT DISK (MS-DOS PROMPT)

Adaptec has developed a Web-based utility to help you create a 3 1/2-inch boot disk that can see your SCSI CD-ROM drive(s). See `http://www.adaptec.com/support/faqs/dosdrvraccess.html`.

Some CD-R/RW drives are designed to use the parallel port, and these are best suited for situations in which you need a portable backup/archive device. The primary disadvantages are that these drives are typically slower than their SCSI or IDE counterparts and that they tend to be more expensive (as is the case for other portable CD-R/RW drives regardless of their interface type). The extra expense is justified because they must be housed in a portable case that is much more shock-resistant than a case snugly sheltered out of harm's reach inside a PC's chassis. Don't forget that you'll also need to find a power outlet for any parallel-port portable drive.

The USB interface is the preferred solution when you need a portable CD-R/RW drive, given some operating system caveats discussed in a moment. Because USB devices provide hot-swappability, all you have to do is plug in—or unplug—the drive to move it from one PC to another. However, USB is not supported by versions of Window 95 prior to OSR2, and it's not supported by Windows NT 3.x or Windows NT 4.x. However, USB *is* supported by Windows 95 OSR2 (marginally), Windows 98, Windows Me, and Windows 2000.

THE BEST TYPE OF CD-R/RW FOR YOU IS...

As previously mentioned, external models tend to be a bit more expensive than their internal counterparts; ditto SCSI versus IDE. But don't let price be the driving factor here. Instead, consider how you will use the CD-R/RW drive. If it must service many PCs and they are not networked, you'll benefit from the portability of an external USB unit. If it must service many networked PCs, an internal SCSI-interface drive would be best. If it is being used in a single standalone PC then an internal SCSI unit would be best. If you don't want to spend the (relatively) few more dollars on a SCSI internal model, go with IDE.

Flash Memory for Firmware Upgrades

As discussed in Chapter 4, "Upgrading the BIOS," many hardware devices have their own onboard BIOS drivers, often called *firmware*. Similar to the system board BIOS, some of these are flashable—meaning you can upgrade them after installation via software. Look for a CD-R/RW drive that supports field-upgradable firmware. This way, as the manufacturer fine-tunes the firmware, you can keep your drive up to date. Upgrades can usually be downloaded from the manufacturer's Web site.

TIP

CD-R/RW DRIVE MANUFACTURERS' CONTACT INFORMATION
Finding your drive manufacturer's Web site and other contact information can be a challenge. To ease the pain, Adaptec has assembled a list of links to 46 manufacturers, including their Web address, contact support Web page(s), U.S. main phone number, U.S. technical support phone number, U.S. fax back phone number, and more. Go to
`http://www.adaptec.com/adaptec/partners/cdrec.html`.

Supported CD Storage Formats

This section describes a variety of—but by no means all—CD storage formats:

- **Bootable CD**—We cover bootable CDs in this chapter's section "Booting Your Computer from a CD."

- **CD Extra (CD Plus)**—This type of disc contains more than one type of data in multiple sessions. Audio tracks are stored in the first session; CD-ROM XA data is stored in the second session. See also the alternative Mixed-Mode format.

- **CD-Audio**—Refers to a CD (or the format thereof) that contains CD-DA audio information. Is synonymous with CD-DA.

- **CD-DA (CD-Digital Audio)**—This format was jointly developed by Philips and Sony in the early 1980s and is the standard that defines how a traditional audio CD is formatted, recorded, and played back. The digital audio data on a CD-DA is in the format 44.1KHz, 16-bit, stereo, uncompressed PCM. Drop a CD-DA disc into your Discman and it will play back audio for your listening pleasure.

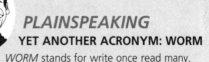

PLAINSPEAKING
YET ANOTHER ACRONYM: WORM
WORM stands for write once read many. You will often see this acronym used to describe storage media such as CD-R that can be written (recorded) once and read back many—effectively an unlimited number of—times. ∎

- **CD-I**—This now effectively vestigial format's purpose was to support multimedia applications on a player attached to a TV set.

- **CD-R**—As you learned early on in this chapter, this acronym stands for CD-Recordable.

- **CD-ROM**—Technically, this format refers to a disc containing computer data only, that is, no audio data. But on the street, many folks use "CD-ROM" to refer to any type of compact disc, whether used for audio, computer data, mixed-mode, and so on.

- **CD-ROM XA (Extended Architecture)**—This CD format is an extension of the ISO 9960 format and was intended to offer enhanced audio/video for multimedia applications. It is no longer in general use.

- **CD-RW**—This acronym stands for CD-Rewritable, and has been described earlier in this chapter.

- **Mixed-Mode**—This type of disc uses a specific format to manage the two types of data encoded on it. Computer (nonaudio) data is stored first on Track 1, and the audio is stored on subsequent tracks. See also the alternative CD Extra format.

- **VideoCD (VCD)**—This CD standard supports full motion pictures with an accompanying audio track.

See Chapter 16, "Adding a DVD Drive," for more information on these DVD format acronyms, along with their pros and cons:

- **DVD-ROM**—Read-only; works like the CD-ROM drive that comes standard on most computer systems. It can read DVD discs, but can't create them.

- **DVD-R**—Write once; the basic equivalent of CD-R. It can record up to 4.7GB per disc.

- **DVD-RAM**—Write many; initially could create discs that contained only 2.58GB of data per side but version 2 supports a full 4.7GB per side.

PLAINSPEAKING

THE RED, YELLOW, GREEN, ORANGE, AND WHITE BOOKS DEFINE CD STANDARDS

There really is order to the confusion and plethora of CD standard names, acronyms, and slang terms. The final and ultimate resting place of The Truth regarding any CD format is contained in one of several standards documents referred to as the Red Book, the Yellow Book, and so on. For a complete breakdown of this taxonomy, go to http://www.licensing.philips.com/ cdsystems/cdstandards.html. ■

■ **DVD-RW**—Write many; 4.7GB capacity.

■ **DVD+RW**—Write many; +RW uses a technology that's slightly different from its DVD-RW counterpart, resulting in less capacity (2.8GB per side for +RW versus 4.7GB for -RW) but improved performance and wider disc compatibility. The next DVD+RW specification is expected to increase the capacity to 4.7GB.

CD Recording and Related Software

To use your new CD-R/RW drive, you'll need some specialized software packages, described in this section:

■ **Backup**—Make backups. Not all backup packages currently support CD-R/RW media; although any backup utility developer worth her salt should by now have extended her wares to cover this burgeoning medium. You might need to upgrade your backup software so you can use it with a CD-R/RW drive.

TIP

T.J. AND LEE'S CHOICE: VERITAS BACKUP EXEC DESKTOP EDITION

Our favorite CD-R/RW–compliant backup tool is Veritas Backup Exec Desktop Edition (`http://www.veritas.com/us/products/backupexec/`), as shown in Figure 15.1. Its current incarnation, as of this writing, is version 4.2 with a street price of $69. Before making a purchase decision, check Veritas's hardware compatibility list at `http://www.support.veritas.com/dsl/index.htm`.

FIGURE 15.1

Veritas Backup Exec Desktop Edition offers a best-of-breed user interface for backing up to a wide variety of devices, shown here recognizing a CD-R/RW drive.

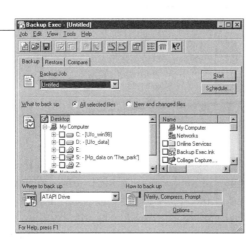

■ **Premastering**—Create data CDs and multimedia CDs (music, photo, video). The majority of modern CD-R/RW drives come bundled with a variety of CD recording and related tools. One of the most common tools creates audio and data discs and is called Adaptec's Easy CD Creator (http://www.adaptec.com/support/overview/ecdc.html; street price is $79). See Figure 15.2. This utility can copy data to a CD/R-RW disc, copy audio tracks to a CD/R-RW disc, and copy one disc directly to a blank disc. (All the usual caveats about preserving intellectual property rights apply.) For a list of Easy CD Creator's supported drives, see http://cdr.adaptec.com/cgi-bin/cdrmain.cgi. This package includes CD Copier for making disc-to-disc copies (see Figure 15.3).

FIGURE 15.2

Adaptec Easy CD Creator offers an easy-to-use Wizard format for creating data and audio CDs; at your option, you can cancel the Wizard and use the intuitive "classic" user interface.

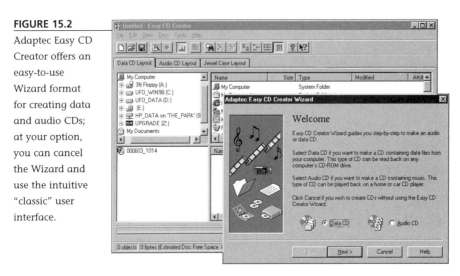

FIGURE 15.3

Adaptec CD Copier ships with Easy CD Creator.

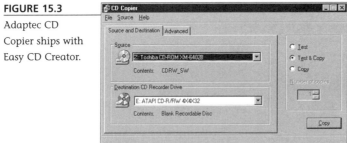

A myriad of specialized tools is available for tasks such as finding, download-ing, storing, and burning audio files (MP3, RealAudio, or Windows Media-encoded); creating and printing disc labels and jewel box covers; enhancing your audio tracks with detailed artist and track information; creating disc-based photo albums; writing video to a disc; and so on. You can find these utili-ties by browsing the online resources listed in this chapter's section "Online Resources."

■ **Packet writing**—Use your CD-RW drive like a 650MB removable hard drive. Your CD-R/RW drive must be designed at the mechanical and firmware level to support packet writing. If it is so designed then you can copy data to (and from) the CD as easily as if it were a plain vanilla hard drive. Adaptec's DirectCD utility is the most common platform for accomplishing this feat.

CD-ROM DRIVES SUPPORTED BY THE UDF READER

Adaptec maintains a table of these drives at `http://www.adaptec.com/tools/compatibility/udfreaderwin.html`. Per Adaptec, "This list has not been updated since early 1999, when it became the responsibility of the CD-ROM drive manufacturers to test and certify their drives as compatible with the Adaptec UDF reader."

In fact, you can use drag-and-drop with a packet-writing drive. A file format called *UDF (universal disk format)* that was specifically developed to support high-capacity optical storage media, such as CD-RW, DVD-ROM, and DVD-Video, works in conjunction with packet writing to offer several significant benefits. You can incrementally add one (or more) file and do so with minimal wasted space on the disc; a UDF-formatted CD can be read on multiple cross-platforms (Macintosh, Windows, and UNIX); and you can randomly erase individual files on such a disc (applies only to CD-RW discs).

TECHNICAL DETAILS ON PACKET WRITING AND UDF

For more information, Michael McMurdie and Robert Griffith of Adaptec have published a very informative, technically detailed article titled "Packet Writing & UDF: CD Recording's Logical Next Step" (`http://www.emediapro.net/MayEM/mcmurdie5.html`).

FREE UDF READERS

Adaptec's UDF readers are free. The UDF Reader for Windows is called UDF Reader Driver. You'll find these readers at `http://www.adaptec.com/products/overview/udfreaders.html`.

Adaptec DirectCD is the interface to your CD-R/RW drive should you want to use it like a floppy, removable, or hard drive. It enables you to set up a CD-R or CD-RW disc so any software application that can read from or write to a drive letter can read/write to it. In addition, it provides an interface for saving files to that CD. Any disc recorded using DirectCD can be read by any other PC with a CD-RW drive using DirectCD, and can also be read by any PC with a standard CD-ROM drive by using Adaptec's freely downloadable UDF reader.

- **Create a bootable CD**—Many premastering tools include this feature. We cover bootable CDs in this chapter's section "Booting Your Computer from a CD."

Writes to Standard CD-R and CD-RW Formats

Be sure you get a CD-R/RW drive that writes to the standard CD-R and CD-RW formats and that supports packet writing.

Installing a CD-R/RW Drive

These steps apply to installing a CD-R/RW drive in an internal drive bay:

1. Shut down and disconnect your system (see Chapter 3's section "Breaking Down Your Computer").

2. Open your PC's chassis and examine the 40-pin IDE cable for the IDE channel on which you're placing the drive. The motherboard diagram in your user's manual will indicate which port is IDE1 and which is IDE2, and it's typically marked on the motherboard surface, too.

   If the target IDE channel's cable is a one-drive cable, as is often the case, you must replace it with a two-drive–type (Y or splitter) cable. This cable is available for about $6 at any electronics parts store, as described in Chapter 3. Some CD-R/RW drives come with such a data cable.

SEE ALSO

➤ For details on the drive-related concepts of master and slave, cable select, and primary and secondary IDE channels, see "IDE Cable," page 165

➤ For tips on installing any type of drive (hard disk, CD, tape, floppy, and so on) see "Handling Tips for Any Drive," page 176

3. Trace your power supply's cable bundles to see whether a free cable exists to power the CD-R/RW drive. If not, you'll need to buy a Y-type splitter power cable available at any electronics parts store. Some CD-R/RW drives come with such a power cable.

4. Follow your CD-R/RW drive's installation instructions. In general, the steps are as follows. Figure 15.4 shows a rear-view diagram of a typical CD-R/RW drive.

5. Select the desired IDE channel.

FIGURE 15.4

Rear view of an Acer CD-ReWriter, model no. CRW4432A.

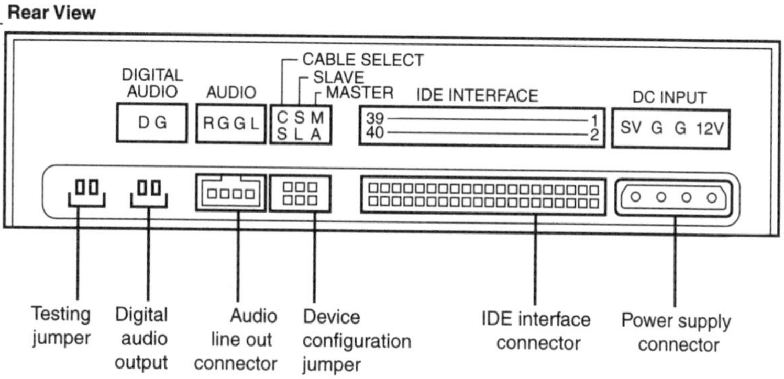

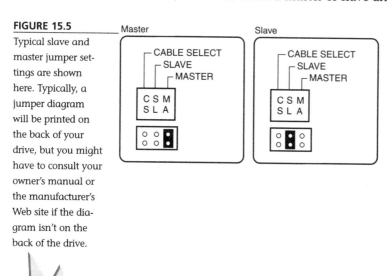

6. Jumper the drive as that channel's master or slave according to the instructions and your system's configuration. Figure 15.5 shows how to jumper a typical CD-R/CD-RW as either a master or slave drive.

FIGURE 15.5

Typical slave and master jumper settings are shown here. Typically, a jumper diagram will be printed on the back of your drive, but you might have to consult your owner's manual or the manufacturer's Web site if the diagram isn't on the back of the drive.

NOTE

A COMMON CD-R/RW DRIVE CONFIGURATION WHEN USING THE IDE INTERFACE

If your system has one IDE hard drive, one CD-ROM drive, and no other removable media drives (such as a Zip), a standard configuration is to leave your standard CD-ROM drive as the master device on IDE2 (or if it isn't set up that way already, to switch it over) and install the CD-R/RW drive as the slave device on IDE2.

7. Connect the four-pin power cable to the drive.

SEE ALSO

➤ *See "Power Connection," page 181*

8. Connect the 40-pin IDE data cable to the drive.

SEE ALSO

➤ *See "Ribbon Cables and Pin 1," page 180*

9. Place the drive in a bay and secure it with the provided mounting screws (if none came with the drive, they're available at any electronics parts store). As with hard drives, you want to ensure the screws you get don't penetrate too far into the CD-R/RW drive's housing (see Chapter 7, "Upgrading the Hard Disk"). If you want your CD-R/RW drive to output audio, connect the audio cable as shown in Figure 15.6.

SEE ALSO

➤ *See "Mounting Brackets and Screws," page 177*

FIGURE 15.6

If you want your CD-R/RW drive to output audio, connect the audio cable to your sound card.

10. Put the chassis cover back on and connect all the power cords.

11. Boot the system.

12. Install the necessary software to test and use your CD-R/RW drive.

13. Copy/create several data discs and audio discs, and then run your drive through its packet-writing/UDF paces. Test the resulting discs on your local CD-ROM drive and at least one other PC's CD-ROM drive.

To use the recording capabilities of your CD-R/RW drive, you'll need some special software (often, but not necessarily, bundled with the drive). These utilities enable you to format CDs to receive data, send data to them as if they were hard disks, add data to them, erase them, set them up so that they can be successfully read by any standard CD-ROM drive, and so on.

AN ALTERNATIVE WAY TO DETERMINE YOUR CD-R/RW DRIVE'S SPECS

If you go to the CD-R Database (http://www.adaptec.com/cgi-bin/cdrmain.cgi) and enter your drive's manufacturer and model information, you'll receive a reasonably full specification sheet on it. This is a great way to find out whether a particular model supports MultiRead, and to find out whether Adaptec software explicitly supports your CD recorder.

Dealing with CD-R/RW Recording Problems

Although countless variations on this theme exist, here is a collection of steps to try when you have problems burning a disc. These steps are arranged in order of increasing pain, so try the easy stuff first, but be aware that you might have to jump through some wild gyrations to get a good disc instead of a coaster. Remember, burning a disc is still an art form, not a science:

1. Power down your PC completely; then restart it. After it's restarted, close all running applications except Explorer and Systray.

2. ScanDisk (in Thorough mode) the partition containing the source data.

3. Defragment the partition containing the data you're burning.

4. Clean out your temporary folder and be sure you have plenty of free hard disk space (at least twice the amount of data being recorded).

5. Set your CD-R/RW drive to record at a slower speed, down to 1x if necessary, as shown in Figure 15.7.

FIGURE 15.7

Adaptec CD Copier enables you to change the recorder's speed on its Advanced tab.

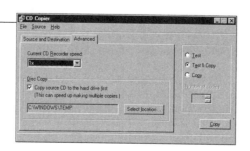

6. Try another brand of media. Some CD-R/RW drive manufacturers have a "preferred media" list on their Web sites—if not, call the technical support line and ask.

7. Switch to another source. For example, if you're burning from one disc to another, see whether the drive can handle burning from a hard disk. Repeat this test for all the permutations available given your current hardware configuration. This helps localize what might be a hardware problem. Always store the source data on the local hard disk, not a network file server.

8. Upgrade the drive's firmware. *If you're running out of options, you might want to do this even if the manufacturer says the latest firmware version doesn't solve your specific problem.*

9. Upgrade your premastering (and other related CD recording) software.

10. Try another firm's premastering package.

11. Study your software's user's guide; look for a troubleshooting section.

12. Check your software's and drive manufacturer's Web sites for support forums, FAQs, and other channels for reporting problems. Post messages on any forums and call the manufacturer's support desk.

13. Check Adaptec's Support Knowledgebase at `http://ask.adaptec.com/ cgi-bin/tic`.

14. Check the resources listed in this chapter's "Online Resources" section.

15. If your CD-R/RW drive is an IDE interface, consider switching to SCSI.

Carrying Your Virtual PC Wherever You Go

We have developed a procedure to help jump-start a new PC into one's own ideal configuration. We call this portable infrastructure a *virtual PC*. The physical PC could be fresh from the factory, a PC that a client or friend asks you to configure for them (set it to your style first; then tweak it for them), or a new bootable partition on an existing PC in your collection. This project has the following two requirements:

- Consolidate all configuration steps into a single Word document.

   You can then publish it as a Web page to retrieve it no matter where you are. Alternately, you can carry it around as a Word document on a CD, saved down to Word 6.0/95 file format so WordPad can open it.

- Consolidate all required software, if possible, onto a single CD-R or CD-RW disc.

You should compress whatever software you consider essential for the proper functioning of a PC. A compact disc is an inexpensive, small, lightweight, high-density medium that's almost universally readable on any CD-ROM drive, perfectly suited for this task.

Here are the steps for configuring your virtual PC. Naturally, adjust things according to your personal preferences:

1. Install the core operating system.

2. Create a startup 3 1/2-inch disk with CD-ROM support and fully test this disk.

3. Verify and optimize BIOS settings. (Skip this step if it's a new bootable partition on one of your existing PCs.)

4. Quickly ensure that each device is working. (Skip this step if it's a new bootable partition on one of your existing PCs.)

5. Burn in the system. The term *burn in* means to continuously test a system's components. You can buy third-party tools to do this for you (such as SiSoft Sandra; see Chapter 2, "Preparing for an Upgrade"). Or you can approximate the same effect by configuring Windows' built-in Task Manager to repeatedly run tasks such as Disk Defragmenter, ScanDisk, Disk Cleanup, and so on. (Skip this step if it's a new bootable partition on one of your existing PCs.)

6. Configure Windows Explorer's Folder Options to your personal preferences.

7. Configure according to our Everybody Do This list (see the following).

   - Organize Windows Start menu.

   - Organize Windows Desktop.

   - Remove unwanted operating system applications.

   - Add missing operating system applications.

   - Maximize performance.

   - Size down the Recycle Bin.

   - Size down the amount of space used by your Web browser for temporary Internet files—for example, in Microsoft Internet Explorer, select Tools, Internet Options, General, Settings, fiddle with the slider control labeled "Amount of disk space to use" until the value is relatively small, click OK, and click OK again to finalize the setting.

   - Fine-tune miscellaneous options.

8. Configure according to our set of Additional Customizations that might not suit everyone, but that we find indispensable (see the following):

   ■ Use the Send To command

   ■ Set up Favorites (copy from your Virtual PC CD)

   ■ PowerToys (we use DOS Prompt Here, Explore From Here, Send To X)

   ■ Fine-tune with TweakUI

9. Verify and optimize the low-level startup files `Autoexec.bat` and `Config.sys`. Ideally, strip them naked (always testing carefully if it's a new PC). We include the command `C:\WINDOWS\COMMAND\DOSKEY` in our `Autoexec.bat` files so `DOSKEY` is available to any MS-DOS window we start.

10. Install your personal Core Utilities list, which is an extension of TUGPCs' Everybody Do This list:

    ■ Nico Mak's WinZip

    ■ Microsoft IntelliMouse (if the PC has one)

    ■ Resource Meter (`Rsrcmtr.exe`, comes with Win9x)

    ■ Alex van Kaam's MotherBoard Monitor

    ■ PowerQuest's PartitionMagic

11. Use PartitionMagic to create an extended partition comprised of one logical partition and about 300MB of free space (you'll use this free space in the next step). This logical partition will serve as the data drive (D:). (Skip this step if it's one of your existing PCs that already has a data partition.) Note: You'll need PowerQuest's CD for this step.

12. Use PartitionMagic to copy the existing primary bootable partition into a new logical partition. When the copy operation is complete, reduce the second logical partition's size as far as possible and hide it. This logical partition—let's call it the "emergency OS partition"—now contains a perfectly configured environment, excluding the larger workhorse applications, such as Office, Visual Basic, and so on, that you'll install momentarily. (Skip this step if it's one of your existing PCs that already has an emergency OS partition, unless this is a different or special OS that requires its own emergency clone.)

13. Install your personal Workhorse Applications list, which is an extension of our TUGPCs Everybody Do This list (we've eliminated some of the personalized items we favor from this list to make it more generic for your benefit):

- Adobe Acrobat Reader 4.0

- Internet Explorer 5 Web Accessories

- Internet Explorer 5 Power Tweaks

- Microsoft Office 2000 and any service releases

- Any other tools you frequently use, such as browser plug-ins, MP3 utilities, Internet connection optimizers, Web page ad blockers, and so forth

14. Configure Task Scheduler for the primary bootable partition to run what we consider mandatory system checks: Disk Defragmenter weekly; Low Disk Space Notification every 30 minutes; Maintenance-Disk Cleanup monthly; ScanDisk Standard daily; and ScanDisk Thorough monthly.

15. Configure for a local area network, if any.

You can use this Virtual PC checklist, personalized for your own preferences, to take your PC with you anywhere. All you need is your latest data, the CDs for your workhorse applications, and a custom-made CD containing the Zip or executable files for whatever assortment of tools and applications are on your must-have list.

Booting Your Computer from a CD

Why would anyone want to boot his system from a CD? Can't you boot from a bootable floppy disk and then access the CD drive to get at any programs or data you want? The short answer is yes, but sometimes you might want to have a self-booting CD disc. A CD that you've created yourself and that can boot your system gives you a virus-free disc to start your system and from which you can access data or a backup image of a partition or an entire drive. In this section, you'll learn how to make your PC boot from the CD drive.

Controlling the Boot Device

To boot the system from the CD drive, you must have two things. First, you must have a reasonably recent BIOS that supports a CD-ROM as a bootable device and a CD drive that will work with that BIOS. Newer IDE and SCSI CD drives have support for being made bootable, depending on the BIOS or the SCSI interface being used. For CD drives connected to the system on the SCSI bus, it depends on the SCSI host adapter and whether the adapter's onboard BIOS supports booting from the CD. The simplest way to determine whether your configuration will support this is by testing it. Be sure you have a data CD disc in the CD drive to begin with.

Start your computer and enter the BIOS/CMOS configuration utility. See Chapter 4 for more information about modifying CMOS settings, especially those that tell the BIOS how the system is configured. The CMOS settings that control boot devices are usually found in the Advanced CMOS settings screen. Often, three or four choices are labeled something like this:

1st Boot Device	Floppy
2nd Boot Device	IDE-0
3rd Boot Device	CD-ROM
4th Boot Device	Disabled
Try Other Boot Devices	Yes

In this example, the 3rd Boot Device would be set to disabled and the 1st Boot Device would be set to CD-ROM. Note that the 2nd Boot Device is the hard disk for this test. When you exit the BIOS utility (having saved the settings), the system restarts and you should be able to observe that the CD drive is accessed as the BIOS tries to read boot information from the drive. Failing to find any boot information on the CD, the system should next access the hard drive and boot up normally.

Creating the Boot CD

Keeping in mind that you can make a CD drive bootable, even a plain vanilla read-only CD-ROM drive, you need a CD-R or CD-RW drive to *create* a boot CD. The creation software must also allow you to create a disc that is "bootable." Adaptec's Easy CD-Creator is a package that we've successfully used to do this (see Figure 15.8).

Part of the process of creating a bootable CD requires that you first have a working bootable floppy disk. Be sure you have already prepared and tested this disk because you'll be prompted for it when burning your boot CD (see Figure 15.9).

The boot disk should contain all the files necessary to boot your system: a `Config.sys` and `Autoexec.bat` file and the necessary drivers for the hardware installed, including the driver for the CD drive itself. The image of the boot disk is burned onto the CD and, when booted, that portion of the CD becomes drive A: (the floppy drive becomes drive B:). Only the boot files will be available on "drive" A:, so in `Autoexec.bat`, you must ensure that the line that loads the `MSCDEX.EXE` file assigns the CD drive its own letter so all the data on the CD disc is available after booting. Use this command:

```
MSCDEX.EXE /D:IDECD000 /L:z
```

In the previous code, *z* is the drive letter you want to assign the CD drive, and *IDECD000* is the identical device name used in the `Config.sys` file for the CD drive.

FIGURE 15.8

Easy CD-Creator
supports
bootable CD
layouts.

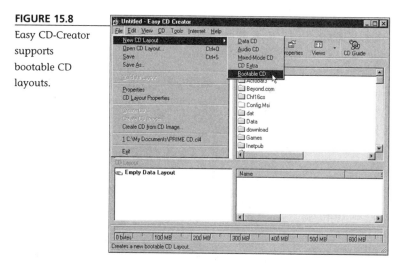

FIGURE 15.9

A boot disk is
required when
creating a
bootable CD.

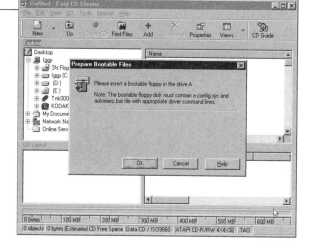

What Else to Put on the CD

Knowing you can make a CD drive bootable is interesting, but what is the practical
use of this feature? Considering that a typical hard disk these days is measured in tens
of gigabytes, you aren't going to fit an entire drive's worth of information on a CD
disc's 650MB. However, you can use software such as Norton's Ghost (http://www.
symantec.com/sabu/ghost/index.html) and Drive Copy (http://www.partitionmagic.
com/drivecopy/index.html) to create an image file containing a drive or a drive
partition.

Granted, it must be a relatively small partition (or a fairly empty drive) because,
even with the compression features of these drive copy programs, the best you'll be
able to squeeze down onto a bootable CD is 1GB (precompression) or less. That's

enough, though, for a clean operating system install so you can readily restore it.

When you create your boot CD, you include the drive image file or any other files you want available on the CD after the system is booted up.

Online Resources

More than any other extant PC component category, CD-ROM, CD-R, CD-RW—in all their myriad configurations and uses—have spawned a vast set of online resources. This is probably also because burning a CD is still far more art than science, and because everyone wants to be able to do it. Meantime, it's a jungle out there, so remember when burning a CD to do so carefully and thoughtfully, or you know what you'll end up

PLAINSPEAKING
BOOTABLE WINDOWS ON A DISC

A very handy thing is a bootable CD that not only fires up your PC but loads and runs the Windows operating system *from the CD disc itself!* What's more, it can actually be done.

However, creating a CD disc that boots Windows 95b or Windows 98 (it won't work with NT or Windows 2000) is not for the faint of heart or the technically unsavvy. If you're not sure how to hack a binary file with a hex editor, maybe you'd better pass on trying this yourself. But it can be done, with know-how, patience, and some luck.

A white paper (in English) on the Computer Technik site (a German computer magazine) outlines all the steps necessary to create a Windows bootable CD-ROM disc, complete with a static Registry that runs in a RAM drive. It's complex but technically very cool information. You can find it at `http://www.heise.de/ct/Service/English.htm/99/11/206.` ∎

with: another coaster for your CD mobile. Check out the following resources for valuable information:

- **Adaptec's CD-Recordable Glossary**—Located at `http://www.adaptec.com/tools/glossary/cdrec.html`, it's an excellent glossary with plenty of links to external information resources.

- **Andy McFadden's CD-Recordable FAQ site**—Located at `http://www.fadden.com/cdrfaq/`, it qualifies for a mandatory bookmark. This site started out as a Usenet newsgroup FAQ and has grown into a stunningly thorough covering of CD-R/RW technology, hardware, software, techniques, and more. Is there a question that's not answered by this FAQ assemblage? We doubt it. The FAQ is updated regularly.

- **CD-R Diagnostic**—Located at `http://www.cdrom-prod.com/body_software.html`, it's a trialware tool that enables you to poke and prod at CD, CD-R, and CD-RW discs. You can test, examine, and even recover (copy) data from discs, as well as examine a drive's properties in minute detail. After a free, 30-day trial period, you can register for $49.95 (see Figures 15.10 and 15.11).

■ **CD-R Resources—** Located at `http://resource.simplenet.com`, it is a premier resource you must bookmark. The author, Mike Richter, is articulate, knowledgeable, and quite funny. Great stuff.

■ **CDRom & Audio Help Links—**Another great resource for help on CD-ROM, hard drive, and sound card issues (`http://mptbbs.simplenet.com/ctech4.htm`).

■ **Public newsgroups—**For example, `alt.comp.periphs.cdr`.

OFF THE WALL

WHY WAS 74 MINUTES CHOSEN AS THE STANDARD LENGTH FOR A CD?

Here's what Andy McFadden (`www.mcfadden.com`) has to say (`http://www.fadden.com/cdrfaq/faq02.html#[2-29]`): "The general belief is that it was chosen because the CD designers wanted to have a format that could hold Beethoven's ninth symphony. They were trying to figure out what diameter to use, and the length of certain performances settled it. There are several different versions of the story. Some say a Polygram (then part of Philips) artist named Herbert von Karajan wanted his favorite piece to fit on one disc. Another claims the wife of the Sony chairman wanted it to hold her favorite symphony. An interview in the July 1992 issue of *CD-ROM Professional* reports a Mr. Oga at Sony made the defining request. The 'urban legends' Web site has some interesting articles for anyone wishing to pursue the matter further." ■

■ **Adaptec's weekly CD-R software newsletters (one for Windows and one for Macintosh)—**You can sign up at `http://www.adaptec.com/adaptec/registration/cdrnews.html`. We monitor the Windows newsletter, and it's a great source of CD-R/RW information. A mailing list also is available.

■ **The Adaptec CD-R Software page—**Located at `http://cdr.adaptec.com`, it provides a set of links for buying Adaptec's line of CD-R software products.

■ **The Adaptec Media Board page—**Go to `http://www.adaptec.com/mediaboard/index.html` to see an up-to-date list of user-submitted tips on CD-R/RW media bargains. You can submit your own tips, too.

■ **Adaptec's Index of CD-R Information—**When you're in a hurry, go to `http://www.adaptec.com/support/faqs/cdrindex.html` for a great starting point. Ditto Andy McFadden's CD-Recordable FAQ (elsewhere in this list). Bookmark both of these pages.

FIGURE 15.10

CD-R
Diagnostic's
analysis of a
multisession,
"open" CD-R
disc with a
buffer underrun
that occurred
during the writing of session 3.

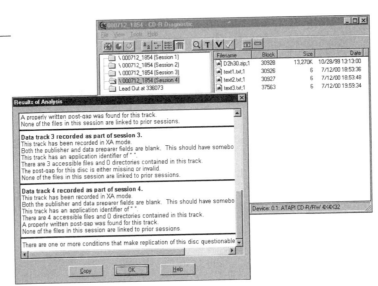

FIGURE 15.11

CD-R Diagnostic
displays its hardware analysis for
an Acer CD-RW
drive.

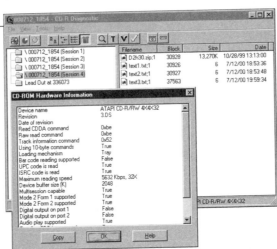

16

ADDING A DVD DRIVE

DVD? Hmmm, isn't that just playing movies on your computer? Yes and no. A DVD drive added to your computer is much more than trying to turn your monitor into an ersatz TV. DVD is the technological successor to the CD-ROM drive. What's more, DVD is backward-compatible in that DVD drives can read data from CD-ROM discs as well as play music CDs. However, the reason an heir to CD-ROM was necessary in the first place is that a CD's 650 megabytes of space is not enough to hold a full-length motion picture. Movies are, at present, what DVD is all about. That places some unique demands on your computer hardware. Is a DVD drive right for you? You must consider a number of factors, the most important being what you plan to do with your computer.

Upgrade Checklist

1. Do your homework.

2. Determine whether your PC supports the planned upgrade. For example, some DVD kits require a free IRQ and a free PCI slot.

3. Determine whether you can perform the upgrade.

4. Purchase or acquire the component. Be mindful that DVD drives can come in SCSI or IDE flavors (see Chapter 7, "Upgrading the Hard Disk"), and that FireWire models are available as well.

5. Organize your tools and work space. See Chapter 3, "Things You Need."

6. Perform the upgrade.

7. Take good notes, and permanently file them in your system log when finished.

8. Update your inventory documentation to reflect the upgraded or newly added component.

Digital Versatile Disc

Digital Versatile Disc is what most people in the computer biz say when asked what DVD stands for. But they're also known as Digital Video Discs in keeping with their genesis as the successor not so much to CD drives but to VHS videotape.

If you're purchasing a brand-new system, DVD might come already installed with the computer instead of a CD-ROM drive. DVD is going to eventually replace CD drives, and some manufacturers are starting to include them with some models. But, if you're upgrading an older system, you have to really weigh the options because even though you can get either a CD or DVD for a reasonable price, a CD-R/RW gives you the ability to burn your own CD discs for a lot less than a recordable DVD drive.

As of this writing, DVD looks better on paper than in real life, after you get past trying to play movies on your computer. The goal is for DVD to replace audio CD, CD-ROM, VHS, and laserdisc, much as they have already done to console game cartridges. What's missing is the killer computer application that spurs everyone to forego CD drives and make the migration en masse to DVD drives. Software still ships on CDs, including computer games, despite the increase in storage that DVD gives you. Music is predominantly put out on CDs, not DVD discs. And you must make some serious hardware considerations when upgrading an older system to DVD. In this chapter, we'll look at both the how and the why of a DVD upgrade.

Data Versus Video

To understand some of the hardware demands DVD places on your computer system and how that complicates upgrading, you must know that a huge difference exists in storage requirements for data as opposed to audio and video. A traditional CD disc can hold 74 minutes of audio. That's more than enough for all the music stored on the old vinyl LP album that audio CDs replaced so effectively. A CD can also hold 650 megabytes of data, or nearly 3/4 of a gigabyte. But that's not enough for a typical movie. Video consumes huge amounts of storage space. On the other hand, a DVD disc can hold 4.7 gigabytes of data, so you have a considerable increase in capacity over CD discs. This added capacity is what has given DVD the boost it needs to become the hot commodity, namely the room to store a two-hour movie including multiple sound tracks and several endings. The standard DVD disc can hold 135

PLAINSPEAKING
SAVE THOSE CARDS AND LETTERS
Hold it—yes, we know more than a dozen DVD formats are available, ranging in size from 1.23GB to a tad under 17GB (that's 6.5 hours of motion picture video). Available are DVD formats that are single-sided, double-sided, single on one side and double on the other, and all sorts of other permutations. But for discussion purposes here, we're talking about single-sided, single-layer DVD discs. That's the typical 4.7GB discs that a movie from your local video rental store comes on. ■

minutes or more of full-motion video, depending on how many audio tracks are included.

First, audio is not a problem if you have a system that can play audio CDs. Pop your favorite CD tunes in a DVD player and strike up the band. Second, data is not a problem, either. Of course, no one is currently distributing much in the way of computer software on DVD. It has yet to catch on even with the computer game manufacturers; the problem being that not enough DVD drives are installed yet. Last but not least, you have that two-hour movie and the demands live-action streaming video places on your system. This is where all the hardware headaches start.

Decoding MPEG Video

To get that movie squished down to fit on even the expanded space available on a DVD required a new compression algorithm. So, the Moving Picture Experts Group or MPEG (pronounced *m-peg*) came up with MPEG-1 to enable streaming video from a CD-ROM. But you still couldn't squeeze a full theatrical movie release on the disc, so they came up with MPEG-2, which was designed to stream video from a DVD disc. The trick is that to uncompress—or *decode*—MPEG-2 video and audio (Dolby Digital), either you need fairly fast system processing power—to handle the decoding using only software—or you need special hardware to uncompress the video and play it out to your monitor. Without the necessary speed, you get jerky video with pauses and jumps instead of a nice, flowing picture.

When we say "fairly fast" we're talking about 300MHz Pentium II or faster, and even then, you won't be as happy with a software-only solution as with a hardware decoder solution. So, for any older system you are upgrading with DVD, you're looking at adding an additional PCI decoder card along with the DVD drive itself to handle the video processing. Even with a decoder card, you'll want to start with a base system of at least a 166MHz MMX (multimedia extensions) Pentium class system with 32MB of system RAM. Windows 98 includes DirectShow 5.2, which supports MPEG-2. However, you can download and install DirectShow on Windows 95 systems (`http://www.microsoft.com/directx/homeuser/downloads`).

Adding a decoder card complicates the upgrade in several ways. First, it takes up a PCI slot. Second, it requires an additional IRQ (see Chapter 2, "Preparing for an Upgrade," for more on freeing up IRQs).

You can get around the decoder card requirement if the video card installed in the system has MPEG decoder hardware built into it. Check to see whether the graphics adapter in the system you're upgrading is DVD MPEG-2–capable. The higher-end graphics adapters all seem to be going in this direction.

If the graphics card is not going to solve your MPEG-2 problem, your best bet is to get a DVD kit that includes a PCI decoder card designed to work with the DVD drive.

DVD Upgrade Kits

An upgrade kit will generally include a DVD drive, a decoder card, and DVD play-back software. The difference between a kit and simply buying a DVD drive for your PC is the inclusion of a decoder card designed to work specifically with the drive.

The decoder card takes up a PCI slot and will require some additional cabling. Generally—and this depends on the specific kit you'll be installing—you'll connect the decoder card to the DVD drive; then, the decoder card can connect to both the system graphics card and the sound card. You should study the documentation that comes with your DVD kit to ensure that you make all the proper connections and that the proper cables are included with the kit. With some decoder cards, your monitor actually plugs into the decoder card, not the graphics card. Again, carefully study the documentation for the kit you're installing.

Numerous DVD playback applications are available on the Internet, but some compatibility issues have been raised with dedicated decoder cards. The playback software included with your kit might be the most compatible with the drive you're installing (see Figure 16.1). Although you can check for a more recent version available on the drive manufacturer's Web site, you'll want to keep the one that came with the drive. This is not to say you can't try running other players, but if you run into problems, you'll want to go back to the one that came with your kit.

FIGURE 16.1
DVD movie playback software lets you use your PC as a virtual DVD player.

DVD Standards and Compatibility

The specifications for CD formats are contained in one of several standards documents referred to as the Red Book, the Yellow Book, and so on. (For a complete breakdown of this taxonomy, go to http://www.licensing.philips.com/cdsystems/cdstandards.html.)

Most DVD drives on the market today read CD-ROMs (specifications as defined in the Yellow Book) and play back audio CDs (Red Book) without any problems. Some problems do exist with DVD drives reading CD-R discs (see Chapter 15, "Adding a CD-Recordable or CD-Rewritable Drive," for more information on CD-R) where the CD-R disc (Orange Book, Part II) appears blank to the DVD drive. This is caused by the dye used in CD-R discs not reflecting the laser beam of the DVD. This problem is most likely to occur in first-generation DVD drives, so you ensure that the drive to which you're going to upgrade comes with a MultiRead label, which guarantees compatibility with both CD-R and CD-RW discs.

Photo CDs are usually recognized by DVD drives, but the viewing software used to display the photos is often incompatible with DVD. As DVD becomes more the standard, expect the companies making this type of software to start supporting DVD.

Writable DVD

Until now, we've been talking about DVD-ROM drives, or read-only, which work like the CD-ROM drives that come standard on most computer systems. They can read DVD discs, but they can't be used to create them.

The DVD recordable drives (DVD-R) that first appeared on the market sold for around $17,000 (January 1999) and have come down to the $5,000 range some 18 months later. Prices will continue to fall, but they have a long way to go to match the price of CD-R or CD-RW drives, which sell for a few hundred dollars or even less.

But the real fly in the writable DVD ointment is that a number of competing writable DVD drive formats exist. Competing standards make for serious compatibility issues; discs created on a particular drive format are not usually readable on another drive format or even a plain DVD-ROM drive. You might want to hold off on a writable DVD drive upgrade until the dust settles and one clear winner emerges.

Currently, four DVD drive formats support recording (burning) your own DVD disc in your PC:

- DVD-R (write once—the basic equivalent of CD-R—recording up to 4.7GB per disc)

- DVD-RAM (write many)

- DVD-RW (write many)

- DVD+RW (write many)

DVD-R

This is a straight DVD burner (much like the CD-R drives discussed in Chapter 15), in that it enables you to create your own DVD disc, but after the disc is created, you can only read the data from it; it cannot be rewritten.

These drives are expensive, but they work, are reliable, and enable you to utilize the full 4.7GB storage space of a standard DVD disc. DVD-R is also the most compatible, letting you read the DVD discs you create in almost any DVD-ROM drive.

DVD-RAM

DVD-RAM drives initially could create only discs that contained 2.58GB of data per side. However, version 2 of the DVD-RAM specification calls for utilizing a full 4.7GB per side.

The real drawback with DVD-RAM is that the discs you burn must be encased in a special cartridge to be written to. As you might expect with a developing standard, more than one type of disc can be used with a DVD-RAM drive. Type 1 is permanently sealed in its recording cartridge, whereas type 2 discs (single-sided only) are in a cartridge that enables the disc to be removed from the cartridge.

When burning two-sided discs, the cartridge must be removed from the drive and physically flipped over and reinserted to enable recording on the other side.

The cartridges cannot be inserted in a standard DVD-ROM drive, so compatibility with other systems is poor. What little good news there is concerns the relatively low cost of DVD-RAM drives (under $1,000) compared to DVD-R drives. But this does not take into account the higher cost of the DVD-RAM media.

DVD-RW

DVD *dash* RW is not to be confused with DVD *plus sign* RW (discussed in the next section). The DVD-RW drives are built on the same foundation as the DVD-R drives; therefore, although they are more compatible with DVD-ROM drives than some of the other writable DVD formats, they also share the higher costs associated with the DVD-R technology. These drives can run from $1,000 to $2,000, depending on the manufacturer.

DVD+RW

The difference between the DVD+RW and DVD-RW drives goes deeper than the plus sign versus the dash in the acronyms. +RW uses a slightly different technology that results in less capacity (2.8GB per side for +RW versus 4.7GB for -RW). However, it is supposed to improve performance and create a disc that is more compatible with DVD-ROM drives and DVD movie players. The next version of the DVD+RW specification should increase the capacity to a full 4.7GB.

Installing a DVD Drive

DVD drives come in both SCSI and EIDE flavors, so the first thing you must determine is on which type of bus you're installing your DVD upgrade. (Some FireWire models are now available from which to choose, so if your system supports FireWire, you might want to consider this architecture.) You should definitely review Chapter 7 to get the scoop on how SCSI and EIDE drives mount in the system chassis and are cabled. Be sure to read the section in Chapter 7 titled "Handling Tips for Any Drive" to ensure a safe drive installation. Adding a DVD drive is also very similar to a CD drive upgrade (see Chapter 15).

In this section, we'll assume you are upgrading to an internal DVD drive. If you have an external model, or if you're installing a DVD drive kit, follow the installation instructions that come with your drive:

1. Shut down and disconnect your system (see Chapter 3's section "Breaking Down Your Computer").

2. Open your PC's chassis.

   Determine in which drive bay you'll mount the DVD drive.

   EIDE drive: Determine on which of the two IDE channels you will install the DVD drive. Generally, you don't want DVD drives on the same channel as your hard drive. In a typical three-drive configuration (hard disk, CD, and DVD drives), the hard disk would be on the primary channel, and the DVD and CD would be on the secondary channel.

   Make sure the drive is jumpered properly. The choices are either Master/Slave or Cable Select. Cable Select is where you use a special ATA/IDE cable, and the position the device occupies on the cable determines its master/slave status. Most of the time, you're simply better off setting the drive to be what you want—master or slave.

   If you're replacing an existing CD (IDE) drive, ensure that the new drive is jumpered the same as the existing drive. If you are adding (instead of replacing), make sure it is set to master or slave as necessary depending on how you want your drive configured. If the drive is on the channel by itself, use the factory default setting of master. Always check the drive documentation and start with whatever recommendations it might have as to master or slave settings. Be sure the EIDE ribbon cable running from the motherboard has a free connector that reaches to the drive bay in which you'll be installing the DVD drive. Obtain a ribbon cable upgrade if necessary.

SCSI drive: Make sure the internal SCSI ribbon cable has a free connector that will reach the drive bay where you'll install the DVD drive. Determine which SCSI ID number is available and set the drive for that number. Always check the drive documentation and go with whatever recommendations it might have.

3. Trace your power supply's cable bundles to see whether a free cable is available to power the DVD drive. If not, you'll need to buy a Y-type splitter power cable, which is available at any electronics parts store.

4. DVD drives must be accessible from the front of the system. If you're replacing an existing CD drive, remove the old drive. If this is a new addition, remove the bezel covering the drive slot on the front of your system. (See Chapter 7, Figure 7.5.)

5. Install the new drive in the appropriate drive bay. DVD drives will usually fit in a full-sized bay without the need for cages or rails. Secure it with the provided mounting screws (if none came with the drive, they're available at any electronics parts store). As with hard drives, you should ensure that the screws you get don't penetrate too far into the DVD drive's housing.

6. Connect the ribbon cable to the DVD drive, either the SCSI or IDE cable depending on the type of drive you are installing. The red stripe that runs along one edge of the ribbon cable goes on the side of the drive connector receptacle marked as pin 1 (this is usually toward the side of the drive where the power connector is). (See Chapter 7, Figure 7.6.)

7. Connect the power lead to the drive. (See Chapter 7, Figure 7.5.)

8. Connect the DVD drive to the sound card with the cable that should have come with the drive. You might have to consult the sound card's documentation and the DVD drive's documentation (see Figure 16.2).

9. Close up the system and boot it.

10. Install any software that accompanied your DVD drive.

Sound card

FIGURE 16.2
A thin cable con-
nects your DVD
drive to your
sound card.

This end connects to
the rear of the DVD drive

PROBLEM CONNECTING TO THE SOUND CARD

If the system you're upgrading has a CD-ROM drive (and you're not replacing it with the
DVD), it probably will already be connected to your sound card. Some sound cards support
both CD audio and CD digital inputs, so you could hook the DVD drive to the CD digital
connector and have both drives connected to a single sound card. If the sound card does
not support multiple input connectors on the card (interior), you might still be able to
hook up both the CD and the DVD, provided the DVD is using a dedicated decoder card.
You can get a micro stereo patch cord (Radio Shack or other electronics stores carry these)
and connect a DVD external headphone jack on the back of the DVD decoder card to the
sound card's line-in jack.

Has DVD's Time Come?

As we've said in this chapter, if you're buying or building a new state-of-the-art
computer system, you might consider going with DVD from the start. As much of a
novelty that watching a DVD movie on your computer screen is (and it is pretty
cool), if your main interest is watching movies, get a nice DVD player for your TV
and let it go at that.

Writable DVD drives are not standardized to the point where we would recommend one at the time of this writing. Compatibility issues are still a major consideration if you need to share the DVDs you plan on burning with other systems, and the costs of both the drives and the rewritable media are much higher than for CDs.

Very little software (business or games) is distributed on DVD media at present, so unless you have some really compelling reason to upgrade (in other words, not just to watch the occasional movie on your computer monitor), you should hold off until prices drop to the levels you see for CD technology and some killer application that takes advantage of DVD technology comes along.

In any event, hold off upgrading to a writable DVD drive until a clear winner emerges from the multiple standards currently fighting it out for dominance.

ANOTHER FINE MESS
FINDING THE MAGIC LETTER
Some decoder cards expect to find the DVD drive defined as a specific drive letter. Check the documentation that comes with your DVD kit to see whether this could be an issue for you. If it is, you must juggle drive letter assignments. You can set the drive letter for certain devices, such as CD and Zip drives. Click Start, Settings, Control Panel, System. In the Device Manager tab, select the device and click Properties. On the Settings tab, you should be able to set Reserved drive letters. Set both the Start drive letter and the End drive letter to the letter you want the device to use. ∎

ADDING REMOVABLE STORAGE

17

D-R and CD-RW drives aren't the only game in town. A plethora of
contenders vie for your hard-earned removable storage dollars, with
more capacity, throughput, interface, and form factor choices than you
can shake a dongle at. In this chapter, we compare these solutions and
rank them on an often-overlooked dimension: media cost per
megabyte. This is because you can, in a drive's life span, spend as
much or more on media as you did on the drive itself.

Upgrade Checklist

1. Do your homework.

2. Determine whether your PC supports the planned upgrade.

3. Determine whether you can perform the upgrade.

4. Purchase or acquire the component.

5. Organize your tools and workspace. See Chapter 3, "Things You Need."

6. Back up everything: data, operating system, mission-critical applications, and BIOS.

7. Test your startup disk.

8. Perform the upgrade.

9. Take good notes, and permanently file them in your system log when you're finished.

10. Update your inventory documentation to reflect the upgraded or newly added component.

Removable Media Primer

Common uses for low- to medium-capacity removable storage drives are

- Backing up files
- Archiving files

- Storing photos in digital photo albums

- Exchanging files with clients, friends, and family (portability)

- Storing large Internet downloads (Internet direct to removable storage, bypassing your hard disk)

Common uses for high-capacity removable storage drives are

- Backing up large files or large numbers of files

- Archiving large files or large numbers of files

- Storing photos in digital photo albums

- Exchanging files with clients, friends, and family (portability)

- Performing personal video recording

- Using MP3 audio jukebox

- Real-time video editing

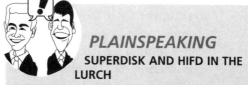

PLAINSPEAKING

SUPERDISK AND HIFD IN THE LURCH

Although the Imation SuperDisk and Sony HiFD were good ideas, and are still being sold in dribs and drabs, we don't recommend them. Their sales are lagging, and it looks like they're both rapidly becoming vestigial technologies. Not to mention, they're awfully slow compared to their competing technologies. ■

The main decision you must make about a removable media drive is how common does the format need to be? If commonality is critical, say, for exchanging files with service bureaus, other vendors, or clients, get an Iomega Zip drive or a CD-R/RW (as covered in Chapter 15, "Adding a CD-Recordable or CD-Rewritable Drive"). These folks are less likely to have Orb or Jaz drives on hand for reading your media. If you're an island unto yourself, or exchange files with only a few people or companies and they share your love of a particular technology, go for Jaz or Orb.

The next criterion is the size of the files you need to store, and their aggregate size when clustered into logical groups. Only you can determine how those values weigh out, both separately and together. Remember to always give yourself some room to grow.

The last important criterion is the interface type. As we've said throughout this book, you always need to look at your existing set of peripherals versus the intended upgrade (or new peripheral), and forecast whatever other growth plans you have for your PC during the next one–two years. An IDE internal drive is fine if you've got a spare channel; SCSI internal is nice if you already have a SCSI controller installed; and USB is by far the best for ease of installation, PnP support, hot-swappability, and portability. We strongly recommend you avoid units that connect to your parallel port because they're too slow and cumbersome.

NOTE

INNOVATIVE REMOVABLE STORAGE FOR NOTEBOOK USERS

Iomega's Clik! drive uses the PC Card interface already built into your notebook (a Type II card slot is required). This is a really cool removable storage solution for road warriors. The drive itself weighs a mere 41 grams (that's 1.4 ounces!) and fits right into the PC Card slot; no dongles, no power or data cables, no fuss, no muss. One Clik! disk holds 40MB. Clik! drives are also good for use with some digital cameras, providing an easy way to get pictures into your home PC or notebook PC. For more information about the Clik! drive, see `http://www.iomega.com/clik/products/pccard.html`.

Table 17.1 analyzes removable storage devices by capacity, throughput, drive cost, and media cost (cost/MB). The table also shows a partial breakdown by interface type; in fact, it shows all the interface types supported by the Iomega Zip 100 and 250 drives. However, we show only one or two interface types for the other drives because we aren't conducting a complete product review of specific manufacturers and models in this chapter. Instead, we want to show you the variety of interface support for what is undoubtedly the most popular device in this product category: the Iomega Zip 100, and in second place, its big brother the Zip 250. Note that CD-R/RW drives are covered in Chapter 15.

Table 17.1   Removable Storage Device Comparison

Drive	Bus	Capacity	Throughput	Drive Cost[1]	Media Cost (Cents/MB)[2]
Castlewood Orb	EIDE	2.2GB	12.2MBps	2.0x ($200)	1.3 cents ($29)
Castlewood Orb[3]	SCSI	2.2GB	12.2MBps	1.6x ($160)	1.3 cents ($29)
Imation SuperDisk LS-120[4]	ATAPI IDE	120MB	0.68– 1.1MBps	1.0x ($100)	7.5 cents ($9)
Iomega Clik! PC Card	PC Card Type II	40MB	0.7MBps	1.5x ($150)	35 cents ($14)
Iomega Jaz 1GB	SCSI	1GB	6.6MBps	1.1x ($110)	9.9 cents ($99)
Iomega Jaz 2GB	SCSI	2GB	5.5– 8.0MBps	3.5x ($350)	6.25 cents ($125)
Iomega Notebook Zip 100	IDE/ EIDE	100MB	1.4MBps	2.0x ($200)	Same as Zip 100
Iomega Zip 100	USB	100MB	1.2MBps	1.0x ($100)	13 cents ($13)
Iomega Zip 100 and 250	Internal ATAPI	100MB and 250MB	2.4MBps	1.0x/ 1.5x ($100 /$150)	—
Iomega Zip 100 and 250	Parallel	100MB and 250MB	0.8MBps	UNK/1.5x ($UNK/ $150)	—
Iomega Zip 100 and 250	SCSI	100 and 250MB	2.4MBps	UNK/1.5x ($UNK/$150)	—
Iomega Zip 250	USB	250MB	0.9MBps	1.8x ($180)	7.2 cents ($18)
Sony HiFD	Parallel[5]	200MB	0.6MBps	1.8x ($180)	7.5 cents ($15)

1. *Rounded to the nearest even $10 increment; then lowest price used as the base to normalize all other prices rel-ative to the base. Drive and media prices reflect average prices for late 2000 and are subject to change, just as is model availability, and so on.*

2. Media unit cost rounded to the nearest whole dollar for single-unit packs wherever possible. The actual media cost is shown in parentheses.

3. Available in all traditional interface configurations, including FireWire.

4. Also available in the following interface configurations: PCMCIA, USB (iMac only), and parallel.

5. Also available in a USB version.

OFF THE WALL
DROP THAT FLOPPY!
Traditional 1.44MB floppy disks, although the cheapest on a per-unit basis, are very expensive on a per-megabyte basis. Floppies tie with the Clik! disk as the most expensive type of removable media storage. ■

Table 17.2 ranks each removable storage drive type based on the media cost in cents/MB. The clear winners on this dimension are CD-R/RW drives (CD-R discs are half as costly as CD-RW because the CD-R discs are not rewritable), the Orb, and Jaz 2GB, followed closely by the Zip 250. Because, over the useful life of a removable storage drive, the media cost can equal or exceed the purchase cost of the drive, carefully consider media cost before making your decision.

CAUTION

IOMEGA JAZ 1GB DRIVES NO LONGER BEING MANUFACTURED
Iomega no longer manufactures Jaz 1GB drives. However, its Web site states, "We will continue to sell Jaz 1GB media and support both the Jaz 1GB drive and the Jaz 1GB disk."

CAUTION

HOW LONG DOES A ZIP DISK LIVE?
According to Iomega, a Zip 100 disk's life span is 2,000 insertion and removal cycles with a shelf life of 10 years (estimated). Two thousand is a relatively large number because, if we assume two disk-insertion/removals per day every day, it would take 2.7 years before the thing gave up the ghost. Still, it's always good to realize that these removable media do have an upper limit for both shelf life (how long they last simply sitting on a shelf) and usage cycles.

In fact, all media types have a shelf life that is not infinity, and are subject to eventual breakdown after so many usage cycles. Check with the specific media and drive manufacturer for their latest values.

Table 17.2 Removable Storage Media Costs in Cents per Megabyte, Shown in Order from Least to Most Expensive

Drive	Capacity	Media Cost (Cents/MB)[1]
CD-R	650MB	0.3 cent ($2)
CD-RW	650MB	0.6 cent ($3.67)
Castlewood Orb	2.2GB	1.3 cents ($29)
Iomega Jaz 2GB	2GB	6.25 cents ($125)
Iomega Zip 250	250MB	7.2 cents ($18)
Imation SuperDisk LS-120	120MB	7.5 cents ($9)
Sony HiFD	200MB	7.5 cents ($15)
Iomega Jaz 1GB	1GB	9.9 cents ($99)
Iomega Zip 100	100MB	13 cents ($13)
Iomega Notebook Zip 100	100MB	13 cents ($13)
Traditional 1.44MB floppy disk	1.44MB	28 cents ($0.40)
Iomega Clik! PC Card	40MB	35 cents ($14)

1. *Rounded to the nearest even $10 increment; then lowest price used as the base to normalize all other prices relative to the base. Drive and media prices reflect average prices for late 2000 and are subject to change, just as is model availability, and so on.*

CAUTION

SONY HIFD ENGINEERING CHANGE IN OCTOBER 1999

Here's an important bulletin from Sony in response to the question, "What should I do if I purchased a HiFD drive or media prior to October 1999?" The answer is "Due to an engineering change implemented in all Sony HiFD drives available starting October 1999, they will not recognize any HiFD disks purchased prior to November 1999. We regret any inconvenience this may cause. For further information, or for information on how to receive free replacements on all HiFD products purchased prior to November 1999, please contact Sony at 1-800-597-5649."

Installing a Removable Media Drive

These Steps Apply to Installing a Removable Media Drive in an Internal Drive Bay

1. Shut down and disconnect your system (see Chapter 3's section "Breaking Down Your Computer").

2. Open your PC's chassis and examine the 40-pin IDE cable for the IDE channel on which you're placing the drive. The motherboard diagram in your user's manual will indicate which port is IDE1 and which is IDE2, and it's typically marked on the motherboard surface, too.

   If the target IDE channel's cable is a one-drive cable, as is often the case, you'll need to replace it with a three-connector IDE cable (one connector for the controller and two for peripherals). This cable is available for about $6 at any electronics parts store, as described in Chapter 3. Some drives, however, come with such a data cable.

SEE ALSO
➤ *For details on the drive-related concepts of master and slave, cable select, and primary and secondary IDE channels, under "IDE Cable," see page 165*

SEE ALSO
➤ *See "Handling Tips for Any Drive," page 176*

3. Trace your power supply's cable bundles to see whether a free cable exists to power the drive. If not, you'll need to buy a Y-type splitter power cable, available at any electronics parts store. Some drives, though, come with such a power cable.

4. Follow your drive's installation instructions. In general, the steps are as follows.

5. Select the desired IDE channel.

6. Jumper the drive as that channel's master or slave according to the instructions and your system's configuration. Figure 15.5 in Chapter 15 shows how to jumper a typical CD-R/RW as either a master or slave drive; that figure applies to other types of removable storage drives, too.

7. Connect the 4-pin power cable to the drive.

SEE ALSO
➤ *See "Power Connection," page 181*

8. Connect the 40-pin IDE data cable to the drive.

SEE ALSO

➤ See "Ribbon Cables and Pin 1," page 180

9. Place the drive into a bay and secure it with the provided mounting screws (if none came with the drive, they're available at any electronics parts store). As with hard drives, you should ensure the screws you get don't penetrate too far into the drive's housing (see Chapter 7, "Upgrading the Hard Disk").

SEE ALSO

➤ See "Mounting Brackets and Screws," page 177

10. Put the chassis cover back on and connect all the power cords.

11. Boot the system.

12. Install the necessary software to test and use your removable storage drive.

13. Test your new drive.

Verify that the drive shows up in your My Computer and Windows Explorer device lists. Create at least one disk and see whether it can be read back successfully. If your drive came with specialty software such as Iomega QuikSync, Iomega 1-Step Backup, Orb Tools 1-Click Backup, Iomega RecordIt, Iomega CopyMachine, or Adobe ActiveShare (a digital photo organizer), test it now. Ideally, take your test output disk to another PC with the same drive and verify that it can be read.

NOTE

INSTALLING A USB DEVICE

Start your PC, connect the USB device—say, an Iomega Zip 250—to a power source (if it's not getting power from the bus), and plug it into a USB port. If the PC hasn't seen this particular device before, Windows runs the New Hardware Found applet, identifies the device, builds a Driver Info Database, and prompts you to insert your master Windows CD (in some cases, you might want to insert a CD that contains a more recent driver). For more information, see Chapter 11, "Adding USB Compatibility."

Case Study: The Iomega Zip 250 USB

When we considered the purchase of a new Zip drive, we first had to choose between the Zip 100 and Zip 250 drives. A Zip 100 drive can't read from or write to a 250MB Zip disk, but a Zip 250 drive is backward-compatible.

This means you can insert a 100MB Zip disk into a Zip 250 drive and it will write to it and read from it. We chose an external USB model because it's portable to any PC or Mac with an unused USB port, hot-swappable, and supports Plug and Play.

As with most USB devices, the Zip 250 drive is quick and painless to install. The unit is deep blue with gray accents, smartly designed to fit right into your hand when you grab its sides, has a very small form factor (0.75" thick by 6.75" long by 4.5" wide), weighs only 9 ounces, and can be mounted vertically on the provided stand. Even when you add the power brick and USB cable, the package weighs in at under a pound: 15.3 ounces to be exact. A great choice for road warriors is an optional $40 PCMCIA card/cable bundle that eliminates the need for the power supply when you're on the road.

The drive's printed documentation and Quick Install pamphlet are excellent.

You're not likely to falter during setup if you follow the instructions. You can option-ally install the user's manual from the supplied CD, and we suggest you do so. A second pamphlet printed on hard-to-miss orange paper and labeled "Read me first!" contains useful tips on getting software updates and a list of USB do's and don'ts.

The bundled IomegaWare software, although satisfactory, wasn't up to the same standard as the drive. (We're reviewing IomegaWare version 2.2.1 here.) IomegaWare can be accessed via the traditional Start menu or desktop icon tech-niques. You can optionally prevent IomegaWare from loading whenever you start Windows.

IomegaWare's interface offers access to help files and allows you to open, explore, find, eject, format, protect, and examine the properties of any Zip drive (you also can perform these operations from inside Windows Explorer). See Figure 17.1.

FIGURE 17.1

IomegaWare's dialog box gives you access to a Zip drive's com-mands and properties and an assortment of bundled tools.

IomegaWare includes the following tools:

- **Iomega QuikSync**—Automatically backs up the contents of one folder to a Zip drive (see Figure 17.2). You can set how often the folder is to be checked for any changes, and whether a file—once changed—is to be backed up to the Zip drive on top of itself or with incrementing filenames, such as Teachpcs.(1).doc and Teachpcs.(2).doc. We were annoyed that QuikSync's Browse for Folder dialog box doesn't display backup source folders in alphabetical order. You can upgrade to QuikSync 2, a version that does support multiple source folders, but you must pay $19.95. (A free 30-day evaluation copy is available for download from IomegaDirect, Iomega's online store, at `http://www.iomegadirect.com`).

FIGURE 17.2

Iomega QuikSync watches a folder for changes and saves those changed files to a Zip drive.

- **Iomega 1-Step Backup**—A quick way to select multiple folders for a backup. You can name and save backup jobs, turn file compression on or off, select files and folders from a multiselect tree view, and turn password protection on or off. IomegaWare also includes a 1-Step Restore tool.

- **Iomega Backup The Works**—This is the bundle's full-featured backup tool (see Figure 17.3). In addition to 1-Step's features, The Works supports a backup scheduler, complete user control over all backup types (full, archive, incremental, and differential), restore and compare, and a Librarian that catalogs all the backups according to volume and filename.

FIGURE 17.3

Iomega Backup
The Works is a
full-featured
backup utility.

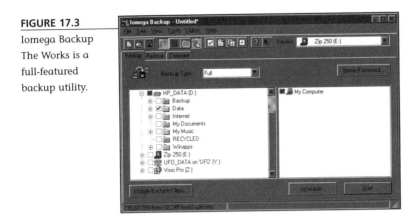

■ **Iomega Copy Machine**—This Wizard lets you copy a Zip disk to a second Zip disk even if you have only one Zip drive.

Iomega Click of Death Syndrome

The dreaded Click of Death syndrome is very real and—when it strikes—catastrophic. However, a free tool is available to help you determine whether your Zip or Jaz drive or cartridges are affected by it. Elsewhere in this book, we've praised the virtues of Steve Gibson and his Gibson Research Corporation. Steve has taken on Click of Death and published some very articulate, thoughtful literature on the subject (http://grc.com/clickdeath.htm). Meanwhile, here's our executive summary.

Click of Death (also called *Click Death* and *COD*) describes the early symptoms of an impending catastrophe with a Zip or Jaz drive or cartridge. An audible, distinctive clicking sound emanates from the drive when a cartridge is inserted or when the heads are reading/writing. Shortly after the clicking occurs, the drive and one or more cartridges dies without warning. (More on data recovery in a moment.) Understandably, this syndrome has angered many customers. To date, Iomega has taken a very quiet approach to handling the problem, and this has exacerbated customer concerns.

The following noteworthy quote comes directly from Steve's site, "Iomega Zip and Jaz drives cause Click Of Death by incorrectly writing to their removable media. This miswriting can damage the user's data, the factory-written low-level formatting, the head's positioning servo information, and the proprietary 'Z-Tracks' that are used internally to manage and maintain the Zip and Jaz drive's cartridge data. The clicking sound itself is … the sound of the heads being retracted from the cartridge into the drive then immediately reinserted. This deliberate strategy is employed by the drive when it is having trouble locating, reading, or writing any of the cartridge's data. This removal and reinsertion of the heads recalibrates the head positioning mechanism, 'scrubs' the heads to remove excessive oxide deposits, and eliminates electrostatic charge buildup on the heads. It is VERY IMPORTANT for you to understand that the clicking sound itself is NOT the problem. The clicking is just an audible indication of a drive that is having trouble accessing the data on a cartridge."

Steve goes on to debunk the myth that COD is contagious. What actually happens when a COD-damaged cartridge is inserted into another drive is that the drive's heads click because, as explained earlier, they are having trouble reading the data *on the damaged cartridge*. Only in extremely—repeat *extremely*—rare cases can a data cartridge actually destroy a drive, and this involves the cartridge media itself tearing so that, when it is inserted into a drive, it actually knocks the heads off and leaves them dangling by their wires. (See `http://grc.com/codfaq4.htm` for more information on this extremely rare, but confirmed, scenario. It has neat pictures, too!)

If you ever hear clicking, clunking, thunking, or thwacking sounds coming from your Zip or Jaz drive, stop everything and run Steve's freeware Trouble in Paradise (TIP) utility. In fact, you should run TIP on all your Zip or Jaz drives and cartridges right now. You can download TIP at `http://grc.com/files/tip.exe`. Because COD can't be prevented by any type of software fix, your best course of action is to run TIP regularly, thus allowing you to save your data should TIP detect an impending problem. Remember, when COD strikes, it does so without warning.

What about data recovery? Iomega has publicly promised that, "If our customers have a problem specific to this issue [COD], whether it's in or out of warranty, we're going to take care of and replace the product if necessary." So, the first step is to get a free replacement for a drive with COD. Next, run TIP on it to make sure it's okay. Gibson reports that running TIP with a healthy drive on a troubled cartridge often restores the cartridge to full health. For a severely damaged cartridge, or a case in which the cartridge's data is so important it must be recovered at any cost, use a data recovery tool instead of TIP. TIP is not designed to recover unreadable data, but data recovery tools are. One such tool is Gibson's own SpinRite 5.0 (`http://grc.com/spinrite.htm`).

Online Resources

■ **An old Iomega Zip FAQ**—Can be found at `http://www.juip.com/zipfaq.html`. Although a bit dated (last updated on June 30, 1998), it nonetheless can be of some value.

- **Castlewood Systems, Inc.**—The manufacturer of the Orb drive maintains a Web site at `http://www.castlewood.com`. There, you'll find product pages, what's new, where to buy, downloads, FAQs, and owner's manuals.

- **IomegaWare software**—Get the latest version of it at `http://www.iomega.com/software/index.html`.

- **SuperDisk FAQs**—If you're a SuperDisk user, you'll find some helpful FAQs at `http://faq.superdisk.com`. See the links for Troubleshooting, Care & Handling, Software Drivers, and User's Guides.

- **Zip Configurator**—Iomega offers this Web-based utility at `http://www.iomega.com/zip/configurator/index.html`. This utility helps you decide which Iomega Zip drive is right for you. Just answer the questions and see what it says.

- **Iomega's QuikSync 2 utility**—Allows you to automatically make a backup copy of any file as you change it. For example, say you edit a Word document called Birthday.doc and save it to your hard disk as usual; QuikSync 2 notices that the file has changed and instantly creates a backup copy to your Zip, Jaz, Clik!, or ZipCD disk. For more information, see `http://www.iomega.com/quiksync/index2.html`.

IOMEGA QUIKSYNC IS NO LONGER FREEWARE

Iomega no longer offers QuikSync as freeware. It now comes bundled with newer drives. You can download a 30-day evaluation copy, or you can buy a copy direct at `http://www.iomega.com/software/index.html`.

- **The Sony HiFD home page**—Located at `http://www.ita.sel.sony.com/jump/hifd/index.html`.

- **FireWire adapter for the Zip 250 USB drive**—You can get this at `http://www.iomega.com/zip/products/accessories.html`. It doubles the read speed. In addition, if you have a 6-pin FireWire port, the drive can get power via the FireWire adapter, thereby avoiding the need for a power supply.

18

ADDING A
TAPE DRIVE

A tape drive for backing up and storing archived copies of data from your hard disk is still one of the best price performance options when you consider you can create multigenerational backups or use an external tape drive with a number of computers. Although other removable media are trying to give the tape drive a run for its money, a number of reasons still exist that recommend going with tape.

Upgrade Checklist

1. Do your homework.

2. Determine whether your PC's operating system supports the planned upgrade. For example, some tape drives have problems with Windows NT4.

3. Determine whether your PC supports the planned upgrade.

4. Determine whether you can perform the upgrade.

5. Purchase or acquire the tape drive.

6. Organize your tools and workspace if you're installing an internally mounted drive. See Chapter 3, "Things You Need."

7. Perform the upgrade.

8. Take good notes, and permanently file them in your system log when finished.

9. Update your inventory documentation to reflect the upgraded or newly added component.

Considering a Tape Drive's Features

As the capacity of hard disks goes through the roof, making a backup copy of your data becomes more of a challenge. Long gone are the days of copying your files onto floppy disks. CD-RW drives make for a good way to store certain subsets of data, but given the relatively low capacity of a CD disc (650MB–700MB), they won't suffice when trying to back up the contents of a 20-gigabyte (GB) drive.

Tape remains the backup medium of choice, although even tape drives have trouble keeping up with the rapidly increasing capacities of hard disks when it comes to backing up an entire hard disk to a single tape cartridge.

There's more to choosing and installing a tape drive than you might think, so we recommend you read this chapter all the way through *before* you pick out a tape drive with which to upgrade your system.

Format

A number of tape formats are available (see Table 18.1).

The Travan (TR) specification was developed by 3M and has replaced the old QIC standard (TR is backward-compatible with QIC cartridges) that had ruled the tape drive roost for years. TR-1 and TR-2 drives used sub-one GB cartridges uncompressed. The current TR-5 tapes holds up to 10GB uncompressed, and the drives can be purchased for well below $500. By the time you read this, the TR-6 drives might be available that promise to double the capacity yet of the TR-5.

Advanced Digital Recording (ADR),

PLAINSPEAKING
TAPE OR DISK FOR BACKUP?

Consider that the cheapest medium for backing up a hard disk is another hard disk. The cost per GB is cheaper than tape, and backing up from disk to disk is faster as well. When you consider that retrieval of backed-up data is nonlinear (no waiting for meters and meters of tape to be spun before the piece of data you are looking for comes up) but random, using a second hard drive as a backup disk is very attractive.

In addition, testing the integrity of your backup by just calling up the data from the backup disk is easier, whereas you never really know whether your tape is good until you go through the restore process and actually pull data off the tape and put it back on the disk.

However, the one major advantage that tape has over a hard disk is that the media, in the form of the tape cartridge, is removable (although you can get USB and FireWire external hard drives and even IDE and SCSI setups where the drive is external and therefore removable). Because the cartridges can be popped in and out of the drive, you can make multigenerational backups—something you can't do by backing up to a hard disk. This also makes offsite storage possible, which can be critical for important data. It also makes transferring information easier because a tape can be delivered overnight from one site to another.

Be sure to weigh the various arguments between tape and disk before running out and upgrading your system. ■

originally developed by Philips Electronics and currently used in OnStream products (www.onstream.com), is a tape format designed for drives that use an eight-channel head that performs read-after-write for better data integrity. The drives also use continuously variable tape speed (meaning that the drives speed up and slow down as the rate that data is supplied from the hard disk changes). Variable speed is supposed to save considerable wear and tear on the physical tape.

Table 18.1 Tape Formats

Format Type	Pros	Cons	Best Use
Travan (TR)	Inexpensive; reliable; internal or external versions	Capacity lags behind larger drive sizes (uncompressed)	Workstations
Advanced Digital Recording (ADR)	Fast throughput; variable speed preserves the life of the tape itself; larger capacity	Proprietary format	Workstations needing faster throughputs than TR provides
Digital Audio Tape (DAT)	Fast throughput; internal or external versions; larger capacity	Higher costs for drives and tape cartridges	Workstations or network servers
8mm	Fastest throughput; high capacity	High cost	Network servers
Digital Linear Tape (DLT)	Fastest throughput; high capacity	High cost	Network servers

Digital Audio Tape (DAT) drives come in various Digital Data Storage (DDS) formats, such as DDS-3 (12GB uncompressed) or DDS-4 (20GB uncompressed), and cost in the neighborhood of $1,000.

At the high end are *8mm* tape offered by Exabyte (`www.exabyte.com`) and `Digital Linear Tape (DLT)` from various manufacturers. These drives cost in the thousands of dollars range and have capacities of 20GB (8mm) all the way up to 35GB for DLT.

Data Throughput

How quickly a tape drive can transfer data from the hard disk to the tape varies depending on the make and model of the drive and the format used. The transfer rates discussed here are the higher ends of their respective formats—again the particular model you choose will be the final determiner of the performance you can expect:

- **TR-5 drives**—These can hit performance levels of 1 megabyte (MB) per second uncompressed (internal EIDE or SCSI interface), but they slow down to around 22MB per minute uncompressed using an external (extended parallel port interface) model. We'd recommend this type of tape drive for a home or small business setup.

- **ADR drives**—These drives from OnStream boast very high transfer rates because of the unique design of the ADR drive technology. They claim their EIDE model transfers a 1MB per second uncompressed, while their SCSI and FireWire models run at 2MB per second. Their USB model runs at .85MB per second uncompressed.

- **DAT DDS-4 drives**—With internal SCSI interface, these can put data onto the tape at nearly 3MB per second uncompressed, rivaling the higher-end 8mm and DLT drives.

- **8mm and DLT drives**—With SCSI interface for either internal or external units, these can store data at speeds of 3MB or even 5MB

ANOTHER FINE MESS
NOTHING LASTS FOREVER

Don't make the mistake of thinking that your archived tapes last forever. Most all backup medium from tape to CD discs have some sort of shelf life, meaning they all break down over time. That shelf life is usually measured in years, but always check to see what the manufacture says. Tapes also wear out through use. Some tapes will list an estimate (similar to the mean time between failures [MTBF] that used to be quoted for hard disk) of how many passes through the tape drive a given tape can be expected to last. If you have long, long storage in mind, be sure to check out the shelf life and expected longevity of use of your tapes. ■

ANOTHER FINE MESS
JUST HOW FAST IS FAST?

Keep the "megabyte per second—wow that's fast!" feeling in perspective. If you have a 20GB drive full of data, copying it all to tape, assuming no compression, will take more than five and half hours. The better your data compresses, the faster the MB per second throughput. But even at a perfect 2:1 compression, you're looking at the better part of three hours for the full 20 gigabytes. Granted, few of us need to perform full backups on a 20-gigabyte drive chock-full of data, but keep in mind that backups can run for hours. You also might have to physically change tapes if your drive does not have the capacity to put everything you want backed up onto a single cartridge. This might influence the type of drive to which you want to upgrade. ■

per second uncompressed, which is pretty darn fast anyway you look at it. But, you pay a premium price for this type of throughput.

Internal Versus External

Tape drives come in several physical configurations and support different buses depending on the individual make and model. The higher-end 8mm and DLT drives usually come in external models connecting to your system only via a SCSI port.

Travan, ADR, and DAT drives can usually be found in either internal or external versions. *Internal* tape drives connect via the SCSI or EIDE bus (see Chapter 7, "Upgrading the Hard Disk," for details on EIDE and SCSI). *External* models come in parallel, USB, and FireWire flavors. OnStream manufactures drives in all configurations and was one of the first to offer USB and FireWire drives (see Chapter 2, "Preparing for an Upgrade," for details on USB and FireWire buses).

External drives are ideal if you want to use one tape drive across several computers, or with a laptop. However, they generally cost more than internal models due to the added expense of the housing that encloses the drive (parallel and SCSI external models also require the addition of a power adapter).

External models are usually easier to install than internal drives, whereas internal drives require opening up the system chassis and physically installing and connecting the drive.

Bus Types

Similar to hard drives, you can choose between EIDE and SCSI type drives (with all the related flavors in each category), with some drives (such as those from OnStream) supporting USB and FireWire buses as well. You'll probably go with whichever drive is compatible with the bus your system currently supports. Most recently manufactured systems support either SCSI or EIDE, and most should support USB (if not, see Chapter 11, "Adding USB Compatibility"). Not all systems currently support FireWire, so make sure your computer fully supports this bus (also known as IEEE 1394) before deciding on a FireWire tape drive.

Between EIDE and SCSI, you'll get somewhat better throughput with SCSI, but it probably won't justify the cost if you have to purchase a SCSI controller to install the tape drive. If your system already supports SCSI devices, you might want to consider a SCSI tape drive. Some tape drives (especially at the higher ends) are available only as SCSI devices. SCSI is one way to go if you're completely out of IRQs (along with USB and FireWire).

You can also get Travan external models that connect to your system via the parallel port. They use the enhanced parallel port (EPP) standard for data transfer, which is slower by nearly half than what you can hope for with EIDE or SCSI models.

Table 18.2 shows the bus types you can use to connect a tape drive to a computer and the pros and cons of the various buses as they relate to tape drives.

Table 18.2 Bus Types That Support Tape Drives

Bus Types	Pros	Cons
Parallel (EPP)	Ease of installation; external	Very slow throughput
USB; FireWire	Ease of installation; external; supports multiple devices	Slow throughput
EIDE	Built in; fast throughput	Limited number of devices
SCSI	Marginally faster throughput than EIDE; supports more devices than EIDE	Usually requires adding a SCSI controller; expensive

Tape Capacity

Much as with hard disk capacity, the more you're willing to pay, the bigger capacity tape drive you can buy. You can find tape drives that will hold from 1GB–35GB on a single tape, or library systems that back up terabytes (TB) across multiple tape cartridges automatically. It all depends on whether you want to spend hundreds, thousands, or tens of thousands of dollars to back up your data.

The key to deciding how much capacity you need is understanding exactly what you're going to want to back up. If you want to back up only current data files, you'll have to analyze just what the phrase "current data files" means in terms of your normal use. If you want to back up your entire hard disk to a single cartridge, you'll need a tape drive that matches your hard disk's storage capacity.

You can, of course, get by with a tape drive capacity smaller than your hard disk. But, you might find yourself having to perform

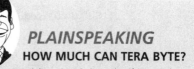

PLAINSPEAKING
HOW MUCH CAN TERA BYTE?

A quick review is in order if just to keep everyone's eyes from glazing over. A floppy disk holds 1.4MB. A gigabyte is 1,000 megabytes (yes, we know we're rounding). That makes a terabyte 1,000 gigabytes. And that's a whole lot of storage. ∎

your backups over more than one tape cartridge. This means you'll need more cartridges and that backing up cannot be done unattended. It all depends on the amount of data you're backing up, how often you make backups, and how many generations of backups you want to maintain.

Another factor to consider when calculating the capacity you want is the cost of the tape cartridges. The larger the cartridge, the higher the unit cost per cartridge. Conversely, the smaller the cartridge, the less expensive but the more cartridges might be necessary to back up all your data.

PLAINSPEAKING
DOUBLE THE CAPACITY? HA!

Manufacturers arrive at the storage capacity for tape cartridges by taking the actual capacity of the tape without data compression (called *native* capacity), and *assuming* that compression will always be 2:1. A tape with a native capacity of 10GB is called a 20GB tape. Some manufacturers note that the listed capacities of their tapes are compressed values, but it's not always clear.

A compression ratio of 2:1 is a poor assumption because file compression is totally dependent on which type of data is being backed up. Some files compress more than 2:1, but a lot of files don't compress that well and might not compress at all. It all depends on which type of data the file contains. Don't assume that you'll get the full capacity of the tape as printed on the box by the manufacturer. Worst-case scenario is that you'll get somewhere between half and two-thirds of the compressed number of gigabytes listed. ■

Installing the Tape Drive

Installing an internal tape drive is nearly identical to installing a hard drive in your system. Installing an external drive, on the other hand, is more akin to connecting a printer. Neither is overly difficult, although the plethora of bus types makes it a bit confusing.

Tape drives come in a number of bus types:

- EPP (Extended Parallel Port)—external

- SCSI—internal and external

- EIDE—internal

- USB—external

- FireWire—external

Only the internal SCSI and the EIDE require you to open up the chassis to perform the upgrade. You should definitely review Chapter 7 to understand how SCSI and

EIDE drives mount in the system chassis and are cabled because these types of tape drives and hard drives connect to the system in the same manner.

Tape drives are not quite as fragile as hard disks, but the same rules apply when handling a tape drive as a hard disk, so be sure to read the section in Chapter 7 titled "Handling Tips for Any Drive" to ensure a safe drive installation.

External Tape Drives

Several flavors of external tape drives should be considered.

External Parallel, USB, or FireWire Drive Installation

Non-SCSI external tape drives are reasonably easy to install.

External Non-SCSI Installations

1. Power down your system and connect the physical drive to the proper port (parallel, USB, or FireWire), depending on the type of drive you've purchased.

2. External power is required for drives connecting to the system via the parallel port. This is usually in the form of a power adapter that plugs into an AC outlet or your UPS unit. USB and FireWire devices get their power directly from the bus, so there's no external power connection to fuss with.

3. Power up the system (and the tape drive if necessary).

4. Install the necessary drivers. If you're installing a drive connecting to the system via the parallel port, you'll have to run the installation software that came with the drive. Install the driver that came with the drive (unless you've gotten a more recent driver from the manufacturer's Web site).

   If you're installing a USB or FireWire tape drive, Windows should recognize the device and prompt you through the installation procedure.

External SCSI Drive Installation

Installing an external SCSI tape drive is only a bit more involved than non-SCSI devices. We'll assume you've done your homework, that your system has a SCSI adapter, and that the port on the controller matches the pin type (50-pin narrow SCSI or 68-pin wide SCSI) for the cable you're going to connect between the controller and the tape drive.

External SCSI Installations

1. Power down your system and connect the physical drive to the external SCSI controller port on your system. This port is usually found on the SCSI controller peripheral card and is accessible from the back panel of your system. If an external SCSI device is already connected, the tape drive will be connected to that device's external SCSI port (daisy-chained).

2. External power is required, usually in the form of a power adapter that plugs into an AC outlet or your UPS unit and then into the external tape drive's housing.

3. Verify that the drive is properly terminated given its location on the SCSI chain. For this, you need to study the documentation that came with the drive for recommendations on where in the chain the drive should be and which SCSI ID setting it requires (if any). For example, some drives need to be the last device on the bus and therefore must be terminated.

4. Power up the system (and the tape drive).

5. Run the installation software as directed by the documentation that came with your tape drive or let the Windows Add New Hardware Wizard walk you through the steps. Use the drivers that came with your disk unless you've downloaded a newer version from the manufacturer's Web site.

Internal EIDE Tape Drives

If you've ever installed an EIDE hard drive or a DVD or CD-ROM, this should all be very familiar. Still, be sure to carefully read the documentation that comes with your tape drive. Some Hewlett-Packard drives, for example, want you to run the installation software that comes with the drive *before* you install the drive itself in the computer. This enables the software to see your system configuration and make some recommendations, which you should write down so you can make the proper choices when you configure the drive after it's installed.

Internal EIDE Installations

1. Shut down and disconnect your system (see Chapter 3's section "Breaking Down Your Computer").

2. Open your PC's chassis and determine in which drive bay you'll mount the tape drive.

3. Determine on which of the two IDE channels the tape drive should be installed. Make sure the drive is jumpered properly as Master, Slave, or Cable Select, depending on your desired configuration (see Chapter 7 for details on these three settings). Always check the drive documentation and start with whichever recommendations it makes as to the initial settings. Make sure the EIDE ribbon cable running from the motherboard has a free connector that reaches to the drive bay in which you'll be installing the tape drive. Obtain a ribbon cable upgrade if necessary.

Because most systems come with a hard disk and a CD or DVD drive, with the hard disk on the primary channel (set as master) and the CD or DVD on the secondary channel (set as master), a number of EIDE tape drives come with slave as the default setting. Hewlett-Packard Travan drives usually come this way, so you can install the tape drive as the slave device on the secondary channel. If the drive is to be the only drive on the secondary channel, use the master setting.

4. Trace your power supply's cable bundles to see whether a free cable to power the tape drive exists. If not, you'll need to buy a Y-type splitter power cable, available at any electronics parts store.

5. Tape drives must be accessible from the front of the system. Remove the bezel covering the drive slot you're using on the front of your system. (See Chapter 7, Figure 7.5.)

6. Install the tape drive in the appropriate drive bay. Secure it with the provided mounting screws (if none came with the drive, they're available at any electronics parts store).

7. Connect the ribbon cable from the appropriate IDE controller on the motherboard to the drive. Note: The ribbon cable already might be connected to an EIDE device as in the case in which the tape drive is to be the slave device on the channel with the CD-ROM as the master device. In this case, the cable runs from the motherboard to the CD-ROM, and then to the tape drive. The red stripe that runs along one edge of the ribbon cable goes on the side of the drive connector receptacle marked as pin 1 (this is usually toward the side of the drive where the power connector is). (See Chapter 7, Figure 7.6.)

8. Connect the power lead to the drive. (See Chapter 7, Figure 7.5.)

9. Close up the system and boot it up.

10. Run the installation software as directed by the documentation that came with your tape drive or let the Windows Add New Hardware Wizard walk you through the steps. Use the drivers that came with your disk unless you've downloaded a newer version from the manufacturer's Web site.

Internal SCSI Tape Drives

If you've ever installed a SCSI hard drive, this should all be familiar. Still, be sure to carefully read the documentation that comes with your tape drive. Some Hewlett-Packard drives, for example, want you to run the installation software that comes with the drive *before* you install the actual drive. This way, the software can see what your system configuration is and make some recommendations, which you should write down so you can make the proper choices when you configure the drive after it's installed.

Internal SCSI Installations

1. Shut down and disconnect your system (see Chapter 3's section "Breaking Down Your Computer").

2. Open your PC's chassis and determine in which drive bay you'll mount the tape drive.

3. Make sure the internal SCSI ribbon cable has a free connector that will reach the drive bay where you'll install the tape drive. Determine which SCSI ID number is available and set the drive for that number. Always check the drive documentation and go with whatever recommendations it makes in this regard. If the drive is to be the last device on the bus, ensure it's terminated. If it is not the last device, ensure it is not terminated. See Chapter 7 for more on SCSI IDs and termination requirements.

4. Trace your power supply's cable bundles to see whether a free cable to power the tape drive exists. If not, you'll need to buy a Y-type splitter power cable, available at any electronics parts store.

5. Tape drives must be accessible from the front of the system. Remove the bezel covering the drive slot on the front of your system. (See Chapter 7, Figure 7.5.)

6. Install the new drive in the appropriate drive bay. Secure it with the provided mounting screws (if none came with the drive, they're available at any electronics parts store).

7. Connect the SCSI ribbon cable to the tape drive. The red stripe that runs along one edge of the ribbon cable goes on the side of the drive connector receptacle marked as pin 1 (this is usually toward the side of the drive where the power connector is). (See Chapter 7, Figure 7.6.)

8. Connect the power lead to the drive. (See Chapter 7, Figure 7.5.)

9. Close up the system and boot it up.

10. Run the installation software as directed by the documentation that came with your tape drive or let the Windows Add New Hardware Wizard walk you through the steps. Use the drivers that came with your drive unless you've downloaded a newer version from the manufacturer's Web site.

Testing the Tape Drive

To actually copy information to a tape cartridge, you must first install backup software on your system. This might happen when you run the install program that comes with the drive, or you might need to do it after the drive is installed.

The backup software that accompanies your drive might suit all your backup needs, or you may want to install backup software from a third party.

Software is available that will make Windows treat the tape drive as though it were a hard drive, even giving it a drive letter and letting you copy to the tape as if you were copying to another hard drive. Some third-party programs try for ease of use and some are jam-packed with every feature you can think of. If you go the third-party route, make sure the manufacturer states the software will work with the particular drive (make and model) you're installing on your computer.

Check to see whether the tape cartridges need to be *retensioned* before use. Retensioning means the tape is run through a process in the tape drive in which the tape is run all the way forward to the end and then rewound back to the beginning. Tapes are sensitive to differences in temperature, and almost every troubleshooting procedure we've seen for tape drives starts off with "try retensioning the tape" first. Some tapes require you to format them before use, as well. This is often a time-consuming process. For some tape formats, you can purchase cartridges already formatted.

After your backup software is installed, you should run as many tests as your backup software supports.

19

ADDING A SCANNER

Once expensive and hard to use, scanners are now a relatively simple addition to most computer systems and offer a wide range of helpful capabilities. Even economy models can handle most small office and household scanning tasks. Moderate-priced consumer units have capabilities beyond those available at professional service bureaus just a few years ago.

Send a photo of the new baby to the relatives? No problem; scan it in. Read an interesting article and want to send a copy to a friend? Don't fax it; scan and email it. Need to convert a paper document into electronic form to use with your word processor? Scan it, and then use optical character recognition (OCR) software. "Digital imaging" is not just for the lofty realm of the corporate world.

Upgrade Checklist

1. Do your homework.

2. Determine whether your PC supports the planned upgrade.

3. Determine whether you can perform the upgrade.

4. Purchase or acquire the component.

5. Organize your tools and workspace.
   See Chapter 3, "Things You Need."

6. Back up everything: data, operating system, mission-critical applications, and BIOS.

7. Test your startup disk.

8. Perform the upgrade.

9. Take good notes, and permanently file them in your system log when you're finished.

10. Update your inventory documentation to reflect the upgraded or newly added component.

Considering a Scanner's Features

Scores of scanners are available on the market, offering users the opportunity to do some extensive comparison shopping. Prices today range from as little as $50 for a rudimentary model to more than $70,000 for high-volume, corporate applications.

The ones of most interest to consumers fall in the $100–$500 range. The investment of a little time and effort will enable you to find a scanner that meets your needs and budget.

Assessing Your Needs

You can do many things with a scanner. But that doesn't mean you are necessarily going to do them all. For example, if you only want to send photographs by email, you don't need professional-level graphic quality. Similarly, a document feeder is of no value to you if you have no plans to convert a large stack of paper documents into electronic form.

The following are some things for you to consider:

- **Is this device strictly for personal use or for business?**—If personal, lower-cost units will more than meet your needs. Business users might need more sophisticated capabilities.

- **Do you use advanced graphics software?**—An application such as Adobe Photoshop can take advantage of high-resolution scans, but high-end scanners would be overkill for Windows Paint.

- **Do you have any reproduction or printing needs?**—The highest image quality primarily is intended for professional print jobs; home or office printers have very modest resolution demands.

- **Are you going to do OCR?**—It's finicky and works best with high-caliber scans.

PLAINSPEAKING
WHAT IS OCR?

Optical character recognition refers to technology that scans the image of words and pictures on a page (say, from a magazine), examines that image, and uses algorithms to convert the stream of words into a format that stores each individual letter of each word. Whether the final conversion is to a Microsoft Word document or a simple text file, OCR transforms the content from an image to a collection of letters—letters that comprise words that comprise sentences and so on—so you can edit the text letter by letter. The most common measure of an OCR system is its accuracy. Although a 99% accuracy rate sounds great, it can be problematic. At 99% accuracy, you've got a 1% error rate on average. This means more than zero errors will occur, so a human must be employed perform some postprocessing to clean them up; with larger documents this can entail considerable work. ■

Scanner Types

Scanners come in four basic configurations:

- **Flatbeds**—These are the small, platform-like units that most users generally think of as a "scanner." You place your documents on a glass "bed" and the system optics run underneath it to perform the scan. Flatbeds look very similar to a small photocopier, minus the printing mechanism; which, in fact, is exactly what it is. Flatbeds typically produce excellent quality scans and can handle the widest range of jobs, including both documents and photographs. When shopping, pay attention to things such as the size of documents it can accommodate, the workmanship of the unit, and the design's ease of use.

- **Document Scanners**—These are compact units into which you feed documents, which then pass over rollers, making the contraption resemble a high-tech pasta cutter. Quite common a few years ago, they have fallen somewhat out of favor as the price of flatbeds has declined sharply. But specialized document units can be a cost-effective and space-effective way to deal with digitizing paper documents. Few choices are available here, but you still want to be attentive to how smoothly documents pass through the roller mechanism. If documents don't go straight through, the scan will go awry.

- **Handhelds**—As the name implies, you hold them in your hand and slide them across the document to make the scan. This is another design that has waned in popularity in favor of flatbeds, but they are still necessary for portable use and can be handy for scanning books or awkwardly shaped items.

- **Specialized Units**—These include scanners for the photographic market and professional production units. However, scanners designed for photographs and slides are beginning to make their way into the consumer market. As prices drop, they could be a useful addition to your computing arsenal.

Another permutation growing in popularity is the so-called "all-in-one" unit, which is a combination scanner, printer, copier, and fax machine. The same evolutionary process that has marked single-purpose scanners is at play here: Document feeder units (essentially, glorified plain-paper fax machines) have given way to units based around flatbed scanners and color inkjet printers.

TIP

"SWEET SPOT" SCANNERS

You can do yourself a big favor when you go shopping for a scanner by starting with the units priced between $100 and $150. This is the current "sweet spot" in the market. You get very solid performance and features at this price, and you should then have a benchmark against which to compare more expensive units. It's not that higher-end scanners don't have advantages, but if you can't figure out what those advantages are while you are shopping, it's a good bet those aren't features you'll need.

TIP

KNOW THE BRAND FOR SUPPORT—NOT QUALITY

The best-known brands in scanning include HP, Visioneer, Epson, Umax, Microtek, and Xerox. Brands are important because you should buy a product that has good technical support and strong warranties. But scanning engines are fungible and manufacturers often share components: Brand A's scanner could well be Brand B's in a different box. So, don't spend time worrying whether A is better than B.

Interface

With scanners, the manner in which you attach them to your PC can have a meaningful effect on performance. The advent of USB technology has been a major plus for scanners, and a plus for users, as well. USB scanners typically are much easier to set up, and they are often priced lower than similar units with the older forms of connection: parallel ports and SCSI. With data transmission speeds of 12 megabits/sec (1.5MB/sec), USB can send data to your PC about as quickly as the scanner can produce it. That's important because a full-color scan of an 8×10 color glossy photo can easily generate a file that's 7MB or larger. USB connections are plug-and-play, meaning that connecting the peripheral automatically triggers the configuration process.

SCSI used to be the interface of choice for scanners, reflecting the graphics professionals' penchant for Macintoshes (which used to come with SCSI standard) and also because SCSI was the only interface capable of moving large amounts of data quickly from external peripherals. As you learned in Chapter 7, "Upgrading the Hard Disk," SCSI can transfer data at rates of 5MB/sec–160MB/sec, as compared to USB's 1.5MB/sec throughput. That actually is more bandwidth than consumer scanners need.

SCSI also can be difficult to configure. Each of the devices on the chain that can be attached to a standard SCSI adapter must be assigned a unique ID number, and the total length of cables connecting all SCSI devices must be less than 6 meters (19.7 feet). Most PCs don't have SCSI as a standard feature, and it must be added on by installing an adapter card. On the other hand, after the setup is accomplished, SCSI is fast and reliable.

As a stopgap, low-end scanners were designed to connect to the PC's parallel printer port, typically using a "passthrough" connection to enable the printer to share the port. Parallel, however, has a data transmission speed of only 500 kilobits/sec (62.5KB/sec). Furthermore, passthrough devices often disrupt printing and especially two-way links between printers and PCs.

Now that most PCs come with USB ports and USB is supported by Windows 98 and 2000 as well as the latest Macs, look for it to be the dominant standard for scanner interfaces. For more information on USB see Chapter 11, "Adding USB Compatibility."

Resolution

So, what exactly do we mean by resolution, anyway? And what's *high*? Or *low*?

Scanners break up the images they see into tiny dots, and the more dots per inch (dpi), the higher quality the image (this is discussed in Chapter 13, "Printer Upgrades"). However, you might find it more convenient—and more accurate—to think in terms of *samples* per inch instead of *dots* per inch when contemplating scanner resolutions. When you see dpi measurements with two numbers, for example, a scanner with a stated optical resolution of 600dpi×1200dpi, this means the device has an asymmetrical optical resolution. In plain English, it takes 600 samples per inch in one direction and 1,200 samples per inch in the other. Manufacturers typically give their scanners' specifications in terms of the maximum dpi and advertise both *optical* and *enhanced* numbers.

Optical, as you might guess, is the actual sensitivity of the scanner's sensors. Enhanced resolution is performed by the scanner's software, which interpolates the actual optical data into much higher resolutions. This enables a consumer type of scanner to emulate much more expensive professional units, which has some value in publishing. However, for most users, the specifications arms race is meaningless because the file sizes at maximum resolution are way too large to be practical (see Table 19.1). The higher the resolution, the larger the file size; and this grows exponentially.

Progress in the realm of resolution has been staggering in recent years. These days a $100 entry-level scanner will deliver 600dpi optical, which not too long ago was unavailable on top-of-the-line consumer models. It's now common to see 1200dpi optical/unlimited enhanced resolution in the more expensive consumer models.

To add a little confusion, scanning resolution is not necessarily the same as the resolution you want to use in your documents or graphics files. For example, by default a scanner might typically scan a color photograph at 150dpi. But your graphics software commonly would have 72dpi as its default. The "extra" resolution is not wasted; rather, it enables you to minimize quality loss when you manipulate the picture with your software, such as by resizing or retouching it.

Table 19.1   dpi Comparisons

8×10 Color Image in .bmp (Uncompressed) Format	75dpi	150dpi	300dpi
Truecolor (24-bit)	1.372MB	5.476MB	21.882MB
256-color; grayscale (8-bit)	0.459MB	1.831MB	7.304MB
Black-and-white (1-bit)	0.059MB	0.229MB	0.915MB

Color Depth

Another measure of picture quality is *color depth*. In the digital world, no physical "picture" is pasted on your hard drive, of course. Similar to all digital data, it is a string of 0s and 1s. The number of digits used to describe each picture element, such as color, determines the number of permutations possible. In digital color, 36-bit color (numbers consisting of 36 binary digits) descriptions allow 68.7 billion possible shades and 30-bit color, a mere 1.07 billion. 30-bit is a rock-bottom spec for cheap scanners, and anything that costs more than $100 will deliver at least 36-bit.

Note that almost no standard PC video card supports anything more than 24-bit Truecolor (a measly 16.8 million shades). So, you will never see the 36-bit picture on your screen. Nonprofessionals likely will have little need for anything more than 24-bit. The advantage of the higher depth is in minimizing image accuracy losses when saved at lower standards.

8-bit color, which permits 256 colors (and also 256 shades of gray—the standard grayscale specification), is commonly used when file sizes are at a premium, such as on the Internet. One of the standard Internet graphic formats, .gif, is 256 colors, for example. Two-color, black-and-white is 2-bit. (4-bit and 16-bit standards also exist, but they are seldom used these days.)

Again, the more color depth, the larger the file size (refer to Table 19.1). Truecolor, in fact, would be totally impractical for consumer use had it not been for the advent of JPEG and other graphic file formats that incorporate data compression, enabling users to shrink file sizes down to 10% or 20% of the original.

Optical Density

Another file size consideration is *document output size*. Scanning software usually produces—by default—an image at 100% of the size of the original. But most scanning software enables you to reduce the size to whatever you want. You also can perform some cropping.

We prefer to scan at 100%, and do the resizing/cropping with graphics software afterward. However, you might want to perform the adjustments during the scanning process if you need to get the output into a form that is immediately usable.

Core Technology

Scanners are complex units, but the underlying technology is pretty straightforward. Take a piece of paper with printing on it, hold the front up to a light, and look at it from the back. That's a scan.

A light source illuminates the item to be scanned, and light-sensitive sensors see the item. Usually, mirrors and other optics are present to direct the light to the sensors, and some kind of mechanism for scanning exists along the item. In a flatbed, the item stays fixed and the optics move; in a document scanner, the optics are fixed and rollers move the document. (With a handheld, the user is the movement mechanism.)

Processors and software then convert the light-sensor data into a digital graphic "picture."

It is worth bearing in mind that, as far as the scanner is concerned, everything it sees is a picture. It does not matter whether the document is text, photographs, charts, whitespace on the page, or any combination thereof. The scanner pays no heed; it just takes an electronic snapshot of whatever is in the bed.

You also should note that while a good scanner is very accurate, it is not perfect. No copy ever can equal an original. And no copy can be better than the original, either.

The imperfections in a document that we often mentally ignore—a scratch in the photograph, say, or the texture of the newsprint in the morning paper—will be picked up by the scanner.

Software

You can be pretty picky about software bundles these days. Even low-priced scanners come with a decent assortment of applications. Here's what should be in any good package:

PLAINSPEAKING
TWAIN

No, *TWAIN* isn't something that runs on twacks. It's the protocol most scanners use to communicate with your PC and its applications. You should make sure that your scanner is TWAIN-compliant. The standard not only makes it possible for scanner output to be placed inside an application, it also provides a software hook that enables many applications to launch the scanner. This ensures that your scans will not disappear into electronic limbo, and will be usable in your system.

The acronym means *technology without an interesting name*. Really. We're not making that up. ∎

- The scanner driver (the software the operating system needs to make the peripheral part of the system) and the scanner's own operating software (the software that serves as the control panel for the scanner). If you are going to have a problem with a scanner, short of manufacturing defects, the most likely cause will be the driver and control software.

- Document management applications (such as ScanSoft's PaperPort) that enable you to index, organize, and manage your scanned images. For many scanners, the scanning software is combined with the document management application.

- At least some rudimentary form of OCR. (The standard procedure is to supply a "lite" version of a commercial OCR product.)

- Software that enables you to make copies using your printer and use scanned documents in faxes.

- A graphics application with the capability to retouch, crop, and resize photographs, as well as to change the file formats of scanned images.

PLAINSPEAKING
ABOUT OCR

Depending on your state of mind at the time, OCR will be one of the greatest technological marvels you have encountered, or a hair-pulling, obscenity-laced aggravation. Here's something to think about: If OCR is 98% accurate, that means it will make 20 errors per 1,000 words scanned. That can be tedious to correct, but just remember that having to retype those 1,000 words would be even more of a pain.

Most OCR programs can be set to automatically examine a document, let's say a magazine page, and sort out the illustrations, headlines, text, and so forth, placing each type into its own recognition zone. It's always worth trying full automatic recognition and seeing what happens (see Figure 19.1). But, you often get better accuracy if you perform the zoning yourself.

Manufacturers claim that their software can accurately reproduce not only the text content of published material, but preserve layout and formatting, as well. This works amazingly well, all things considered. However, you must resign yourself to the fact of having to do a lot of tinkering afterward. Typically, after the OCR processing is completed, the data gets transferred to your word processor for editing and use.

The truth is that the more sophisticated the job you ask the OCR application to perform, the greater the possibility of error. Furthermore, exotic fonts and the exotic layouts now in vogue at many publications also diminish accuracy. The rule of thumb is don't ask the OCR to do anything more than you actually need. If plain text will do, don't bother with preserving layouts. ■

FIGURE 19.1

Pagis Pro's OCR software works its magic on a magazine page.

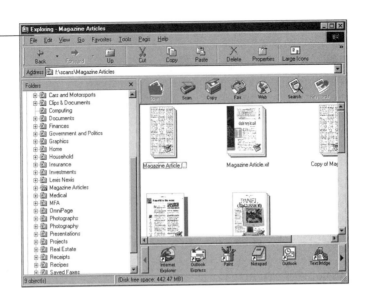

WHEN TO UPGRADE THE SOFTWARE

For routine use, the included software bundles probably will suffice. However, if you expect to be using your scanner all the time, especially for business purposes, it is worth taking a look at some of the enhanced software packages on the market. Which is to say, the application suites produced by ScanSoft, Inc. Through a series of mergers, the Massachusetts-based firm (a Xerox spin-off) now owns the leading brand names in the field.

The product it originally offered, Pagis, has been positioned as a package for the small-office or moderately sophisticated graphics users. PaperPort has been aimed at home users, and newly acquired Caere's product lineup is pitched at larger companies (see Figure 19.2).

What you get for the money (about $100 for Pagis Pro Scanning Suite) is upgraded OCR, the capability to extend document management to all the data on your hard drive and even Internet pages, and more flexibility in working with file formats and other applications.

FIGURE 19.2

ScanSoft's Pagis
Pro Millennium
Scanning Suite.

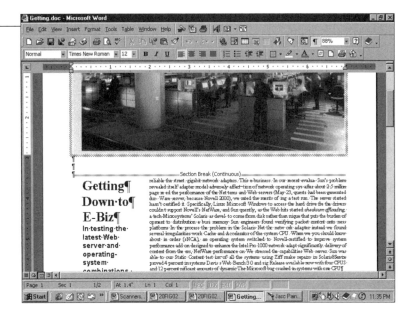

FIGURE 19.2

ScanSoft's Pagis
Pro Millennium
Scanning Suite.

Document Feeders

Combine the old-style document roller–style of scanners with a flatbed and what do you have? A flatbed with a *document feeder*.

At present, these are seen primarily in more expensive scanners, either as part of the unit or as an add-on attachment. For casual use, this is an expensive toy. But if digitizing paper documents is a routine part of your business operations, a document feeder is a must. Both the software that ships with scanners and the major aftermarket applications are programmed to recognize when a document feeder is in place, and the software automatically inputs each page as it makes its way through the feeder.

If you are scanning in volume, picking up the lid of a flatbed, removing the just-scanned document and inserting a new one gets old quickly.

The mechanism is similar to that of a fax machine or copier and is subject to much the same problems, primarily paper jams. You should ensure that documents are neatly aligned in the feeder, free of staples, and have as few wrinkles as possible. Remember also that the feeder does extract a toll in the form of a little extra wear and tear on your documents, especially because the feeder usually routes the paper in a U-shaped path. So, it's not a good choice for fragile documents or photos.

You do not lose the ability to manually feed documents, however. The feed mechanism serves as the cover for the flatbed, and you simply lift it up to access the scanning bed. Similarly, adding on a feeder generally is a matter of unsnapping the latches that hold the cover in place, snapping in the feeder mechanism, and plugging in a cable to connect it to the unit's electronics.

Nonpaper Sources

Flatbeds demonstrate their versatility by their capability to handle many sources of images. You are not, for instance, limited to traditional print media. You can stick three-dimensional objects—a flower; a trinket; heck, a beer can if you want—on the bed and make an image of it.

For the most part, nonpaper sources will be photos and artwork. There is no special ritual you need to perform. You place them on the scanning bed like any other document. However, you should use relatively high resolution to enhance quality. Scanner software enables you to make contrast/brightness and color adjustments if you want.

One of the typical weak spots of scanning, though, is working with photographic slides. Because these transparencies come to life only when light is being shined from their back through the front, but the scanner needs to shine the light from the front to the back, you need mirrored contraptions to bounce the light around so that the scan can succeed. We have found the results to be unreliable. With patience, you can get usable images from the occasional photographic slide. But scanners specifically designed for slides are more reliable and less tedious for larger jobs.

Overhead slides are not subject to the same limitations and can be scanned as if they were paper documents. As for photo negatives, they really are best handled with a special-purpose scanner.

NOTE

FIND THE BUTTON

Visioneer's One-Touch series of scanners introduced the concept of putting buttons on the unit itself so that you can execute functions without having to touch your PC first. The company's product lineup still leads the league in number of buttons, but the competition is catching up fast. The button functions are programmable and typically can be set to perform such tasks as printing a copy on your printer, starting a fax, or simply beginning a standard scan. Although the buttons give the impression that the scanner can operate independently of your PC, the buttons merely run software on your computer. However, they can save you some time and motion, avoiding having to shuttle back and forth from the scanner to your PC.

Footprint

One thing to remember about scanners is that they take up a lot of room. By definition, to handle 8 1/2×11-inch documents, a flatbed needs to be at least that size, plus a margin on all sides for its components. A typical unit might be 18×15 or so, which means it will take up more desktop space than almost any other single component you have. And a scanner capable of handling larger documents will, of course, be even bigger.

Scanners aren't very tall, but you can't put anything on top of them because you won't be able to open the lid. Plus, with a document feeder in place, they will take up vertical space, also.

That was one of the charms of the old document scanners—they took up very little space. As the performance of the all-in-ones improves, they become an option to consider for space reasons alone.

Installing the Scanner

The following is a scanner installation checklist.

Installing a scanner is easier than it used to be, but it is not an absolutely bullet-proof process. Some simple steps will enable you to make the job as painless as possible:

1. Work out the physical placement of the scanner in your office.

   This is not a trivial matter. You must physically place items in the scanner. Therefore, you need easy access to it. If you are sharing it with other users, you need to place it in a location where a person at the scanner won't disrupt someone else's work. If it is for personal use, you want to be able to reach it easily. Having to go back and forth from your desk to the scanner every time you need to change the document being scanned quickly gets tiresome. A scanner is an input device just like a keyboard, and it will be helpful to think of it that way in judging its placement.

2. As with any major system change, back up your system before you get started.

   You particularly want to ensure that Windows registration settings are saved so that you can undo any installation that goes awry. Remember, installing a scanner is as much a software job as a hardware task.

3. Read the documentation that came with the scanner, especially the "quick start" guide that should be included.

If a scanner doesn't have a "quick start" guide, that's a good reason to be wary of buying it. The key item to check is the hardware versus software installation sequence. This is not identical from machine to machine. Typically, you connect a peripheral and then install software. But on many scanners, you do the reverse.

4. If your scanner does require the software to be installed first, start there.

   One useful tip: You are under no obligation to install everything the manufacturer has provided. You need the scanner driver and basic operating software, but you are free to pick and choose among the other applications. You don't need to add another graphics program to your system if you already are using something else. So, look for a custom installation option rather than going with the default.

5. Next, shut down your computer and turn off the power to it and all attached peripherals.

6. Unpack the scanner and connect its power cord and connection cable. Do not plug it in to a power outlet yet.

7. For SCSI, set its SCSI ID as per the manufacturer's instructions and the available IDs on your system. (See Chapter 7 for more details.)

   If that requires plugging it in, unplug it when you're finished. Next, connect the SCSI cable to your SCSI chain. SCSI scanners usually are designed to be the last peripheral in an external chain and are terminated, which means you must turn off the termination for the component that previously was at the end of the chain.

8. For a parallel connector, disconnect your printer from the PC parallel port, attach the scanner's cable to the PC, and attach the printer cable to the scanner's passthrough.

9. Have the software that came with your scanner at hand. Now, plug in the scanner and turn your PC and peripherals back on. (Note that for USB, the USB cable should be connected to the scanner but not the PC. See step 10.)

10. For USB only: After Windows has booted up, plug the scanner cable into one of your PC's USB ports. This will trigger a USB Device Found dialog box and prompt you to install the necessary drivers. Follow the manufacturer's installation instructions.

11. For SCSI and parallel port scanners, the customary New Hardware Found dialog box and Wizard are automatically triggered when Windows starts up. Follow the manufacturer's instructions, which typically tell you to use the Wizard's specified path option to look for drivers on the manufacturer's disk.

12. Occasionally, the normal process does not work.

   The manufacturer should have included instructions on how to install the device manually. In addition, one trick to try is to unplug the scanner and then plug it back in. (Or, if your scanner actually has a power switch—typically they don't—turn that off and then back on.) Scanners have power-saving features that put the units into a sleep mode when they aren't being used. Sometimes the boot process is long enough that your unit is asleep by the time Windows starts up, and Windows won't recognize it.

Testing the Scanner

This section provides a scanner test checklist.

Having survived the installation, you are now ready to test and use your scanner. The following are some steps to try:

1. You should begin by performing an uncomplicated scan.

   That doesn't refer to what is scanned—anything will do—but rather to running the scan through the unit's own software. You want to see whether the scanner actually runs, and assess the quality and accuracy of the images it produces.

2. If you have control buttons on the unit itself, test them to ensure that they work.

   Be sure you read the manual for instructions on how to configure the buttons; depending on the software, those controls can be part of the main scanning software, a separate application, or even in an applet in Control Panel.

3. Check whether the TWAIN function is working.

   See whether you can launch a scan from inside another application. Most of the Microsoft Office 2000 applications support scanning (Insert, Picture, From Scanner, or Camera), as do graphics and faxing programs.

4. If OCR software is included, test it by feeding a plain-text document, using standard fonts, through the scanner.

5. Take a closer look at the quality of the scans by scanning a complex text-and-color-image page. You are testing how effective the scanner software is at getting the colors right and at how clear the text is.

6. Test the functionality of the scanning software package. For example, see which kinds of tools you have for changing file formats or cropping a photo.

If your scanner installation passes the tests, you are off and running. If it does not, think about returning it. Although a call to technical support might be justified for some very specific quirk of your system, too many good scanners are available on the market that really do plug-and-play for you to waste your time on one that doesn't.

Online Resources

These online resources are good sources of information about scanners and related technologies:

- **PC Techguide**—An excellent source of "how does that work?" and "what are the specs?" information; located at http://www.pctechguide.com/18scanners.htm.

- **ZDNet's guide to scanners**—Located at http://www.zdnet.com/products/filter/guide/0,7267,1500124,00.html.

- **PC World's guide to scanners**—Located at http://www.pcworld.com/top400/category/0,1377,Scanners,00.html.

- **cNet's guide to scanners**—Located at http://computers.cnet.com/hardware/0-1073-7-1473841.html.

- **http://www.image-acquire.com**—An independent resource for news and reviews of scanners, digital cameras, and the software that drives them.

- **HP scanning tips and projects**—Admittedly plugging its own products, it's located at http://www.scanjet.hp.com/workshop/index.htm.

- **ScanSoft**—Another product plug, but also with helpful hints; located at http://www.scansoft.com/scanners/.

- **Imaging Magazine**—Aimed at business users, it's located at http://www.imagingmagazine.com/index.shtml.

- **Digital photography reviews**—Located at http://www.inconference.com/digicam/index.html

PART VI

SOLVING PROBLEMS

20

UPGRADING YOUR OPERATING SYSTEM

An operating system upgrade is not a trivial matter. You should exercise the same care in performing such an upgrade as you would upgrading your CPU, motherboard, or hard disk. If you, or the upgrade's setup program, hiccup during the process, you can easily be left with a lifeless, useless PC. Caution and careful planning are the watchwords for this chapter.

To be honest, we should tell you that there have been circumstances when we—due to time or other resource constraints—had to just shove a new operating system CD in and let 'er rip. About half the time we survived; the other half, well, we got what we deserved. In those wild and woolly cases, we knew the risks, and accepted them, but we genuinely hope you won't set foot down that harried path. It's not worth it! If you need to upgrade your operating system, please read this chapter, study the Web resources we provide, ask questions on public newsgroups, talk to friends and neighbors, and definitely sleep on it. Then, follow our checklists and you'll be fine.

Upgrade Checklist

1. Do your homework.

2. Determine whether your PC supports the planned upgrade.

3. Determine whether you can perform the upgrade.

4. Purchase or acquire the component.

5. Organize your tools and workspace.
   See Chapter 3, "Things You Need."

6. Back up everything: data, operating system, mission-critical applications, and BIOS.

7. Test your startup disk.

8. Perform the upgrade.

9. Take good notes, and permanently file them in your system log when you're finished.

10. Update your inventory documentation to reflect the upgraded or newly added component.

Installing Clean Versus on Top

Installing *clean* means installing the new operating system to a partition that currently has no operating system on it. Either this could be a second partition in a multiboot scenario, or you could reformat your existing operating system's partition and install to it. Installing *on top* means letting the new operating system install itself right on top of the existing operating system.

There's a widespread notion that you should never perform an operating system upgrade on top of the existing operating system, that you should instead reformat your hard disk and start from scratch. Whether this is a good idea or not depends on the PC in question, the existing operating system, and the operating system to be upgraded. Up until the arrival of Windows 2000, we advised the "why borrow trouble" approach: If a specific PC has no history of problems with Windows 95/98 and you're upgrading it to Windows 98 Second Edition, Millennium Edition (Me), or NT 4.0, upgrade on top; but if the target PC has a history of OS-related problems, nuke it and start over with a clean install.

The exception to all these tenets is Windows 2000. Given the extensive amount of post-installation work you might have to endure for a functional Windows 2000 upgrade on top of a previous version of Windows, we advise always performing a clean installation of Windows 2000.

Operating System Upgrade Checklist

The checklist in this section covers all the bases for an upgrade, whether you're installing clean or on top. In fact, this checklist can be so useful that we have distilled it down to just the bare-bones steps in a Note later in this chapter.

You'll see some references to Windows 2000 in this section. That's because we wanted this book to suit the needs of folks who are interested in that operating system as well as those of you who use Windows 95, 98, or Millennium. Windows 2000 is a more complex operating system to install and use than Windows 95, 98, or Millennium. On the other hand, it offers more stability and security than members of the Windows 9x family. For example, ZD Labs' reliability tests show that the average system uptime of Windows 2000 Professional was more than 50 times that of Windows 98 and 17 times that of Windows NT Workstation 4.0. However, stability and security aren't the only two reasons you might consider migrating to Windows 2000—for example, if you have a laptop, Windows 2000's use of the latest power management technologies makes it an ideal OS for a mobile PC. It is also a good operating system candidate for a networked workstation.

But all this stability, security, mobility, and so forth comes at a price: There's quite a lot to learn. If you're ready to make the leap to Windows 2000, get a copy of *Special Edition Using Microsoft Windows 2000 Professional*.

1. Verify that your PC meets the new operating system's general hardware requirements.

NOTE

THE WINDING WINDOWS MILLENNIUM UPGRADE PATH

It is *not* possible to upgrade from Windows 3.1 to Windows Millennium. It *is* possible to upgrade from Windows 95 or Windows 98 to Windows Millennium.

TIP

WINDOWS MILLENNIUM HARDWARE REQUIREMENTS

These system requirements are from Microsoft's Millennium home page, which doesn't distinguish between minimum and recommended. Contrary to Microsoft's position, we recommend 64MB of RAM as the minimum level for Windows Millennium. The requirements are as follows:

- Pentium 150MHz or higher processor
- 32MB of RAM or better
- 480MB–645MB free disk space
- VGA or higher-resolution monitor
- Microsoft mouse or compatible pointing device
- CD-ROM drive
- 28.8Kbps modem or faster with Internet connection
- Sound card
- Speakers or headphones

TIP

WINDOWS 2000 HARDWARE REQUIREMENTS

According to Microsoft, the *minimum hardware requirements* for running Windows 2000 are as follows. These values represent the absolute minimum necessary for the operating system to function. Microsoft also publishes *recommendations*, which are a guideline for average use and efficiency; these are shown in parentheses. In our opinion, for a PC running Windows 2000, you should have 128MB of system memory (twice Microsoft's recommended level). The requirements are as follows:

- Intel Pentium or compatible 133MHz or higher processor
- 32MB of RAM (64MB)
- 650MB free disk space (2GB)

- VGA-compatible or higher monitor (SVGA PnP monitor)
- Keyboard, mouse, or other pointing device
- CD-ROM or DVD drive (12¥ or faster)

2. Verify that your BIOS meets the new operating system's requirements (see Figure 20.1).

   If you need to upgrade your BIOS, do so now. Windows 98 needs a BIOS that's Plug and Play compatible. Windows 2000, on the other hand, needs a BIOS that's ACPI compatible. For detailed instructions on getting information about your current BIOS, see Chapter 4, "Upgrading the BIOS."

CAUTION

WINDOWS 2000 BIOS REQUIREMENTS

Windows 2000 might not function properly if your PC does not have a BIOS that supports Advanced Configuration and Power Interface (ACPI). Before you upgrade a Windows 98 PC to Windows 2000, you can easily check for ACPI compliance. Look at your Device Manager tab and expand the System Devices node. If, at the top of the list, you see the entry Advanced Power Management Support, ideally you should upgrade to a newer BIOS that supports ACPI (Windows 2000 might still function under APM, but why risk it). If you see the entry Advanced Configuration and Power Interface (ACPI) BIOS, your system's BIOS supports ACPI, as shown in Figure 20.1. For more information, go to the Windows 2000 Web Resources page (`http://www.microsoft.com/windows2000/library/resources/reskit/WebResources/`) and follow the Hardware Update link.

FIGURE 20.1

This Windows 98 PC's BIOS supports ACPI.

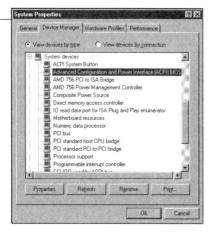

3. Verify that your PC's existing devices are supported by the new operating system.

NOTE

WINDOWS MILLENNIUM'S TESTED HARDWARE LIST

Microsoft's hardware compatibility page for Windows Millennium is at
`http://www.microsoft.com/windowsME/upgrade/compat/default.asp`.

Windows 2000's setup has a Check Upgrade Only mode that you can run prior to an actual installation. It produces a report that highlights any potential hardware or software problems. The report goes to the file `Upgrade.txt` in the Windows directory. To run this check, insert your Windows 2000 master CD, select Start, Run; then, (assuming your CD drive letter is Z:) type `z:\i386\winnt32.exe /checkupgradeonly` and click OK. This mode's dialog box is titled Microsoft Windows 2000 Readiness Analyzer and includes a progress meter, descriptive text, and the exact path to which `Upgrade.txt` is being saved.

We performed a Windows 2000 upgrade on a PIII/450 running Win98 SE with a fairly standard application load, including (but not limited to) Microsoft Office 2000 Developer, Microsoft Visual Basic 6, and Norton AntiVirus 2000. The Analyzer took about seven minutes to evaluate this system. During this process it prompted us with `Please ensure that Microsoft Outlook Express is not running so that Norton AntiVirus can unconfigure it for email scanning.` If you get this or other prompts, answer them as appropriate to keep the Analyzer moving forward.

Here's what the final dialog box of the Windows 2000 Readiness Analyzer reported during this test: `Microsoft found some compatibility problems you might encounter after you upgrade to Windows 2000. This report describes those problems. In most cases, new software updates from the hardware or software vendor can correct these problems. If you are concerned about the results of this report, you should not upgrade to Windows 2000 until these problems are corrected.` This same text appears at the top of `Upgrade.txt` (see Figures 20.2 and 20.3).

TIP

CHECKING THE LATEST WINDOWS 2000 HARDWARE COMPATIBILITY LIST

The Readiness Analyzer is the fastest way to determine a PC's compatibility with Windows 2000. However, you also can look at a version of the Windows 2000 Hardware Compatibility List (HCL), which might be more current than the one that ships on the CD; browse to `http://windows.microsoft.com/windows2000/reskit/webresources` and click the Hardware Compatibility List link (see Figure 20.4). On the Web-based version of the HCL, you can search by computer, hardware device, and software categories.

FIGURE 20.2

The final dialog box of the Windows 2000 Readiness Analyzer files a report on one of our test systems.

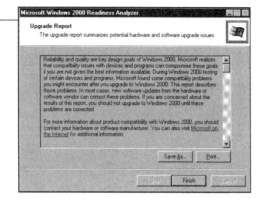

FIGURE 20.3

The Software Incompatible with Windows 2000 section of the Upgrade.txt file for one of our test PCs.

4. If your PC is on a network, gather relevant network data.

   At a minimum, you should know your PC's name and workgroup (or domain) name.

5. Print your system's settings.

   Right-click My Computer, choose Properties, select the Device Manager tab, click the Print button, select the All Devices and System Summary option, click OK, and when done click Cancel to dismiss the dialog box. Store this output in your NEAT box.

FIGURE 20.4

Microsoft's online version of the Windows 2000 Hardware Compatibility List might be more up to date than the version on your CD.

6. Print device settings not revealed by Device Manager's System Summary.

   Take screen shots of each device's current dialog box settings; then print and save these in your NEAT box. For example, start Control Panel, run the Display applet, click the Settings tab, take a screen shot, click the Advanced button, and take screen shots of the desired tabs in that dialog box.

TIP

HOW TO TAKE A SCREEN SHOT

You can use a Windows keyboard shortcut to take a screen shot of the current application: Press Alt+PrintScrn. If you need a screen shot of your entire desktop, press PrintScrn. Next, start up WordPad, Word, or any other editor that accepts graphic images, and paste the screen shot in from the Clipboard.

---

7. Print your CMOS settings.

   Print or write down your current CMOS settings. Store this information in your NEAT box. For more information, see Chapter 4.

8. Copy your PC's current `Autoexec.bat` and `Config.sys` files (if you have any) to a safe, write-protected medium.

   `Autoexec.bat` and `Config.sys` files exist on the start disk that Windows 98 produces for you, but these are specialized for use by the start disk. You should preserve your original boot files separately.

9. Print listings of your PC's current `Autoexec.bat` and `Config.sys` files (if you have any).

   To print either file, edit it with Notepad and select Print. Store these listings in your NEAT box. Close the file without making any changes to it.

10. Verify that you have all your applications' source media. You might have your applications stored on original manufacturer CDs, 3 1/2-inch disks, or some form of removable media you've created yourself (CD-R, Zip disk, and so on). Perform an inventory of all the applications you want to run under the new operating system and make sure you have the corresponding media on hand. In the case of a clean installation, you'll need these media to reinstall your applications. Even if you're performing an on top install, the installation can go south, leaving you without your applications.

11. Verify that you have all your latest device drivers. Look in your NEAT box for either 3 1/2-inch disks or CD-ROMs from the manufacturer. If you've downloaded or upgraded any drivers since you last configured your PC, copy these drivers from your hard disk to standalone media if you haven't done so already.

12. Confirm that your start disk works and includes real-mode drivers for your CD-ROM drive. Turn off your PC, insert the start disk, turn on your PC, and make sure it boots properly and that you can see all your hard drives and CD-ROM drives. (Type each drive letter and a colon; then press Enter and perform a `DIR` command on the drive to ensure that it's available.) You *must* do this for your CD-ROM drive. On many occasions in the field, we've discovered a problem with the start disk's real-mode drivers such that it couldn't detect the CD-ROM drive. It's much better to discover this and correct it before you start the upgrade than afterward, when it's too late.

CAUTION

DON'T SKIP THE BOOT DISK!
Later in this chapter, we point you to a Web page that describes how to uninstall Windows 2000 after you have installed it in a dual-boot mode along with Windows 95/98. *If you want to be able to successfully uninstall Windows 2000 in that scenario, you must have a functioning Windows 95/98 start disk.*

13. Clean up your drives.

    See this chapter's section "Cleaning Up a Hard Drive" for suggestions on how to quickly clean up your hard drives and recover wasted space. This gives the Windows setup routine the maximum amount of free space with which to work.

NOTE

HOW MUCH FREE SPACE IS ENOUGH?

If you can't find out exactly how much free space a new operating system requires during setup, as opposed to when it has finished setup, here's a rule we use. In the absence of any other information, always have as much disk space free as is occupied by your current operating system plus your standard applications minus any data. Say you're running Window 98 Second Edition with a fairly standard application load that includes (but is not limited to) Microsoft Office 2000, Microsoft Visual Basic 6, and Norton AntiVirus 2000, and the total space on your primary partition excluding data is 2.0GB. You should have 2.0GB free if you're going to attempt an on-top installation of Windows Millennium or 2000.

14. Perform a full backup of your drives.

15. Defragment your drives.

TIP

RUNNING LEAN AND MEAN BEFORE A DISK DEFRAG

Before running Disk Defragmenter, close all running applications, including Task Scheduler (right-click its system tray icon and choose Pause Task Scheduler). Also, disable your screensaver.

NOTE

SPRING CLEANING

As you read in Chapter 3, the accumulation of a few months' worth of dust can be very damaging to your PC. When you perform an operating system upgrade, take the opportunity to rid your PC of dust, inside and out.

16. If you intend to upgrade any peripherals or components, do so before you upgrade to a new operating system.

Don't just install a new peripheral, run it for a few minutes, and then upgrade to a new operating system. Test the new device for a few days before performing the OS upgrade.

17. Start your PC clean. This means shut down your PC and then restart it; close all running applications, including those in your System Tray; and disable any antivirus software.

18. Run setup. For the detailed steps on upgrading to Windows 2000, see the section "Upgrading from Windows 95/98 to Windows 2000."

19. Perform any postinstallation tasks. Create a new start disk or emergency repair disk (ERD) *immediately*. Verify that all devices are functioning properly. Add the PC to a network if appropriate. Configure your desktop and environment, and then install your utilities and applications.

NOTE

OPERATING SYSTEM UPGRADE CHECKLIST

Here is a reminder checklist covering what we've discussed so far in this chapter, with the steps condensed down into as compact a list as possible.

1. Verify that your PC, BIOS, and existing devices all meet the new operating system's requirements.

2. If your PC is on a network, gather relevant network data.

3. Print all your system's settings (system, device, and CMOS).

4. Copy your PC's current `Autoexec.bat` and `Config.sys` files (if you have any) to a safe, write-protected medium; then print them and store the listings.

5. Verify that you have all your applications' source media.

6. Verify that you have all your latest device drivers.

7. Confirm that your start disk works and includes real-mode drivers for your CD-ROM drive.

8. Clean up, back up, and defragment your drives.

9. If you intend to upgrade any peripherals or components, do so before you upgrade to a new operating system.

10. Start your PC clean.

11. Run setup.

12. Perform any postinstallation tasks.

Upgrading from Windows 95 to Windows 98

Insert the Windows 98 upgrade CD and follow the installation instructions. Your PC will reboot itself many times during the install; that's normal for this upgrade. When you're asked to register online, go ahead and do so, but we recommend you not allow the installer to send your PC's inventory back to Microsoft. The choice of whether to save your prior Windows 95 installation is strictly up to you. Of the many Win95-to-Win98 upgrades we've performed for clients in the field, we've never found it useful to retain the prior installation files. Your mileage might vary.

The benefits of upgrading to Windows 98 from Windows 95 include built-in support for USB, improved Plug and Play, a FAT system called FAT32 that can increase the amount of available disk space by using your drive more efficiently (Microsoft claims FAT32 can provide up to 28% more space), an improved disk defragmenter that's smart about where to put your applications' files for fast starting, built-in Internet Connection Sharing software (for Windows 98 Second Edition), a variety of new maintenance and troubleshooting tools and wizards to make it easier to care for your PC, support for DVDs (in Windows 98 Second Edition), and improved dial-up networking.

TIP

UPGRADING FROM WINDOWS 95 OR 98 TO WINDOWS MILLENNIUM

You can use this chapter's Operating System Upgrade Checklist when upgrading from Windows 95 or 98 to Windows Millennium. Be aware that Millennium has some new features that you would be better off knowing about before you upgrade—just so you're not surprised. Millennium doesn't enable you to boot to the MS-DOS command prompt (the desktop still supports MS-DOS command windows, though). Millennium uses the desktop found in Windows 2000, which is somewhat different from the Windows 95/98 desktop. In addition, Millennium's System Restore feature works in the background to automatically prevent you from deleting or overwriting any important files from the Windows and Program Files folders (you can turn off System Restore if you want, but it is active by default). Millennium's AutoUpdate feature is on by default (you can customize or turn off AutoUpdate).

Upgrading from Windows 95/98 to Windows 2000

We recommend you keep your existing Windows 95, 98, or Millennium operating system and give Windows 2000 a test drive, rather than installing it on top of your current operating system. In this section, we explain how. First, let's cover the various file systems available to Windows 95, 98, Millennium, NT, and 2000 so you can choose the best one for you. A *file system* is the way an operating system organizes the files on a disk. See Table 20.1 for a comparison of how various operating systems support these file systems. The available file systems are as follows:

- **FAT (File Allocation Table)**—FAT is a 16-bit file system used primarily in MS-DOS, Windows 3.x, and Windows 95 (Windows 95.0b, also called Windows 95 SR2, can support FAT32 also). FAT is often referred to as *FAT16* to avoid confusion between the 16-bit version of FAT and the 32-bit version (FAT32); we'll follow that convention for the remainder of this chapter.

■ **FAT32 (File Allocation Table, 32-bit)**—FAT32 was introduced in Windows 95.0b and is available in Windows 98, Millennium, and Windows 2000. Windows NT 3.x and 4.x cannot see FAT32 partitions.

■ **NTFS (NT File System)**—NTFS is not supported by and is not visible to any of the Windows 9x/Millennium operating systems. NTFS is available to only Windows NT (2000 is actually NT 5.0, meaning that Windows 2000 uses the NTFS 5.0 file system) operating systems. This introduces a complication when multibooting Windows 2000 and Windows 98. Because Windows 98 can't see an NTFS partition, data on the Windows 2000 partition is invisible to Windows 98. The workaround is to add a third partition, formatted with FAT32, which can be read by either OS.

Table 20.1   FAT16, FAT32, and NTFS File System Support by Operating System

Operating System	FAT16	FAT32	NTFS
Windows 95	Yes	No	No
Windows 95.0b (OSR2)	Yes	Yes	No
Windows 98	Yes	Yes	No
Windows Millennium	Yes	Yes	No
Windows NT 3.x	Read-only	No	Yes
Windows NT 4.x	Read-only	No	Yes
Windows 2000	Yes	Yes	Yes

UPGRADING TO WINDOWS 2000

1. Use a third-party partition tool such as PartitionMagic to create a second primary partition intended for Windows 2000.

   This partition should be 650MB minimum, 2.0GB recommended. This enables you to have a known-good operating system that you can fall back on if the Windows 2000 install fails (if you want to, later you can use PartitionMagic to delete the original Windows 95/98 partition and redistribute the space to other partitions). See Chapter 22, "Managing Disk Partitions," for more information on PartitionMagic.

Microsoft's documentation states that in a multiboot operating system scenario in which Windows 2000 is one of the systems, you can use either FAT, FAT32, or NTFS (unlike Windows NT in which the boot partition must be FAT, not FAT32). We recommend in this scenario that you use FAT32 for Windows 2000 to simplify things, but you could also use NTFS if you prefer.

2. Start your PC's existing operating system, insert the Windows 2000 CD, and run `Setup.exe` from the CD's root folder.

3. When Setup prompts `Would you like to upgrade to Windows 2000?`, click Yes.

   In step 6, tell Setup that you're installing Windows 2000 to a partition other than the one you just booted into.

4. When Setup prompts you with a dialog box containing two option buttons— Upgrade to Windows 2000 (Recommended) and Install a New Copy of Windows 2000 (Clean Install)—select the Install a New Copy of Windows 2000 (Clean Install) option and click Next.

5. You'll see the End User License Agreement (EULA) screen, and in the next screen you'll be prompted to type in your product key.

6. You next see the Select Special Options screen.

   Click the Advanced Options button and mark the checkbox labeled I Want to Choose the Installation Partition During Setup. *This is very important; this step tells Windows 2000 to install itself somewhere other than the current operating system's partition.*

7. Continue following Setup's instructions to the point where it displays a list of existing partitions and, if present, unpartitioned space. *Select the partition that does not have Windows 95/98 on it.*

8. Setup will eventually finish installing components.

   You'll be notified with the message `You have successfully completed Windows 2000 setup. If there is a CD in your drive, remove it. Then, to restart your computer, click Finish`. Do as the prompt advises.

9. When your PC reboots, you see the Boot Loader screen.

   This screen lists all the installed, bootable operating systems. In the scenario we've described in this section, the boot loader would look like this:

   ```
   Please select the operating system to start:
   Microsoft Windows 2000 Professional
   Microsoft Windows 98
   ```

```
Use ↑ and ↓ to move the highlight to your choice.
Press Enter to choose.
Seconds until highlighted choice will be started automatically: 29
For troubleshooting and advanced startup options for Windows 2000,
➥press F8.
```

10. Choose the operating system you want to load and press Enter.

NOTE

HOW LONG DOES A CLEAN INSTALL OF WINDOWS 2000 TAKE?

Plan on at least 1 1/2 hours for just the setup process after you start `Setup.exe`. Configuring your desktop and other preferences and installing your favorite applications will take somewhere around 1–3 hours thereafter. Your mileage may vary, particularly if you have a complex network setup.

NOTE

MAKING WINDOWS 2000 BOOT DISKS

You can install Windows 2000 via a set of four 3 1/2-inch boot disks. You create these Windows 2000 boot disks by running the Makeboot tool from the CD. Click Start, Run, and type `z:\bootdisk\makeboot a:` (where `z:` is the drive letter of your CD-ROM drive); then press Enter. To set up Windows 2000 using these disks, simply insert Disk 1 in the floppy drive, reboot your PC, and follow the instructions from there.

If your PC's BIOS supports booting from a CD, the Windows 2000 CD is bootable. So, you also can start a setup that way.

TIP

UNINSTALLING WINDOWS 2000

Jason Anderson, Windows 2000/NT Forum Manager at MSN's Computing Central, has written an excellent article describing how to do this when you have Windows 95/98 and Windows 2000 established on a dual-boot system. Go to `http://computingcentral.msn.com/topics/windowsnt/uninstall.asp`.

Cleaning Up a Hard Drive

The amount of free hard disk space you need to upgrade your operating system, especially if you're performing a clean install to a separate partition, is staggering. Consider cleaning up your hard disk prior to performing an operating system upgrade. Cleaning up a hard drive, and keeping it clean, is amazingly simple—no matter how small or large the drive. Follow this checklist to avoid having your hard drive overflow with junk.

TIP

GUARANTEEING DRIVEWIDE FILE SEARCHES
When using Find for drivewide searches, check the Include Subfolders checkbox. After it's checked, it will stay checked forever—across Windows sessions—until you uncheck it. To limit a search to a specific folder, uncheck the box; just remember to check it again when you're finished.

NOTE

WINDOWS 95 DOES NOT INCLUDE THE DISK CLEANUP TOOL
Windows 95 doesn't have a Disk Cleanup tool, so you must perform most of these steps manually.

1. Delete any rubbish files.

   A rubbish file is one you don't have use for any longer. Don't let these files tie up precious hard disk real estate or be a distraction.

2. Zip infrequently used files.

   Zip any files you rarely access but that aren't yet old enough to be archived off your hard drive.

3. Archive old files.

   These are keepers, but if you haven't accessed a file in over a year, it's a good candidate for archiving off your hard drive onto removable media.

4. Use the Add/Remove applet's Windows Setup tab to uninstall unused Windows 98 components.

   For example, the Online Services component (typically C:\Program Files\Online Services) represents about 350KB of wasted space if you already have an ISP. Granted, this isn't a Grand Canyon-size chasm in your hard disk, but every little bit helps.

TIP

WINDOWS 98'S DISK CLEANUP TOOL
The Disk Cleanup tool can help you with many disk cleanup tasks. To start this tool, select Start, Programs, Accessories, System Tools, Disk Cleanup; pick any drive; and click OK (see Figure 20.5). You can schedule Disk Cleanup to run at regular intervals via Task Scheduler; we set our PCs to run it daily at noon.

FIGURE 20.5

Windows 98's
Disk Cleanup
dialog box.

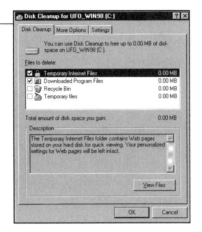

FIGURE 20.5

Windows 98's
Disk Cleanup
dialog box.

5. Use the Add/Remove applet's Install/Uninstall tab to uninstall applications you don't use.

    The Disk Cleanup tool can also perform this task.

6. Manually uninstall any unwanted applications that, for whatever reason, aren't in the previously mentioned Install/Uninstall list.

7. Empty your Recycle Bin.

    The Disk Cleanup tool can also perform this task.

8. Empty your browser's temporary Internet cache.

    In Internet Explorer select View, Internet Options; then in the Temporary Internet Files section, click the Delete Files button, click OK, and click OK again. In Netscape Navigator select Edit, Preferences, expand the Advanced node, choose the Cache node, click the Clear Disk button, and click OK. The Disk Cleanup tool can also perform this task. Note that this emptying of the Internet cache has the side effect of taking slightly longer to load a page the very first time you browse to it after having emptied the cache.

9. Optimize your browser's history setting.

    The fewer the days that pages are kept, the less disk space will be wasted.

10. Delete spurious `File*.chk` files in each primary partition's root folder.

    These files are left over from ScanDisk's efforts to correct cross-linked files. The Disk Cleanup tool can also perform this task.

11. Delete spurious log files.

    Sometimes you might unintentionally set an application's logging mechanism to append instead of replace mode. These files can reach gargantuan proportions. Perform a drivewide search for `*.log`.

12. Delete out-of-date document backup files.

    For example, a candidate for deletion in Microsoft Word would have a name of `Backup of Surfing Journal.wbk` (Backup of...wbk), in Microsoft Excel `Backup of Net Worth.xlk` (Backup of...xlk), and so on. A drivewide search for `backup*.*` would do the trick. Check your individual applications' help files for details on their backup filenaming conventions.

13. With Microsoft Word closed, delete any `~*.tmp` and `~*.doc` files.

    These are junk files left hanging around by errant Word sessions. They tend to be in your document folders but can, on occasion, stray and end up getting stored anywhere.

14. If you're running Microsoft Office, uninstall the Find Fast tool.

    Find Fast is a tool Office installs by default along with Office. It indexes your hard drive to supposedly make it faster for you to find documents. However, in our long experience (we've written six books on Microsoft Office and have been developing Office applications since before Office was Office), it's inherently buggy and slows your system's performance down when it is updating its indexes. We strongly suggest you uninstall it. Start Microsoft Office 2000's setup application in Maintenance Mode, click the Add or Remove Features button, click Office Tools, choose Not Available from the Find Fast Control Panel control, and click Update Now.

15. Remove any unwanted messages from your email client's Deleted Items folder.

    Move or archive any important messages still hanging around in Deleted Items.

16. Compact your email storage file.

    Start by noting the size of your email storage file. Use your email client's interface to compress your email storage file. (In Microsoft Outlook 2000, the steps are right-click the Personal Folders folder, choose Properties, click the Advanced button, click Compact Now, click OK when done, and click OK again.) Check again to see this file's reduced size and notice the difference.

17. If your Windows 9x operating system supports it, activate FAT32. (As mentioned earlier in this chapter, under Windows 95, FAT32 is available for only the OSR2 version, sometimes called Windows 95.0b.) If you're not running OSR2 and don't have access to it, install PowerQuest's PartitionMagic and use it to optimize your cluster size.

TIP

USING THE WINDOWS UPDATE TOOL TO VIEW CRITICAL UPDATES AND PRODUCT UPDATES

Windows 98, Millennium, and 2000 include a built-in feature called Windows Update. It's visible at or near the top of your Start menu, as shown in Figure 20.6. You can also access it from Microsoft Internet Explorer by selecting Tools, Windows Update. A steady stream of operating system, browser, and email interim updates, patches, and bug fixes are being released daily. These updates are especially important when they affect your system's security. To address this issue, Microsoft has created a tool called Windows Critical Update Notification. You can download it from the Windows Update page (`http://windowsupdate.microsoft.com`), and we suggest you do so. It runs silently at regular intervals, checks the Windows Update page in the background to see whether any new critical update items exist, and then prompts you whether to view the updates now or later. The Windows Update page also contains noncritical product updates such as new media players, browser font packs, and so on. All these updates are optional.

In the case of formal application or operating system Service Packs, we suggest you upgrade these from only a CD. That's for two reasons: first, because a Service Pack is a major upgrade (for example, Windows 2000 Service Pack 1 was just released as of the time of this writing), it would be risky to install it over the Internet and second, a Service Pack is usually so large that even with high-speed Internet access downloading it wouldn't be efficient.

FIGURE 20.6

The Windows Update command appears at or near the top of your Start menu.

Online Resources

- **The Naked PC**—Our free newsletter routinely covers Windows-related news, products, books, and resources. Subscribe at `http://www.TheNakedPC.com`.

- **Paul Thurrott's SuperSite for Windows**—Located at `http://www.winsupersite.com`, it has excellent FAQs, reviews, and news. If you're interested in Windows news and tips, you'll want to subscribe to the free *Windows 2000 Magazine UPDATE* and *WinInfo Daily UPDATE*, among others from their extensive offerings.

- **Newsgroups managed by Microsoft**—Currently, 30 are available that are dedicated to Windows 2000, 31 covering Windows 98, and 12 covering Windows 95. Look for `microsoft.public.win2000.*`, `microsoft.public.win98.*`, and `microsoft.public.win95.*`, respectively, and choose the right newsgroup for you.

- **Microsoft's hardware compatibility page for Windows Millennium**—Located at `http://www.microsoft.com/windowsME/upgrade/compat/default.asp`.

- `http://www.dell.com/us/en/biz/topics/win2k_home.htm`—For all you Dell aficionados, they've done an excellent job of organizing an extensive set of resources for Dell customers interested in migrating to Windows 2000. Other PC manufacturers take note. Highly recommended.

- **Frank Condron's World O' Windows site**—Located at `http://www.worldowindows.com`, it covers Windows 95, 98, NT, 2000, and CE, including drivers/company search, news, commentary, book reviews, a cool Windows timeline, discussion groups, and more.

- **Jim Forbes's "A Brief History of Microsoft Windows"**—This fascinating stroll down memory lane includes screen shots and commentary, although it doesn't yet cover Windows NT or 2000. Go to `http://www.primenet.com/~jforbes/winhist/windows.html`.

21

UPGRADING YOUR APPLICATIONS: STRATEGIES AND ADVICE

Software suites, browsers, utilities, games, Internet downloads …, after you install them, you start on the never-ending upgrade trail. Trying to keep up with the latest version along with the interim patches, bug fixes, and service releases can make you crazy. Unless you have a plan.

Upgrade Checklist

1. Do your homework.

2. Determine whether you can perform the upgrade. Some application and service pack upgrades require you to have a prior version or patch already installed.

3. Purchase/download the software component.

4. Determine how best to prepare your PC prior to performing the planned upgrade. This is in case you must roll back to a preinstall point if an upgrade destabilizes your system. This can involve making backups of data, the operating system, and mission-critical applications and files.

5. Perform the upgrade.

6. Take good notes, and permanently file them in your system log when finished.

7. Update your inventory documentation to reflect the upgraded or newly added software component.

Application Upgrade Strategy

To understand why software upgrades are necessary more often and have become more complicated, you have to understand how the entire software sales model has changed. Companies used to turn out fairly stable, feature-complete versions of their products, and you as a consumer would evaluate, purchase, and install the program that best suited your needs. New versions of existing products came to market only every 18 months to 2 years.

That is the old sales model; you chose an application, paid for it, and would spend only incremental dollars on the same product again if the manufacturer came out with a version that had compelling new features. This model worked well for manufacturers while a constantly expanding market of users existed to which to sell their wares.

But, as development cycles got shorter and the market for new users got tighter, software companies started shifting to a subscription model in which they're willing to practically give away the software as long as they can charge for a continuous stream of upgrades. Consider the primary software suite you use on your computer. Chances are good you're using the software that came preinstalled on the system because it was provided free (or for a nominal fee) and came on the computer ready to go. You didn't shop for—or evaluate—programs to get what you wanted; you just took what came with the computer. The software developer gave the original equipment manufacturer a sweetheart deal if they'd preinstall the software on the hard disk that came in your system. This is how programs such as Microsoft Office develop market share. Microsoft figures they'll own the market and make up the profit in upgrade fees.

Another factor in this equation is the explosive growth in the Internet as a means to distribute software of all sorts. New features can be added and versions instantly distributed to millions of users over the Internet. To stay competitive, software developers have gone to shorter and shorter development cycles to keep their products looking new and fresh. The downside from the consumer's perspective is that software is commonly released in what can only be considered a beta stage of development, a semiunfinished state with the intention to fix any stability and feature problems in a series of ongoing upgrades to the application over time. The software companies like this scenario because the more often they come out with new versions, the more often they can charge you for upgrading.

New versions, interim service releases, bug fixes, and patches all make keeping your software upgraded to the current version a time-consuming and complicated mess. You need a well–thought-out strategy to keep things from getting out of hand.

Finding the Version Number

To know what you need to upgrade, you must know the version of the software you currently have installed. Determining the latest version of a given product is

ANOTHER FINE MESS
CHECK THAT VERSION NUMBER!
Keeping track of what you've updated is critical in case you ever have to restore your system after a crash. Checking the version number in the Help, About dialog box usually gives you the correct number, but you can't always count on it. Every time you patch or upgrade a program, immediately check the version number to see whether it has incremented. Some patches don't increment the version number, so you'll have to carefully note the upgrade you've performed in your system journal. ■

not always easy. Generally, you should start the application in question and choose the About option on the Help menu (see Figure 21.1).

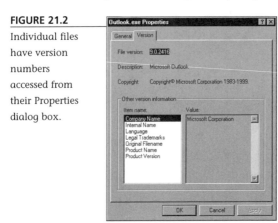

The version numbers, as you can see in Figure 21.1, are a lot more complex than the old 1.0, 1.1, and 1.2 version numbers of days gone by. Service releases don't always change the number, but oftentimes just tack on something like "SR-1" or "SR1a" at the end of the version number to indicate the current service release that has been applied. Service release numbers have become more important because some patches and fixes require that a particular service release be installed *prior* to installing the fix.

A way to determine a specific version for an individual file is to check the version number of the executable file that starts the application. Continuing with our Outlook example, we found the executable file in `C:\Program Files\Microsoft Office\Office\Outlook.exe` in Windows Explorer. Select `Outlook.exe`, right-click it, and click the Properties option from the pop-up menu. Select the Version tab, and you'll see that the file version is 9.0.2416, which is different from that shown in the Help, About dialog box (see Figure 21.2).

Keeping Track of Upgrades

The version of each important program installed on your system, including every interim bug fix, patch, and service release you've applied, is something you need to track.

First, some patches cannot be applied unless you've previously installed some other patch. Consider the Outlook E-Mail Security Update released in June 2000. It requires you to have installed the Office 2000 Service Release 1a (SR-1a) for all of Office 2000 *before* you can install this security patch for Outlook. As software becomes more complex and integrated (especially Microsoft's family of products), the interplay between patches, upgrades, and fixes becomes more important.

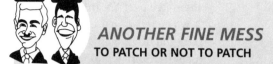

ANOTHER FINE MESS
TO PATCH OR NOT TO PATCH

Before you install a patch, be sure you understand which problem it corrects and what it does to the functionality of the program, if anything. For example, Microsoft came out with a security patch for Outlook in the aftermath of the I Love You virus. The patch "secured" the user from being able to access executable attachments, which caused a big problem for users who needed that feature. Some patches cannot be uninstalled without removing the program entirely and reinstalling the unpatched version, so don't blindly start installing patches without doing your homework first. ■

Second, you probably have your major applications, such as Microsoft Office, on CD-ROM. Therefore, in the event of a disaster, you can simply reinstall from the original CD program disc and restore your applications. Except that the patch and service releases you've installed no doubt were downloaded directly from the Internet. If you reinstall from CD disc, you're actually restoring an earlier version, sans the patches and service releases you had so meticulously installed.

In addition, you must consider all the programs you've purchased and downloaded in their entirety from the Internet and for which you don't have physical CDs. You need a strategy and methodology to keep track of these programs so you can restore them if necessary. This includes all the interim patches and fixes you've picked up along the way. In the next section, you'll see one approach that has worked well for us for a number of years.

Downloading Programs and Patches

The first rule of application upgrades (we're including bug fixes, patches, service releases, and so on, as well as applications purchased over the Internet under the general term "upgrade" in this section) is that it's okay to download them over the

Internet but to *never* install them live over the Internet. Always, repeat *always*, download the upgrade file to your local hard drive and install it—after the download has completed—from that local file.

This method lets you make a backup or storage copy of the upgrade so you have it on tape or removable media and can archive it in case you must reinstall it at a later time. Although you could just go back to the Internet to get any software you need to reinstall, consider the problems you could run into:

- A site gets moved and you have to start searching for it.

- A piece of software you are fond of gets discontinued (this happened to us a year or so ago with Luckman's Anonymous Cookie).

- You can't remember the name of the company that wrote the software, much less its URL.

- Software purchased over the Internet can't readily be redownloaded without going through a number of time-consuming steps.

ANOTHER FINE MESS
AVOID GETTING CUT ON THE CUTTING EDGE

The Internet makes it easy to get the latest upgrades for full-blown applications, service releases, patches, bug fixes—you name it and it's only a download away. Save yourself some grief and be prudent about how quickly you grab the latest and greatest and slap it on your system. Avoid "public" betas unless you have a very good reason to climb out there on the bleeding edge. These public betas are fraught with peril in regard to bugs and can expire at some point after the beta period. Or, when you get the final release, it might require you to completely uninstall the beta—or even reformat your hard disk—before you can safely install the release version, all of which can result in a loss of data or other inconveniences.

If you can, wait awhile before installing service releases and patches to see whether the fix turns out to be worse than the problems the upgrade purports to solve. Often, a major service release comes out and, after bugs in the update have ravaged the early adopters, a second service release comes out to fix the problems caused by the first one. Also, some fixes cannot be easily uninstalled or unwound, leaving you stuck with an upgrade that can turn out to create more problems than it solves. Be smart and wait to see what problems are reported before you jump in. ■

Downloading and Running

Create a Downloads folder on a drive with the necessary room to store these sometimes multimegabyte upgrade files that you'll be downloading. Then, create subfolders to categorize the downloaded files. For example

```
c:\Downloads\Applications\
c:\Downloads\Windows\
c:\Downloads\Drivers\
c:\Downloads\Utilities\
c:\Downloads\Browsers\
```

You would include categories that make sense for the types of applications and files you downloaded. Create additional subfolders for various service releases or patches. For example

```
c:\Downloads\Windows\ActiveSetupControl\
c:\Downloads\Windows\scriptlet.typelib.Eyedog\
c:\Downloads\Windows\ShutdownUpdate\
```

TIP

SAVE INSTRUCTIONS RIGHT OFF THE WEB

Most updates and patches come with installation instructions, usually on the Web page you go to in order to download the upgrade file. Save the instructions by saving the Web page as an HTML file in the same folder in which you've downloaded the file. In your browser, click File, Save As, and save the page to your local disk.

After you have the upgrade file on your local system, you must install it. Some upgrades make this easy, letting you simply double-click the executable file, which triggers an installation program that takes care of the install. But some upgrades are packaged as Zip files, requiring you to unzip the dozens of files contained therein and then search for the one executable that either triggers the patch or runs an installation program.

The best way to handle the upgrade is by copying the downloaded file to a temporary directory—for example, *d:*\Downloads\Temp\—and unzipping or running the installer from there. After you have upgraded, you can delete the contents of this folder. This keeps the installation files separate from the download file.

Finding Upgrades

Information on upgrades these days is most often found on the Web sites of the software manufacturers. But don't count on the manufacturer proactively notifying you of a new patch, fix, or version no matter how many times you've filled out a registration card (physical or electronic). It's up to you to stay on top of your application upgrades.

A trend exists for applications themselves being made smart enough to check on the Internet to see whether a newer version or patch is available. If one is available, they application lets you know by popping up a dialog box or message window telling you you should upgrade. This requires an Internet connection and assumes you have not blocked applications on your local machine from accessing Web sites to check for new versions (see Figure 21.3).

FIGURE 21.3

Some programs provide a mechanism for checking for upgrades via the Internet, such as the wizard shown here.

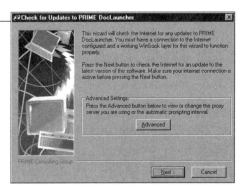

An application can provide a button or menu option that lets you tell it when to check for upgrades, or it might just periodically do this on its own. Some concern exists about what, if anything, an application might be telling its parent company about your local system while it's gallivanting around the Internet checking on upgrades. We don't consider this much more than a minor annoyance—at least so far.

You also can install software whose sole purpose is to find out whether newer versions of the software you're using are available.

Again, the best bet is to check on what's happening with a particular upgrade on the software manufacturer's Web site. Of course, finding a given manufacturer's URL is not always easy. Often, a company will put contact information, including its Web address, in the program's Help, About dialog box. Program documentation might also list this information. After you're at the manufacturer's Web site, look to see whether it offers an email notification on new upgrades or perhaps a free electronic newsletter that would announce new upgrades as they become available.

FINDING AND UPGRADING DRIVERS

If you want to locate a driver upgrade for a particular piece of equipment, a software service release, or updates for things such as the latest multimedia drivers and you're not sure where to start looking, go to the WinDrivers.com database page:

`http://www.windrivers.com/company.htm`

Here, you can find USB drivers, updates for graphics cards, and so on—you name it and they can help you find it. You can even search for a particular company to find updates for a given product. You'll find links to service releases for Microsoft Office and Windows 95/98/NT. Overall, WinDrivers.com is an incredible online resource.

Third-party utilities are available that search your local system for installed applications, and then these applications are compared to a database of information on the latest versions of popular software. A list is presented to you showing which upgrades are available for your software. These programs often also help you download the appropriate files and install the upgrades.

McAfee's Oil Change Online offers a Software Update Finder that works over the Internet to help you locate and install upgrades available for your installed applications. Oil Change Online is available for an annual subscription fee:

`http://www.mcafee.com/myapps/clinic/oilchange/ov_softupdatefinder.asp`

Symantec offers their Norton Web Services subscription for free, and it includes LiveUpdate Pro (formerly Quarterdeck's TuneUp). This is also a Web-based program that scans your local applications and offers to help you find and install the latest upgrades:

`http://www.nortonweb.com/home.shtml`

CNet offers CatchUp, a free utility (Windows 95/98/NT/2000) that installs on your local drive and, similar to the offerings from Symantec and McAfee, runs over the Web to check for new upgrades:

`http://www.catchup.com`

For more generic and news-oriented information on software upgrades, you should stop by the ZDNet/Updates.com site and subscribe to its free, weekly newsletter delivered via email. It keeps you apprised of new software releases and patches:

`http://updates.zdnet.com/`

Microsoft offers a Web service for upgrading Windows 95/98/NT:

`http://windowsupdate.microsoft.com`

The upgrades are categorized as Critical, Pick of the Month, Recommended Updates, and Additional Windows Features. The downside to Microsoft's approach is that upgrades are downloaded and installed in a single step without giving you the opportunity to save the upgrade file to disk (see Figure 21.4). This prevents you from archiving the upgrades you've installed on your system and forces you to go back to the Microsoft Web site if you ever need to reinstall a given upgrade.

This might not sound onerous. However, given our experience with Microsoft moving Web pages without redirection links, and of just abandoning pages when a site is remodeled, it makes it difficult to feel confident that a particular upgrade will be readily available later on should you need to find it again.

Windows ME boasts a feature called AutoUpdate that downloads and installs what Microsoft calls "critical system file upgrades" in the background while you are online. While you surf and do other things, Windows ME checks on current upgrades that might be available for itself and offers to install them for you.

FIGURE 21.4

The one-step download/install process makes it impossible to archive the upgrades you get through Windows Update.

Archiving the Files

Now that you have the upgrade file on your local system, you must think about archiving the file so it's available in case of a system or disk problem that causes you to lose files on your hard drive. If you have a writable CD drive (see Chapter 15, "Adding a CD-Recordable or CD-Rewritable Drive"), one of the best solutions is to copy your Download folder and subfolders to a CD disc. If you have too many files to fit on a single CD, you can create a Download1 and Download2, where the contents of each folder (including subfolders) is less than the maximum burnable area of the CD. This enables you to put each set of folders onto a separate CD disc.

You can do the same sort of thing using a tape backup drive (see Chapter 18, "Adding a Tape Drive"), a Zip drive (see Chapter 17, "Adding Removable Storage"), or other removable media. This archives your software upgrades in bulk, making retrieval possible in the event that you lose the original file(s) on your hard disk.

KEEPING THINGS PHYSICALLY TOGETHER

Minor fixes, patches, and the like might be small enough to fit on a floppy disk. If this is the case, consider copying the download to a floppy and storing it with the CD-ROM disc that contains the last full version of that particular program. This keeps everything together "on the shelf," as it were. Larger service releases might fit on Zip disks (admittedly, a more expensive solution on a per-disk basis) or might be massive enough to require their own writable CD discs. In any event, physically keeping together the original software and all subsequent patches, upgrades, and service releases is a good idea.

Record All Upgrades

Back in Chapter 3, "Things You Need," we discussed the importance of the system journal. This journal is a simple spiral notebook you keep next to your computer. In it, you record every crash and glitch, odd noise, and those "hmmm, that was odd" incidents. You also record every upgrade, patch, and service release you install on your computer.

This gives you a chronological history of all the software installed on your system. Before you install a software upgrade, check the current version number and record it in the system journal. Immediately after performing the upgrade, check the version number again and note the new number (or if the number did not change, be sure to note that, too). You want to know when you performed the upgrade, the software you upgraded, the version numbers before and after, and any other relevant information.

Keeping track of upgrades can save you a lot of headaches if you must restore a system. A missed upgrade could put you at risk for errors or compromise security. This is a situation made worse because you might think you've already protected yourself by installing the upgrade in the first place and not realize you missed a key fix when you have to restore your system.

Using System Recovery Tools

It's a sad fact of computer life that upgrading a system does not always work out as planned. This is especially true of application and operating system upgrades. Many is the time when a serious system instability can be traced back to a recent software upgrade.

Your computer is working fine, but then you install a software upgrade and suddenly you start experiencing all sorts of problems. What can cause this is the complex interdependency of various system and application files working under a complex operating system such as Windows (in all its various flavors).

The program you've just installed might work great, but another program may crash unexpectedly or Windows might start giving you troubles. This can be caused by a shared system DLL being overwritten by one supplied by the new software application you just installed. Or, a critical Registry entry might be moved or changed, thereby causing the system to become unstable. Uninstalling the new application may not alleviate the problem because most uninstall programs just delete Registry entries, files, and folders and might not restore overwritten system files.

What you used to do in the old days was to make a complete backup of your system, install something new, test to see whether your system remained stable, and if the upgrade caused problems, you had to restore your entire system from the backup. Fortunately, restoring a system after a less-than-satisfactory application or software upgrade is much easier these days. A number of utilities and services make it possible to roll back your system to a preinstall state.

Manual Registry Rollback

You should always make a backup copy of your Registry files before performing any upgrade to your computer system. For Windows 95/98 systems, the Registry is composed of two files, System.dat and User.dat, found in the C:\Windows folder. Copy both files to make a complete backup of your Registry.

Windows 98 comes with a utility called the Registry Checker. Every time you boot the system, it does just what you'd think: It checks the Registry. If it decides no problem exists with it, a backup of the Registry is per-

ANOTHER FINE MESS
REGISTRY CHECKER ISN'T FOOLPROOF

As handy as the Registry Checker is, you have to understand its limitations. If your Registry gets corrupted, but the corruption does not cause you any immediate problems, the Checker might not notice something is wrong. From there on out, every time you boot your system, the bad Registry gets backed up. It's possible that some or all five of the default backup copies of the Registry are bad, meaning you'll be unable to restore a good copy. That's another good reason to back up your data frequently. If you have to nuke the machine and start over to recover from a corrupted Registry, at least you won't lose irreplaceable data. ■

formed automatically. By default, the last five "known good" copies of the Registry are saved as compressed CAB files in the C:\Windows\Sysbckup folder. The CAB file contains the System.ini and Win.ini files, as well.

You can manually restore any of these CAB backups by running Windows in MS-DOS mode and typing **scanreg/restore** at the DOS prompt. The last five backups named RBnnn.cab are listed, where nnn is an incremental number starting at 000. Select the file you want restored and choose Restore. You can increase the number of Registry backups that the Registry Checker keeps by editing the scanreg.ini file, found in the C:\Windows folder. Change the MaxBackupCopies setting to the number of backups you want kept. For example, to increase the number of backups to 10, you'd change the setting in scanreg.ini as follows:

MaxBackupCopies=10

Windows NT creates a series of what it calls *hive* files that make up the Registry. Your best bet for manually creating a backup of the Registry on an NT system is by using the NTBackup program. This creates a copy of the Registry files along with other key files when the Backup Local Registry option is selected.

Like Windows 98, NT has a mechanism faintly similar to the Registry Checker for creating automatic backups of the Registry. When you boot NT, you can invoke the Hardware Profile/Last Known Good menu. From this menu, you can boot from what

NT has determined is a "good" Registry—in other words, the last Registry in effect when NT booted successfully.

Windows 2000 also keeps a backup copy of its Registry and other key files and lets you try booting from this, which it calls the *Last Known Good Configuration*. It does not provide an easy method for you to create your own backups of its Registry, though.

Both Windows NT and Windows 2000 are designed for a networked environment where it is anticipated that the network administrator will centralize the backup of key files, including Registry and boot files. Also, Windows 2000 has a feature called Windows File Protection that prevents applica-

ANOTHER FINE MESS
DIFFERENCES BETWEEN WINDOWS NT AND WINDOWS 2000

With Windows NT, you can update your Emergency Repair Disk (ERD) to include a new copy of your current Registry files (assuming your Registry has not gotten too big to fit on the disk). Windows 2000 also lets you create an ERD but does not provide an option for updating it later. In fact, the Windows 2000 ERD does not include the Registry as part of the disk contents at all because the Windows 2000 Registry is larger and won't fit on a single disk.

What's doubly confusing is that an option exists on the ERD creation dialog box that you can check to "back up the Registry to the repair directory." This does not put the Registry on the ERD, but backs it up to a folder on your local hard drive. ■

tions from overwriting protected system files (.sys, .dll, .ocx, .ttf, .fon, and .exe), hopefully reducing the chances that an application upgrade will seriously destabilize your system. If a protected file is overwritten, the System File Checker automatically replaces the incorrect file with the correct Microsoft version from the \system32\ dllcache folder.

In any event, for backing up files to roll back your system, you'll have to look to third-party utilities (discussed shortly).

Windows Me System Restore

Windows Me comes with an option called System Restore that improves mightily upon Win98's Registry Checker. Using System Restore, you can roll back your system to an earlier point, thereby undoing an upgrade installation that causes problems.

System Restore creates system checkpoints, which are created automatically by Me, and enables you to manually create the same thing yourself—but the documentation calls them *restore points*. Me will automatically create an installation restore point when it detects certain programs being installed, such as Microsoft Office. Rolling back is as simple as clicking a calendar icon to select a given date and then choosing from a list of all the points created on that day (listed chronologically).

Third-Party Utilities for Rolling Back

GoBack is a utility sold by Adaptec that enables you to roll back the current state of your system to some point in history that you choose. It keeps track of everything you do, as you do it, and then offers to let you decide to undo an event or a series of events in the hopes of being able to restore your system to stable operation.

The price of this type of protection is up to 10% of your available disk space for GoBack to use in keeping track of every single thing you do so that each action can be undone. GoBack works with Windows 95/98 and Windows ME. A version for NT has been promised but has not been released as of the time of this writing. You can find GoBack at
`http://www.adaptec.com/products/overview/goback.html`

Another utility to consider for this type of duty is Second Chance by PowerQuest (for Windows 95/98 only). Second Chance enables you to set checkpoints in time (up to 24 checkpoints per day) and to roll back changes on your entire system or just for an individual file. You can exclude folders, such as a temp directory, from being monitored to save on the number of extraneous changes being tracked. Similar to GoBack, you must sacrifice disk space to keep track of all the changes you make to your system as you use your computer. But it's handy to set a checkpoint before performing an application upgrade, thereby giving you the option to easily return the entire system to a preupgrade condition. Second Chance is available at
`http://www.powerquest.com/secondchance/index.html`

If you're running Windows 2000, you should check out WinRescue from Super Win Software. WinRescue performs full system backups, in addition to backing up the Registry and key boot files. You can also use WinRescue to create boot disks and recovery disks, making it a very versatile and handy utility. Super Win Software has versions of WinRescue for Windows 95, Windows 98, and NT4: `http://www.superwin.com`

22

MANAGING DISK PARTITIONS

Did you know that you can turn your PC into several individual PCs? It's true, and it's easy to do. In this chapter we show you how.

When a PC comes from the factory, it is usually configured with a single partition. If you want to use that PC to boot more than one operating system, you must create another partition (one for each additional OS you intend to use). In addition, if you want to separate your operating system and applications from your data (a good idea, as we've said throughout this book), you must create a new partition for your data. A partitioning utility can make these ominous-sounding chores relatively mundane, and certainly safe.

Upgrade Checklist

1. Do your homework.

2. Determine whether your PC supports the planned upgrade.

3. Determine whether you can perform the upgrade.

4. Purchase or acquire the component.

5. Organize your tools and workspace. See Chapter 3, "Things You Need."

6. Back up everything: data, operating system, mission-critical applications, and BIOS.

7. Test your startup disk.

8. Perform the upgrade.

9. Take good notes, and permanently file them in your system log when you're finished.

10. Update your inventory documentation to reflect the upgraded or newly added component.

Partition Terminology

CAUTION

THIS CHAPTER ASSUMES YOU'VE INSTALLED PARTITIONMAGIC

This chapter assumes that you have already purchased and installed a copy of PartitionMagic. If you're new to disk partitioning, we recommend you use only a partitioning tool such as PartitionMagic to perform the tasks described in this chapter and not use the MS-DOS command `FDISK`. For those of you comfortable with `FDISK`, you can, of course, use that tool for many of these operations. Keep in mind, however, that `FDISK` is a powerful tool that can, with a simple typographical error, wipe out all the data on a partition.

Here's a list of the many uses you'll find for partitioning and boot manager utilities:

- Clone a known-good bootable partition and hide it, to be kept for safekeeping in the event that the original bootable partition becomes damaged.

- Clone a known-good bootable partition to be used for testing beta software or troubleshooting hardware.

- Run two or more operating systems on the same PC.

  A large number of combinations is possible—for three examples, (1) Windows 98 and Windows 2000, (2) Linux and Windows NT, and (3) Windows 98, Windows Millennium, and Windows 2000.

- Separate your operating system(s) from your data by creating a data-only partition.

  This data-only partition can be shared, or not, by multiple operating systems. This configuration simplifies data backup/archives and makes repairing a wrecked bootable partition much easier.

- Implement password-restricted access to one or more operating systems.

  You could have your own Windows 98 partition that's inaccessible to your children (they don't have the boot manager password for your partition), and your children could have their own Windows 98 partition. The two partitions are totally independent (read: they can crash their Windows and yours will still run fine).

- Set various convenient boot options, such as the default operating system and how long to count down before starting the default OS (or not to count down at all).

- Use a friendly graphical interface to perform operations that would otherwise be daunting or impossible.

  PartitionMagic includes these functions: copy, create, resize, move, label, format, check (integrity), scan, hide, activate, convert, and delete partitions; redistribute free space; and merge adjacent partitions.

- PartitionMagic includes additional convenience tools.

  DriveMapper, MagicMover, and PartitionInfo are described in more detail in the section "Additional PartitionMagic Tools."

For a simple example, let's assume your 8.0GB physical hard disk is composed entirely of one 8.0GB partition with the drive letter C: (a typical scenario when a PC comes from the factory). In a common multi-OS scenario, you would use a partitioning utility to clone a known-good partition as a safety measure so you could recover the cloned partition to replace another partition that has been damaged somehow (say, by a software beta test gone awry). You would use the partitioning utility to reduce the size of your C: partition so that it occupies half your hard disk (4.0GB), and then copy it into the unallocated 4.0GB of space you just freed up. The copy operation automatically would create a new partition for you, so you would then have your original C: partition still bootable as before (only it would be half its original size) and a second partition that would be an exact replica of C:. (We cover the detailed steps later in this chapter.)

Like so many things in life, understanding the terminology is half the battle. Partition terminology is not as scary as say, understanding how a hard disk is physically put together. But it does help if you have a basic understanding of the following terms.

A single hard disk can be divided into different *partitions*, or it can be configured as one partition that uses the entire disk. A disk must be partitioned before you can format it, and a disk must be partitioned for it to have a drive letter.

Partitioning a disk is useful for organizing the contents of the disk. Each partition behaves as though it were a separate hard disk. You can even run various operating systems from the same drive by booting into different partitions. Because different operating systems can use different file systems, each partition can be formatted differently (FAT, FAT32, NTFS, and so on).

A good way to work through this conceptual material is to install PartitionMagic and then start it on your PC. Meditate on PartitionMagic's user interface; study the way it represents your hard disk(s) as a horizontal bar with different colors and borders to reveal the various attributes of the partitions. If your PC's hard disk currently comprises only one partition, that's okay; look at Figures 22.1 and 22.3. Keep in mind that if adequate free space is available on your hard disk, there's nothing to prevent you from simply creating partitions and trying to produce this chapter's case studies right on your own PC—even if you don't want to implement these scenarios long-term, they make great exercises.

Currently, most hard disks support up to four primary partitions. That is, four partitions that behave as though they were separate drives, and onto which you can install various operating systems and file systems. However, you can create a type of partition called an *extended* partition, and within this extended partition you can have as many *logical* partitions as you want. The entire extended partition, however, must use the same type of file system. The following are the types of partitions available:

- **Primary partition**—A partition that behaves as though it is a separate hard disk (remember, a hard disk might have only one primary partition covering the entire disk space). A hard disk must have at least one primary partition. An example of a primary partition is the 8.0MB C: partition we mentioned in the example earlier in this section.

- **Extended partition**—An extended partition is a primary partition that can be further subdivided into logical partitions, with each logical partition assigned a separate drive letter. An extended partition can contain as many logical drives as can be accommodated based on available disk space and drive letters. Think of an extended partition as a shoebox into which you can place several smaller jewelry boxes (logical partitions). No one jewelry box can be bigger than its container shoebox, and all the jewelry boxes together can't exceed the size of the shoebox.

- **Logical partition**—A logical partition is a subdivided zone of disk space within an extended partition. Some operating systems can be booted from a logical partition by making it the active partition.

- **Active partition**—One partition (primary or logical) on a drive must be marked as active so that, when the PC boots, it knows which OS to use. Only one primary partition can be active and therefore bootable at one time.

- **Hidden partition**—A hidden partition is invisible to any other partitions on a hard disk. At bootup the partition is not assigned a drive letter thereby rendering it unseen and inaccessible to the booted OS. Earlier in the chapter, we described making a clone of a partition with a known-good operating system and then setting the copied partition as hidden; this way, you won't inadvertently interact with it in Windows Explorer, for example. An operating system cannot generally see file systems that are foreign to it, so a partition might not be visible or accessible from a given operating system even though the partition is not officially marked as hidden. For example, Windows NT 3.x and 4.x can't see a FAT32 partition (for more information on file systems, see Chapter 20, "Upgrading Your Operating System").

Before you decide to start carving out partitions, be very aware that certain operating systems require that their host partitions physically start within so many gigabytes of the beginning of the disk. For example, Windows 95, Windows 98, Windows 2000, and Linux have a boot code boundary of 8GB, whereas the limit for Windows NT is 2GB.

Installing PartitionMagic and BootMagic

CAUTION

REPEAT: THIS CHAPTER ASSUMES YOU'VE INSTALLED PARTITIONMAGIC

This note repeats what another cautionary note similar to it said earlier in this chapter. We assume that you have already purchased and installed a copy of PartitionMagic. *If you're new to disk partitioning, we recommend you use only a partitioning tool such as PartitionMagic to perform the tasks described in this chapter and not use the MS-DOS command* FDISK. Even folks who use FDISK regularly do so very gingerly. Be kind to yourself: Use a third-party partitioning tool for these delicate tasks.

PartitionMagic and BootMagic have very well-behaved setup programs. However, here are some valuable tips to make your first encounter with these applications even smoother:

1. Verify that your start disk is fully operational.

2. Perform a backup before installing these programs because you're going to be using them shortly to modify your hard disk's partition structure. You also should defragment the hard disk you'll be repartitioning (using the built-in Windows Disk Defragmenter utility).

3. If you're not familiar with disk partitioning concepts, or if you are but this is your first time using PartitionMagic and BootMagic, read their user's guides carefully before proceeding.

4. Unless you're severely space-constrained, install all the PartitionMagic tools along with BootMagic. We predict you'll find them immensely useful, and if not then you can easily remove them later.

5. If you have earlier versions of PartitionMagic or BootMagic already installed, allow the setup program to remove them (it will prompt you about this).

6. After PartitionMagic is installed, if you have several physical hard disks and don't want one or more of them to be operated on by PartitionMagic, you can tell it to consider a disk read-only. Select General, Preferences, and check the appropriate entry in the Set as Read-Only for PartitionMagic list; then click OK, as shown in Figure 22.1.

NOTE

BECOMING FAMILIAR WITH PARTITIONMAGIC'S USER INTERFACE

If you're new to PartitionMagic and just want to play around with the interface without placing your drive at risk, activate the read-only switch. Select General, Preferences, and check the appropriate entry in the Set as Read-Only for PartitionMagic list; then click OK, as shown in Figure 22.1. This works just fine even if you have only one hard disk. Later, when you're ready to effect a change to your disk, simply clear that checkbox.

FIGURE 22.1

As a safety pre-caution against unintended or unauthorized changes, you can tell PartitionMagic not to operate on a specific hard disk.

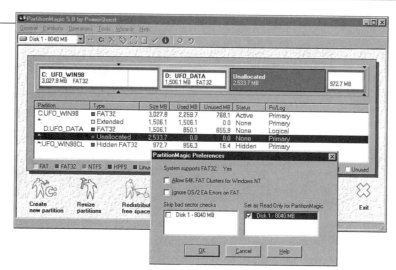

7. During setup when PartitionMagic and BootMagic prompt you to create rescue disks (two for PartitionMagic and one for BootMagic), *you absolutely should do so.* It is critical that you have these disks on hand immediately. You might need them yourself at any time; furthermore, if you contact PowerQuest's technical support staff, the user's guide warns that they might not be able to help you if you haven't created these disks.

CHOOSING A WAY TO CREATE PARTITIONS

You can run many of PartitionMagic's functions either as Wizards or as traditional menu commands. For example, Figure 22.2 shows the Create New Partition wizard and Figure 22.3 shows the dialog box that appears when you select any unallocated space and then choose Operations, Create.

FIGURE 22.2

PartitionMagic's Create New Partition wizard walks you through the steps of creating a new partition.

FIGURE 22.3

You also can create a partition using PartitionMagic's classic command interface.

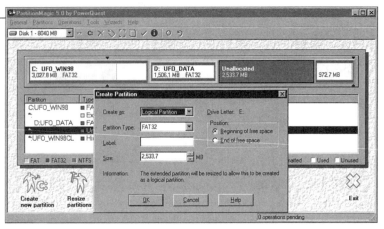

Case Studies

The goal of the following sections is to give you some real-world cases in which multiple partitions and multibooting are put to use. You might find that your own partitioning preferences are different, but if you study these cases, you'll see how to apply the tools to real situations. Then, you'll be able to apply what you learn to your own requirements.

Cloning a Known-Good Bootable Partition and Hiding It

This case study assumes your hard disk is currently configured as a single partition and that the current OS is Windows 98. (For information on configuring a data-only partition, see the section "Implementing a Data-Only Partition.")

1. Start PartitionMagic.

2. Resize the current primary partition (we'll refer to this as PRIMARY-1 for "Primary Partition #1") to half the size of the physical disk (see Figure 22.4).

NOTE

REDUCING PRIMARY-1

You don't have to follow this "reduce to half" step religiously. You can reduce PRIMARY-1's size down to enough space to cover its current state—the OS, applications, and data—and a matching amount of free space. Say you have a 20GB disk, your OS/apps/data use 4GB now, so multiply 4 by 2 to get 8GB. Resize PRIMARY-1 from 20GB to 8GB so it has roughly equal amounts of used and free space.

FIGURE 22.4

Reduce the size of your existing, active primary partition to make room for a new partition.

3. Create a new primary partition.

In PartitionMagic's main window, select PRIMARY-1 and choose Operations, Copy. PartitionMagic automatically sets the copy destination to the unallocated space to the right of PRIMARY-1 (see Figure 22.5). Click OK to begin. This creates a new, hidden primary partition that we'll refer to as PRIMARY-2 (for "Primary Partition #2") even though, when it is first created, it has the same label as its source—PRIMARY-1. PartitionMagic creates the new primary partition as hidden to protect you. Keeping nonactive primary partitions hidden helps prevent them from being accidentally used or tampered with. You can change this attribute if you want (select the partition, and choose Operations, Advanced, Unhide Partition).

Select the second primary partition (the rightmost partition in PartitionMagic's main window); choose Operations, Label; type in a new label, **PRIMARY-2**; and click OK. Note that PartitionMagic queues up some of these operations for processing in DOS mode, so be prepared in the next step to have the program take you there.

FIGURE 22.5

When you copy a partition, you must tell PartitionMagic the destination; here it's the unallocated space to the right of the existing, active primary partition.

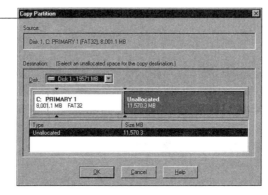

4. Exit PartitionMagic.

PartitionMagic now boots itself into DOS and actually effects the copy operation. When it is done, it reboots your PC back into the originally active partition, PRIMARY-1.

NOTE

APPLYING CHANGES IN PARTITIONMAGIC

After you have one or more actions queued up for PartitionMagic to process, you can apply them by clicking the Apply Changes button, choosing General, Apply Changes from the menu, or exiting PartitionMagic (you'll be prompted to apply or discard changes).

5. Run BootMagic Configuration.

   The program gives you the following message: `BootMagic is currently installed on more than one partition. To fix this problem, insert the BootMagic rescue diskette, reboot your computer, and follow the instructions on the screen.` This is normal. (You can avoid this scenario if you don't install BootMagic on PRIMARY-1 before you clone it, but then you'll have to remember to install it after the cloning process.) BootMagic runs PQBoot in DOS mode and lists the partitions containing BootMagic. They are listed by ID number (1, 2, and so on), and you can see their Volumes (labels), Types (FAT, FAT32, NTFS, and so on), Status (Primary, Logical, and so on), Visible (Yes/No), and Size in MB. Choose the partition on which you want to keep BootMagic active (in this example, select ID 1 Should Be Shown as PRIMARY-1). Next, you see a DOS-based GUI of BootMagic's configuration dialog box; all you should do here is click the Save/Exit button. Now, you're back at a DOS prompt, so remove the rescue disk and reboot (BootMagic knows that PRIMARY-1 was the active partition so it takes you back there automatically).

   Results: PRIMARY-1 is your active partition; PRIMARY-2 is hidden from PRIMARY-1 (test this for yourself in Windows Explorer); and PRIMARY-2 is not on BootMagic's boot list because you—purposefully—haven't put it there.

6. If you don't want BootMagic to control your boot operations (and at this point you don't), you should run BootMagic Configuration, clear the BootMagic Enabled checkbox and click Save/Exit. From this point on, until you re-enable it, BootMagic won't control your PC's boot operations.

Cloning a Known-Good Bootable Partition and Using It

This case study assumes your hard disk is currently configured as a single partition and that the current OS is Windows 98. This scenario enables you to safely test beta software or perform hardware troubleshooting on a second partition while having a reliable production partition to use for normal work.

A few important differences exist between a clone that's for safekeeping only, as discussed previously, versus one that you intend to use. Follow these steps:

1. Follow all the steps in the previous section, "Cloning a Known-Good Bootable Partition and Hiding It."

2. Enable BootMagic.

   Run BootMagic Configuration and check the BootMagic Enabled checkbox.

3. Add the cloned operating system to the boot menu.

   Click Add, select the cloned OS, click OK, and click Save/Exit. You might also want to set other BootMagic preferences at this point, such as a default OS, how long the countdown timer should run (if at all), and so on (see Figure 22.6). Consult your BootMagic user's guide or help file for more information.

FIGURE 22.6

Click the BootMagic Configuration dialog box's Add button to access the BootMagic Add OS dialog box (shown here). This is where you add an operating system to your boot menu list.

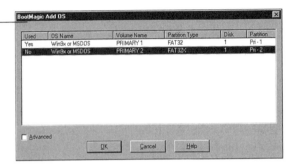

4. Reboot your PC.

   The BootMagic menu appears. Select the desired operating system and verify that it works as expected.

5. Reboot your PC again.

   When the BootMagic menu appears, boot into the other operating system (the one you didn't boot into in step 4) and verify that it works as expected.

TIP

HOW TO KEEP YOUR MULTIPLE OPERATING SYSTEMS STRAIGHT AFTER YOU'RE AT THE WINDOWS DESKTOP

You can do this several ways, but here are two we fancy. If the two operating systems are different then skip this tip. If they are the same, you can change the desktop's background color (or theme or bitmap, you get the idea) on one versus the other. Also, you can create an empty folder in each partition's root drive and name it Z_<something>, and then copy it as a shortcut to the desktop. Now you can quickly glance at the last desktop folder icon's label and see which OS you're running (assuming you alpha-sort your desktop icons). For example, in the case we've been discussing, you might use the names Z_WIN98 on PRIMARY-1 and Z_WIN98_BETA on PRIMARY-2.

Implementing a Data-Only Partition

This case study assumes your hard disk is currently organized into two primary partitions, PRIMARY-1 and PRIMARY-2, and that Windows 98 is the OS in both. If you ever want to run Windows NT (3.x or 4.x) or a version of Windows 95 prior to OEM SR2 on this PC and have it read/write data on your data partition, you should create the data partition as FAT—not FAT32. However, as mentioned in Chapter 20, Windows 2000 supports FAT and FAT32. Follow these steps:

1. Follow all the steps in the previous section "Cloning a Known-Good Bootable Partition and Using It."

2. Boot your PC into PRIMARY-1.

3. Create an extended partition to host the data partition.

   Start PartitionMagic and select the unallocated space to the right of PRIMARY-2. Choose Operations, Create, and in the Create Partition dialog box, make these selections: Logical Partition in the Create As control; FAT32 in the Partition Type control. Enter **DATA** in the Label field; make sure

ANOTHER FINE MESS
PITFALLS OF RUNNING DIFFERENT OPERATING SYSTEMS ON ONE PC

What we are warning you about here is not running two instances of the same operating system on one PC, but two different operating systems on one PC. For example, Windows 98 and Windows NT.

Running different operating systems on the same hardware can cause problems if, for example, a certain peripheral on your computer has good solid drivers that enable it to work well with one operating system but that might not be supported at all under another. If you install a program on your PC, you must install it twice if you expect it to be available under both operating systems. In many cases, you'll need to purchase different versions of the same programs to run them under various operating systems. Windows 2000 is a good example of this phenomenon.

If you are running multiple operating systems on the same physical drive in different partitions and anything happens to the drive, you lose not just one but multiple operating systems. This can make recovering from a disk crash much more involved than if the PC used only one OS.

Finally, there's the issue of sharing data between the various operating systems. This can be very difficult and assumes a common file system format so the different operating systems can access a common data partition (a partition that each of the bootable partitions can see when they are active). Then, you must have versions of your core applications that work properly under each operating system; otherwise, there won't be any applications to manipulate the common data on the data partition.

Despite these caveats, we highly recommend multi-booting and have done so with all our personal and work PCs for many years, always to our benefit. ■

Position is set to Beginning of Free Space (the default); select the desired size (in this example, 4MB); and click OK. PartitionMagic now creates two partitions—one extended partition serves as a host for this (or other) logical partition, and one logical partition is used as your data partition. The logical partition is drive D: (an extended partition itself never has a drive letter). In this case, the logical partition is as large as its host extended partition, but you can, as described earlier in this chapter, create and maintain several logical partitions within one extended partition.

4. Exit PartitionMagic.

   PartitionMagic finishes these queued operations without needing to exit to DOS and reboot.

5. Reboot your PC.

   Although this isn't mandatory, your OS might not immediately recognize the new drive letter. Therefore, we recommend you reboot at this time. You now have access to a C: drive (PRIMARY-1 or PRIMARY-2, depending on which you boot into) and a D: drive (DATA).

NOTE

DUAL-BOOTING WINDOWS 98 AND WINDOWS 2000
We cover this scenario in Chapter 20 during a discussion of performing a clean install of Windows 2000 on a system that's already running Windows 95/98, while preserving the existing Win95/98 partition.

NOTE

OPERATING SYSTEMS SUPPORTED BY BOOTMAGIC 2.0
The following OSs are supported by BootMagic 2.0:

- Windows 95
- Windows 98
- Windows NT 3.51 and 4.0
- Windows 2000
- Windows 3.x (must be installed with DOS 5 or later)
- MS-DOS 5.0 or later
- PC-DOS 6.1 or later

- Open DOS

- OS/2 2.0 or later

- Linux

- BeOS

- Most other versions of DOS

- Some other PC-compatible operating systems

Additional PartitionMagic Tools

PartitionMagic's claim to fame is certainly its outstanding partitioning utility, but it also includes in the box some very handy ancillary tools that make using your partitions easier:

■ **DriveMapper**—One problem with using partitioning tools to hide, unhide, create, and delete partitions is the effect these actions can have on assigned drive letters. Drive letters are assigned in sequence when the system starts up, with the first active partition becoming the C: drive. If you change the sequence of partitions, you can cause drive letters to change. This can throw the Windows Registry for a real loop. If you're using Windows NT or Windows 2000, you can permanently assign drive letters to your partitions (Operation, Advanced, Change Drive Letter). But if you're using Windows 9x, you can use the DriveMapper utility to lock in your drive letter assignments (assuming you have only FAT or FAT32 partitions and have no more than one CD-ROM drive and one removable drive).

■ **MagicMover**—If you remember fondly the good old days when you could relocate an application by simply moving its folder to a new partition or physical drive, you'll love MagicMover. Nowadays, with everything being logged deep into the Windows Registry, moving an application folder usually results in an unusable application. But MagicMover moves application folders and automatically changes every reference throughout Windows to the new drive/path location. Shortcuts, menus, everything automatically knows the new home of your program.

■ **PartitionInfo**—This is a disk diagnostic tool you might find helpful if you're having problems with a drive or partition. To run it, select Start, Programs, PowerQuest PartitionMagic 5.0, PartitionInfo (see Figure 22.7).

FIGURE 22.7

PartitionInfo generates a detailed onscreen report of disk geometry, along with disk and partition errors. The report can be saved to disk or printed.

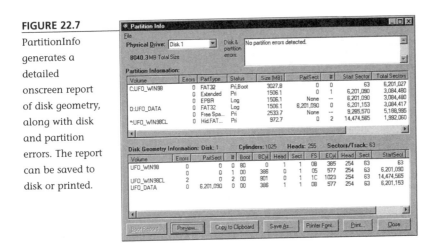

Online Resources

We've used PartitionMagic in our examples because it's a utility we've used for many years and can therefore wholeheartedly recommend.

The PowerQuest Web site contains a number of technical support information pages:

- PowerQuest Technical Support

  http://www.partitionmagic.com/support/index.html

- PowerQuest Technical Support—General FAQ

  http://www.partitionmagic.com/support/PM-faq.html

- PowerQuest Technical Support—Technical FAQ

  http://www.partitionmagic.com/support/PM-faqt.html

V Communications makes System Commander, a product we've used in the past (although less so than PartitionMagic). It worked well for us when we did use it, and it has garnered critical acclaim from the trade press. The System Commander folks have recently come out with a product called Partition Commander, which we've not used ourselves, but it looks very promising. It comes with a personal version of System Commander to handle any boot management needs:

http://www.partitioncommander.com

Quarterdeck made a product called Partition-It, but because Symantec acquired Quarterdeck, that product has not been upgraded in some time. Although the commercial favorites are PartitionMagic and Partition Commander, freeware and shareware versions of partitioning utilities are available on the Internet, as well. However, as a general rule, we would not recommend them because PowerQuest and V Communications have such a well-established customer base and track record.

23

TROUBLE-SHOOTING HARDWARE AND SOFTWARE PROBLEMS

*D*espite best efforts, sometimes an upgrade does not go as planned. When you run into a problem with an upgrade, don't panic and immediately call technical support. Instead, take a deep breath and spend a little time tinkering first. The problem is most likely one that you can diagnose yourself using the checklists and suggestions in this chapter. Should you run into something that you cannot fix yourself, you can still narrow down the possibilities regarding where the problem is and be better able to discuss the problem with a qualified technician should the need arise. Before you pick up the phone, surf the Web, or take your system into a repair center for an answer, try the troubleshooting procedures described in this chapter. These procedures will save you aggravation aplenty.

Upgrade Checklist

1. Double-check each upgrade step to see whether you missed anything obvious, such as an unplugged cable.

2. Review the documentation that came with the upgrade component to verify you did not omit a step or miss a jumper setting.

3. Back up everything: data, operating system, mission-critical applications, and BIOS. Do not back up over your prior backup. Create a new set of backup files.

4. Organize your tools and work space. See Chapter 3, "Things You Need."

5. Troubleshoot the upgrade.

6. Take good notes, and permanently file them in your system log when finished.

7. Update your inventory documentation to reflect the upgraded or newly added component.

System Triage

The good thing about computers is that they have very few moving parts and on the whole, if they start out working okay from day one, they tend to continue working without problems. (Note we said *tend*.) But problems do arise, especially after an upgrade of either hardware or software. When you encounter a problem, you need to determine its severity and its cause. Is the problem one you can troubleshoot and quickly remedy yourself, or do you need to escalate to some form of technical support?

Hardware or Software?

One of the first things you'll want to determine is whether your problem is software or hardware related. It's not always as clear cut as it might sound.

If you've just installed a new video card and suddenly applications are crashing, you might assume that you have a hardware problem and that the graphics adapter is the culprit. But the hardware might be fine while the software for the adapter, the video driver, might be the true cause of the problem. Keep an open mind when you encounter a problem and don't automatically assume the fault is with either hardware or software without some due consideration.

The graphics adapter might have a compatibility problem with Microsoft's DirectX drivers. A driver upgrade might be the solution to what at first appears to be a hardware problem.

General Software Troubleshooting Procedures

Here is a list of things you can try to troubleshoot and resolve for software problems following an upgrade. However, before you start troubleshooting, you must decide whether the nature of the problem you're encountering is serious enough to put your data in jeopardy. A complete backup of all your data is something you want to consider early whenever your computer starts acting up. Try these troubleshooting steps:

- *Make sure you have a current, functional Windows Startup disk (you already should have done this prior to performing any upgrade to your system).* If you haven't yet created a Windows Startup Disk, grab a blank floppy disk and click Start, Settings, Control Panel, Add/Remove Program, click the Startup Disk tab, and then click Create Disk. Have some blank, preformatted 3 1/2-inch disks handy as well.

- *Don't panic.* If you get a GPF (general protection fault) or any other system-level error message, try shutting down all running applications and saving any data as you close the programs. Shut down Windows and then power down the system. Wait several minutes and power up the system. A full shutdown and reboot (called a *cold boot*) forces all files to be closed and all temporary files and buffers to be purged. You might find this fixes a number of transient problems.

TIP

RECOVERING DATA WHEN A GPF HITS

When you get a GPF, any unsaved data in the failed application as of the moment of the GPF is usually lost. But you might be lucky and find that the application that died was writing temporary files and these files might contain some or all of your lost data. Look for

Continued

files with a .tmp extension, usually found in the Windows Temp folder (C:\Windows\Temp) or in the main folder of the application that failed.

■ *If the problem you're experiencing is sporadic and difficult to attribute to a particular application, try running ScanDisk (Start, Programs, Accessories, System Tools, ScanDisk) using its Thorough setting.* Some of your files might have become cross-linked, and ScanDisk can correct that problem. Running Disk Defragmenter (also found on the System Tools menu) is also a good idea.

■ *If you suspect the video driver, try starting Windows in Safe Mode.* Reboot your system and when you see the text Starting Windows appear, press F8. Select the third option, Safe Mode, from the Startup menu. This forces Windows to load a generic 16-bit video driver and resets your screen resolution to 640×480, which is 16 colors. Change your video driver to Standard Display Adapter (VGA) or Super VGA and reboot your computer into normal Windows. If your display problems stabilize, check with your graphics adapter manufacturer to see whether a newer driver is available.

■ *If you're having trouble discerning where in the boot process an error is occurring, start Windows in Safe Mode and select the Logged (\BOOTLOG.txt) start option.* Windows will attempt to boot normally and will record each step it takes, and every driver it loads (marked as successful or failed), to a file in the root folder of your boot drive named BOOTLOG.txt. Examination of this file can shed light on just what is happening when the system fails.

■ *In addition to Safe Mode, you can press F8 at the appropriate time and select Step-by-Step Confirmation mode.* During this mode, Windows prompts you as it processes each of its boot files during startup. Again, this can help you determine where in the boot process the problem is located.

■ *Prevent anything but the operating system from loading.* During the boot process the BIOS loads; then individual peripheral drivers are loaded, and software that has been configured to start automatically at startup loads. A conflict or problem with automatically loaded software could be causing a problem, so this is a good troubleshooting procedure. If this corrects the problem, you can add the autostarted applications back in one at a time to eliminate the one causing the problem. To see which applications are being loaded at boot time, click Start, Run, type **msconfig**, and click OK. Click the Startup tab in the System Configuration Utility dialog box. By unchecking the checkboxes in the displayed list, you can prevent those applications from loading at startup. Also, click the Win.ini tab and expand the Windows folder. Check for files being started via the RUN= or LOAD= lines. If any exist, uncheck the boxes next to them so they won't be started.

Change Video Drivers in Windows 98

1. Right-click the desktop and select Properties from the pop-up dialog box.

2. On the Settings tab, click the Advanced button and then select the Adapter tab.

3. Click the Change button to start the Update Device Driver Wizard.

4. When prompted, tell the Wizard to "Display a list of all the drivers in a specific location...."

5. When prompted, check the box labeled Show All Hardware.

6. Under Manufacturers, select (Standard Display Types) and choose a generic VGA or Super VGA driver as listed on the right.

PLAIN SPEAKING
WHAT DOES SCANDISK SCAN?

ScanDisk checks your hard disk for certain errors and attempts to correct errors it recognizes. ScanDisk can be run in either of two modes: Standard or Thorough. In *Standard* mode, every directory entry on the disk is checked, and ScanDisk attempts to detect and correct any corrupted or invalid filenames, creation or modification dates, and file sizes. ScanDisk checks the File Allocation Table (FAT) and corrects errors where a disk region is neither allocated (used) nor free (unused) or both allocated and free. In *Thorough* mode, every sector (the smallest amount of disk space that can contain data) is tested and, if a sector containing data is deemed bad, ScanDisk tries to recover the data and move it to a good sector. ■

General Hardware Troubleshooting Procedures

Don't overlook the obvious when it comes to troubleshooting a hardware problem that crops up after you've performed an upgrade to your system. Again, if you suspect your data might be at risk, be sure to perform the necessary backups:

■ *Check that all cables were connected (or reconnected) after you performed your upgrade.* Many a journey down the cold, lost rabbit trail of troubleshooting can be saved if you simply check every cable connection. We've been called out to troubleshoot many client problems only to find that the printer cable was never reconnected or another cable had come loose. We've seen dead hard drives come to life when the ribbon cable that was forgotten was finally connected.

■ *Make sure the PC's power cable is plugged into the external AC power source.* If you're using a UPS or surge suppressor power strip, make sure they're functional and that the power is actually turned on.

■ *Check that the red stripe on ribbon cables is matched to pin 1 at both the drive and controller connections (see the pin 1 markings on the back of your drive or consult your owner's manual).* Visually inspect the cable ends and make sure that a pin inside the connector has not become bent. On newer systems, the connectors are notched to ensure you don't connect a ribbon cable backward, but you don't get this safeguard on some older systems.

■ *Make sure the connections are well seated.* This means cables are properly connected and that any adapter cards are properly inserted into their slots. Make sure any RAM modules you've upgraded are properly installed and seated. You might want to remove and reinsert the cards you had out of the system during the upgrade to ensure they're properly seated.

OFF THE WALL
BEEP, I SAY, BEEP!

Excuse me, but your computer is beeping. When you fire up your system and everything is ducky, you hear a single beep (assuming you have an AMI BIOS). You probably don't even notice it, but this single beep is your computer telling you, "I'm fine, thanks for asking." Built into the BIOS of your system are some basic self-diagnostic routines, and the results of the diagnostic process are translated into a number of beeps that your computer makes at bootup. With an AMI BIOS, one beep is good, whereas seven heralds disaster. Sequences with up to eleven beeps let you know what your PC thinks is wrong with it. The Phoenix BIOS uses a series of beeps for each of its diagnostic results. For example, one - pause - four - pause - one indicates that your motherboard is bad. The full list of codes for both AMI and Phoenix can be found on the Hardware Central Web site:

`http://www.hardwarecentral.com/`
`hardwarecentral/tutorials/13/1/`

The Award BIOS is sold to motherboard manufacturers who then are free to customize the BIOS however they want. So, although the beep codes for an Award BIOS generally conform to those described here, at the EFA site, you can count on it. When in doubt, check with the motherboard manufacturer:

`http://www.efacorp.com/support/notes/`
`980216.htm`

You'll find beep code information about a number of lesser-known BIOS makes at Eric's BIOS Post Codes:

`http://www.webenet.net/~ntuser/` ■

- *Verify that all internal devices that require power have a power connector properly plugged in and seated.*

- *Is the fan on the chassis power supply running?* If it isn't and you can verify that the PC is plugged into a power source that is turned on, you might have run into a bad power supply. When a power supply goes out, you don't fix it—you replace it with a new one.

- *Review the map and make sure you didn't miss reconnecting something.* In Chapter 3, we discussed the importance of drawing a map of your chassis's internal layout, noting all the connections and writing down all the steps you made in performing the upgrade. Ditto the notes you put on all the connections. Finally, work through each step you made going backward to see whether you missed something.

ANOTHER FINE MESS
DID IT WORK BEFORE?

It is very easy to start chasing a problem down the wrong path by making quick assumptions. Always go for the obvious first. If you flip the power switch on a computer and absolutely nothing happens, don't assume the computer is dead until you've plugged a table lamp or some other appliance into your power source. A client once called us out to his home to troubleshoot a bizarre problem he had with his new computer. Sometimes the system would work, other times he'd turn it on and get nothing at all, as though it were unplugged. It turned out that he had plugged his power strip into a wall outlet that was controlled by a light switch next to the door. When he turned on the light switch to turn on the lamp in that room, the PC had power. Otherwise, it acted like it was completely dead.

Always check to see that the AC outlet has power before trying to fix a nonexistent problem. Or that a phone jack at that wall is actually connected and provides a dial tone before trying to troubleshoot what appears to be a nonworking modem. ■

Studying Your System Journal for Clues

If you have a system that is working fine and then stops working when you try to upgrade the video card, the problem is fairly easy to pinpoint even if it is not easy to fix. Some kind of problem exists with the card or the card's driver. But, often it's not quite that easy to locate the cause of a problem. You can upgrade something on your system and have everything work fine for a while, only later to start experiencing problems. Worse is when you've made several upgrades before problems surface, making pinpointing the cause of the problem more difficult. Keeping proper records can help you in these situations.

In Chapter 3, we discussed at length the necessity of having a system journal. This is a day-to-day record of everything you do to your computer by way of upgrades, applied patches, service releases, bug fixes, and new software installations. It's also where every little glitch and problem you have with your system is recorded. You note the date and time, the nature of the problem you've encountered, and *exact* error message the system displayed, as well as what you were doing when you had the problem. In Chapter 2, "Preparing for an Upgrade," you learned how to set up and maintain a system inventory where information on all installed components of your computer is compiled. These two pieces of documentation can help you zero in on the malfunction's culprit.

Being able to flip back through the pages of the journal can reveal whether any pattern exists to the problem you're experiencing. If a problem crops up only when you're working with particular programs or devices, some kind of interapplication or interdevice conflict might be occurring. This gives you a logical starting point for focusing your troubleshooting efforts.

The journal also tells you when you last upgraded your system and what the upgrade was. Very often, an upgrade will appear to have gone fine until you start having problems some days later. From your inventory list, you can look up the exact model number (for hardware upgrades) or version number (for software upgrades) of the upgrades you've recently performed.

The system journal should enable you to answer the following questions. The answers to these questions are required whether you troubleshoot the problem yourself or have to resort to technical support of some kind.

Troubleshoot to Determine Whether Professional Help Is Needed

1. Since the last upgrade or change, how long did the system function without problems?

2. When was the first occurrence of the problem?

3. What is the exact text of the error message (if it's in a message box or dialog box, note both the caption text and the interior prompt text)?

4. What other programs were running when you experienced the problem?

5. What task were you performing when you had the problem?

6. How frequently does the problem occur? What day and/or time?

7. Were any upgrades performed on your system prior to the first occurrence of the problem?

If you perform an upgrade on your system and then get an error, the logical candidate for the cause is, of course, the upgrade. However, if a review of the system journal reveals that you've also experienced this problem *prior* to the upgrade, you might want to reconsider.

The inventory you keep on your system should have the exact name, model number, manufacturer, and so on listed for each upgrade you perform on your system. This information is necessary if you must track down new drivers, for example, from the manufacturer's Web site. It's also necessary if you wind up having to call their technical support line.

Common Problems and How to Fix Them

We can't give you the definitive solution for your computer problem because we don't know your system configuration, which upgrade you're performing, and what troublesome symptoms your computer is displaying. But we can touch on some of the more common problems and give you some good ideas about how to troubleshoot them.

Should these basic troubleshooting procedures fail to correct the problem, it's time to get technical support, which is discussed at length in Chapter 24, "Dealing with Technical Support."

Out of Memory Errors

If, while running your applications, you suddenly start getting "insufficient memory" errors, it's probably due to one of three things:

- You actually do need to add more RAM.

- Running software does not release memory back to the system even when it is no longer running (beta software is notorious for this).

- Your hard disk is out of space.

Insufficient memory and errors when attempting to print can point to a lack of free disk space on the drive where the swap file (a file used by Windows that acts as additional RAM) is located. Or, they can be caused by a lack of free space on the drive where print files are spooled before printing. Without enough free room to write files, you can get errors that don't immediately make you think of disk space.

TIP

FREEING UP DISK SPACE

To check free space available on a hard disk, open the My Computer window, right-click the icon for the drive you want to check, and choose Properties from the pop-up menu. You can also do the same thing from the Windows Explorer application: Select the drive, right-click it, and choose Properties. The General tab on the Properties dialog box shows how much of the disk is used space and how much is free space.

If you need to clean out temporary files, Internet cache files, or the Recycle bin, you can use the Windows 98 utility Disk Cleanup. Click Start, Programs, Accessories, System Tools, Disk Cleanup and select the drive you want. Windows generates a listing of the type of files you can have Cleanup remove. Check the boxes representing items you want to get rid of and click OK.

Intermittent Lockups or Sudden Restarts

A system that intermittently freezes or spontaneously reboots itself might be suffering from overheating. Make sure the air intakes are open and that adequate ventilation exists around the system box.

Open up the chassis and dust it out thoroughly (see Chapter 3 for more on breaking down your system and cleaning it). With the chassis open, very carefully power up the system and check to see whether all cooling fans are working properly, including the main fan on the power supply and any fans mounted on peripheral cards.

NOTE

ADDING A FAN

If you've installed heavy-duty multimedia sound and video cards, you also might need to install an extra case fan to deal with the extra heat generated by these surround-sound and 3D visual wonder cards. These cards get so hot that they now require their own heat sinks and fans be mounted right on the cards. Even though those do a fair job of cooling down the card, that extra heat is still in your system case.

A great place to look for the latest and greatest in keeping your system cool is the 3DCool.COM INC site:

`http://www.3dcool.com/`

Another cause of sudden shutdowns and spontaneous reboots can be power fluctuations. This problem and its solution are discussed in some detail in Chapter 10, "Adding Power Protection."

IRQ Conflicts

The shortage of available interrupt requests (IRQs) has caused more problems when upgrading a computer system than all the other potential problems put together. Devices that want to get the attention of the CPU have to do so on an interrupt request line.

If two or more devices try to use the same IRQ, you can experience errors. What's maddening is that you might install a new device and that item works fine, but some other device on your system might start acting up because it's in conflict with the newly added device. This makes troubleshooting all the more difficult.

Another vexing problem is that not all adapter cards will use any IRQ but insist on having a particular IRQ—such as IRQ 5, or either IRQ 5 *or* IRQ 10. These are usually older ISA cards; hopefully you don't have many of these still in use on your system.

Using Windows Device Manager

To see your IRQ assignments and to check for conflicts, you must call up Windows Device Manager:

1. Right-click the My Computer icon on your desktop.

2. Select Properties from the pop-up menu.

3. Click the Device Manager tab.

4. Select the first item in the list, Computer, and make sure the option button View Devices by Type is selected. At this point, you can print a listing of your devices and their IRQ assignments by clicking the Print button. (To see them listed onscreen, click the Properties button.)

5. To see whether any conflicts exist, you must expand each device category in the System Properties dialog box by clicking the small plus symbol (+) for each category (see Figure 23.1).

FIGURE 23.1

Here, each device category has been expanded. Note the exclamation point in the yellow circle on the Creative Labs IDE controller.

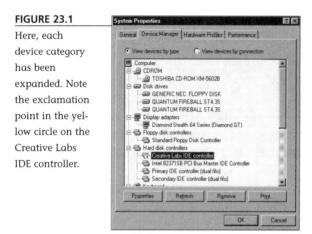

Any conflicting devices should have an exclamation mark inside a yellow circle next to the device name; disabled devices will be marked with a red X. One conflict is noted in Figure 23.1—the Creative Labs IDE controller. This is a good example of how you can't take the information in the System Properties dialog too literally. This system does not have a Creative Labs IDE hard disk controller.

This error cropped up on one of our test systems when we replaced a dead serial mouse with a new PS/2 mouse. The old serial mouse used IRQ 3, and the sound card (from Creative Labs) used IRQ 5. When the PS/2 mouse was installed, it grabbed IRQ 5 and Windows played musical chairs with the remaining IRQs. So, the sound card wound up without an IRQ to call its own. Reassigning the PS/2 mouse to IRQ 12 and putting the sound card back on IRQ 5 resolved the problem.

The heart of the problem with IRQs is that only 16 (numbered 0–15) of them exist on your computer, and a number of them are already assigned to basic system components. Table 23.1 shows how IRQs are initially assigned on most systems.

Table 23.1 Default IRQ Assignments

IRQ Number	Default Assignment
00	System timer
01	Keyboard
02	Redirected
03	COM2 (serial port)
04	COM1 (serial port)
05	LPT2 (parallel port)

Table 23.1 continued	
IRQ Number	**Default Assignment**
06	Floppy disk controller
07	LPT1 (parallel port)
08	CMOS clock
09	Redirected
10	Available
11	Available
12	PS/2 mouse
13	Math coprocessor
14	Primary IDE channel
15	Secondary IDE channel

IRQ 2 is redirected to IRQ 9, so trying to assign both IRQs causes conflicts. If you assign IRQ 2 to a device, it appears to other software as IRQ 9. This is because IRQ 2 is really a conduit for IRQs 8–15, which is just as confusing as it sounds. Newer systems use IRQ 9 for the Plug and Play BIOS, which works and relieves you from trying to figure out whether you can use IRQ 2 at all.

IRQs 1, 2, 6, 8, and 13 are taken by system resources right off the bat. That translates into 9 IRQs available. But consider how fast those 9 IRQs can be used up. On a typical system you have to provide an IRQ for a printer, network card, sound card, modem, mouse, hard disk, and CD or DVD drive. Those 8 devices would leave you with only 1 free IRQ for future upgrades.

Freeing up some IRQs is possible, depending on which devices you are using with your system. If, for example, you are not using any serial devices, you can go into your CMOS setup (see Chapter 4, "Upgrading the BIOS") and disable COM1 and/or COM2 (they might be listed as Serial 1 and Serial 2 in the CMOS administration screen). Disabling one or both serial ports frees up the IRQ it would normally use.

If you're using a serial mouse, you might be able to disable IRQ 12, normally reserved for a PS/2 mouse, and thereby free up that IRQ.

Using Plug and Play (PnP) PCI cards is another way to work around the limited number of available IRQs. In theory, the PCI bus can enable up to four devices to share a single IRQ and manage things so that no more than one device uses an IRQ at a time. In practice, however, this does not always work flawlessly.

Old ISA adapter cards required you to set IRQ numbers using DIP switches mounted right on the card. PnP cards work with the Windows operating system, and between them, they decide on which IRQ should be assigned to which cards. When it works, it's great. When it doesn't work, it's terrible because you can't force a PnP PCI card to use a specific IRQ. You must ensure you are running a current, up-to-date BIOS that fully supports Plug and Play. Poor PnP support at the BIOS level can cause you grief as you try to untangle device conflicts.

TIP

FINDING THE LUCKY PCI SLOT

If you have a PnP PCI adapter card that continually causes IRQ conflicts, try moving it to a different physical PCI slot on the motherboard. Oftentimes, this causes the card to use a different IRQ and thereby resolves the conflict.

To resolve conflicts, select the problem device in the Device Manager list and click the Properties button (see Figure 23.2). Next, click the Resources tab to change the assigned IRQ. Uncheck the Use Automatic Settings checkbox; you can then click the Change Setting button.

FIGURE 23.2

To change settings on the individual device's Resources tab, you must uncheck the Use Automatic Settings checkbox.

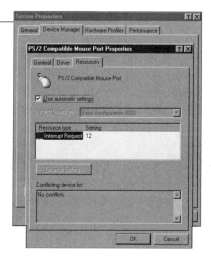

TIP

USB: MANY DEVICES, ONE IRQ

One way to work around the IRQ shortage is to use USB devices wherever possible. The port itself uses only one IRQ. By using hubs to connect multiple devices, you can have many USB peripherals all on a single USB port. The theoretical maximum is 127 devices on a single port.

I/O Address Conflicts

In addition to an IRQ, any device you add to your system requires a block of system memory to call its very own. Some devices require more than one block of memory. Only so many contiguous blocks are available, so once again the potential for a conflict between devices trying to use the same memory block exists.

The device with the conflict will be marked with the exclamation point in Device Manager. Select the device, click the Properties button, and select the Resources tab. Then, select the Memory Range that is in conflict and click the Change Settings button (see Figure 23.3).

FIGURE 23.3

Select a memory range that is not in conflict with any other device.

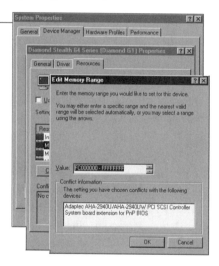

The available memory addresses can be scrolled through so you can find (hopefully) a free block that is not being used by another device.

DMA Channel Conflicts

Newer systems support the use of Direct Memory Access (DMA) channels in which a device can directly access the system memory, bypassing the CPU, which greatly increases the data transfer rate. However, similar to IRQs, a limited number of DMA channels is available, and conflicts can occur when more than one device tries to use the same channel.

To check for DMA conflicts, do the following:

1. Right-click the My Computer icon on your desktop.

2. Select Properties from the pop-up menu.

3. Click the Device Manager tab.

4. Select the first item in the list, Computer, and make sure the option button View Devices by Type is selected. At this point, you can print out a listing of your devices and their DMA assignments by clicking the Print button.

5. Click the Properties button. In the Computer Properties dialog box, check the Direct Access Memory (DMA) option button (see Figure 23.4).

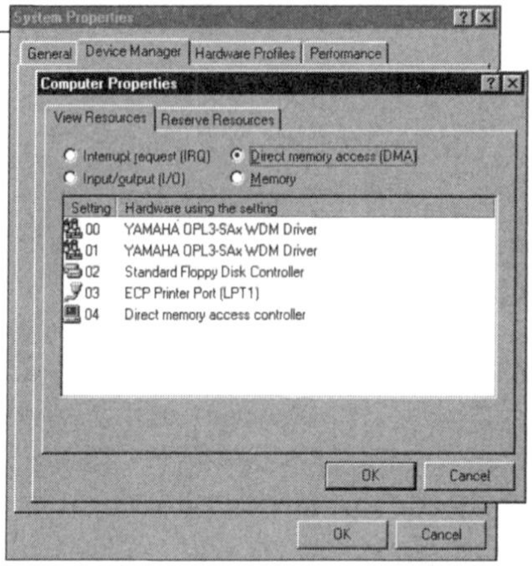

FIGURE 23.4

Devices such as the floppy disk, ECP printer ports, and the DMA controller itself all use channels.

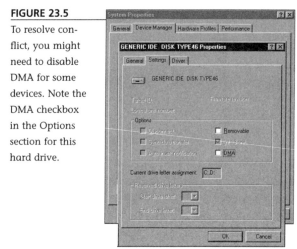

You try to find available channels the same way you do for IRQs: You select the device in Device Manager, click Properties, and click the Resources tab. Some devices will not let you change the DMA channel number. Enable or disable DMA usage for hard drives by selecting the drive in Device Manager, clicking Properties, selecting the Settings tab, and checking or unchecking the DMA checkbox option (see Figure 23.5).

FIGURE 23.5

To resolve conflict, you might need to disable DMA for some devices. Note the DMA checkbox in the Options section for this hard drive.

Adapter Card Problems

Should you pop in a new peripheral adapter card and that card does not seem to be recognized by the system, try moving the card to a different slot. This sometimes helps Windows recognize a card and get it properly assigned to a free or PCI shared IRQ address.

If you're upgrading to an AGP graphics card, note that it will fit into only the AGP slot on the motherboard. Trying to force it into a PCI or ISA slot will damage the card, the slot, or both. The AGP slot is usually closest to the CPU on the motherboard.

If it's a card that has seen prior use, you might need to clean the *contacts*, which are the metal tabs that extend down the part of the card that goes into the slot on the motherboard. You can clean these contact points with a cotton swab dipped in alcohol. Be gentle and make sure you leave no cotton bits on the card. Older ISA cards can get so tarnished that you might have to take a new pencil eraser and gently scrub them. Be careful that no eraser bits remain on the card when you reinsert it into the PC (gently dust-bust it before reinserting it).

When you install a new adapter card, you usually install an appropriate driver as well. Chances are good that the Windows hardware wizard will have a driver for the card right on the Windows CD. However, if your peripheral card came with a disk or CD of its own, it generally contains a more current driver. To get the absolutely latest driver for your new device, stop by the manufacturer's Web site and download the latest version (if one is available). A word of caution, though—don't use drivers the manufacturer has listed as "beta" unless you have no other choice. No sense in going looking for trouble.

Printer Won't Print

As we've mentioned several times already, check the obvious. The first thing to be done is determine whether the printer itself is working properly.

Checking the Obvious

1. Does the printer have power? Is the Ready light on? Most printers have a light or other indicator that comes on when a problem exists with the printer. Check for this and refer to your printer's documentation to see what any error code means.

2. Make sure the printer cable is well seated at both the printer and PC connections. Make sure you're using the right cable. For example, if you need a bidirectional cable, ensure it supports the IEEE 1284 standard (see Chapter 13, "Printer Upgrades").

3. Verify the printer is not jammed with paper and that the paper tray is not empty.

4. Turn off the power on the printer to clear its memory buffer. After five seconds, turn on the printer and see whether this corrects the problem.

5. Run the printer self test (see your printer's documentation on how to perform this test).

Printers are often good at letting you know what problem they're having internally by displaying an error code number or a sequence of lights. The printer manual that came with your printer usually has a section that deciphers the error codes so you can determine the best way to correct the problem.

If the printer passes the self test, the printer itself is probably not the problem. Next, you must check things out on the computer side.

Printer Is Fine; Now Check the Computer

1. Check to see that the hard disk to which applications are spooling the print job has adequate free space. This is usually C:\Windows\Temp, unless you've defined a specific temp folder in the Autoexec.bat file with a line such as TEMP=D:\Temp.

2. Go into Windows Device Manager and expand the Ports (COM & LPT) category.

3. Select the Printer Port (LPT1) device (or the port you have your printer connected to) and click the Properties button.

4. Confirm that under Device status no conflicts are reported. It should read This device is working properly (see Figure 23.6).

5. If an IRQ or other conflict exists, click the Resources tab and make the necessary changes to resolve the conflict. You probably have to uncheck the Use Automatic Settings checkbox to make changes to IRQ or I/O (memory block) settings.

6. Check with the manufacturer's Web site for a more current printer driver or technical bulletins for your model printer. Download the newer driver if one exists. If a newer driver is not available, you should try reinstalling the printer using the driver you already have.

7. Click Start, Settings, Printer and delete the icon for the installed printer.

FIGURE 23.6

Device Manager Properties should show no conflicts for the printer port.

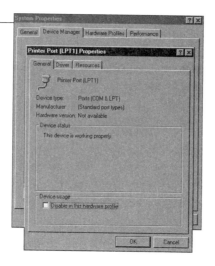

8. Double-click Add Printer; this starts the Add Printer Wizard. Install your printer using the new driver.

PRINT DIRECTLY TO THE PRINTER

The purpose of print spooling is to free up the application sooner so you can start working with it again. The application sends the print job to disk, and you regain use of the application while the print job goes from disk to the printer. That's why in Microsoft Word you print out a huge document and are able to exit the document and shut down Word while pages are still coming out of the printer.

If your printer is physically connected to your computer (you're not using a networked or shared printer connected to someone else's computer), you can bypass print spooling. This is very useful if you're short on hard disk space and print large files. The tradeoff is that your application is tied up longer while it prints the job.

Click Start, Settings, Printers. Right-click the printer you want, and select Properties on the pop-up menu. Click the Details tab and then click Spool Settings. Select the Print Directly to the Printer option button and click OK.

ONLINE PRINTING TROUBLESHOOTERS

Microsoft has posted a troubleshooter on its Web site designed to resolve problems when printing from the Windows operating system. By clicking the problem you are having, MS offers possible solutions. It's available at

```
http://support.microsoft.com/support/windows/tshoot/printing98/
default.asp
```

Continued

Hewlett-Packard also has printer problem information posted on its Web site. You select the type of printer, make, and exact version from drop-down lists. The results include care and maintenance information, drivers, and other downloads for your printer, along with step-by-step instructions on how to resolve common problems. You can find it at

`http://www.hp.com/cposupport/jsnav/prhome.html`

Hard Disk Problems

Hard disks are the main component in your system that have moving parts, which makes them more susceptible to failure than other parts of your system. They are also very fragile. If you drop your hard disk while installing it, you do it permanent damage—so be very careful when performing hard disk upgrades.

When you're performing a hard disk upgrade and you're having a problem, try the following procedure first:

Difficulty with a Hard Disk Upgrade

1. Verify that the drive is mounted properly in the drive bay/cage. See Chapter 7, "Upgrading the Hard Disk."

2. Check to see that the power connector is plugged in and properly seated.

3. Verify the ribbon cable is connected to the drive and that the red-striped edge is connected to the drive connector at pin 1. This is usually on the same side of the connector as the power connector is located.

4. Check the drive for proper configuration.

   For EIDE drives, check to see that the other end of the ribbon cable is properly connected to the EIDE connector on the motherboard. Usually, two EIDE connectors exist, so make sure the drive is on the channel (primary or secondary) it's supposed to be on.

   Ensure that the EIDE drive is properly configured as master, slave, or Cable Select as dictated by your configuration.

   For SCSI drives, check to see that the other end of the ribbon cable is properly connected to the SCSI controller (usually an add-in card unless the motherboard supports SCSI directly).

   In addition, for SCSI drives, make sure the drive has been assigned a unique number and that it has the proper termination depending on its position in the SCSI chain (see Chapter 7).

If you've verified that the drive is physically installed correctly, you next must check to see whether the drive controller is recognizing the drive. Boot the system and enter the CMOS program (see Chapter 4, "Upgrading the BIOS"). For EIDE systems, the CMOS should be set by default to autodetect any EIDE devices on the two EIDE channels. If no drive information is shown (things such as drive type, drive size, number of cylinders,

> ### PLAIN SPEAKING
> #### BOOT-TIME ERROR MESSAGES
> Trying to decipher the various errors you can get when you boot up a hard disk is not easy. Fortunately, a Web resource exists that lists all the common error messages you might run into, with a detailed explanation and a recommendation on a course of action to take to correct the problem:
>
> `http://www.pcguide.com/ts/x/comp/hdd/`
> `fail_Failure.htm` ■

and so on), see whether the CMOS supports a manual detection process. This is run from the CMOS setup program and forces the BIOS to try to detect any drives. If you still cannot get the CMOS to recognize the installed drive, the drive itself might be bad and require replacement.

If the system is SCSI, run the SCSI setup program. This is a program similar to the CMOS setup program and is run by pressing a key combination at a certain point during bootup. See the documentation that came with your SCSI controller card to learn how to access this utility. See whether the setup program recognizes the drive. Diagnostic utilities might be available in the SCSI setup utility that can help determine the cause of the problem you're experiencing. You should verify that the entire SCSI chain is properly configured, that all ID numbers are unique, and that the end of the chain is properly terminated (and that it's not terminated anywhere else).

If the hard disk is recognized by the controller, the problem is most likely one of preparation or software.

Verify that the hard disk has been properly prepared with the FDISK utility and that it has been formatted. Check to see that the proper partitions have been created and that, if the drive is to be bootable, the first partition has been made active. You also must check that the drive has had the proper system files copied to it (see Chapter 7).

Misbehaving Device Driver

When you go into Windows after having installed a new device, Windows should automatically run its Add New Hardware Wizard. If it doesn't then you must run it yourself (Start, Settings, Control Panel, Add New Hardware) to get Windows to recognize the new device.

When the Add New Hardware Wizard asks whether you want Windows to search for new hardware, select No, I Want to Select the Hardware from a List. Then, select the hardware type.

You should have gotten a driver with your new device, either on a 3 1/2-inch disk or CD-ROM disc. Or, you might have downloaded the latest driver from the Internet (we always recommend you get the latest driver when performing an upgrade). Click the Have Disk button and use this newer driver, as opposed to using the drivers that came with Windows (see Figure 23.7).

FIGURE 23.7

You should always use the latest driver available (not including beta releases of drivers) when installing new hardware.

When a piece of software crashes with a GPF, you often get the name of the DLL that died and a cryptic error code to indicate what went wrong. A useful utility is available for Windows 95/98, called DLLShow (shareware), that displays all currently running applications:

`http://www.gregorybraun.com/DLLShow.html`

Select an application in the upper window and all the DLLs that the application is subject to call on are displayed in the lower window (see Figure 23.8).

FIGURE 23.8

DLLShow will let you see all the DLLs accessed by a given running application.

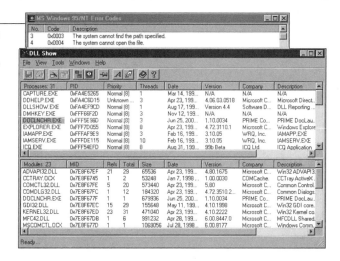

DLLShow gives you detailed information about the version number and who wrote the DLL. It also shows you where it is on your hard disk. Another nifty feature is a list of error codes and their English-language equivalents. When you get a GPF with an obscure error code, such as 0x000F, you can look it up in DDLShow to see what it actually means (see Figure 23.9).

FIGURE 23.9

Track down the meaning of the oddball error codes you get with a GPF in DLLShow.

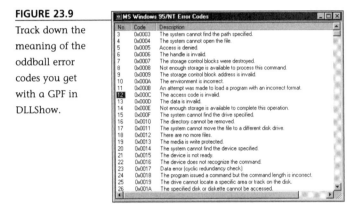

Troubleshooting with Windows Troubleshooting Wizards

Windows 98, Windows Millennium Edition, and Windows 2000 provide built-in troubleshooting help topics that can walk you through a series of questions on a given subject. As you select the answers that describe your problem, the troubleshooter tries to come up with the solution (see Figure 23.10).

FIGURE 23.10

The Windows help system has troubleshooters that try to resolve problems with a number of devices and programs.

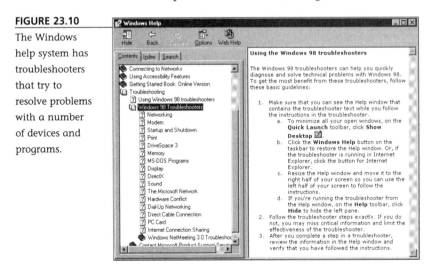

To access these troubleshooters, do the following:

1. Click Start.

2. Select Help.

3. Select the Contents pane.

4. The last entry on the Contents list is Troubleshooting. Double-click this entry to expand the topic.

5. Select the device or process that is causing you trouble and follow the steps/questions that appear in the right pane of the Help window.

If you're using Windows 95, you can still access the Microsoft Troubleshooting help, but you have to do so from the Microsoft Web site:
`http://support.microsoft.com/support/tshoot/default.asp`

These troubleshooters are fairly basic but are worth a try when diagnosing an upgrade problem.

Restoring Your Registry

Windows keeps track of changes to your system by recording information about hardware and software in the Registry. If an upgrade goes bad, it can leave you unable to run Windows. Rolling back to a version of the Registry that predates the upgrade installation is a quick way to restore your system to operation.

Rolling back the Registry won't help you troubleshoot or fix whatever went wrong with your install, but it can get your system operational again.

How to back up and restore the Windows Registry under Windows 95 and 98, Windows Millennium Edition, and Windows 2000 is covered in detail in Chapter 21, "Upgrading Your Applications: Strategies and Advice," in the section titled "Manual Registry Rollback."

Third-party utilities are available that monitor changes to your system and that can help you recover your system from an upgrade gone bad. See Chapter 21's section titled "Third-Party Utilities for Rolling Back."

24

DEALING WITH TECHNICAL SUPPORT

t some point, everyone has to bite the bullet and seek out help from a qualified technical support engineer. If you're desperate enough, you don't really care how qualified the engineer is—you just want someone to suggest something you can try to get your system working again. Before you start waving dead chickens over your monitor and reciting incantations, here's what you need to do to prepare before you hit a Web site or dial the phone looking for help.

Upgrade Checklist

1. Do your homework.

2. Gather as much information about your problem as you can. Write down the exact text of error messages, or the steps you performed that resulted in the problem. Your own initial problem-solving notes should be in your system journal, as should all your notes with the technical support staff. See Chapter 23, "Troubleshooting Hardware and Software Problems."

3. Know the exact hardware involved (name, model number, version number, and so on) and the specifications of the system you're working on when the problem occurs. See Chapter 2, "Preparing for an Upgrade," and Appendix C, "PC Inventory Form," for more information about a PC inventory checklist.

4. Determine the most suitable keywords for Knowledge Base or Web searches to optimally target information related to your problem.

5. If you're using telephone technical support, be sure to take good notes; get the name of the technician; note the date, time, and duration of the call; and get a direct line call-back number first thing in case you get cut off during the call.

6. Do your research and make sure you understand the steps you'll be trying to correct the problem.

7. Perform the troubleshooting steps.

8. Take good notes, and permanently file them in your system log when finished.

Know Thy Problem

In Chapter 23, we covered the methods of figuring out what's gone wrong and what is most likely causing the problem. We'll assume that you've done everything recommended in that chapter to troubleshoot your problem and are now looking for answers in the wild and woolly world of technical support. Whether you're calling a technical support hotline and speaking with someone in real time, are posting questions and follow-ups on a Web-based bulletin board, or are searching knowledge bases and Web sites for information, you'll need to arm yourself with everything you can about your problem before you storm the gates of the technical support fortress. To paraphrase the great military philosopher Sun Tzu, "Know your problem and know your technical support venue and you will be victorious in solving any computer glitch."

Contacting Your PC and Peripheral Manufacturers

In the event that you ever need to contact the manufacturer of your PC—or the maker of one of its component parts—for technical support, the odds are good that you'll save time and frustration if you go straight to the help line phone number or the Web site address found in the manual or other related documentation provided by the manufacturer. That's why it's important that you keep all PC collateral material that comes with each and every component, device, software package, cable, printer, joystick, ad infinitum, or with any upgrade you install on your computer. This includes manuals, 3.5" disks, CDs, instruction sheets, shipping slips, packing slips ... anything that has writing on it.

The best place to keep all this stuff is in your NEAT box, discussed back in Chapter 3, "Things You Need." (See Chapter 3's section "Clear the Clutter.") In a perfect computer world, whenever you need to contact a manufacturer, the phone number, address, or URL would be right there in the documentation, safely within your NEAT box. Of course, we don't live in a perfect computer world, so even if you do have every scrap of paper that came with a peripheral, you might still have to go searching for the contact information for a given component.

Finding a Software or Peripheral Manufacturer

If all you have is a company name or a component description—such as the model name of a motherboard, for example—then some searching on the Internet is called for. You can try a number of places. Sometimes, just having a driver name can help you track down a component manufacturer by searching for an updated driver for the troublesome device. Try these resources:

- **Guide to Computer Vendors Search Engine**—Lets you search by a company name, a description of the service or goods they produce, or by a category of company types:

  `http://guide.sbanetweb.com/SBA_search.html`

- **Computer Technical Support PC Drivers HeadQuarters**—Although this is a site designed primarily to help you find device drivers, you can get an alphabetical listing of computer hardware manufacturers and links to their Web sites by first selecting the category a driver for the troublesome component falls under:

  `http://www.drivershq.com/main_home.html`

- **Frequently Asked Questions Part 5**—This is the old `comp.sys.ibm.pc.hardware` newsgroup FAQ and, though it's a bit out of date, it's still a good source for tracking down manufacturers of legacy components:

  `http://www.faqs.org/faqs/pc-hardware-faq/part5/`

- **Manufacturers' Technical Support Site**—This About.com site is hosted by Holly Henry-Pilkington and provides direct links to manufacturer technical support sites for a number of computer component and peripheral categories:

  `http://pcsupport.about.com/compute/pcsupport/msubmfrs.htm`

After you find a manufacturer's Web site, it might not be easy to find the right link to reach its online technical support. Look for links labeled as shown in the following list (listed alphabetically) that might appear at the bottom of the main Web site page:

- Contact (and any variations thereof)

- Customer Service

- Feedback

- For More Information

- Help (and any variations thereof)

- Press Room

- Send Email

- Support

- Technical Support

- Webmaster

One of these links might at least lead you to a page where you can ask a question or find a link to the real technical support page. Failing to find anything useful on the Web site, you can try sending an email to the site's base domain name using one of the following addresses. Think of this as email of a last resort:

- feedback@*domain*.com

- info@*domain*.com

- support@*domain*.com

- tech@*domain*.com

- webmaster@*domain*.com

- sales@*domain*.com

Online Support Resources

A tremendous number of resources are available for technical support on the Internet. Most are static listings of tips or solutions to known problems. One of the nice things about online resources like these is that they're available 24 hours a day, 7 days a week. It's amazing how poorly computer problems conform to any type of reasonable working schedule. It's almost a law of nature that as soon as you pick up the telephone to call technical support, you realize that they closed five minutes ago. Try these online support resources:

- **Tom's Hardware Guide**—Technical news and detailed information covering every major component of a computer system, plus a message board, make Tom's a major resource:

  http://www.tomshardware.com/

- **Windows 98 Troubleshooter site**—You drill down through questions about common problems with Windows 98 and hopefully zero in on the solution to your particular problem:

  http://support.microsoft.com/support/windows/tshoot/

- **ZDNet Help and How-To site**—Help on hardware and operating system problems, along with software tips and fixes make this a site worth bookmarking. It also has handy step-by-step and beginner tutorials covering the installation of a number of hardware components:

  http://www.zdnet.com/zdhelp/

- ***Upgrading and Repairing PCs, 12th Edition* Web site**—This is the companion site to Scott Mueller's PC upgrade opus and contains a FAQ, industry updates, and a form to email technical questions directly to Scott. This site also contains streaming video segments:

  `http://www.upgradingandrepairingpcs.com`

- **HelpTalk Online**—A collection of 30+ software and hardware forums where you can post questions and ask for help and advice:

  `http://www.helptalk.com/`

- **Techmommy FAQs**—Basic "what do I do when this happens" collection of questions and answers:

  `http://www.techmommy.com/FAQs.html`

  Techmommy also offers a Talk to the Expert support service; for a small fee ($6.95 last time we checked), you can send in an email question and get a response:

  `http://www.techmommy.com/fee_consultation2.html`

- **Microsoft Technical Support Plans**—A gateway page to the various support sites provided by Microsoft. Some pages are free; some require you to pay for a particular support plan:

  `http://support.microsoft.com/directory/customer.asp`

- **Microsoft Personal Online Support**—Search the Knowledge Base or browse all the available information from this page. Includes links to Maxwell, Microsoft's AskJeeves front end to its Knowledge Base that lets you type in your questions in plain English:

  `http://support.microsoft.com/support/default.asp`

- **Microsoft Personal Support Phone Numbers**—A listing of all the phone numbers available under Microsoft's personal-use support plan. Some lines are available for only 90 days after your first call, but some are unlimited:

  `http://support.microsoft.com/directory/directory/phonepers.asp`

- **Microsoft FAQs by Product**—Microsoft's Frequently Asked Questions pages for specific products. Covers Windows, Office, BackOffice, and Developer categories. A great place to visit to determine whether your problem is a known one and, secondly, whether it has a readily available solution:

  `http://support.microsoft.com/directory/faqs.asp`

■ **Microsoft Expired Warranty Support**—If you had 90-day free support on a purchased Microsoft product and you are past the warranty period, you can call for technical support for a fee of $35 per service request. This service is available 24 hours a day, 7 days a week. When you're pulling your hair out at 3:00 a.m. after having worked on a problem for the last 16 hours, that $35 doesn't look so outrageous:

```
http://support.microsoft.com/directory/directory/exp_warranty.asp
```

Newsgroups and Bulletin Boards

When you call a technical support phone number, you get instant satisfaction because you get to speak with a live human being in real-time (after being on hold for an eternity, of course). Granted, she might not be able to help you solve your problem, but it feels more immediate in terms of getting help than any other technical support venue.

Posting your problem on a newsgroup or bulletin board also puts you in touch with live humans, but in what we call a *delayed correspondence* mode. You don't get spontaneous feedback and you have to work harder to ensure you provide all the relevant information because you don't have a technician on the other end of the conversation willing to sit with you for however long it takes. Also, you have the added hassle of having to go back and check to see whether someone has posted an answer to your question.

However, the support you can find on newsgroups and bulletin boards can make up for the lack of immediacy. Plenty of smart people are willing to help you with your problem if you ask nicely and provide the information they need. And, you can post to every relevant newsgroup and bulletin board you can find to increase the likelihood of finding someone who can help resolve your problem. Plus, newsgroup advice is *free*.

Newsgroups

Newsgroups are Internet special interest groups that act like bulletin boards. Newsgroups predate Web sites and still have a large following. Newsgroups exist for any topic you can imagine, and they can be a good technical resource for finding answers to computer problems or discussing planned upgrades with other computer users.

Many newsgroups can be accessed via a Web browser through sites such as Deja.com or the newsgroups covering Microsoft products. However, many newsgroups require you to have access to a news server. Your ISP usually provides you with access to a news server as part of your Internet service package.

TIP

NEW TO NEWSGROUPS?

A very good primer on using newsgroups is available on Deja.com:

`http://www.deja.com/info/usenet_faq.shtml`

Information found in newsgroup FAQs is generally of a very high quality. Of course, the usefulness of individual posts on the newsgroups themselves is dependent on who is making the post. On a public newsgroup, anyone can post anything, so you have to be careful and make some judgments as to the quality of posted information. However, some companies host newsgroups for their own products and have technical support people to monitor the posts. On these types of newsgroups, the quality of the information can be excellent. Try these newsgroups:

- **Usenet Newsgroups**—FAQs for All Usenet Newsgroups contains lists of the questions most frequently asked on various Usenet newsgroups. Most of the FAQs listed include pointers to Web sites, books, mailing lists, newsletters, and other helpful information for a given topic. Keep in mind that a FAQ is not the same as accessing the newsgroup itself. Before posting to a newsgroup, always review the associated FAQ to see whether your question/problem is a common one that has already been answered in the FAQ. FAQs will have links to the actual newsgroup at the top of the FAQ, but to access them, you must have a properly installed newsgroup reader (such as Outlook Express or Netscape Communicator) as well as access to a news server to read messages or post messages to a newsgroup:

  `http://www.faqs.org`

- **Search Discussions**—Search Usenet discussions from your browser. You can browse by category or search across all available discussion groups:

  `http://www.deja.com/usenet`

- **Microsoft Newsgroups**—600+ newsgroups covering Microsoft products are available, and you can access them directly from your browser (a newsgroup reader is not required). See Liszt's Usenet Newsgroups Directory for Microsoft newsgroups:

  `http://www.liszt.com/news/microsoft/`

  You can also use the official interface provided by Microsoft to access Microsoft's peer-to-peer newsgroups:

  `http://support.microsoft.com/support/news/`

Bulletin Boards

Web-based bulletin boards are a good resource, however, like newsgroups, they're not as responsive as the telephone technical support. The upside is that you can post to several bulletin boards and thereby increase your chances of getting some help in a hurry.

Keep in mind that you're counting on someone with more knowledge about your problem than you reading your post and then taking the time to answer it. In this regard, a bulletin board is no different from posting to a newsgroup. But some bulletin boards have a very helpful community of technically savvy users who might very well have already solved the problem you're wrestling with.

PLAIN SPEAKING
CALIBER OF NEWSGROUP SUPPORT

Although some manufacturers host and provide support via their own newsgroups, most are not directly supported by the manufacturers of the software or hardware on which the newsgroup focuses. More often, they're what are called *peer-to-peer* support forums, which means the people who answer questions are doing so out of the goodness of their hearts (Microsoft newsgroups fall into this category). (While on the subject, a tip of our hats to all the diligent and knowledgeable Microsoft Most Valuable Professionals—also called *MVPs*—who frequent the Microsoft newsgroups.) Even though they might be grass roots, don't discount this type of support because some of these folks are extremely knowledgeable about the topics they discuss and have experience that can help you out of a sticky spot. However, you do get some postings that, while well meaning, are not terribly well informed. Keep this in mind when using newsgroups as a technical support resource. ■

Post a concise, cogent summary of your problem and any ancillary information—such as the system type, speed, memory, hard disk capacity, BIOS version, and so on—that might have a bearing on the problem. Remember, anyone answering your query is doing so on his own nickel (in other words, for free), and you don't want to make him have to play 20 questions to get enough background information on your problem or your system to help you. Trust us, in these situations, it's much better to give what you think is too much information than too little.

Here are a few general purpose bulletin boards that we've found helpful:

- **The Annoyance Board**—A strong, mutual support community of computer users. Covers a wide variety of topics:

  `http://www.PRIMEConsulting.com/annoyanceboard/`

- **The Cork Board**—Forums on hardware and software, Windows 95/98/NT, and Outlook. Post questions and get answers:

  `http://www.onlinesupport.com/main/corkboard/`

- **CNet Help.Com**—Provides a number of forums where you can post questions and read answers on computer support topics covering both hardware and software. A nice feature is that you can display only messages that have had a response:

  `http://www.help.com/`

As with newsgroups, some companies host Web-based bulletin boards to provide support, both direct and peer-to-peer. Check with the manufacturer of the component to see whether it offers a Web-based bulletin board when you first perform your upgrade. Having this information can help cut the time it takes to get a problem resolved.

Newsletters

Newsletters are not what you'd call a rapid-response type of technical support venue. They're more like regular technical updates and are good for alerting you to known problems with existing or just released software and hardware. Often, you can find an answer to something that has been troubling you in an article or a response to a reader's question. Searching back issues is also a good source of technical support data. Here are some of the computer-oriented newsletters we find worthwhile:

- **The Naked PC (TNPC)**—The format of TNPC is article-based along with high-productivity "favorite reviews" of Web sites, books, FAQs, and hardware/software products, plus current news tidbits blended in for a delicious and informative mix. The newsletter discusses the latest technologies, low-tech solutions to high-tech problems, and tips on the best free or low-cost programs and hardware around. This free bulletin is published every other week by the authors of the book you are holding in your hand right now. (Subscribe today, okay?)

  `http://www.TheNakedPC.com`

- **Neat Net Tricks**—A collection of tips and comments focused on Internet use but also covering general computer problems and tips on resolving them. Published twice a month:

  `http://www.NeatNetTricks.com`

■ **Langa List**—Fred Langa puts out this gem every week. He answers reader questions and talks about the latest and greatest bugs and boons in computerdom:

```
http://www.Langa.com
```

■ **Microsoft free newsletters**—Microsoft offers a number of free informational newsletters. They cover topics ranging from Windows announcements, tips, tricks, and techniques to Office information to TechNew news flashes. Be aware, though, that in their typically innovative style, you must register with the Microsoft site and give them your email address *before* you can even see the list of newsletters to which you can subscribe. After you register, you're dumped back to the main Microsoft page where you have to select Newsletters from the Subscribe pull-down menu option:

```
https://register.microsoft.com/regsys/logon.asp
```

■ **Paul Thurrott's WinInfo newsletter**—This daily newsletter is focused on the latest news and information dealing with the Windows operating systems. Very informative:

```
http://www.wininformant.com/
```

Knowledge Bases

A *knowledge base* is similar to a FAQ that has grown so large it cannot be contained any longer in a single file. With a knowledge base, you have to search among a number of articles to find the ones with information relevant to your current problem.

Probably the best-known knowledge base is the one used by Microsoft and that is made available to users via the Web and as part of a monthly CD subscription to TechNet. This knowledge base started out as a resource used by Microsoft telephone technical support people. This was back in the days when a software company actually did its own technical support and people expected technical support for free. Now, not only is free technical support a thing of the past, but most manufacturers outsource their technical support operation to companies that handle dozens of products from various companies. Try these knowledge bases:

■ **Microsoft Knowledge Base Search**—Microsoft's extensive Knowledge Base of searchable information provides access to white papers, articles, and problem/solutions, covering all their released products:

```
http://search.support.microsoft.com/kb/c.asp
```

MICROSOFT TECHNET: SUPPORT DELIVERED TO YOUR DOOR

For a fee, you can get the Microsoft Knowledge Base delivered right to your door every month by subscribing to TechNet. For $299/year, you get a one-year subscription (delivered on CD or DVD discs) that includes the Knowledge Base as well as information on all Windows products, including copies of service packs and services releases, drivers and patches, technical training material, case studies, reviewers' guides, resources kits, and deployment guides. For an additional $150, you can get TechNet Plus, which adds select beta software releases. Imagine that—you get to pay Microsoft to test their beta software. Seriously, though, if you need early looks at upcoming software and can't qualify for Microsoft's technical beta programs, this might be just the ticket for you:

`http://www.microsoft.com/technet/subscription/about.asp`

- **Indiana University Support Center's Knowledge Base**—This database of computer information is geared toward how computers are used on the university's campus but includes many topics that apply to anyone using a computer:

  `http://www.kb.indiana.edu/`

- **Search 4 AnyThing: Computers**—Not strictly a knowledge base but a Web search engine focused on computer-related information:

  `http://www.4anything.com/4/0,1001,5,00.html`

- **Experts Exchange**—This is another site that is not strictly a knowledge base, but you can ask questions and get answers from volunteer "experts." It's not apparent from the main page, but they do cover a number of hardware topics:

  `http://www.experts-exchange.com`

USING YAHOO! TO FIND KNOWLEDGE BASES

Yahoo! can give you a good list of knowledge bases. Just go to `http://www.yahoo.com` and search for "knowledge base" (including the quotation marks). To narrow it down to computer-related knowledge bases, use this as your search string:

`+"knowledge base" +computer`

Friends and Colleagues

More and more people are installing computers in their homes and home offices. Find out whether anyone you know has or is setting up their own system and performing upgrades. Network (in the social sense) with your friends and colleagues, be they gurus or newbies. Sometimes just explaining the problem you're facing can give you new insights into what the solution might be or something to try that you hadn't thought of before.

NOTE

START YOUR OWN USERS' GROUP

If you decide to enter the big time with your casual group of like-minded computer-ites, you can always start your own formal users' group. All you need is some interested people who want to help out and support each other. A great resource for getting your user group started is called the Association of Person Computer User Groups at

`http://www.apcug.org/`

Searching the Web and Knowledge Bases Effectively

We discussed knowledge bases earlier in this chapter; you can always fall back on the major Web search engines when looking for technical support information. However, effectively searching in a knowledge base or a search engine requires some forethought to ensure you have the best chance of getting back relevant references.

Here are 10 general tips that will help you keep your queries focused when searching for information:

1. *Write down the problem you're having.* The exercise of putting it down on paper helps you organize your thoughts. Focus on keywords that you'd expect to see when reading about your problem.

2. *Check your spelling.* Misspellings waste your time by not producing any returns on your search or by returning items that are not relevant to your query.

3. *Place quotation marks around multiple words and phrases.* Use, for example, "hard drive" or "power supply" so that the search knows the words must be adjacent to one another.

4. *Write down relevant synonyms for each keyword in your search.* Adding synonyms is an easy way to improve the quality of your search results.

5. *Browse through Yahoo!'s categories.* Yahoo!'s categories are professionally categorized, and you might hit on a mother lode of sites targeted to the information you want.

6. *Try your favorite search engine to see whether you can luck into a quick hit that's right on target.* If that fails, try a metasearch engine, such as www.dogpile.com, that performs a general search across several search engines simultaneously.

7. *Study your favorite search engine's syntax.* Although advanced search syntax can be tedious (and annoyingly different from one search engine to another), it's one of the best ways to improve the quality of items returned.

8. *If you keep getting poor results, try reducing the number of keywords in your query to better focus the search.* (Many search engines default to a logical OR if you use more than one keyword in a search. This results in a larger hit list than an AND-ed search expression.) You can also try to build a better Boolean search (see item 7) by using the syntax recommended for advanced searches for the engine you are using.

9. *Use wildcard characters sparingly.* Too many wildcards tend to produce off-target returns.

10. *Know when to quit a dead-end trail.* If you don't find something relevant in the first 20 or 30 returns, don't keep looking through all 200 returns. It's better to rework your query to force the relevant returns to the top than to scan page after page of information that's not what you're looking for.

TIP

SEARCHING THE SEARCH ENGINES

The Internet itself is rife with guidelines on using search engines to effectively search the Internet. Check out an article we wrote for Ziff-Davis called *Search Engine Secrets*; it's all about how to get more out of your Web searches:

http://www.zdnet.com/pccomp/stories/all/0,6605,405202,00.html

Making Phone Sense

Calling a telephone technical support department requires you to do more than be able to endure hours at a time listening to elevator music while on hold. You must be able to explain your problem so the technician on the other end of phone can grasp your situation (remember, she's trying to do this sight unseen, like a blind-folded fortune teller trying to do a cold reading). You have to be able to translate what the technician tells you over the phone into action on your end. And you have to determine whether the problem is being corrected. Follow these guidelines:

1. *Write everything down.* Start with the problem or question you want to ask the technician when she answers the phone. After a 45- or 60-minute wait, you might go blank when she finally picks up the phone. Have a pad of paper handy and something to write with. Remember, if you don't write it down, it never happened. If you can't remember the exact steps the technician gave you, or the URL to the FAQ that answers your question or that has the driver upgrade you need, you have to start all over again.

2. *Get the technical support representative's name and a* direct *call-back number (or his extension) for follow-up calls or in case you get cut off.*

3. *Take notes on every conversation you have with technical support.* Start with the date and time (and how long the call lasted when you're finished). Always get a name. Every piece of information can be priceless later. Jot down everything you can as you go along. Don't be shy about asking the technician to wait a moment while you write something down or to repeat something. Have him spell out URLs, and if possible, try to access them while the technician is still on the phone just to see whether what you wrote down works.

4. *Consider calling back and talking to another technical support representative and seeing whether you get the same answer.* You might be surprised. The third time might even be the charm. If you get a solid answer that sounds very plausible, you probably won't have to go for the second opinion. But, if the fix sounds crazy to you or if you work through the suggested procedures and don't get the results you wanted then a second, and possibly a third, opinion are definitely called for. Try a different engineer just to see whether she offers the same advice as the last one did.

5. *Get (and write down, of course!) the case number, tracking number, or whatever the support person calls the number that identifies the service call/problem you've gener-ated.* Not all support organizations use tracking numbers, but most do so be sure to get it. In the event you have to call back, you might not have to start completely from scratch.

6. *Don't hesitate to escalate to a supervisor if you're dissatisfied for any reason.* If you wind up going back to the technical support person you started with because his suggested fix didn't correct your problem, and he doesn't do any better his second time at bat, insist on talking to a supervisor. Generally, the frontline phone people can handle the simple stuff and a technical support supervisor that can handle the more complex stuff oversees the phone jockeys. You want to talk to the supervisor at this point. When you ask to speak with a supervisor, be nice but firm. Your time is invaluable, and at some point you have to stop the runaround while you ask a question and the phone technician puts you on hold while he asks the supervisor, who tells him, who tells you, and so on. Cut out the middleman.

7. *An angry tone of voice works against you at all times.* No matter how frustrated you are, taking it out on the technical support person is not going to help. And most likely, the technician on the other end of the phone is genuinely trying to help you. But she's working at a disadvantage because first, she can't see the problem for herself, and second, she's not as intimately familiar with it as you are (you who have been beating your head against it for the last how many hours). Keep a grip on your temper and forge ahead.

BUILDING A PC
FROM SCRATCH

Off-the-shelf computers are cheap and continue to get cheaper. You can get an inexpensive PC from mail order giants such as Micron, Dell, and Gateway, and more computer manufacturers are selling "made-to-order" models in which you can select various options and components for the machine you're buying. However, nothing gives you as much control over the final product as building it yourself from scratch. *But know going in that it probably won't be cheaper.* The primary reason for building your own PC is to get a quality system that is exactly what you want. This approach almost always costs more when compared to machines from mass-market manufacturers who use the cheapest components available by the boatload. If you factor in your time as well, it always costs more to build custom than buy ready-made.

Pre-Upgrade Checklist

1. Do your homework.
2. Purchase or acquire all your components.
3. Organize your tools and workspace.

   Be sure to read Chapter 3, "Things You Need," and have the following tools:

   - Flashlight
   - Nutdrivers (3/16" and 1/4")
   - Screwdrivers (Phillips and slotted without magnetic tips)
   - Tweezers (larger types suitable for picking up and holding machine screws, not the smaller type found in the medicine cabinet)
   - ESD wrist strap or comparable ESD equipment (antistatic mat, sprays, and so on)
   - Magnifying glass
   - Cable ties
   - Suitable container for holding screws and other small parts
   - Electrical extension cord (three-prong)
   - Extra PC power cable (and power cord-to-extension cord converter)
   - An assortment of splitters and connectors, depending on the upgrade project you're about to tackle
   - The computer's system journal and NEAT box

4. Perform the upgrade.
5. Take good notes, and permanently file them in your system log when finished.
6. Create your inventory documentation as discussed in Chapter 2, "Preparing for an Upgrade."

Cost Versus Having It Your Way

It used to be that you could save a bundle by building your own PC, or by having what is commonly called a *clone shop* assemble the machine of your dreams to your specifications. With computers selling at discount chains and computer superstores for under $500 *with* a color ink jet printer tossed in, don't plan on a build-it-yourself (BIY) PC saving you any money. In fact, it will probably wind up costing you more than if you could buy the exact model you want, with the exact components you want, from a mass-market PC manufacturer. The problem is that you aren't likely to find the *exact* system you want off the shelf.

Made to Order

Plenty of computer resellers will build a semicustom PC for you. You get to choose from among a couple of basic product lines as a base model, and then make selections for components to customize your PC. Here are the sort of options you can choose:

- **Processor**—Don't look for choices between various CPU makers; most resellers have a deal with Intel or AMD, but rarely both. You can generally choose from a few CPU models and from several chip speeds.

- **Chassis**—Usually desktop or tower. Some have graduated choices, so you could get a slimline desktop model or a minitower if you wanted. But choices are limited to the chassis the reseller stocks.

- **RAM**—Here, you get to choose quantity only. You don't get to choose SIMM or DIMM configurations or the type of memory you're getting.

- **Drives**—Again, you get to choose size (how many gigabytes the hard drive has), not the brand name of the drive itself. That goes for removable media, as well. For CD or DVD drives, you might get to pick speed or rewritable versus recordable, but not the brand or subfeatures.

- **Video**—Usually limited to the amount of memory onboard the graphics adapter, but they might offer one or two brand names.

As you can see, you get to pick from only a limited selection of *sizes*. You're not really picking the brands of the components or the individual models, meaning you have no control whatsoever over the feature sets of the components going into your computer.

Cherry-Picking Components

To get the system you want, and to justify the added hassle of going the BIY route in the first place, you'll want to pick the best of breed for the individual components going into your system.

If you're building a SCSI system, you'll want one of the better cards from Adaptec, the name brand leader in SCSI interface cards. It might cost more than if the same card came in a mass-marketed system (after all, you're buying only one card, whereas system manufacturers buy them by the boxcar load), assuming you could even get an off-the-shelf system with the card you want in it.

The same goes for a video adapter. If you're a game buff, you'll want something special (and more expensive than what comes on the discount systems) that can handle a high frame rate and that's loaded to the gills with high-speed RAM. If you're an audiophile, a higher-end sound card is definitely on your list.

For a monitor, you might already have the one you want from your last system (fortunately, most made-to-order resellers allow you to buy a system sans monitor, letting you use one you already have or purchase one separately), or you might want some state-of-the-art unit in flat-screen digital. As we discussed back in Chapter 12, "Monitor and Graphic Card Upgrades," your choice of monitor can seriously impact what you want in the system by way of a graphics card.

Choosing the name brand and the individual models offered by your vendor of choice is the best way to get the system of your dreams. Oftentimes, it's the only way to go. Selecting the components gives you the most flexibility in configuring your system for your particular needs.

The downside, of course, is that it costs more. Sometimes a little more; sometimes a lot more depending on the specific components you want. But the ultimate effect on the system you wind up with can make it a very worthwhile decision.

Clone Shops

Putting together a system from scratch can sound frightening, especially if you are not comfortable with the more technical side of computer hardware. It's one thing to contemplate upgrading an old hard drive and installing a new one, but it's another thing to picture an empty chassis and having to install every component yourself. Even though the two extremes are not really all that far removed from one another, it can still be a very scary proposition.

One compromise between creating a BIY system and buying a mass-market, off-the-shelf unit is having your system built by a local clone shop to your own specifications.

Similar to your local car repair shop, you must find a shop that is reputable and that you feel comfortable dealing with. Ask around to see whether someone you know can recommend a good local shop that builds systems to order. Go in and talk to the people working there. See how they answer your questions and what type of suggestions they make when discussing your specifications.

Over the past several years, we have had excellent dealings with just such a firm, Computer Repair Center (CRC), located in Canoga Park, California. We recently needed to build a PC literally overnight but were overbooked with other consulting work, so CRC to the rescue. Using the very information you've read in this book, we selected the desired components—from processor to chassis to the bells and whistles—we wanted on the DVD drive and graphics card and put together the specification list with their technicians. CRC's staff built the system, tested it, and shipped it to our offices pronto. We got exactly the system we wanted, with every component we wanted, for a very good price. We paid some labor costs and shipping, but we saved our time and still got a system built to our exact specifications.

Another advantage of using a clone shop in a BIY scenario is for troubleshooting. Having a technical shop you can call on if you run into any serious problems is a very good idea before going down the BIY road.

Comments on Components

Before you stop off at the computer superstore and start buying motherboards and a chassis, you'll want to spec out your BIY system on paper. As in so very many things, the more upfront planning you do, the smoother the building process will go.

You build a PC from its core components outward—these being the processor, motherboard, and chassis.

The first decision you must make is the motherboard make and model and the processor chip that will be mounted on it. This is the heart of your system and the key cost component. The motherboard and its form factor will influence what type of chassis you'll get. The motherboard must mount properly in the chassis.

Consider the following when making up the specification sheet for your BIY system. The overriding concern when you are going to purchase your own components and assemble them into a system is to always, repeat always, buy from a reputable vendor who has been around for a while. You'll be dealing directly with the vendor on any warranty work, so you want them to be around in case you need them to make good on a component.

TIP

USE THE 800 NUMBER WHEN ORDERING

If you are buying components for your BIY system over the Internet, avoid the Web page order form and call the 800 number. If the vendor is too exclusive to have an 800 number, find another vendor. If you need additional service with your purchase, you'll want to talk to someone in real time. So, the sooner you start a person-to-person relationship with the sales rep, the better.

Motherboard

We discussed motherboards and CPUs in some detail in Chapter 6, "CPU and Motherboard Upgrades." The basics apply whether you are upgrading the motherboard in an existing system or creating a BIY computer from scratch. The key to winding up with a functional system when you're all done is to start with a name brand, mainstream motherboard and a proven CPU chip. We've worked with motherboards from ASUS, EpOX, and Micro-Star (MSI), but a number of good manufacturers exist, including Abit, BIOSTAR, Gigabyte, Intel, Supermicro, and Tyan, to name some of the more popular ones. Most come with USB ports, but not all support FireWire (see Chapter 2). If a certain feature is important to you, be sure to consider it here at the motherboard level.

The motherboard form factor will impact the chassis in which you can mount it. Most of the motherboards sold currently are ATX or micro-ATX (see Figure A.1). This form factor relocates the CPU and memory module sockets away from the expansion card slots so each slot can accept a full-length adapter card.

When deciding on which bells and whistles you want on your motherboard, keep in mind how you intend to use your system. Does having a built-in SCSI controller on the motherboard make more sense than getting a SCSI adapter card? Is saving a slot better than having a SCSI controller you can swap out? The same applies to audio, networking, and other goodies built into the motherboard.

If the motherboard goes out, all the components built into it go out as well, even if it was something else on the board that broke. Later, if you decide to upgrade the video adapter, you'll have to fuss around with disabling the video on the motherboard to use the adapter card. This adds to the hassle of performing future upgrades.

As we mentioned back in Chapter 6, one of the best motherboard resources on the Internet is the Motherboard Homeworld site. A large amount of information on evaluating and buying motherboards is available on this site. It has a page called

MOBOT that lets you enter your criteria and then suggests motherboards that meet your specifications:

`http://iceberg.pchomeworld.com/cgi-win/MoBotGen/MoBot.asp`

The motherboard vendor might sell CPUs and offer a bundled deal price if you buy both at the same time. The CPU is usually shipped separately from the motherboard, although it is possible to purchase a motherboard with the CPU already installed.

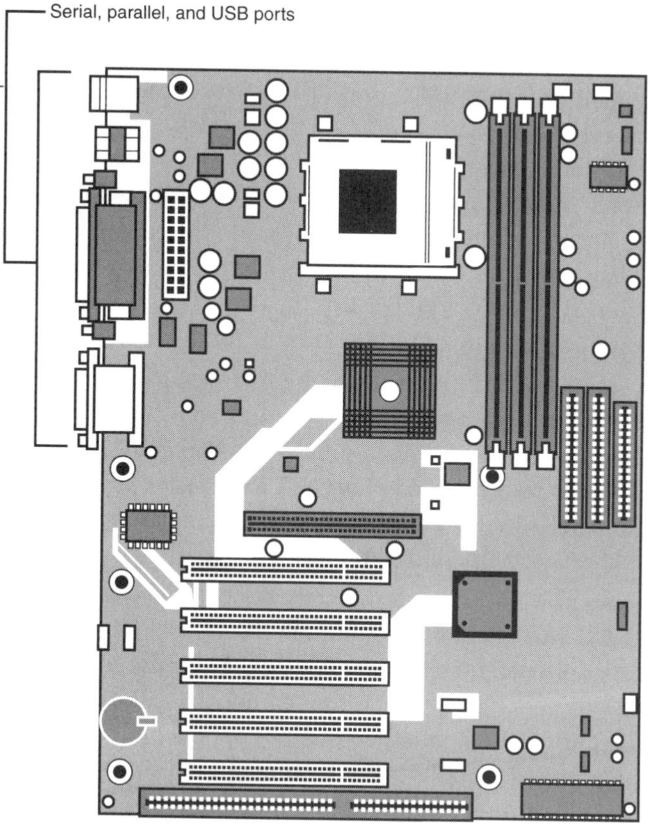

FIGURE A.1

Here you see an ATX mother-board. Note the input/output ports mounted on the mother-board itself. They must align properly with the cutouts on the chassis in which you're mounting the board.

Serial, parallel, and USB ports

TIP

MATCHING THE MOTHERBOARD AND THE CPU

A motherboard is rated for the type of CPUs it supports. Do yourself a huge favor and never try to plug a CPU chip into a motherboard that's not rated for that chip. No matter how many of your friends tell you what a good idea it is or how well it's working for them, it's not worth all the trouble, glitches, and incompatibility problems this can cause.

Chassis

The motherboard must fit the chassis in which you're going to install it, which means more than just lining up a few screw holes. It used to be that you'd run small ribbon cables from motherboard connectors to the port cutouts on the chassis back to create the ports for the system. However, motherboards for the large part now have ports that open onto the

ANOTHER FINE MESS
WATCH THE POWER SUPPLY PLACEMENT

Working inside a computer chassis is a study in claustrophobia. You rapidly wish for three hands, all about the size of a first grader's. This is one reason we favor a midsize tower case. As tower cases go, they're roomy inside, and you can avoid some grief if you get one that doesn't force you to remove the power supply to mount the motherboard. ■

back of the system mounted right on the epoxy. This means you have to be sure the ports will align with the cutouts on the back of the chassis. Match the form factor of the motherboard you're going to use to the chassis you want. Note that many computer cases will accept any of several form factors.

Most of the motherboards made today are ATX or micro-ATX form factors. A *micro-ATX* is a smaller motherboard usually used in smaller chassis. However, if you're planning to mount a micro-ATX in a full-size tower chassis, it should fit without any problems. Most chassis that accept an ATX form factor motherboard will take the smaller micro-ATX. See Figure A.2 for a visual of the four primary case designs—full tower, minitower, desktop, and slimline.

If you're going to be installing a motherboard using a less common format, such as a WTX or NLX, make doubly sure that the chassis will mount it and that the slots and ports align properly. The former is generally for use in servers; the latter for use in small desktop systems that use a riser card to provide only a few expansion slots. The slots are parallel to the motherboard, as opposed to being perpendicular as on an ATX motherboard. See Chapter 6 for a figure showing the NLX form factor.

We prefer a tower chassis using an ATX (or micro-ATX) form factor. The larger chassis provides lots of room for upgrades and is easy to work inside. What's important is that you get a chassis that works with the motherboard you want and that is the proper size for where you'll be installing the system.

FIGURE A.2

Chassis range from the giant full-sized tower to the midsize tower to the desktop and down to the slimline case.

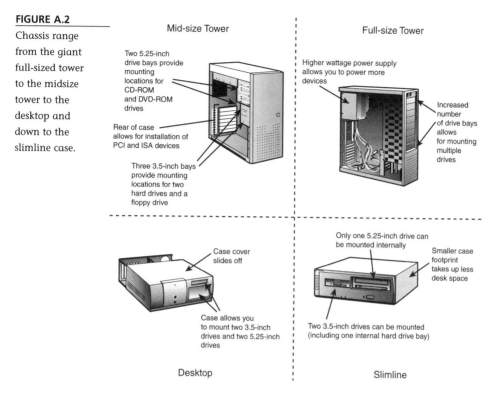

Mid-size Tower

Two 5.25-inch drive bays provide mounting locations for CD-ROM and DVD-ROM drives

Rear of case allows for installation of PCI and ISA devices

Three 3.5-inch bays provide mounting locations for two hard drives and a floppy drive

Full-size Tower

Higher wattage power supply allows you to power more devices

Increased number of drive bays allows for mounting multiple drives

Case cover slides off

Case allows you to mount two 3.5-inch drives and two 5.25-inch drives

Desktop

Only one 5.25-inch drive can be mounted internally

Smaller case footprint takes up less desk space

Two 3.5-inch drives can be mounted (including one internal hard drive bay)

Slimline

Power Supply

Get a chassis that comes with a power supply already installed. Chapter 10, "Adding Power Protection," touched on how the power supply must supply enough wattage to run all the peripherals you plan to install on your system. Given the way PC systems tend to grow over time (as you add new components), you can't really have too much in the way of a power supply. So, don't short yourself; go for something in the 250–300 range and make sure it is UL approved. As mentioned earlier, things will go more smoothly if you don't have to remove the power supply to install the motherboard.

Memory

In Chapter 5, "RAM," we discussed the various types of memory available for your system. Again, the motherboard you decide on for your BIY system will dictate which type of memory you can use in your system by the type of module sockets it has: SIMM, DIMM, or RIMM. The more sockets, the more flexibility you'll have in memory configurations.

Sound

Right now, audio capabilities are fairly standardized, so you might not really miss much if you get a motherboard with built-in sound. It saves you a slot, and you can always drop in a sound card if some new wrinkle comes along in PC audio.

Video

You can get a motherboard with onboard video, but this is one area where you probably want to go with a graphics adapter card to get more resolution or other advanced features. See Chapter 12 for more about the bells and whistles available in graphics card adapters.

Drives

The motherboard you select can have EIDE, SCSI, or both types of controllers built in. More commonly, motherboards come with onboard EIDE and provide two channels for connecting drives (see Chapter 7, "Upgrading the Hard Disk").

ANOTHER FINE MESS
A CASE FOR THE CASE

Sure, the chassis is just a box that holds all your components, but think through all the features you want before you buy the first ATX minitower you see. You can get cases that are very colorful (putty is no longer your only color choice) and that have sections of transparent plastic, making for visually intriguing systems.

Be wary, though; we've never worked on one of these wild, avant-garde designer chassis that wasn't a tremendous pain to get things installed properly. Some chassis have slide-out trays that hold your drives, slide-out motherboards, and many other gimmicks, some of which work nicely and some of which are hokey. Unless you're going to be constantly taking your system apart, many of these features might not be cost-effective.

Think about things such as removable panels on each side of the case (in the case of tower-based systems) that can be removed easily. This gives you ample access to the interior, making upgrades easier but without adding much more cost to the case. ■

Assembly Order

After you have secured all your components, you need to assemble them all into the finished computer. Here is the general order in which to install the individual components. Your individual situation might differ from what we set forth here, depending on the type of system you're assembling and the associated components involved.

At each step, please read and follow any instructions provided by the component manufacturer. Individual components might require special treatment, so always follow what the manufacturer tells you to do. Chapter 3, which discusses handling components; protecting yourself from ESD; and keeping track of material, packaging, and related items is definitely required reading before tackling a BIY system. It also covers the tools and work area layout, so we'll assume you're up to speed on that. In addition, you should have another system available for making boot disks and accessing the Internet for information, drivers, and so on. Things will go much more smoothly if you have the boot disk that comes with Windows 98 or can prepare a 3.5-inch boot disk before you assemble your system. This boot disk should have the necessary files to enable you to SYS, FDISK, and FORMAT your hard drive. If you can create one with the drivers for the DVD or CD drive going into your new system, so much the better.

TIP

BUILDING A BOOT DISK

A boot disk with drivers that support the CD drive in your BIY system is a good thing to have as you perform the assembly and install an operating system. Windows 98 comes with a boot disk with generic drivers that will boot your fledgling system and enable you to access the CD drive. The Tweak Central site has a great page with detailed instructions on building boot disks with CD support, as well:

`http://www.2e.org/bootdisk.htm`

Be sure to start assembly without the PC power supply being connected to its power source—in other words, an AC wall outlet or UPS system. Follow these steps:

1. Before you start working on the motherboard, study the documentation that came with it and verify that any and all jumpers are set correctly. Review all the connectors on your motherboard (as shown in your documentation) and make sure you can identify them on the physical motherboard. The more familiar you are with where the various connectors are, the easier installing the remaining components will be.

2. Install the CPU chip per the manufacturer's instructions. Mount the heat sink(s) and cooling fan(s) on the CPU as necessary and connect the power wires coming from the cooling fans to the motherboard (newer motherboards) or the power supply (older motherboards), as necessary.

TIP

ATHLON HELP GUIDE

AMD has a help guide for building PCs around their Athlon processors:

`http://www.amd.com/products/cpg/athlon/howtobuild/howtobuild.html`

3. Install your memory modules (see Chapter 5) on the motherboard.

4. Mount the motherboard in the chassis. Align the mounting holes and insert the screws that secure the motherboard to the case. Be careful not to twist, tweak, or bend the motherboard when handling it or mounting it in the case. Applying too much pressure at any one point has been the death of many a motherboard.

With some chassis, you can remove what is called the *pan* or *motherboard tray*, which is a flat metal plate you mount the motherboard to; the pan is then screwed into the chassis (see Figure A.3).

Be very careful whenever mounting a motherboard that none of the component leads on the motherboard wind up touching the metal walls of the case.

FIGURE A.3

Here you can see a motherboard mounted on a tray or pan.

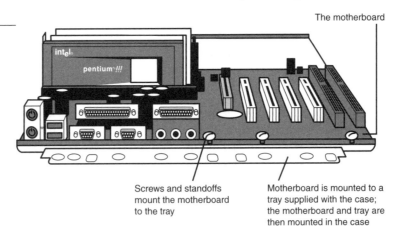

The motherboard

Screws and standoffs mount the motherboard to the tray

Motherboard is mounted to a tray supplied with the case; the motherboard and tray are then mounted in the case

TIP

ALIGNING THE I/O PORTS

Take care to align the I/O ports with the cutouts on the chassis's back panel (sometimes, you'll see this panel called the I/O *shield*). You might need to punch out the metal covers on the system's back panel where the I/O ports will show through. Some chassis don't have cutouts but rather have a rectangular opening where the motherboard I/O ports protrude from the inside of the system. A metal template is provided with the chassis that matches the layout of the I/O ports for your particular motherboard. This template lines up with the I/O ports and attaches to a larger opening on the back panel of the chassis.

5. Connect the primary power lead (the thick bundle of wires) from the power supply to the connector on the motherboard. On newer systems, the power cable connector is keyed so it fits into the motherboard only one way. Don't force anything; use firm, steady pressure until the connector is well seated.

6. Connect the wires leading from the system lights (LEDs) and buttons on the front of the chassis to the motherboard (see Figure A.4). Also, connect the lead from the tiny speaker mounted in the front of the chassis to the proper connection on the motherboard so you can hear the various beeps and noises a system makes as it boots up. Consult the motherboard documentation for the proper connection details. New systems switch power on and off through the motherboard instead of a mechanical switch on the power supply, so getting the on/off button connected correctly is important.

7. Install the floppy drive (if the system will have one).

8. Install the graphics adapter in the dedicated AGP slot and connect the monitor to the graphics card.

9. Review the previous steps to ensure that everything that should be connected at this point is in fact connected and that all the connections are secure. Make sure nothing is left in the chassis that does not belong there. If you are safety conscious, you can close up the case, but you'll be opening it up again shortly.

10. Connect a keyboard, plug your AC power into the power supply receptacle on the back of the system, and turn on the computer. You should hear a beep from the PC's speaker and see something on the monitor. Enter the CMOS setup (see Chapter 4, "Upgrading the BIOS," for information on CMOS settings). Set the correct date and time; then, exit the CMOS setup program and see whether you can access the A: (floppy) drive. Power down and unplug the computer from the wall or UPS.

FIGURE A.4

FIGURE A.4

Getting the LEDs and front panel button connections hooked up correctly on the motherboard is important.

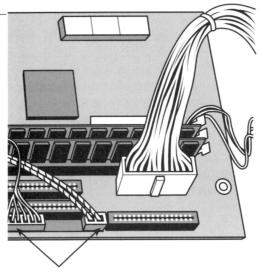

These connectors supply power to the power supply switch, reset button, and so on

11. Shut down the system and install your hard drive(s). Most motherboards provide EIDE controller connections on the motherboard, although you can also get a motherboard that provides a built-in SCSI connection. Connect the drives to the motherboard or to the controller card as necessary for your system (see Chapter 7).

This is where your boot disk comes in handy. Booting your fledgling system from this boot disk enables you to SYS, FDISK, and FORMAT your drive(s). If you don't have a boot disk, proceed to the next two steps where we discuss booting a new system from the CD drive.

The following steps should be performed one at a time. In additon, the system should be tested by powering it up and seeing whether the component works before shutting down everything and proceeding to the next step. That's not to say you couldn't slap all the remaining components into the system and go from there; however, if you get each individual item installed properly before going on to the next one, you have less chance of compatibility problems and make troubleshooting any problems that much simpler.

12. Install the CD or DVD drive as necessary. See Chapter 15, "Adding a CD-Recordable or CD-Rewritable Drive," and Chapter 16, "Adding a DVD Drive." If you got the hard disk formatted and bootable back in step 11 then you

should not have any problem installing the CD or DVD drivers from the install disks provided by the component manufacturer. If you do not have the hard drive booting yet, see step 13.

13. At this point, you should install the operating system because the remaining components will have to be recognized by the OS before they're useful. Of course, it's not as easy as you might think because, like the eternal question about which came first, the chicken or the egg, you must deal with getting the CD-ROM to be recognized by the OS when the OS is not installed and can be installed only from the CD-ROM.

One method requires you to have a bootable disk for the OS you're going to install (we'll assume Windows 98 Second Edition) that has drivers that will recognize the CD drive. If you have such an animal, just boot the system with it; then, you can proceed to install Windows from its master CD.

CD-ROM DRIVERS

The good news is that Windows 98 SE and Windows Me include generic CD-ROM drivers that will work with almost any CD drive, making your life easier. If, however, you're installing Windows 95 or Windows 98 (not the Second Edition version), you must ensure you have the CD-ROM driver for your particular drive available on floppy so you can install it after you boot your system. If your CD drive did not come with such a disk, check the manufacturer's Web site for the proper driver before performing the install. Most CD drive manufacturers provide the necessary drivers on their sites for free download.

If you're installing Windows NT or Windows 2000 and you don't have a bootable disk, you can go into the CMOS settings and change the boot order of the devices (see Chapter 15). This works well on newer systems with a BIOS that supports booting from a CD drive. Set the system to boot from the CD or DVD before the hard drive. Pop your Windows disc in the drive, and you should be able to boot right up into the Windows installation. You can use this method to let Windows format your hard disk if you did not do so manually back in step 11.

14. Install your sound card (unless this is built into the motherboard).

15. Install any additional peripheral cards as required for your system.

If you press the on/off button on the front of your case and nothing happens, check that the wires from the chassis's front panel (LEDs and buttons for power on and reset) are correctly connected to the motherboard and that the manual power switch on the power supply is switched on.

The LED lights on the front of the case should light up when you power up the system, and the LED for the hard drive should stay on during the boot process. You should hear the hard drive spin up as the system fires up; the fans on the CPU should start spinning; and the fan on the power supply should come on, as well. The CD/DVD drive has power if you press the button and the disc tray ejects.

If you run into problems at this point, review Chapter 23, "Troubleshooting Hardware and Software Problems." You also can find a good reference on troubleshooting a system that won't boot on the Motherboard Homeworld site: `http://www.motherboards.org/build/build-28.html`

Still, if something is fundamentally wrong with your system—say a motherboard failure, a broken wire, or bad connector—you'll probably be unable to diagnose it on your own. Here's where a clone shop or reliable system repair company comes in very handy because it will have the diagnostic hardware necessary to locate the specific problem you're having.

Burning In a New System

After you have your system assembled, you need to test the various components to see whether they are functioning, as you'd expect. You can do this manually using the procedures in this section. We'll also mention some of the diagnostic software we've used in testing and burning in systems.

We'll assume at this point that the computer boots properly and that you've installed an operating system such as Windows 98 SE. After Windows has been installed, right-click the My Computer icon and click Properties in the pop-up dialog box. Click the Device Manager tab and review all the installed components. You should not see any warnings, such as the yellow exclamation point that indicates a conflict or a red X indicating a device is nonoperational.

Disk Drives

Test your floppy drive by creating a Windows 98 SE startup disk. Insert an empty, formatted 1.44MB disk in the floppy drive; then, in Windows click Start, choose Settings, click Control Panel, run Add/Remove Programs, click the Startup Disk tab, and finally Create Disk. The creation process should run without problem. Test the startup disk by shutting down Windows and rebooting the system with the startup disk in the floppy drive.

You tested your hard drive(s) when you ran FDISK on it and partitioned and formatted it. You can further test your hard disk(s) by running ScanDisk in Windows. Close all running applications and in Windows click Start, Programs, choose Accessories, System Tools, and click ScanDisk. Run ScanDisk on all your hard drive partitions.

CD or DVD Drive

The easiest way to test your CD or DVD drive is to insert an audio music disc and play it. You should hear music through your system's speakers.

Then, take a data CD and try copying several files from the CD to the hard disk. If you are using a DVD drive, perform the same test with a data DVD disc.

To test your DVD movie-playing capability, make sure you've installed your player software and insert a DVD movie disc. With a little luck, all you'll need is some popcorn.

Display Adapter

If your system can display any image at all, you know the graphics adapter is doing something. To give it more of a workout, you can make some changes in the Display Properties dialog box. Right-click the Windows desktop and choose Properties to access the video settings. In the Properties dialog box, click the Settings tab. Try changing the resolution in the Screen Area setting. You should be able to change the resolution to any resolution supported by both your graphics adapter and your monitor.

Burn-In Utilities

We've used a number of burn-in and diagnostic utilities to test new computers (whether purchased off the shelf or BIY units). The ones we like run under Windows and provide a number of informative reports:

- **Microsoft System Information Tool**—This tool is provided with Windows 98 and is also known as MSInfo. Click Start, Programs, Accessories, System Tools, and then System Information. Double-click the Hardware Resources category and select the Conflicts/Sharing item. Review the displayed information for any indications of trouble. Double-click the Components category and click Problem Devices to see what MSInfo has to report on your installed components.

- **SANDRA**—SANDRA (System, Analyzer, Diagnostic, and Reporting Assistant) from SiSoft Software is one of the most well-designed, informative, and easy-to-use Windows applications we've run across in a long, long time. SANDRA generates up to 50 diagnostic reports (called *modules*). The modules are full of documented and undocumented information about your system. It returns the exact CPU model installed on your system and lists the BIOS and CMOS settings, how much memory is installed, and which type of memory is installed.

Resources for This Appendix

- **Abit**—http://www.abit-usa.com/

- **Adaptec, Inc.**—http://www.adaptec.com/

- **AMD**—
  http://www.amd.com/products/cpg/athlon/howtobuild/howtobuild.html

- **ASUS**—http://www.asus.com/

- **BIOSTAR**—http://www.biostar-usa.com/

- **Computer Repair Center (Southern California)**—(818) 347-7534

- **Dell Computer Corporation**—
  http://www.dell.com/us/en/gen/default.htm

- **EpOX**—http://www.epox.com/

- **Gateway, Inc.**—http://www.gateway.com/home/index.shtml

- **Gigabyte**—http://www.giga-byte.com/

- **Intel**—http://www.intel.com/

- **Micro-Star (MSI)**—http://www.msicomputer.com/

- **Micron PC, Inc.**—http://www.micronpc.com/index.html

- **Motherboard Homeworld**—http://www.motherboards.org/index.html

- **SANDRA**—http://www.sisoftware.demon.co.uk/sandra/

- **Supermicro**—http://www.supermicro.com/

- **Tweak Central**—http://www.2e.org/bootdisk.htm

- **Tyan**—http://www.tyan.com/products/products.html

LAPTOP UPGRADES

pgrading a laptop typically involves adding more system memory, adding a new external peripheral of some kind, or upgrading a removable hard drive. This is because a laptop—relative to its desktop cousin—is a wholly integrated unit with far fewer upgradable parts and a higher manufacturing cost. This higher production cost is driven by a laptop's small size, its need to be ruggedized (some models more than others), and the power constraints imposed by the competition between requirements for a small/lightweight form factor and long battery life.

Upgrade Limitations

Know that for most laptop upgrades, you'll be limited to only the components offered by the laptop manufacturer. If your removable CD drive can be upgraded to a DVD drive, it's almost a certainty that you'll be forking over a premium price for the proprietary model offered by the company that made your laptop. Laptops are proprietary by design and do not enjoy the interchangeability of components such as their larger PC cousins.

You probably won't be upgrading the motherboard or CPU. Likewise, the keyboard or monitor. On some laptops, you can change out the "standard" LCD panel offered with the unit for a better one, but it is usually so costly as to not make economical sense. The upgrades you'll want to make pertaining to a laptop will be for memory and peripherals. Memory is a way to get extended life out of an aging laptop. Peripherals, even though they tend to cut down on portability, are a way to add more features.

Adding more system memory is relatively easy, and the good news here is that some of the major third-party memory providers might offer memory upgrades that work with your laptop. Just follow our advice from Chapter 5, "RAM," and use third-party memory configurator tools such as those provided by Crucial or Kingston to find the best upgrade for your particular laptop model.

One way to expand a laptop's capabilities is by adding or changing a PC Card (sometimes referred to as *PCMCIA*). This offers you a lot of flexibility because you aren't locked into only the choices from your laptop manufacturer. As discussed in Chapter 2, "Preparing for an Upgrade," PC Card technology offers small form factor and high portability (see Figure B.1), support for PnP and hot-swapping, and backward-compatibility between the three PC Card type architectures (I, II, and III). You can add DVD drives (with the decoder built in), CD drives, external hard disks, and a wide range of peripherals—all via the PC Card interface.

FIGURE B.1

A PC Card's dimensional specifications.

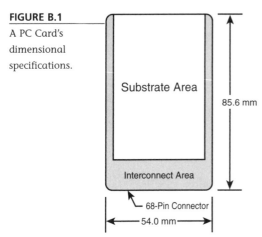

Substrate Area

85.6 mm

Interconnect Area

68-Pin Connector

54.0 mm

Upgrading with a Port Replicator or Docking Station

Because little, if any, space exists within the laptop case into which you can install new components, the only way to connect peripherals is via the ports installed on the laptop. If you have maxed out your laptop's built-in ports, you need either a port replicator or a docking station. A port replicator is a less expensive, less complex solution. For example, IBM's Tpad Port Replicator for 380/390/560/570a comes with the following ports and has a street price of $160:

■ One serial port

■ One parallel IEEE 1284 (EPP/ECP) port

■ One PS/2 keyboard port

■ One PS/2 mouse port

■ One VGA port

■ One floppy interface port

A docking station is designed to turn a laptop into a desktop PC. After the laptop mates with the docking station, it draws power from the docking station's AC line; its video display is deactivated (the signal is shunted instead to an external monitor); its keyboard is disengaged (a free-standing keyboard takes over); and its pointing device is cut off (you instead use a traditional mouse). In addition to the traditional ports provided by a port replicator, a docking station can provide other services, too, including but not limited to these:

■ Network interface card and connector (RJ-45)

■ RJ-11 modem port

■ Various audio ports

■ Infrared port (IrDA)

■ Battery charger

■ USB port(s)

■ Additional bay(s); for example, CD-ROM, CD-R/RW, LS-120, and hard disk

■ Additional PC Card slot(s)

■ PCI slot(s)

A docking station such as the IBM ThinkPad Dock (model 26311OU) with all the previously mentioned features has a street price of $499–$540. That's three times that of a port replicator.

Here are the Web pages for five of the most popular notebook manufacturers:

- **Compaq portables**—http://www.compaq.com/products/portables/

- **Dell notebooks**—http://www.dell.com/us/en/bsd/products/ line_notebooks.htm

- **IBM ThinkPads**—http://www.pc.ibm.com/us/thinkpad/index.html

- **Sony VAIO Notebook Computers**—http://www.ita.sel.sony.com/ products/pc/notebook/

- **Toshiba Portables**—Go to http://www.csd.toshiba.com/cgi-bin/tais/ product/community_home.jsp and then follow the "Portables" link

NOTE

THE MILITARY DOES RUGGED RIGHT

There really is such a thing as a military notebook torture test. It's called the Military Standard 810E (MIL-STD-810E). For more information, see http://www.panasonic.com/ computer/notebook/rugged/mil_std.htm.

Your need for laptop accessories will depend on how you use it. If you use your laptop within the domestic U.S., here is our "absolute bare essentials" list of the accessories you shouldn't be without, ever. (If you're traveling internationally, see the Roadnews Web site for hot tips in that arena.) Literally hundreds of "laptop travel" accessory lists are available; ours is pared down to the lean and mean, domestic minimum. See the "Online Resources" section at the end of this chapter for places to go to buy laptop accessories:

- Security, security, security: laptop lock, camouflaged carrying case, and heavy-duty protection/encryption for sensitive data files

- Spare battery

- Small toolkit

- Startup disk

- Backup copy of your operating system's master CD

- Three-prong AC adapter

- Long modem cable and RJ-11 extender (a two-female adapter)

- One CD-RW disc for emergency data backups

- Automobile cigarette lighter adapter

- A spare power cord that is in-flight capable (has a special connector); interfaces with a power jack on the back of your fellow passenger's seat and enables you to use your laptop while flying without draining the batteries

- Laptop-specialized surge protector

- Digital phone line signal tester

Online Resources

These resources will keep you and your laptop operating safely and soundly, no matter how bumpy the ride:

- **Roadnews**—If you travel with a laptop (or even if you don't), you should bookmark this site, located at `http://www.roadnews.com`. It has tips and tricks galore; publishes an email discussion list; and maintains a stellar list of accessory vendors (conveniently organized by product category), an extensive resources link, and periodic product reviews.

- **iGo Mobile Technology Outfitter**—Located at `http://www.igo.com`, it is a popular source for batteries, power-related gear, laptop stuff, and travel gear, as well as cellular, PDA, and handheld doodads. It has plenty of cool stuff to keep your laptop well stocked and well heeled.

- **The Frequently Asked Questions About Batteries page**—Located at `http://www.cadex.com/cfm/index.cfm?Pg=55&Lp=1&Db=&Mo=`, it offers a wide variety of answers to the many battery questions we've all had but were afraid to ask. (And, if you tote a portable, we know you've got battery questions!) Some of the FAQs come from Isidor Buchmann's book *Batteries in a Portable World: A Handbook on Rechargeable Batteries for Non-Engineers* (Isidor is the founder of Cadex Electronics), and others have been recently added or updated. These FAQs range from "What do I need to know about chargers?" to "How can I make a battery more reliable and longer lasting?"

- **The Laptop Guide**—Located at `http://www.laptopguide.com`, it might offer you some useful information if you dig. However, it has accumulated some dust recently. The news section hasn't been updated since December 1999, and the most recent reviews date back to early 1999.

- **The Microsoft whitepaper "Mobile Computing in MS Windows 98: The Power Is in Your Hands"**—Located at `http://www.microsoft.com/Windows98/usingwindows/work/articles/004Apr/mobile.asp`, it provides a brief overview of laptop power management, sharing strategies, and wireless options.

- **The *Microsoft Windows 98 Resource Kit*—**Chapter 19, "Remote Networking and Mobile Computing," is primarily about remote networking, but does includes two informative sections on mobile computing features and troubleshooting. Buy it online at `http://www.amazon.com/exec/obidos/ASIN/1572316446/`.

- `comp.sys.laptops`—This public newsgroup is the place to go for lively, unfettered discussions of laptop topics.

PC INVENTORY FORM

You can download our Excel template from a variety of sources listed in the front matter of this book. For those of you who prefer to fill out forms with paper and pencil, you have our permission to photocopy the pages in this appendix.

Use these forms to document the hardware and software that makes up your computer(s). Keeping a detailed record of this information is an invaluable tool for troubleshooting, repairing, and upgrading PCs. Keeping documentation is important, whether you own a single machine or are lucky enough to manage a stable of machines at the office.

General Information

PC Name: _____

PC Username: _____

Manufacturer Technical Support: _____

Manufacturer Customer Service: _____

Manufacturer Service/ID Number: _____

Order Number: _____

Order Date: _____

Customer Number: _____

Internal Asset Number: _____

PC Model

Manufacturer: _____

Model: _____

Serial Number: _____

Web Site: _____

Warranty: _____

Comments: _____

Case

Bus/Interface: _____

Manufacturer: _____

Model: _____

Quantity: _____

Serial Number: _____

Driver Info: _____

Web Site: _____

Warranty: _____

Latest Driver Version: _____

Latest Driver Download Info: _____

Comments: _____

CPU

Manufacturer: _____

Model: _____

Quantity: _____

Serial Number: _____

Web Site: _____

Warranty: _____

Comments: _____

Processor Socket/Slot

Manufacturer: _____

Model: _____

Quantity: _____

Serial Number: _____

Web Site: _____

Warranty: _____

Comments: _____

L1 Cache

Manufacturer: _____

Model: _____

Quantity: _____

Web Site: _____

Warranty: _____

Comments: _____

L2 Cache

Manufacturer: _____

Model: _____

Quantity: _____

Web Site: _____

Warranty: _____

Comments: _____

System Bus (MHz)

Quantity: _____

Comments: _____

Motherboard

Manufacturer: _____

Model: _____

Serial Number: _____

Web Site: _____

Warranty: _____

Comments: _____

Chipset

Manufacturer: _____

Model: _____

Web Site: _____

Warranty: _____

Comments: _____

BIOS

Manufacturer: _____

Model: _____

Driver Info: _____

Web Site: _____

Warranty: _____

Latest Driver Version: _____

Latest Driver Download Info: _____

Comments: _____

BIOS Plug and Play

Manufacturer: _____

Model: _____

Web Site: _____

Warranty: _____

Latest Driver Version: _____

Latest Driver Download Info: _____

Comments: _____

RAM

Manufacturer: _____

Model: _____

Quantity: _____

Serial Number: _____

Web Site: _____

Warranty: _____

Comments: _____

Hard Drive #1

Bus/Interface: _____

Manufacturer: _____

Model: _____

Quantity: _____

Serial Number: _____

Driver Info: _____

Web Site: _____

Warranty: _____

Latest Driver Version: _____

Latest Driver Download Info: _____

Comments: _____

Hard Drive #2

Bus/Interface: _____

Manufacturer: _____

Model: _____

Quantity: _____

Serial Number: _____

Driver Info: _____

Web Site: _____

Warranty: _____

Latest Driver Version: _____

Latest Driver Download Info: _____

Comments: _____

Floppy Drive

Bus/Interface: _____

Manufacturer: _____

Model: _____

Quantity: _____

Serial Number: _____

Driver Info: _____

Web Site: _____

Warranty: _____

Latest Driver Version: _____

Latest Driver Download Info: _____

Comments: _____

SCSI Controller

Bus/Interface: _____

Manufacturer: _____

Model: _____

Serial Number: _____

Driver Info: _____

Web Site: _____

Warranty: _____

Latest Driver Version: _____

Latest Driver Download Info: _____

Comments: _____

SCSI BIOS

Bus/Interface: _____

Manufacturer: _____

Model: _____

Driver Info: _____

Web Site: _____

Warranty: _____

Latest Driver Version: _____

Latest Driver Download Info: _____

Comments: _____

PCI Bus

Manufacturer: _____

Model: _____

Comments: _____

CD-ROM Drive

Bus/Interface: _____

Manufacturer: _____

Model: _____

Serial Number: _____

Driver Info: _____

Web Site: _____

Warranty: _____

Latest Driver Version: _____

Latest Driver Download Info: _____

Comments: _____

CD-R/CD-RW Drive

Bus/Interface: _____

Manufacturer: _____

Model: _____

Serial Number: _____

Driver Info: _____

Web Site: _____

Warranty: _____

Latest Driver Version: _____

Latest Driver Download Info: _____

Comments: _____

DVD Drive

Bus/Interface: _____

Manufacturer: _____

Model: _____

Serial Number: _____

Driver Info: _____

Web Site: _____

Warranty: _____

Latest Driver Version: _____

Latest Driver Download Info: _____

Comments: _____

Zip Drive

Bus/Interface: _____

Manufacturer: _____

Model: _____

Serial Number: _____

Driver Info: _____

Web Site: _____

Warranty: _____

Latest Driver Version: _____

Latest Driver Download Info: _____

Comments: _____

Tape Drive

Bus/Interface: _____

Manufacturer: _____

Model: _____

Serial Number: _____

Driver Info: _____

Web Site: _____

Warranty: _____

Latest Driver Version: _____

Latest Driver Download Info: _____

Comments: _____

Other Removable Media Drive

Bus/Interface: _____

Manufacturer: _____

Model: _____

Serial Number: _____

Driver Info: _____

Web Site: _____

Warranty: _____

Latest Driver Version: _____

Latest Driver Download Info: _____

Comments: _____

Modem

Bus/Interface: _____

Manufacturer: _____

Model: _____

Serial Number: _____

Driver Info: _____

Web Site: _____

Warranty: _____

Latest Driver Version: _____

Latest Driver Download Info: _____

Comments: _____

Monitor

Bus/Interface: _____

Manufacturer: _____

Model: _____

Serial Number: _____

Driver Info: _____

Web Site: _____

Warranty: _____

Latest Driver Version: _____

Latest Driver Download Info: _____

Comments: _____

Video Card

Bus/Interface: _____

Manufacturer: _____

Model: _____

Serial Number: _____

Driver Info: _____

Web Site: _____

Warranty: _____

Latest Driver Version: _____

Latest Driver Download Info: _____

Comments: _____

Sound Card

Bus/Interface: _____

Manufacturer: _____

Model: _____

Serial Number: _____

Driver Info: _____

Web Site: _____

Warranty: _____

Latest Driver Version: _____

Latest Driver Download Info: _____

Comments: _____

Speakers

Bus/Interface: _____

Manufacturer: _____

Model: _____

Quantity: _____

Serial Number: _____

Web Site: _____

Warranty: _____

Comments: _____

Keyboard

Bus/Interface: _____

Manufacturer: _____

Model: _____

Serial Number: _____

Driver Info: _____

Web Site: _____

Warranty: _____

Latest Driver Version: _____

Latest Driver Download Info: _____

Comments: _____

Mouse

Bus/Interface: _____

Manufacturer: _____

Model: _____

Serial Number: _____

Driver Info: _____

Web Site: _____

Warranty: _____

Latest Driver Version: _____

Latest Driver Download Info: _____

Comments: _____

Network Interface Card

Bus/Interface: _____

Manufacturer: _____

Model: _____

Serial Number: _____

Driver Info: _____

Web Site: _____

Warranty: _____

Latest Driver Version: _____

Latest Driver Download Info: _____

Comments: _____

Printer

Bus/Interface: _____

Manufacturer: _____

Model: _____

Serial Number: _____

Driver Info: _____

Web Site: _____

Warranty: _____

Latest Driver Version: _____

Latest Driver Download Info: _____

Comments: _____

Scanner

Bus/Interface: _____

Manufacturer: _____

Model: _____

Serial Number: _____

Driver Info: _____

Web Site: _____

Warranty: _____

Latest Driver Version: _____

Latest Driver Download Info: _____

Comments: _____

Operating System

Bus/Interface: _____

Manufacturer: _____

Model: _____

Serial Number (Product Key): _____

Driver Info: _____

Web Site: _____

Warranty: _____

Latest Driver Version: _____

Latest Driver Download Info: _____

Comments: _____

Slots 1–8

Slot 1: _____

Slot 2: _____

Slot 3: _____

Slot 4: _____

Slot 5: _____

Slot 6: _____

Slot 7: _____

Slot 8: _____

Comments: _____

PC Card Slots 1–2

Slot 1: _____

Slot 2: _____

Comments: _____

IDE Bus

Primary IDE—Master: _____

Primary IDE—Slave: _____

Secondary IDE—Master: _____

Secondary IDE—Slave: _____

Comments: _____

GLOSSARY

10BASE-T Refers to a specific (and quite common) Ethernet implementation that uses a particular type of cable, specifically, twisted-pair. 10BASE-T has a maximum run length of 100 meters and uses a connector called an RJ-45 connector. This cable is also referred to as Category 5 (or Cat-5) cable and can be used for LAN implementations other than 10BASE-T.

adapter card See *peripheral card.*

AGP Accelerated Graphics Port. This bus architecture was initially released by Intel in 1996. Its primary purpose is to give high-performance, memory-hungry video cards faster access to system resources (AGP's base frequency is 66MHz, twice that of PCI). If present, there is only one such slot on the motherboard. When a video card uses the AGP slot, this frees the PCI bus to attend to other devices. Actually, AGP is really a port; not a bus.

ATAPI AT Attachment Packet Interface. An extension that provides support for peripherals using the IDE interface, such as tape and CD-ROM drives.

bezel A plastic cover, located in the front panel of the computer, used to cover an empty drive bay.

BIOS Basic input/output system. A little bootstrap program that jump starts your computer and enables it to deal with the peripherals attached to it as the system starts up.

brownouts Low-power brownouts, called *sags*, are sometimes planned by your local power utility to deal with high demand caused by extremely hot summer days when everyone cranks up their air conditioning. The power company reduces power in selected areas, shifting the brownout around to cut down on overall demand.

bus A set of physical wires that transfer data and other information to and from the various components of a PC. In the computer realm, a bus is primarily characterized by its width—that is, how many bits it can carry at a time. The other key descriptor is speed—measured in megahertz (MHz)—which is how many trips data can make along the bus in one second (one megahertz equals one million trips, or cycles).

chipset A set of chips that, taken together, provide a motherboard's core functionality, meaning, what the motherboard can do in addition to housing a microprocessor. This includes, for example, how the processor communicates with memory, peripherals, ports, and so forth. In the analogy of microprocessor as brain and PC as human body, a brain is of little use to a human being without a central nervous system to communicate with the body's organs and limbs. Often, you'll hear the individual chips referred to as the North Bridge and South Bridge.

cluster The smallest amount of disk space to which a file or portion thereof can be allocated. The larger the cluster size, the more wasted space on a drive.

CMOS Complementary Metal-Oxide Semiconductor. This chip is where the BIOS gets all its settings so it can recognize and work with the PC's installed hardware. The CMOS is capable of retaining these settings when the PC is powered down by use of read-only memory and a small battery. See also *BIOS*.

cold boot The process of rebooting the computer from a completely shut-down (powered-off) state. This is as opposed to a warm boot in which the system is running and you restart it via the reset switch or the Restart option in Windows. See also *warm boot*.

continuity module The C-RIMM does not provide any memory, just allows the data to flow through all the RIMM connectors. A C-RIMM looks like a standard RIMM without any memory chips on it. If your PC uses RDRAM, you must place a continuity module in all empty RIMM sockets.

controller A device that controls the bidirectional flow of data between a peripheral and the computer. An example is a hard disk controller.

CPU Central processing unit. A collection of exceedingly small transistors crammed together into a very small integrated circuit package no more than a few inches square. Think of a CPU as the brain of your computer.

C-RIMM See *continuity module*.

DIMM Double In-Line Memory Module. Physical RAM comes packaged as a series of small chips soldered on a narrow strip of epoxy, called a memory module, that looks like a miniature peripheral card and is usually an inch or so high and three to four inches wide. A DIMM plugs into a slot on the motherboard. DIMMs are usually found on Pentium IIs and later systems; they fit into 168-pin slots.

DRAM Dynamic random access memory. This is the basic memory of PCs today. You'll also see it referred to as *FPM (fast page mode) RAM*. It's cheap and dense (you can pack a lot of memory into a small chip), but rather slow, especially compared to the processors on the market today.

DVD Digital versatile disc or digital video disc. The apparent goal is for DVD to replace audio CDs, data CDs, VHS tapes, and laserdiscs, and give console game cartridges a run for their money, as well. A DVD has a minimum storage capacity of 4.7GB. The acronym itself no longer has a real meaning; it has simply become the vernacular for the latest optical disc storage technology.

ECP Enhanced Parallel Port. This is a bidirectional parallel port specification, also known as the IEEE 1284 standard. Windows 98 and Windows 2000 natively support ECP.

EDO RAM Extended data output RAM. This type of system memory was developed by Micron Technology for use in the first Pentium-class computers. To use EDO RAM, your motherboard's chipset must support it and accept SIMMs. It's faster than standard DRAM by 15%–20% and is a good choice for systems with bus speeds up to 66MHz.

EIDE Enhanced IDE. See *IDE*.

ESD Electrostatic discharge. ESD is caused by your body acquiring a surplus of electrons. Given a chance, nature likes to keep things balanced, and those electrons will leave you if they can by jumping to something else. See also *ESD wrist strap*.

ESD wrist strap Electrostatic discharge wrist strap. This device consists of an attachment that makes contact with your wrist with a conductor wire and a cord you attach to a ground. This lets any static buildup flow from your wrist to ground. See also *ESD*.

expansion card See *peripheral card*.

external cache See *L2 cache*.

FAP Fair Access Policy. A controversial Internet connection bandwidth monitoring and balancing protocol implemented by Hughes for its DirectPC customers.

HomePNA Home Phone-line Networking Alliance. This is a nonprofit association of industry leaders who share the goal of a single, unified phone-line networking industry standard.

hot plugging See *hot-swapping*.

hot-swapping A feature whereby a device can be plugged in (or unplugged) at any time, even when the device and PC are powered on. Once swapped, the system automatically reconfigures itself to support the device.

hub A device that gathers all the cables together into a central location and passes signals among connected devices.

ICS Internet Connection Sharing. A built-in feature of Microsoft Windows 98 Second Edition, Windows Millennium, and Windows 2000 that enables multiple PCs to share a single Internet connection.

IDE Intelligent Drive Electronics or Integrated Drive Electronics. An interface for storage devices. Although in the vernacular IDE and ATA are used synonymously, ATA is actually an implementation of the IDE standard.

integral cache See *L1 cache*.

interface Officially, "a point or means of interaction between two systems, disciplines, or groups." In the context of PC hardware, an interface is a card, plug, or other mechanism that connects devices. In fact, the terms *interface card, adapter card, expansion card*, and *peripheral card* are synonyms. An interface card uses one of a PC's peripheral buses.

interface card See *peripheral card*.

internal cache See *L1 cache*.

IRQ Interrupt request. A number assigned to various devices on your system to identify them to the CPU. Conflicts arise when two devices try to use the same interrupt to communicate with the CPU. Only a limited number of IRQs are available on a PC, making IRQ assignments a potential trouble spot when performing upgrades.

jumper Connects the pins being jumped and completes a circuit between them.

L1 cache L1 stands for Level 1. This is a memory cache built into the Intel 486 and later-generation processors, so it runs at the processor's full core speed (read: faster than any other cache in the system). Synonyms for L1 cache are *internal cache, integral cache*, and *primary cache*.

L2 cache L2 stands for Level 2. This is the second memory cache to which a processor turns. Traditionally, it is larger in size than its upstream L1 counterpart, and—for P5 generation systems—is located on the motherboard, thus running at the motherboard bus speed (meaning, more slowly than the processor's full core speed). In the P6 family, the L2 cache migrated into the processor (in the Pentium II MMX and Pentium III, the internal L2 cache runs at half the core speed). Synonyms for L2 cache are *external cache* and *secondary cache*.

mask A mask focuses the electrons being streamed through the CRT onto the phosphor dots. The glass tube in your monitor looks similar to a funnel with the small end at the back of the monitor and the large end at the front. A number of electron guns sit at the back and blast electrons onto the larger screen end of the tube. A mask sits between the electron guns and the phosphor dots to better direct the electrons onto the phosphors.

MCA Micro Channel Architecture. This bus was invented by IBM in 1987 to replace the performance-constrained ISA bus. The architecture never caught on outside IBM and is no longer in use.

megabyte   One million bytes. When describing storage, the value is 1,048,576 bytes exactly (2 to the 20th power); when describing transfer rates, the value is 1,000,000 bytes. For example, one megabyte of system RAM is 1,048,576 bytes, and a transfer rate of one megabyte per second is 1,000,000 bytes per second.

memory module   A collection of memory chips on a small card, usually an inch or so high and three to four inches wide, that plugs directly into the motherboard.

metal-oxide varistor (MOV)   A technology used in surge suppressors, MOVs sit across the hot wire and the ground wire and under normal conditions do not conduct electricity. At higher voltages, they become conductive and "shunt" the electricity to the ground wire.

motherboard   The primary circuit board in a personal computer; this circuit board contains the CPU, chipset, sockets for memory, expansion cards, and so on.

motherboard bus   See *system bus*.

nonvolatile memory   Most computer memory is volatile in that when the computer is shut down, the memory is cleared. Nonvolatile memory (also referred to as read-only memory, or ROM) is maintained between computer sessions, powered by a battery inside the computer.

North Bridge chipset   This motherboard chipset contains the cache controller, the main memory controller, and an interface between the motherboard bus (processor bus) and the PCI and AGP buses. See also *chipset*.

packet writing   A technology that enables a CD-RW drive to behave like a traditional hard drive. Your CD-R/RW drive must be designed at the mechanical and firmware level to support packet writing. If it is so designed then you can copy data to and from the CD as easily as if it were a plain vanilla hard drive. Adaptec's DirectCD utility is the most common implementation.

parity bit   Used to check whether the entire data unit has been transmitted correctly. If a communication session gets garbled or corrupted, the system knows it because of the parity bit and can proceed accordingly.

PC100, PC133   The PC100 and PC133 memory standards were devised by Intel and define the specifications memory must meet to run in a system running a 100MHz bus speed and a 133MHz bus, respectively.

peripheral card   A circuit board that plugs into a peripheral slot on the motherboard. See also *adapter card*.

peripheral slot   A receptacle that accepts a peripheral card and connects it to one of the PC's peripheral buses. These peripheral cards are themselves small, printed circuit boards that provide features such as networking, sound, video acceleration, telecommunications, and support for a plethora of additional devices.

pixel   Picture element. A pixel is the smallest resolvable area of an image displayed on a video monitor.

port   The outlet that acts as a connection between a PC and a device. A bus typically involves (and can expand to include) more than two devices, whereas the term port typically signifies communication between only two devices.

primary cache   See *L1 cache.*

processor bus   See *system bus.*

processor core speed   The processor's internal speed, which is a multiple of the motherboard speed. For example, a Pentium III Xeon 500MHz system has a motherboard bus speed (processor bus speed) of 100MHz. Its clock multiplier is 5, so its processor core speed is 5×100, which is 500MHz.

processor full core speed   See *processor core speed.*

product code   A series of characters, usually alphanumeric, that a manufacturer uses to identify one of its devices. It is usually printed on or near the device's serial number label.

RAM   Random access memory. The primary memory where your computer stores data. RAM is volatile in that when power to the computer is interrupted, any data in RAM is lost. See also *ROM.*

RDRAM   Rambus DRAM. A product of Rambus, Inc. Therefore, unlike SDRAM, it's a proprietary technology rather than an open standard. See also *DRAM* and *SDRAM.*

receptacle analyzer   A small device that plugs into a three-prong wall outlet and lets you know whether you have a good ground. While working on electrostatic-sensitive equipment, you plug your ESD wrist strap into the analyzer, which is in turn plugged into the wall.

RIMM   Rambus In-Line Memory Module. A new technology presently found in only a few high-end systems. These modules are used exclusively for the new RDRAM type of memory and use 184-pin connectors.

ROM   Read-only memory. Most computer memory is volatile in that when the computer is shut down, the memory is cleared. Read-only memory (also referred to as non-volatile memory) is maintained between computer sessions. See also *RAM.*

SCSI   Small computer system interface. This term is pronounced "scuzzy" and is a standard for a device interface used in a variety of operating systems and platforms. The first incarnation of SCSI was introduced by the American National Standards Institute in 1986. Wintel PCs don't come with SCSI built in; you must add a SCSI host controller to a peripheral slot to attach SCSI devices.

SDRAM   Synchronous DRAM. The current workhorse of PC memory. SDRAM provides a 25% speed increase over the older EDO technology without any appreciable increase in cost, which is why it is used in so many systems. See also *DRAM.*

secondary cache   See *L2 cache.*

SIMM   Single In-Line Memory Module. Found on 486 and earlier Pentium computers. They can be 30 or 72 pins—the shiny metal connectors that run along the bottom edge of the module.

slot   In the context of a microprocessor and its motherboard, it refers to the microprocessor's connection to the motherboard. However, it also can be used in the context of other device connections—for example, when referring to a peripheral card's connection to the motherboard. A slot is thin and rectangular, similar in appearance to a peripheral card slot. See also *socket*.

socket   A PC's microprocessor is connected to the motherboard using either a socket or a slot. A socket connector is square in appearance, whereas a slot is thin and rectangular, similar in appearance to a peripheral card slot. See also *slot*.

South Bridge chipset   Contains the interface to the PCI bus, the interface to the ISA bus, dual IDE hard disk controller interfaces, the interface to the USB, and the CMOS RAM and clock. See also *chipset*.

splitter   A Y-splitter connects to one of the power cables inside your computer, effectively giving you an extra power connection.

SRAM   Static random access memory. A type of memory that is much faster than traditional DRAM—so fast that it can keep up with the galloping processor. However, SRAM's fast speed makes it very costly. Also, consider that SRAM is physically much larger than a comparable quantity of DRAM. See also *RAM* and *DRAM*.

S-spec number   A four- to six-digit alphanumeric code used by Intel Corporation to identify its microprocessors.

surge suppressor   Sits between the wall outlet and your computer. If a spike occurs on the power line, the surge suppressor is supposed to shunt it harmlessly to the ground, thereby preventing it from ever reaching your system. The suppressor usually gives up the ghost when this happens, sacrificing itself to protect your computer.

switch   A switch is a type of traffic-routing device used in local area networks. Switches go hubs one better by separating traffic on each port and knowing—to a limited degree—which packets should be sent to a specific port. This dramatically reduces signal collisions and thereby increases the speed of the LAN.

system bus   Connects the microprocessor and a crucial chipset, the North Bridge (more on this later). It is the highest-speed bus in a system. Synonyms for system bus are *motherboard bus* and *processor bus*.

Torx   A special screwdriver that has a tip in the shape of a six-pointed star.

UDF reader   Universal Disk Format reader. UDF is a file format that was specifically developed to support high-capacity optical storage media such as CD-RW, DVD-ROM, and DVD-Video. It works in conjunction with packet writing to offer several significant benefits. See also *packet writing*.

UPS   Uninterruptible power supply. A backup power system for your computer. Should the power go out, the UPS battery kicks in automatically and gives you time to save your work and power down your system gracefully.

USB   Universal serial bus. USB is a
medium-speed serial bus. The main advocate of the bus is Intel, aided by Compaq,
Digital, IBM, Microsoft, NEC, and Northern
Telecom; together these firms comprise the
USB Implementers Forum. USB was developed in 1996, but users didn't become interested until 1998 when Apple released the
iMac with USB ports in place of serial and
Apple Desktop Bus connectors. Most recently
manufactured motherboards provide built-
in USB support in the form of two USB connectors. Many modern monitors and
keyboards also serve as USB hubs. USB's
main features are support for up to 127
devices, Plug and Play, and hot-swapping. It
can provide power to devices over the bus
and does not require any peripheral cards or
free IRQs.

warm boot   The process of restarting your
computer when it is already running via
the reset switch or the Restart option in
Windows. This is different from a *cold boot*
in which you reboot the computer from a
completely shut-down (powered-off) state.
See also *cold boot*.

Index

Symbols

A